KU-588-602

The Royal Commission on Historical Manuscripts

Guides to Sources for British History
based on the National Register of Archives

11

WITHDRAWN
FROM STOCK

PRINCIPAL FAMILY AND ESTATE COLLECTIONS

Family Names L–W

London: The Stationery Office

© *Crown copyright 1999*
Published with the permission of the Royal Commission on Historical Manuscripts
On behalf of the Controller of Her Majesty's Stationery Office

Applications for reproduction should be made in writing to the Copyright Unit,
Her Majesty's Stationery Office, St Clements House, 2-16 Colegate, Norwich, NR3 1BQ

First published 1999

ISBN 0 11 440276 0

Published by The Stationery Office and available from:

The Publications Centre
(mail, telephone and fax orders only)
PO Box 276, London SW8 5DT
General enquiries 0171 873 0011
Telephone orders 0171 873 9090
Fax orders 0171 873 8200

The Stationery Office Bookshops
123 Kingsway, London WC2B 6PQ
0171 242 6393 Fax 0171 242 6394
68-69 Bull Street, Birmingham B4 6AD
0121 236 9696 Fax 0121 236 9699
33 Wine Street, Bristol BS1 2BQ
0117 926 4306 Fax 0117 929 4515
9-21 Princess Street, Manchester M60 8AS
0161 834 7201 Fax 0161 833 0634
16 Arthur Street, Belfast BT1 4GD
01232 238451 Fax 01232 235401
The Stationery Office Oriel Bookshop
18-19 High Street, Cardiff CF1 2BZ
01222 395548 Fax 01222 384347
71 Lothian Road, Edinburgh EH3 9AZ
0131 228 4181 Fax 0131 622 7017

The Stationery Office's Accredited Agents
(see Yellow Pages)

and through good booksellers

Preface

This volume is the eleventh in the series *Guides to Sources for British History*, and the second part of a guide that has set out to describe the most extensive and important family and estate collections of the United Kingdom. These accumulations of legal, business, personal, political and other papers represent some of the country's richest private archives. Many of the 118 collections in the guide have been known to the Commission since the 1870s, but the collections themselves have grown over the last hundred years, and discoveries of hitherto unknown or unrecorded material have continued to be made. Although firmly based on the resources of the National Register of Archives, this guide also represents the results of much supplementary research, and prints a considerable body of information not previously available to scholars.

This work would not have been possible without the support of owners of privately-held manuscript collections, who generously made papers available, gave permission to publish, and in many cases made helpful comments on drafts. For help and hospitality the Commission is indebted both to them and to a number of country house librarians and archivists, on whose expert knowledge it was fortunately able to draw. The Commission is also most grateful to those librarians and archivists who care for family and estate collections in national, local, university and specialist repositories, in this country and abroad, and who so patiently and expertly responded to requests for help.

As recorded in the preface to part one, the guide has been the work of several hands. Part two has been the responsibility of a team led by Anthony Smith and including David Prior, Giles Mandelbrote, Rosemary Hayes, Andrew Rowley and John Gurney. Anthony Smith, and Richard Olney as the Commission's Director of Guides and Surveys, have been principally responsible for preparing the volume for the press.

CJ KITCHING
Secretary

Quality House, Quality Court
Chancery Lane, London WC2A 1HP

December 1998

Contents

Introduction

The introduction to part one of this guide, covering family names A-K, explained why the country's leading family and estate collections were chosen for treatment in the Commission's series of Guides to sources for British history. It also set out the criteria adopted as the basis of selection and the methodology of the research project on which the publication has been based. The purpose of this introductory note is rather to look briefly at the material presented in the two volumes and attempt a preliminary assessment of its significance.

The extent and wealth of this material can scarcely be in doubt. Cumulatively these 118 collections represent a vast historical source, covering all parts of the country, several centuries of English, Welsh, Scottish and Irish history, and a wide range of topics from legal, administrative and political to social, economic, local and cultural history. Some of this variety could have been predicted from the selection criteria, which required collections to have very substantial and significant runs of deeds, legal papers and estate papers covering long periods. In fact, in addition to series of deeds going back to the middle ages and estate records from the sixteenth century and earlier, many of the collections described have further riches in the form of household and local papers, political and family papers, and a range of collected manuscripts.

The guide, taken as a whole, represents the most complete summary yet published of the country's leading country house collections. Yet it has had to exclude a large number of similar collections, many of them scarcely less substantial or interesting than those chosen for inclusion. In the course of the survey that preceded and accompanied the preparation of the guide the Commission accumulated much information about these other collections, and this is being made publicly available (where owners have given their consent) through the National Register of Archives and its newly developed Family and Estate Index.

Looking in more detail at the collections selected for the guide, the reader may be struck first of all by how representative they are of the nation's leading landed families. Supported by great estates, they maintained in many cases a position of prominence in national affairs over several generations. It is not surprising therefore that most of these families belong or have at some time belonged to the British peerage. In 1883 Bateman listed forty peers in Great Britain and Ireland who owned 50,000 or more acres worth upwards of £50,000 a year.[1] Of these, thirty-two are represented in the guide.

1. John Bateman, *The Great Landowners of Great Britain and Ireland*, 3rd edn 1883, repr Leicester University Press 1971.

The reader may next be impressed by the geographical diversity of these collections. Every English county is represented, although some, such as Nottinghamshire with its great ducal domains, are better represented than others. Some collections are exclusively Scottish or Welsh, but a significant number bestride the borders, outstanding examples being the Powis and Beaufort collections for the Welsh borders and the Buccleuch and Sutherland collections with their large English as well as Scottish components.[2] The guide contains no exclusively Irish collection, but several that have important Irish elements, among them most notably Londonderry and Downshire for Ulster and Devonshire and Fitzwilliam for the south of Ireland.[3] A few collections, such as those of the Dukes of Marlborough (no 98), the Earls of Dartmouth (no 59) and the Earls of Zetland (no 32), have qualified for inclusion despite a paucity of medieval records, but the guide as a whole exemplifies the great medieval riches to be found in country house collections, in the form not only of charters and accounts but also of cartularies and other manuscripts. Some of the great medieval families, such as the Berkeleys (no 7), managed to retain (or in some cases recover) their estates and their archives over the centuries. But it was not necessary to belong to a family of Norman origins in order to acquire substantial quantities of medieval records. Many of the finest collections of medieval records described in the guide were accumulated by families such as the Seymours, Russells, Thynnes and Pagets, that rose to national prominence in the sixteenth century and whose newly acquired estates included former monastic properties. Many monastic charters survive in country house collections because they became part of the muniments of title to properties purchased at a later date, but some records of religious houses, such as those of Glastonbury Abbey now at Longleat (see no 104), were acquired directly or indirectly from the monasteries themselves following their dissolution. By a somewhat similar process parts of the archives of medieval families that failed, either in the male line or altogether, found their way into the archives of other families that have survived to the present day. Thus, although the Hungerford and Botreaux families have no modern successors, some of their records can be found among the Hastings muniments (see Rawdon-Hastings, Earls of Loudon, no 88; Pleydell-Bouverie, Earls of Radnor, no 85).

It is clear that just as inheritance played a major part in the evolution of the country's greatest landed families, so many of the most important family and estate collections are composite archives, with large components inherited from other families. Even families founded principally on the fortune of one individual, made in the counting house, the government office or the law-court, were further enriched and aggrandised through judicious marriages, and their archives reflect the consequent growth of their estates in successive generations. In the case of the Montagu-Douglas-Scott family, Dukes of Buccleuch (no 70), three ducal archives have come together in one collection, creating the longest individual entry in the guide. At a less exalted level, several major collections represent the junction of two family archives, neither of which might have qualified for inclusion on its own

2. Herbert, Earls of Powis, no 51; Somerset, Dukes of Beaufort, no 96; Montagu-Douglas-Scott, Dukes of Buccleuch and Queensberry, no 70; Sutherland-Leveson-Gower, Dukes of Sutherland, no 101.

3. Hill, Marquesses of Downshire, no 52; Vane-Tempest-Stewart, Marquesses of Londonderry, no 110; Cavendish, Dukes of Devonshire, no 17; Wentworth-Fitzwilliam, Earls Fitzwilliam, no 113.

merits. A significant number of these are Scottish collections, reflecting perhaps the way in which Scottish law and custom has been particularly successful in preserving estates despite the failure of families in the male line.

The foregoing cases, where an estate passed intact from one family to another and then remained with its family of adoption, so to speak, are comparatively straightforward. The guide also illustrates a number of other ways in which inheritance could affect estates and their archives, some less obvious than others. An estate might be divided between two co-heirs, as in the case of the Devereux estates in Ireland (see Thynne, Marquesses of Bath, no 104; Shirley of Ettington, no 94). The great Wriothesley estates were divided on the death of the fourth Earl of Southampton in 1667, the co-heirs being the Russell family, Dukes of Bedford, the Montagu family, Dukes of Montagu, and the Noel family, Earls of Gainsborough; but in the next generation the Gainsborough portion was again divided between female heirs, who married respectively the first Duke of Portland and the second Duke of Beaufort. All five of these families are represented in the guide, although not all inherited significant quantities of Wriothesley papers.[4] The most notable instance, however, is that of the estates of the Seymour Dukes of Somerset, a family deriving from Protector Somerset (d1552). The Seymour estates and family archive had a somewhat chequered history between 1552 and 1750. On the death of the seventh Duke of Somerset in 1750 his paternal (Seymour) estates were divided between co-heirs, but the splendid Percy inheritance, that had entered the Seymour family on the marriage of the Percy heiress to the 'proud' sixth Duke in 1682, was divided between two further heirs.[5]

Sometimes estates came together in the same family for only one generation, being separated again in the next. The Duke of Newcastle who died in 1768 was the only member of his family to hold both the Pelham estates inherited from his father (see Pelham, Earls of Chichester, no 80) and the Holles estates inherited from his maternal uncle (see Pelham-Clinton, Dukes of Newcastle, no 81). Similarly, on the death of the third Duke of Bridgewater in 1803 part of his estates went to his nephew Lord Gower, later first Duke of Sutherland, but when the Duke of Sutherland died in 1833 they passed to his second son Lord Francis Leveson-Gower, later Earl of Ellesmere (see Egerton, Earls of Ellesmere, no 33). But estates divided to provide for a younger son might be re-united in a later generation due to a failure of heirs, either in the main line or in the junior branch. Such failures played an important part in the family and archival history of the Lowthers, Earls of Lonsdale (no 63) and the Pierreponts, Earls Manvers (no 84), to name but two. In a few cases, such as that of the Finch and Finch-Hatton families (nos 35 and 36), there are family and archival links between two collections even though the principal estates concerned were never held together.

4. See Russell, Dukes of Bedford, no 90; Montagu-Douglas-Scott, Dukes of Buccleuch and Queensberry, no 70; Noel, Earls of Gainsborough, no 74; Cavendish-Bentinck, Dukes of Portland, no 18; Somerset, Dukes of Beaufort, no 96.

5. For the Seymour estates before 1750 see principally Seymour, Dukes of Somerset, no 92; Brudenell-Bruce, Marquesses of Ailesbury, no 12; Thynne, Marquesses of Bath, no 104. For the division of the paternal Seymour estates in 1750 see Manners, Dukes of Rutland, no 68; Wyndham of Orchard Wyndham, no 118. For the Percy estates see Percy, Dukes of Northumberland, no 82; Wyndham, Barons Leconfield and Egremont, no 117.

Although bringing out the central importance of family inheritance, the guide also provides many examples of the various other routes by which archival material can find its way into these large family collections. At the time of a major estate purchase more records may have been acquired than were strictly necessary to prove legal title to it, as in the case of Sir John Thynne and the Glastonbury Abbey records. The same may be true of executorship or trust papers, where family papers not directly needed for the immediate legal purpose may have passed into the hands of the executor or trustee, as with the Somerset papers in the late seventeenth century (see Thynne, Marquesses of Bath, no 104) and the Crawford papers in the 1830s (see Lindsay, Earls of Crawford and Balcarres, no 61). Where the head of a family had an antiquarian bent he might make the most of such opportunities, but he might also acquire manuscripts through gift or purchase: hence the enrichment of the Towneley collection in the seventeenth century (see no 106) and the Bute and Rutland collections in the twentieth (see nos 100, 68). Traditions of record keeping and accumulation, once established in a family, could be maintained over several generations, and, as at Petworth House or Hatfield House, the country house muniment room could become a repository for papers of family or local interest, voluntarily offered by other owners lacking their own facilities for storage.

* * *

In 1900 the collections described in this guide were almost all in family possession and custody, in most cases at the principal country seat of the family but in a few cases at its London house.[6] Of the 118 collections in the guide, 79 had been reported on by the Commission in these locations between 1870 and 1900. Nearly one hundred years later the picture is very different. Only 33 collections remain principally in private custody, although an estimated further 13 are only partially deposited, with substantial sections of the archives retained in private hands. Nearly two-thirds of the collections have moved, either wholly or mainly, into the public domain, having been deposited, on loan, by gift or by purchase, in a wide range of libraries and record offices.

The other notable phenomenon in the twentieth-century history of these collections is the variety of solutions adopted to the problem of custody. Some collections are mainly concentrated in one repository, be it a record office or a country house muniment room, but others have been fragmented in a sometimes bewildering way, with over twenty identifiable groups in a few cases. In 1900 the situation may not have been very much simpler in terms of physical location, since within a country house papers might have been kept variously in a muniment room, library or study, and outside it in various solicitors' or estate agents' offices, but at least the archive remained in single ownership, and its different components by and large in the places in which one would have expected to find them. (Accessibility for research was of course a different matter.) The trend in collections that remain in private custody has been

6. Some families parted with groups of personal or political papers in the late nineteenth century, mostly to the British Museum. The Towneley family left Towneley Hall in 1901, but there had been a major sale of manuscripts in 1883. The only major collection, however, whose dispersal, including deeds and estate records as well as family and collected MSS, began before 1900 was that of the Pelhams, Earls of Chichester (no 80).

towards concentration in one location, as town houses have been given up,[7] secondary seats disposed of, estate offices closed and solicitors' basements cleared. Where collections have moved into the public domain the trend conversely has been to divide them among a number of repositories, according to geographical relevance and specialist content, although in many cases there has been one major deposit that has kept the bulk of the archive intact.

The transfer of collections from private to public custody may have different reasons in different cases. The owner may decide on public-spirited grounds that his papers can be better preserved, and made more accessible to scholars, in a library or record office. Other owners may be forced by circumstances to sell their papers, either by private treaty to a public repository or through the sale room. Of the latter fate there are several examples in the guide,[8] although auction sales, especially of library manuscripts, are a phenomenon by no means confined to the twentieth century, and in recent years the private-treaty sale has been the preferred course of action. In general, however, families prefer to retain their archives in their own custody if practicable, and when sales are contemplated the family archive is more often the last rather than the first asset to be considered.

It is the fate of the country house in the twentieth century that has often been the key factor in the fate of the family archive associated with it. The sale of a principal seat may not necessarily precipitate the sale or deposit of its archival contents: some families manage to move with their archives to smaller houses. But the high rate of survival among these very large and important collections, already referred to in this introduction, must be connected with the relatively high rate of survival of the major country houses that in a significant number of cases still accommodate them. In exactly half of the collections described in the guide (59 out of 118) the principal seat in 1900 is still occupied by the family today. In an estimated 17 further cases the family, though no longer resident in the principal seat, lives near it (and in one or two instances still uses it to store papers) or has moved to a secondary seat. In the case of 20 of the collections held privately the owner currently (1998) employs an archivist. In all 20 cases the estate survives as well as the house at its centre, although generally speaking the acreages given in the guide have been considerably reduced in the last hundred years. It is at the next level of landed estates, typically those of the greater gentry rather than those of the great noble landowning families, that the losses of country houses have been higher and the complete sale of estates more frequent.[9] It is more than likely that the loss of collections at this level has been proportionately greater.

---

7. Examples of London houses with important muniment rooms were Spencer House (see Spencer, Earls Spencer, no 97), Montagu House (see Montagu-Douglas-Scott, Dukes of Buccleuch and Queensberry, no 70), Bridgewater House (see Egerton, Earls of Ellesmere, no 33) and Norfolk House (see Fitzalan-Howard, Dukes of Norfolk, no 37).

8. For instance Chichester-Constable of Burton Constable, no 21; Hill, Marquesses of Downshire, no 52; Montagu, Dukes of Manchester, no 69; Towneley of Towneley, later Barons O'Hagan, no 106; Townshend, Marquesses Townshend, no 107.

9. See Heather A Clemenson, *English country houses and landed estates*, 1982, *passim*. Of her sample of 500 country houses in 1880, only 30% were held by the same family one hundred years later. For the 'great landowners' the figure was 41%, but for the greater gentry as low as 26% (*ibid*, p 151).

On the other side of the park wall, a major factor has been the availability of public repositories able and willing to receive large family and estate collections. In 1900 it was difficult to find an alternative home for such a collection as a whole. The British Museum Department of Manuscripts, then and later, might be willing to purchase the papers of a prominent national figure, or a selection of medieval and early modern deeds and estate papers, leaving the remainder with no obvious place of deposit.[10] The situation was not much better after the first World War, when a number of large estates were broken up, and when country house archives became for the first time seriously at risk. In the period 1917-27 three major family collections, those of the Egertons, Earls of Ellesmere (no 33), the Grenvilles, Dukes of Buckingham (no 44) and the Hastings family, latterly Earls of Loudon (no 88), were exported to the Huntington Library in California. But thereafter matters improved, with the development, slow at first, of English record offices and the foundation or expansion of national libraries or record offices in Wales, Scotland and Northern Ireland willing to take large estate archives. With increased choice, however, has come reduced predictability, and the guide illustrates on almost every page how important it is for the scholar not to assume that, in finding part of a collection, he or she has found it all.

* * *

The collections in this part of the guide are defined in the same way as in part one, as set out in more detail in the introduction to that volume. They include records accumulated by the owners (or life-tenants) of the estates and their families, and by their agents, stewards, solicitors, housekeepers, librarians and other employees. The families themselves are defined as they existed around 1900, although twentieth-century records are included in the summary descriptions if they are known to the Commission, and if their owners have sanctioned their inclusion. Papers are also included if they have passed out of family possession into other ownership through gift, sale or accidents of custody, both before and after 1900, but papers passing through *inheritance* into other collections are noted in the *Related collections* section at the end of the relevant entry. In general the emphasis in the guide is on legal and estate rather than personal papers, and it has not been possible to give much space to the description of single items rather than groups of papers, with particular restraint having had to be exercised in the case of collected manuscripts.

The guide represents the state of the Commission's knowledge at the end of 1997 (with a few later additions), and the opportunity has been taken, in an appendix, of noting those groups of papers from collections in part one that have come to our notice since the end of 1994. But the guide cannot claim completeness, and indeed the appendix demonstrates the rate at which material from these archives continues to come to light. The Commission therefore remains grateful to custodians and scholars for their help in keeping its knowledge as up-to-date as possible.

---

10. See Pelham, Earls of Chichester, no 80, for papers acquired by the British Museum in 1886 and later; Verney, Barons Willoughby de Broke, no 111, for papers acquired in 1917; and Capell, Earls of Essex, no 16, for papers acquired in 1922.

Access to privately owned papers

Privately owned collections of papers deposited on loan in libraries, record offices and other public institutions are normally available for research without restriction. Special conditions, however, may sometimes apply, particularly if a collection is as yet uncatalogued, and advice on access and related matters should be sought from the institutions concerned.

Permission to study papers that remain with a private owner should be sought from the owner in writing, either direct or, where indicated, through an intermediary. The inclusion of such material in this guide does not imply that it is available for research. Where papers can be made available, applicants are reminded that it is often at considerable inconvenience to their owners, and that access for the purpose of research is a privilege and not a right. The conditions of access cited in the guide are those that prevailed in December 1998. Details of the present location of collections whose ownership or whereabouts is not specified in the guide may, where appropriate, be obtained from the Commission.[1]

Those wishing to study papers in private hands are also advised to consult catalogues or other finding aids available in the Commission's search room or elsewhere before approaching owners or custodians.

---

1. Enquiries to the Commission should be addressed to the Secretary, The Royal Commission on Historical Manuscripts, Quality House, Quality Court, Chancery Lane, London WC2A 1HP. Where indicated, enquiries about Scottish collections should be addressed to the Secretary, National Register of Archives (Scotland), West Register House, Charlotte Square, Edinburgh EH2 4DF. For addresses of repositories generally, see the Commission's *Record Repositories in Great Britain*, tenth edition, PRO Publications, 1997.

Table of family names and peerage titles

The following table provides a list of the collections described in parts I and II of this guide, with cross-references from the peerage titles of those families as they appear in the entry headings. Other family names and titles connected with the contents of the guide may be traced through the Select Index of the appropriate volume.

Principal family and estate collections
Family names L–W

[59] LEGGE, Earls of Dartmouth

William Legge (d1670), Lieutenant of the Ordnance under Charles II, received royal grants of property in County Louth and the Minories (London) and the lieutenancy of Alice Holt and Woolmer forests in Hampshire. His son George Legge (d1691), created Baron Dartmouth 1682, gained Bromley Park (Staffordshire) through his marriage in 1667 to the heiress of Sir Henry Archbold, and purchased Lewisham (Kent) in 1673. The second Baron (d1750), created Earl of Dartmouth 1711, bought Sandwell (Staffordshire) from the Whorwood family in 1701 and Morley (Yorkshire, West Riding), a former estate of the Marquess of Halifax, in 1716. He also owned property in Westminster. The Woodsome estate at Farnley Tyas (Yorkshire, West Riding) was acquired through the marriage of the first Earl's son George Legge, Viscount Lewisham, to the daughter and heiress of Sir Arthur Kaye, third Bt, in 1722. The second Earl (d1801), grandson of the first Earl, married in 1755 the daughter and heir of Sir Charles Gunter Nicoll, from whom came estates in Sussex (Racton, Woodmancote), Buckinghamshire (Olney, Warrington), Middlesex (Kentish Town) and London (Aldersgate, Charterhouse Square, Old Jewry), with small amounts of property in Berkshire, Hampshire, Kent, Nottinghamshire, Suffolk and Surrey.

In the eighteenth century the Sandwell estate was augmented by purchases in Handsworth, Smethwick and West Bromwich (Staffordshire), and other Staffordshire property (Needwood Forest, etc) was leased from the Duchy of Lancaster. Sandwell Hall (built 1703-11) was given up in the mid-nineteenth century and a more secluded estate at Patshull (Staffordshire), including land in Pattingham (Staffordshire) and Albrighton (Shropshire), was bought from Sir Robert Pigot, fourth Bt, in 1848. Sales of Handsworth and London property occurred in the nineteenth century, and much of the Staffordshire estate was alienated in the twentieth century.

In the late eighteenth century property was briefly held in Florida, and in the twentieth century purchases were made in Kent (Godmersham Park), Leicestershire and Rhodesia. From the mid-nineteenth century the management of the family's estates was largely in the hands of the estate agents Thynne & Thynne of London.

Estates in 1883: Yorks WR 8,024 acres, Staffs 7,316 acres, Bucks 2,195 acres, Salop 1,096 acres, Sussex 454 acres, Kent 391 acres, Middlesex 42 acres, total 19,518 acres worth £58,657 a year.

[a] Deeds 17th-19th cent, mainly Staffs (Abbots Bromley, Pattingham) but incl some for Co Louth; Mountjoy (Co Tyrone) cartulary 1664-84; wills and settlements 18th-19th cent; trust papers 19th cent; legal papers rel to estates in Ireland 19th cent; Staffs and Derbys manorial records 15th-19th cent, incl Patshull court rolls 1486-1661 and Pleasley (Derbys) manorial accounts 1425-6; Staffs estate records 18th-19th cent, incl surveys, rentals, accounts and corresp; Yorks WR (Morley, etc) estate papers 18th-19th cent, incl surveys, valuations and corresp; rentals, accounts, corresp and papers rel to estates in Bucks, Hants, Kent, Lincs, London and Sussex 18th-19th cent; Co Louth estate papers mainly 17th cent, incl rentals, accounts and corresp; Woodsome Hall (Yorks WR) building papers 1784 and inventory 1740; Staffs militia and volunteer papers 1779-95 and late 19th cent; Hants shrievalty account rolls 1687; papers rel to the lieutenancy of the forests of Alice Holt and Woolmer 17th cent.

Official, political and personal papers 16th-19th cent, incl papers of William Legge (d1670), the 1st Baron Dartmouth and the 1st-4th Earls; other family corresp and papers 17th-20th cent, incl accounts 17th-18th cent and sketches of the

Sandwell estate and servants 19th cent; papers rel to the Kaye and Nicoll families 18th cent.

Staffordshire and Stoke on Trent Archive Service, Staffordshire Record Office (D(W) 515, D(W) 1778, D 1501). Deposited by the 6th, 7th and 9th Earls of Dartmouth 1930-75 in the William Salt Library (transferred to Staffordshire Record Office *c*1980) and directly in the Staffordshire Record Office. HMC *Second Report, App*, 1874, pp9-12; *Eleventh Report, App V*, 1887; *Thirteenth Report, App IV*, 1892, pp495-506; *Fourteenth Report, App X*, 1895; *Fifteenth Report, App I*, 1896; *Guide to the Location of Collections*, 1982, p16. *Staffordshire Family Collections*, 1992, pp22-3. NRA 5197.

[b] Staffs deeds 16th-20th cent, incl some for Abbots Bromley 17th cent, Handsworth, Smethwick and West Bromwich 17th-20th cent, Sandwell 16th-18th cent and Patshull 17th-19th cent; deeds for Bucks 16th-19th cent, Yorks WR 17th-19th cent, Kent 17th-20th cent, Suffolk 18th cent and Salop 19th cent, with some for Florida 18th cent and Rhodesia 20th cent; abstract of title to Pigot (Pattingham) estates 1802-23; schedule of Kaye family deeds (Warwicks and Yorks) 1674-1723; settlements, trust papers and mortgage papers 19th-20th cent; legal papers rel to the Florida estate 19th cent; manorial records, Kent 17th-19th cent (incl Lewisham court rolls and surveys 1605-1851) and Bucks 17th cent.

Staffs (Abbots Bromley and Sandwell) estate records 17th-20th cent, incl leases, maps, rentals, accounts and sale papers, with an honour of Tutbury particular 1683; Lewisham (Kent) estate papers 18th-20th cent, incl leases, rentals, corresp, steward's papers and Blackheath Fair rent roll *c*1740; Godmersham (Kent) tenancy agreements and papers 20th cent; estate records for Yorks WR (Morley and Woodsome) 18th-19th cent, incl valuations, rentals, accounts and corresp, and for Bucks 18th-20th cent; misc estate papers, incl London rentals 1782-98 and Florida plans and valuations late 18th cent; Patshull Hall inventory 1936; papers rel to Staffs affairs 18th cent; papers of William Legge (d1670) and the 1st Baron Dartmouth, incl some rel to the Civil War 1639-61, the Ordnance Office 1660-83 and the Tangier expedition 1663-4; political papers of the 1st and 3rd Earls; other family papers 17th-20th cent, incl papers of the 5th Earl.

Staffordshire and Stoke on Trent Archive Service, Staffordshire Record Office (D 742, D 3629, D 4544). Deposited by Gamlen, Boardman & Forward, solicitors, London 1964-86. *Solicitors' papers in Staffordshire County Record Office*, p3. HMC *Papers of British Politicians 1782-1900*, 1989, p60. NRA 5197.

[c] Salop and Staffs deeds 17th-19th cent, incl some for the Pigot family; deeds for Kent, Middlesex and Sussex 18th-19th cent and Yorks

WR (Kaye family) 1710; abstracts of title, Staffs estate 19th cent; schedule of deeds, Minories estate 1670-85; wills and settlements 17th-19th cent, Astley and Pigot families; Pigot family mortgages and grants of annuity 1700-1830; Staffs manorial records 18th cent, incl Pattingham court book 1740-99; misc estate papers 17th-19th cent, incl survey of Berks, Hants, Suffolk, Surrey and Wilts estates 1797, Kentish Town particulars 1805, accounts of Cambs, Lincs, Middlesex, Staffs and Warwicks fee farm rents 1685-1820, and papers rel to exchanges with the Earl of Shrewsbury 1882; Ordnance Office papers 17th cent, incl saltpetre accounts 1683-7.

Staffordshire and Stoke on Trent Archive Service, Staffordshire Record Office (D 3074). Deposited by JM Findlay 1976. NRA 5197.

[d] Kent, Leics and Yorks WR deeds, wills, settlements and trust papers 19th-20th cent; Patshull Estate Company papers 20th cent.

Staffordshire and Stoke on Trent Archive Service, Staffordshire Record Office (D 5128, D 5372). Deposited by Penningtons, solicitors, London, through the British Records Association 1992-5. NRA 5197.

[e] Legge family wills and financial papers 19th cent; Whorwood family mortgages 17th cent; misc daybooks, accounts, reports and papers for all Dartmouth estates 17th-20th cent; Sandwell estate records 17th-20th cent, incl leases, maps, rentals, accounts, vouchers, corresp and memoranda; leases, accounts and papers rel to Staffs mines and collieries 19th-20th cent; estate records for Patshull and Bromley Park 18th-20th cent, incl leases, maps, rentals, accounts, corresp, memoranda and Bromley Park timber papers; Handsworth sale papers 1867; Sandwell Hall inventories 18th cent and garden accounts 1892-4; official, personal and estate corresp of the 2nd Earl; corresp and papers of the 3rd and 4th Earls.

Staffordshire and Stoke on Trent Archive Service, Staffordshire Record Office (D 564, 761, 857). Deposited from the archive of Thynne & Thynne, estate agents, London, through the British Records Association 1958 and through AR Martin of Blackheath 1964, 1966. NRA 8863.

[f] Staffs estate plans 19th cent, mainly Patshull but incl some for Albrighton and Sandwell; misc Blackheath estate plans 19th cent; architectural plans and drawings for Patshull Hall and garden 19th cent.

Staffordshire and Stoke on Trent Archive Service, Staffordshire Record Office (D 1517). Deposited by FW MacMillan 1975. NRA 3515.

[g] Schedule of Patshull deeds 1665-1921 (copy); personal and family corresp 19th-20th cent, incl some of the 5th-8th Earls and of Lady

Dorothy Meynell (eldest daughter of the 6th Earl) 1899-1962.

Staffordshire and Stoke on Trent Archive Service, Staffordshire Record Office (D 859). Deposited by Lady Dorothy Meynell 1966. NRA 5197.

[h] Commonplace books of William Legge 1686 and Frances Charlotte Chetwynd Talbot (wife of the 4th Earl of Dartmouth) 1821; journal of the 3rd Earl 1795-8.

Staffordshire and Stoke on Trent Archive Service, Staffordshire Record Office (D 1548). Purchased from Messrs Phillips, auctioneers, London 1975. NRA 3515.

[i] Pattingham manorial records 1615-1780; Patshull estate papers 1783, 1817; corresp rel to militia 1817; postal service and Ordnance Office papers 1645-86.

William Salt Library, Stafford (WSL 11/20, 250/ 27, 293-358/27, 54-58/28, 426-471/27, M/591/ 1-2, SMs 260, 261, 463). William Salt Collection, with additional papers presented by the 6th Earl of Dartmouth 1920-8. NRA 3516, 7279.

[j] Yorks WR deeds and muniments of title 13th-20th cent (mainly former Kaye estates); deeds for Lancs (former Kaye estates) 14th cent, and for Bucks (former Longville estates) and Hants 16th-18th cent; Kaye family settlements 14th-16th cent and legal papers 1627-41; manorial records, Yorks WR 16th-17th cent, incl Woodsome and Farnley Tyas court rolls 1565-1611, and Bucks (Bradwell, Wolverton) 17th cent; Yorks WR estate records 17th-20th cent, incl leases, maps, plans, surveys, rentals, accounts, vouchers and letter books; records of Yorks WR coal and ironstone mines and textile mills 19th-20th cent, incl mill leases and accounts and Morley Main Colliery papers; Woodsome Hall inventory 1813 and accounts and papers 1878-86; accounts of the dowager Countess of Dartmouth 1891-2.

West Yorkshire Archive Service, Leeds (DT). Formerly amongst the archives of Thynne & Thynne, and deposited in part through Staffordshire Record Office 1962 and in part by AR Martin 1964, 1967. NRA 16328.

[k] Yorks WR manorial records 15th-16th cent, incl court rolls for Slaithwaite and Lyngarths 1541-93 and Woodsome 1498-1524.

West Yorkshire Archive Service, Kirklees (M/SL). Deposited before 1960 from an unknown source. NRA 26729.

[l] Yorks WR agent's letter book and audit memorandum 1804-10.

West Yorkshire Archive Service, Kirklees (KC 161). Deposited 1985. NRA 26729.

[m] Abstracts of title, Morley 1700-54; wills and settlements 19th-20th cent; manorial records 18th-19th cent, incl Slaithwaite court papers 1797-1881; Yorks WR (Morley) estate records 19th-20th cent, incl leases, agreements, accounts, corresp, and bankruptcy papers rel to collieries and textile mills, with Honley (Yorks WR) chief rent books 1789-1857.

The John Goodchild Collection, Wakefield. Presented by an unnamed solicitor *c*1970. NRA 23594.

[n] Misc deeds 18th-20th cent; executorship papers 1801-3, 1857-66; cash books and accounts for all Dartmouth estates 1909-16; Kent (Lewisham, Blackheath, etc) estate records 18th-20th cent, incl leases, surveys, rentals, accounts, vouchers, letter books, memoranda and papers; Lewisham tithe and glebe accounts 1796-1923; estate records for London and Middlesex properties (Kentish Town, Westminster, etc) 18th-20th cent, incl leases, rentals, accounts, vouchers, letter books and memoranda; estate records for Bucks (Olney) and Sussex (Racton) 18th-20th cent, incl rentals and accounts; misc estate papers, incl Sandwell letter book 1861-2, and corresp and papers for Berks, Hants and Patshull estates 18th-19th cent; misc Legge family corresp and papers 18th-20th cent.

London Metropolitan Archives. Deposited by Thynne & Thynne, estate agents, London, through the British Records Association and AR Martin 1958-74. Access restricted while the collection is being catalogued. HMC *Annual Review 1996-1997*, pp32-5.

[o] Family corresp and papers 19th cent, mainly that of Lady Caroline Legge (d1885) and Lt Col EH Legge (d1900).

London Metropolitan Archives (F/LEG). Deposited by Miss Virginia Legge 1957. NRA 40391.

[p] Journals, letter books, order books, corresp and official papers of the 1st Baron 1672-89, incl maps and drawings of fortifications, Tangier expedition papers and corresp of Prince Rupert.

National Maritime Museum (DAR). Deposited by the 7th Earl 1936; the maps were purchased 1948. HMC *Eleventh Report, App V*, 1887; *Fifteenth Report, App I*, 1896. *Guide to the Manuscripts in the National Maritime Museum*, 1977, pp106-7, 1980, pp108, 117. NRA 28836.

[q] Papers of the 2nd Earl rel to North America 1765-82; papers of Francis Legge, governor of Nova Scotia 1773-82.

National Archives of Canada (MG 23, A I). Presented by the 6th Earl 1926. HMC *Eleventh Report, App V*, 1887; *Fourteenth Report, App X*, 1895. Microfilm copy at Staffordshire Record Office (H 992-4). NRA 25410.

[r] Corresp of William Legge (d1670) and the 1st Baron Dartmouth (copies).

Yale University, Beinecke Library (Osborn MSS fb 190/1-3). Purchased 1948. HMC *Second Report, App*, 1874, p9. NRA 18661.

[s] Letter book of the 2nd Earl of Dartmouth 1775.

Boston University, Mugar Memorial Library, Massachusetts. Purchased 1948 (Quaritch catalogue no 660, lot 80). PM Hamer, *A Guide to Archives and Manuscripts in America*, 1961, p238. HMC *Fourteenth Report, App X*, 1895, p410.

[t] MS volume rel to offices in America and West Indies 1775.

University of Michigan, William L Clements Library, Ann Arbor (Misc MSS, 25). Purchased c1948. AP Shy, *Guide to the Manuscript Collections of the William L Clements Library*, 1978, p94.

[u] Thomas Gardiner's 'Generall Survey of the Post Office' 1682.

British Library, Manuscript Collections (Add MS 62091). Presented to the 1st Baron Dartmouth 1682, sold to FW Bond at Sotheby's, 9 Mar 1948, lot 449, and purchased at Sotheby's, 17 Dec 1981, lot 110. Published in *Postal History Society*, Special Series, no 5, 1958.

[v] Papers of Mary, Countess of Dartmouth (d1929) and Lady Joan Legge (d1939).

In private possession. See RH Trainor, *Black Country Elites*, 1993.

Related collection: Earls of Guilford (Bodleian Library, Oxford MSS North, NRA 837), including trust, legal and Yorks estate papers of the Kaye and Legge families 18th cent.

[60] LEIGH, Barons Leigh

The London merchant Sir Thomas Leigh (d1571) acquired estates in Bedfordshire (Cranfield), Gloucestershire (Adlestrop, Longborough), Warwickshire (King's Newnham, Fletchamstead and Stoneleigh) and elsewhere. The Gloucestershire property passed to his son Rowland Leigh, ancestor of the Leighs of Adlestrop. King's Newnham (Warwickshire) passed to another son, William Leigh, from whose descendant the Earl of Chichester (d1653) it passed to the fourth Earl of Southampton (see Montagu-Douglas-Scott, Dukes of Buccleuch and Queensberry, no 70).

Sir Thomas Leigh's Stoneleigh estate was acquired by his second son Thomas (d1625), who bought Hamstall Ridware (Staffordshire) in 1601 and was made a baronet in 1611. His grandson and heir Thomas (d1671), created Baron Leigh 1643, was succeeded as second Baron by his grandson, who acquired property in Bedfordshire, Buckinghamshire and Kent through his marriage to Elizabeth, daughter and heir of Sir Richard Brown of Shingleton (Kent). Fillongley and Maxstoke (Warwickshire) entered the family on the marriage of the third Baron (d1738) to the daughter and heir of Thomas Holbeche. The third, fourth and fifth Barons purchased property in Warwickshire (Watergall, Wibtoft), Leicestershire (Claybrooke) and Staffordshire (Yoxall). Estates at Leighton Buzzard (Bedfordshire) and Stewkley (Buckinghamshire), acquired on the marriage of the first Bt's son to the heiress of Sir Christopher Hoddesdon, were settled on Charles Leigh, second son of the first Baron, and subsequently on Charles Leigh (d1749), second son of the second Baron, who bought Bradenham (Buckinghamshire) in 1734 and Little Leigh (Cheshire) c1737. They were inherited by the fifth Baron and descended with his other estates after his death in 1786.

On the death of the fifth Baron the barony expired, and his estates passed successively to his sister the Hon Mary Leigh (d1806), the Revd Thomas Leigh (d1813) and James Henry Leigh (1765-1823) of Adlestrop, whose son Chandos Leigh (d1850) was created Baron Leigh in 1839. The Leighs of Adlestrop had augmented their Gloucestershire estates in the eighteenth century through marriages with the Lord family, which brought property in Kent and Surrey, and the Brydges family, Dukes of Chandos, which brought Holborn (Middlesex) property. Sales took place in the earlier part of the nineteenth century (including Egham and Leighton Buzzard) and after the First World War (including Holborn and parts of the Warwickshire estate).

Estates in 1883: Warwicks 14,891 acres, Staffs 2,350 acres, Gloucs 2,232 acres, Cheshire 1,198 acres, Leics 294 acres, total 20,965 acres worth £32,013 a year.

[a] Deeds and muniments of title 13th-19th cent, mainly Warwicks but incl some for Beds, Bucks, Cheshire, Gloucs, Leics, London, Northants, Staffs and Surrey; Stoneleigh Abbey ledger book c1392 and cartulary 16th cent; Hailes Abbey (Gloucs) cartulary c1539; wills, settlements and inquisitions *post mortem* 16th-19th cent, Leigh, Holbeche, Lord, Paulet and Watson families; executorship and trust papers 18th-20th cent, Leigh, Turner and Wentworth families, incl some for the 1st Duke of Buckingham 1771-1856 and the 6th Earl of Aylesford 1846-65; abstracts of title and schedules of deeds 14th-19th cent; legal papers 16th-20th cent, incl some rel to the Duchess of Dudley's charity 1545-1884, the lunacy of the 5th Baron (d1786), claims on the Leigh estates 1806 and the Leigh peerage 1828-9; bonds and financial papers 16th-20th cent; manorial records 13th-19th cent, mainly Warwicks

(Stoneleigh, etc) from 13th cent but incl some for Beds (Leighton Buzzard *alias* Grovebury) and Bucks (Stewkley) 15th-19th cent, Cheshire (Little Leigh) 18th-19th cent, and Gloucs (Adlestrop, etc) and Staffs (Offlow with Hamstall Ridware, Yoxall) 16th-19th cent.

Warwicks estate records 16th-20th cent, incl leases, maps, plans, particulars, surveys, valuations, rentals, accounts, vouchers and corresp; Warwicks farm and game records 18th-20th cent, foresters' accounts and timber sales papers 17th-20th cent, and accounts and papers rel to enclosure and tithes 13th-20th cent; Staffs estate agreements, particulars, surveys, rentals, accounts, corresp and papers 17th-20th cent; estate records for Cheshire 18th-20th cent and Beds and Bucks 18th-19th cent, incl leases, maps, plans, surveys, rentals and accounts; papers rel to Beds and Bucks enclosures and tithes and Cheshire timber and salt 19th cent; Adlestrop and Longborough (Gloucs) estate records 16th-20th cent, incl leases, maps, plans, surveys, valuations, rentals, accounts, vouchers and corresp; rentals, accounts and estate papers for Herts and Surrey (formerly Lord family) 18th-19th cent and Holborn (formerly Brydges property) 18th-20th cent; misc papers rel to estates in Leics, Northants and Oxon 17th-20th cent; Stoneleigh Abbey (house and park) building plans, drawings and accounts 16th-19th cent, incl Humphry Repton's designs 1809; inventories, household accounts, garden accounts, cellar books and provisions books for Stoneleigh, Adlestrop and London houses 17th-20th cent.

Papers rel to Warwicks affairs 16th-20th cent, incl lieutenancy and shrievalty papers 16th-19th cent (Leigh family), records of Thomas Southern's charity (Stoneleigh) 1863-1970 and Temple Balsall hospital 17th cent, corresp and papers rel to volunteers 1850-1905, and misc papers rel to schools, elections and railways 18th-19th cent; papers rel to Beds, Bucks, Cheshire, Gloucs and Staffs affairs 18th-20th cent; Beds shrievalty papers 1588-92 (Hoddesdon family); Longborough overseers' orders and accounts 1738-68; Needwood Forest (Staffs) accounts and papers 17th-19th cent; patents, appointments and commissions 17th-20th cent; inventories of the Leigh, Holbeche and Paulet families 16th-19th cent; family accounts, diaries, corresp and papers 17th-20th cent, Leigh of Stoneleigh, Leigh of Adlestrop, Holbeche, Brydges, Turner and Wentworth families, incl diaries of the 3rd Baron Leigh 1876-1909 and the Revd Henry Brydges 1710-16; volume of historical and local MSS 13th-14th cent; recipes 18th cent; sketches, photographs and genealogical papers 18th-20th cent.

Shakespeare Birthplace Trust Records Office (DR 18, 553, 554, 662, 671, 762, 823, 961, 962). Deposited by the 4th and 5th Barons Leigh, and the Trustees of the Stoneleigh Settlement and the Stoneleigh Abbey Preservation Trust

1942-98. HMC *Second Report, App*, 1871, p49; *Guide to the Location of Collections*, 1982, p37. A Kingsbury and Little Packington (Warwicks) mortgage 1711 was deposited by the Stoneleigh estate office in 1931 (ER 3/2829). NRA 4523, 21856.

[b] Yoxall (Staffs) manorial papers 1882-1918.

Shakespeare Birthplace Trust Records Office (DR 188). Deposited by Messrs Field & Son, solicitors, Leamington Spa, through Warwickshire County Record Office 1964. NRA 21856. (See also [h] below.)

[c] Stoneleigh maps and plans 1800-9; Leigh family accounts and papers 19th-20th cent, incl papers rel to Warwicks, Staffs and Gloucs charities.

Shakespeare Birthplace Trust Records Office (DR 339). Deposited by Warwickshire County Record Office 1975. NRA 21856. (See also [h] below.)

[d] Holborn estate leases 18th-20th cent; map of Stoneleigh estate *c*1938; marriage settlement of Sophia Leigh and GWG Leveson-Gower 1861.

Shakespeare Birthplace Trust Records Office (DR 520, 659). Deposited by Boodle Hatfield, solicitors, London 1982, 1989. NRA 4523, 21856.

[e] Inventory of Lord Leigh's property at 31 Grosvenor Square, London 1929.

Shakespeare Birthplace Trust Records Office (DR 950). Deposited by Stoneham, Langton & Passmore, solicitors, London, through the British Records Association 1997.

[f] Cheshire estate maps and misc papers 19th cent.

Shakespeare Birthplace Trust Records Office (DR 675). Formerly in the possession of the Jones family of Warwickshire, agents and solicitors to the Leigh family, and deposited 1989. NRA 33911.

[g] Agency papers 1749-66, incl trust accounts.

Warwickshire County Record Office (CR 2855). Purchased 1991 (Sotheby's, 13 Dec 1990, lot 362).

[h] Yoxall (Staffs) manorial records 1741-1934.

Staffordshire and Stoke on Trent Archive Service, Staffordshire Record Office (D 960, D 1306). Deposited by Messrs Field & Son, solicitors, Leamington Spa, through Warwickshire County Record Office 1968, 1972. NRA 19798.

Related collections: Leigh of Adlestrop family correspondence 1654-1788 (Bodleian Library, Oxford MS Dep. a. 55-6, 622-5, c. 562-85, d. 501-9, e. 261-2); Montagu-Douglas-Scott,

Dukes of Buccleuch and Queensberry, no 70, including King's Newnham estate papers.

[61] LINDSAY, Earls of Crawford and Balcarres

The statesman John Lindsay, Lord Menmuir (d1598), second son of the ninth Earl of Crawford, bought Balcarres and Pitcorthie (Fife) in 1587. His son was created Baron Lindsay in 1633 and his grandson Earl of Balcarres in 1651. In 1808 a claim to the earldom but not the property of the twenty-second Earl of Crawford was inherited by the sixth Earl of Balcarres (1752-1825) and in 1848 this earldom was confirmed to his son the seventh and twenty-fourth Earl. The Fife estate was sold in 1791 by the sixth Earl to his brother Robert Lindsay (d1836), who also bought property at Leuchars (Fife). The sixth Earl settled at Haigh (Lancashire), a coal-rich estate near Wigan, acquired through his marriage to the daughter and heir of Charles Dalrymple. Dalrymple had inherited it from his maternal grandmother Elizabeth Edwin, daughter of Sir Roger Bradshaigh, third Bt (d1746), whose family, created baronets in 1679, had been settled there since the fourteenth century.

The seventh and twenty-fourth Earl (d1869), created Baron Haigh of Haigh Hall in 1826, married the daughter of the first Baron Muncaster, bought Dunecht (Aberdeenshire) in 1845 and also acquired an estate at Llanarthney, Llanon and elsewhere in Carmarthenshire, mainly disposed of during the 1890s. The sixth Earl's Jamaican estate was sold in 1847. The ninth and twenty-sixth Earl (d1913) repurchased Balcarres (from Sir Coutts Lindsay, second Bt) in 1886 and sold Dunecht in 1899. Property at Warboys (Huntingdonshire) came through the tenth and twenty-seventh Earl's marriage to a daughter and co-heir of Sir Henry Pelly, third Bt, but was soon sold. The Lancashire estate was given up in 1947.

The earlier earls of Crawford and their estates are represented in the Lindsay family muniments. David Lindsay, created Earl of Crawford in 1398, inherited property in Forfarshire (Glenesk, etc) and Lanarkshire (the lordships of Crawford and Lindsay) and by the mid-fifteenth century his descendants had extended the Forfarshire property and settled at Finhaven. Auchtermonzie (Fife) entered the family through the marriage of the fourth Earl (d1453) to the daughter and heir of Sir David Dunbar. Some property of the eighth Earl was forfeited to the Crown and on his death in 1542 the earldom and remaining estates passed to his cousin David Lindsay of Edzell (Forfarshire). When Edzell died in 1558 the Crawford title and estates descended to the eighth Earl's grandson while the Edzell estates were inherited by Edzell's son Sir David Lindsay (d1610), brother of Lord Menmuir (see above). (About this time

Glenesk seems to have entered the possession of the Edzell line, being afterwards sold with the other remaining family property by David Lindsay to Lord Panmure in 1703.) The fourteenth Earl of Crawford sold Finhaven to the second Baron Spynie in 1630 and the royalist sixteenth Earl forfeited what remained of his family's property in 1644, having agreed in 1642 to settle his earldom upon the Earl of Lindsay.

John Lindsay, tenth Baron Lindsay of The Byres, was created Earl of Lindsay in 1633. His ancestor, created Baron Lindsay in 1445, had inherited the barony of Byres (East Lothian) and the Ochterotherstruther or Struthers (Fife) estate but in 1608 Byres was sold by the eighth Baron to the first Earl of Haddington. John Lindsay, fourth Earl of Lindsay and twentieth Earl of Crawford (d1749), was succeeded in his titles and estates by his cousin the fourth Viscount Garnock (d1781), who had inherited Kilbirnie (Ayrshire) from his grandfather the first Viscount (so created 1703), to whom it had come from his mother, a daughter and co-heir of Sir John Crawford of Kilbirnie. The fourth Viscount built Crawford Priory on the Struthers estate and was succeeded by his son George Lindsay-Crawford, twenty-second Earl of Crawford. On Lord Crawford's death in 1808, he was succeeded in the Crawford Priory and Kilbirnie estates by his sister Lady Mary Lindsay-Crawford (d1832), upon whose decease they passed to the Earl of Glasgow (see Boyle, Earls of Glasgow, no 9). The title to the earldom of Crawford (though not the other honours) devolved, however, upon the sixth Earl of Balcarres (see above).

The *Bibliotheca Lindesiana* at Haigh Hall was created by the eighth and twenty-fifth Earl, the earlier collection of books and papers at Balcarres having largely been dispersed when the seat was given up. This Earl appears also to have inherited the contents of Crawford Priory, including some muniments, and to have collected writs and papers in connection with the Crawford and Montrose peerage cases.

Estates in 1883: Earl of Crawford: Lancs 1,931 acres, Westmorland 24 acres, Carmarthenshire 1,670 acres, Aberdeenshire 9,855 acres, total 13,480 acres worth £39,252 a year (of which the Lancashire estate contributed £31,763 a year); Sir Coutts Lindsay: Fife 4,672 acres worth £9,619 a year.

[a] Charters, titles and writs rel to the estates of the earldom of Crawford 14th-17th cent (mainly Fife, Forfarshire and Perthshire) and the Lindsay family of Edzell 15th-18th cent (mainly Forfarshire), with collected titles and writs of related families 16th-19th cent; Fife (Balcarres estate) titles and writs 15th-20th cent; Lancs (Haigh) deeds 14th-20th cent; misc deeds for Carmarthenshire 18th-20th cent, Hunts c1799-1824, Cumberland (Muncaster estate) 16th-

18th cent, etc; wills, inventories, marriage contracts and settlements, executorship papers and trust papers 16th-20th cent, Lindsay of Balcarres, Lindsay of Edzell and related families; Bradshaigh wills, settlements and related papers 17th-18th cent; executorship and trust papers, 1st Baron Muncaster (d1813) and Sir David Erskine of Cambo (Fife) 1840-54; legal papers, abstracts, inventories of title and financial papers 15th-20th cent, incl Crawford and Montrose peerage case papers; minutes of the barony courts of Glenesk 1543 and Edzell 1579-1609 and Lethnot (Forfarshire) head court 1576.

Lancs (Aspull and Haigh) manorial records 15th-19th cent; Lancs estate papers 17th-20th cent, incl leases, terrier 1796, survey 1721, rentals and accounts; accounts, corresp and papers rel to Lancs coal mining and ironworks 18th-20th cent, with Wigan Coal & Iron Co records c1865-1947; Fife (Balcarres and Leuchars) estate records c1782-20th cent, incl accounts, vouchers and corresp; Fife feu duty receipts 1749-1876; misc estate papers for Carmarthenshire 18th-20th cent, Dunecht 1845-99 and Hunts c1898-1919; misc papers rel to the estates (Cumberland, Yorks ER, etc) of the 1st Baron Muncaster (d1813), with related corresp 1813-49; Jamaica estate accounts and papers c1795-1847; Edwin family rent book 1754-9 and chief rent accounts 1673-81; misc estate papers 15th-18th cent, incl Struthers (Fife) farm accounts 1763-8, 1806-7.

Haigh Hall staircase bills 1716-19 and plans, accounts, corresp and papers 19th-20th cent; papers rel to houses in London and elsewhere 18th-20th cent, incl Berkeley Square household accounts 1825-53, papers rel to Lady Balcarres's Edinburgh house 1783-1819 and corresp rel to the Villa Palmieri (Florence) 1879-81; Muncaster household papers 1819-21; Balcarres building, household and garden accounts and papers c1790-1855; Struthers (afterwards Crawford Priory) household accounts 1755-67, 1785-7; Edzell household inventory 1573 and accounts 1592-1697; misc inventories 17th-19th cent, incl the 1st Earl of Dunfermline's books at Pinkie (Midlothian) 1625, the 9th Earl of Argyll's Stirling household 1682, the 2nd Viscount Garnock's books (? at Kilbirnie) 1727 and Lady Mary Lindsay-Crawford's Westminster house 1834.

Papers rel to Cheshire, Lancs and Wigan affairs 17th-20th cent, incl Lancs high shrievalty accounts 1678-9, Wigan mayoralty accounts 1680 and Wigan election corresp 1692-1747, 19th cent; papers rel to Haigh, Rivington and Blackrod schools c1684-1876; papers rel to Fife politics and local affairs mainly c1794-1854, incl election accounts 1832-5.

Patents and commissions 15th-19th cent; family accounts and papers 16th-20th cent, incl some of Lord Menmuir, Sir David Lindsay (d1610),

the 1st Baron Lindsay (d1641), the 3rd, 5th and 6th Earls of Balcarres and the 24th-28th Earls of Crawford; MSS of the 3rd Earl's narrative of Scottish affairs 1688-9; papers of Sir Ronald Charles Lindsay (d1945); literary, South African and other papers of Lady Anne Barnard (d1825), with some of Andrew Barnard (d1807), colonial secretary at the Cape; accounts and Indian papers of Robert Lindsay (d1836); papers of Lt-General James Lindsay (d1855), Sir Edward Nicholas (d1669), John Gunning of Castlecoote (Co Roscommon) 1735-50 and Sir Robert Murray Keith (d1795): letter book of Robert Hamilton of Bourtreehill (Ayrshire) 1750-8; Bradshaigh and Dalrymple family papers 17th-19th cent; accounts of the 24th, 63rd and 71st regiments 1778-1823 and the 4th Earl of Balcarres's troop of dragoons 1731-5; letter book, 37th regiment of foot 1773-4; account book of the steamer *Lady Lindsay* 1855-6; extensive records of the *Bibliotheca Lindesiana* at Haigh 1831-20th cent.

Genealogical papers 16th-19th cent, incl Bradshaigh pedigree 1647; literary and misc papers 16th-20th cent, incl MS proceedings of the Border commissioners 1605-6, MS of Robert Lindsay of Pitscottie's *Historie and Chronickillis of Scotland*, MS narrative of military events in the Carnatic by JS Lindsay (d1783), memoirs of Lady Charlotte Lindsay (d1849), and minutes of the National Union of the Working Classes 1831-3; extensive printed collections, incl English civil war and French revolutionary newspapers and tracts, royal proclamations, etc.

National Library of Scotland (Acc 9769). Mainly deposited at the John Rylands University Library of Manchester by the 28th and 29th Earls of Crawford 1946-80 and transferred 1988. HMC *Second Report, App*, 1874, pp181-2; *Papers of British Politicians 1782-1900*, 1989, pp62, 65, 82. GA Matheson and F Taylor, *Handlist of personal papers from the muniments of the Earl of Crawford and Balcarres*, 1976. NRA 11004. Journals and other papers of the 27th Earl remain in the private possession of the present Earl of Crawford.

[b] Sederunt book 1790-7.

National Library of Scotland (Dep 301/112). Deposited by Tods, Murray & Jamieson, WS, Edinburgh 1979. NRA 29083.

[c] Titles and printed petitions 1586-1830.

National Library of Scotland (Acc 11351). Deposited by Tods, Murray & Jamieson, WS,

Edinburgh in the Scottish Record Office 1958 (GD 237) and transferred 1996.

[d] Papers of Lord Menmuir (d1598) as Secretary of State and master of metals and minerals, incl drafts of state papers and papers rel to the University of St Andrews and the Church in Scotland; corresp, accounts and papers of and rel to Queen Mary of Guise (d1560); other papers of or collected by the Lindsays of Balcarres, incl letters of the 4th Earl of Morton (d1581) and papers of the 1st Earl of Balcarres (d1659).

National Library of Scotland (Advocates MSS 16.2.3, 19.1.24, 29.2.1-9a). Presented by the 3rd Earl of Balcarres to the Faculty of Advocates 1712.

[e] Corresp and papers of the peerage lawyer John Riddell (d1862), incl Crawford peerage case papers and collected books and MSS 16th-19th cent.

National Library of Scotland (Advocates MSS 25.8.1-26.7.37, Chs A 245-51). Riddell's papers were bought by the 25th Earl of Crawford (d1880), who presented some in 1867 and bequeathed the remainder in 1881. Other Riddell papers, including Crawford and Montrose peerage case papers, were presented by Miss Susan M Riddell c1906 (Advocates MSS 81.2.1-10, Chs A 205-9).

[f] Further corresp and papers of John Riddell, with papers of the antiquary James Maidment (d1879).

National Library of Scotland (MS 5312). Purchased from the 28th Earl of Crawford at Sotheby's, 19 May 1947, lot 188.

[g] Kilbirnie and Glengarnock (Ayrshire) rental 1757-82.

National Archives of Scotland (CS 96/3612).

[h] Haigh (Lancs) manor map 1796; extensive Haigh estate records 19th-20th cent, incl rentals, accounts and vouchers, wages books, letter books, corresp and farm records; architectural drawings, Haigh Hall stables 1865; misc Haigh Hall household accounts 1864-1946; Haigh Conservative Association minutes 1884-1935; records of Woodlands Red Cross Society 1914 and the Prince of Wales's National Relief Fund 1914-16; personal accounts of the 27th Earl 1919-34; misc papers, incl schedule of deeds at Warter Hall (Yorks ER) c1800, Carmarthenshire abstracts of title 1833-1925 and Llanon valuation 1911.

Wigan Archives Service (D/D Hai). Deposited by the 28th Earl of Crawford with Wigan County Borough and transferred c1970-9. NRA 41241.

[i] Corresp and papers rel to the Wigan Coal & Iron Company and other Lancs mining and business interests c1816-1947, incl Lancs railway papers c1842-1906; misc papers rel to Carmarthenshire properties 19th-20th cent; Dunecht report 1853 and accounts 1880.

Wigan Archives Service (Acc 1811, D/D Hai). Deposited by Ellis, Sayer & Henderson, solicitors, Wigan 1976. NRA 41242. For further Wigan Coal & Iron Company records see HMC *Records of British Business and Industry 1760-1914. Metal Processing and Engineering*, 1994, p74.

[j] Legal and financial papers 1869-75, incl Haigh, etc rental 1870.

Wigan Archives Service (Acc 1984, D/DX.EL boxes 73-4). Deposited with other clients' papers by Ellis, Sayer & Henderson, solicitors, Wigan 1979. NRA 19719.

[k] Haigh colliery orders 1635-98; Haigh library bills and book catalogues 1909-12; misc collected papers 1792-1815.

Wigan Archives Service (D/DZ A2, A13/34). Deposited by the 28th Earl of Crawford.

[l] Architectural drawings for the Crawford chapel in Wigan parish church 1850; misc illuminated addresses 1874-1922.

Wigan Archives Service (D/D Hai and Acc 739, D/DZ A 13/51-61). Presented by the 28th Earl of Crawford 1947.

[m] Haigh estate foreman's diaries 1880-4.

Wigan Archives Service (Acc 2676). Presented by L Smith 1990.

[n] Lancs estate rental 1870.

Lancashire Record Office (DDX 291/121-2). Deposited by the Society of Genealogists 1977. NRA 3510.

[o] Leases, legal and misc papers rel to Lancs coalmining c1840-60.

Birmingham University Information Services, Special Collections Department (Business records 14/iv-15/i-ii, boxes 10-11). Provenance unrecorded. NRA 31928.

[p] Papers of the 6th Earl of Balcarres as governor of Jamaica 1798-1801.

National Army Museum (6807/183). Presented amongst papers of Sir George Nugent by the Royal United Service Institution 1968. HMC *Private Papers of British Colonial Governors 1782-1900*, 1986, pp35-6. NRA 20793.

[q] Collected MSS of the Earls of Crawford and Balcarres from the *Bibliotheca Lindesiana*, incl English medieval and illuminated MSS, armorials, pedigrees and family histories, corresp of the naturalist Henry Baker (d1774), papers of Sir Frederic Madden (d1873), German and

European language collections, and Middle Eastern, Oriental and other MSS.

John Rylands University Library of Manchester. Purchased by Mrs Rylands from the 26th Earl of Crawford 1901. Further books and papers from the *Bibliotheca Lindesiana* were dispersed by sale at Sotheby's in 1924 (1-4 Dec), 1925 (27-8 April, 30 Nov-3 Dec), 1947 (24-5 Mar, 5-7 and 19 May, 5-6 July) and 1948 (1 Nov, 21 Dec). MSS relating to French history were acquired by the British Museum (Add MSS 41170-3, 41192-4, 41289-90). For the earlier history of the collections see N Barker, *The Bibliotheca Lindesiana*, Roxburghe Club, 1977.

[r] Misc literary and other papers of Brigadier-General Colin Lindsay (1755-95).

John Rylands University Library of Manchester (Eng MS 1135). Presented by Ronald Hall 1948.

[s] Diary of Lady Charlotte Lindsay 1814.

Bodleian Library, Oxford (MS Eng. misc. d. 226). Purchased 1931.

[t] Dunecht observatory papers of the 26th Earl c1871-96.

In private possession. Enquiries to the National Register of Archives (Scotland) (NRA(S) 2657). NRA 9504.

[u] Papers of the 27th Earl rel to the Education Bill 1906 (1 vol).

Liverpool University Library, Department of Special Collections and Archives (MS 24.30). Provenance unrecorded but known to be from the library of the Earl of Crawford.

Related collections: Boyle, Earls of Glasgow, no 9; Hope-Johnstone of Raehills, no 54, including papers of the 18th Earl of Crawford; Eaglescairnie papers (National Library of Scotland Advocates MSS 23.3.26-30), including letter book 1746 and other papers of the 20th Earl of Crawford; Barons Muncaster (Cumbria Record Office, Whitehaven D/Pen, NRA 12093; Hull University, Brynmor Jones Library DDWA, NRA 13797; John Rylands University Library of Manchester, see *Accessions to Repositories 1982*, p10); Barons Overstone (London University Library MS 804, NRA 17743; Northampton-shire Record Office, NRA 4952); Red Cross papers of Lord Wantage 1870-1905 (British Red Cross Archives D/Wan, NRA 30569); Berry papers and Sheffield Park papers (British Library, Manuscript Collections Add MSS 37726-61, 61979-87), including journals and papers of Lady Charlotte Lindsay (d1849).

[62] LLOYD-MOSTYN, Barons Mostyn

Ieuan Fychan (d1457) of Pengwern (Denbighshire) and Tre Castell (Anglesey) acquired lands in Mostyn (Flintshire) through marriage to Angharad, daughter and heir of Hywel of Mostyn. Gloddaeth (Carnarvonshire) was brought by marriage shortly before 1460. The Mostyn surname was adopted by Thomas ap Richard ap Hywel (d1558) and by his brother Peter, ancestor of the Mostyn baronets of Talacre. The Mostyns of Mostyn were created baronets 1660. Beeston and Peckforton (Cheshire), and the former estates of the Hough and Whitmore families in Leighton, Great Neston and Thornton Hough (Cheshire), came with the marriage of Bridget, daughter and heir of D'Arcy Savage, to Sir Thomas Mostyn, second Bt (1651-92). The bulk of the Mostyns' Anglesey property was disposed of c1732, but the marriage in 1766 of the fifth Bt to Margaret, daughter and heir of Dr Hugh Wynn, brought further estates at Berth Ddu (Denbighshire) and Bodysgallen (Carnarvonshire), as well as the former Lloyd estate of Bodidris (Denbighshire) and the Vaughan estate of Corsygedol (Merionethshire).

Following the death in 1831 of the sixth Bt, his brother-in-law Sir Edward Pryce Lloyd, second Bt, of Pengwern (Flintshire) and Bodfach (Montgomeryshire), was created first Baron Mostyn. The latter's son Edward Mostyn Lloyd inherited his uncle's estates, took the additional surname Mostyn and succeeded to the title in 1854. Beeston (Cheshire) was sold to John Tollemache in 1840, and the Mostyn Estates Act of 1842 was followed by substantial sales of land in Carnarvonshire, Cheshire, Denbighshire, Flintshire, Merionethshire and Montgomeryshire. Mostyn and Gloddaeth were retained, as were the family's mining interests and its involvement in the development of Llandudno (Carnarvonshire).

Estates in 1883: Flintshire 5,462 acres, Carnarvonshire 2,025 acres, Denbighshire 292 acres total 7,779 acres worth £14,752 a year.

[a] Deeds 13th-19th cent, mainly Flintshire and Merionethshire 13th-19th cent, Denbighshire 14th-18th cent, Carnarvonshire 15th-19th cent and Cheshire 13th-18th cent, with some for Anglesey 14th-19th cent and Montgomeryshire 16th-19th cent; abstracts of title 16th-19th cent; wills, settlements, executorship, trust and legal papers, Mostyn, Lloyd and Lloyd-Mostyn 16th-19th cent, Vaughan and Wynn 16th-18th cent, Lloyd of Bodidris 18th cent, and Hough, Whitmore and Savage (incl recusancy papers) 15th-17th cent; manorial records for Carnarvonshire, Flintshire and Montgomeryshire 15th-19th cent, incl Edern (Carnarvonshire) court books and precepts 1741-1816, Pwllheli (Carnarvonshire) borough court and entry books 1708-98, Caerwys (Flintshire) suit rolls 1741-54 and Llanidloes

(Montgomeryshire) borough court rolls 1781-1818.

Anglesey estate rentals (Mostyn family) 1611-1736; records of the Mostyn and Lloyd-Mostyn family estates in Carnarvonshire 16th-19th cent, Denbighshire 17th-19th cent, Flintshire 16th-20th cent, Merionethshire 18th-20th cent and Cheshire 17th-20th cent, incl leases 16th-19th cent, surveys, maps and plans from 17th cent, particulars, valuations, rentals and accounts from 16th cent and corresp 18th-19th cent; papers rel to tithes 16th-20th cent, enclosures, allotments and drainage 18th-19th cent, timber, hunting, quarries, roads and railways 18th-20th cent, and the Dee navigation 1738-1852; records of mines, quarries, shipping and industrial undertakings 17th-19th cent, incl Mostyn colliery and wharfage accounts 18th-19th cent, and of urban development at Llandudno (Carnarvonshire) *c*1827-90; papers rel to Lloyd family estates in Carnarvonshire (Pantglas), Flintshire (Pengwern, etc), Montgomeryshire (Bodfach) and Radnorshire 17th-19th cent; Carnarvonshire and Merionethshire estate papers 17th-18th cent, Wynn and Vaughan families; Cheshire (Great Neston, Thornton Hough, etc) surveys, rentals, accounts and papers 16th-17th cent, incl Leighton commons papers 1569-82.

Bodidris house building accounts 1818-24; inventories of Mostyn family houses at Bloomsbury Square (Middlesex) 1721, Gloddaeth (Carnarvonshire) 1854 and Bodysgallen (Carnarvonshire) 1859, with misc household accounts and papers 18th-20th cent; Corsygedol building accounts 1760-4, with Corsygedol and Nannau (Merionethshire) household inventories 1698-1777 and Corsygedol household papers 17th-18th cent; household inventories for Ruthin (Denbighshire, Wynn family) 1746, the Lloyd (of Bodidris) family 1664-71 and the Hough and Whitmore families 16th cent; Carnarvonshire, Flintshire and Merionethshire shrievalty papers 16th-18th cent, Mostyn and Vaughan families; papers rel to Carnarvonshire, Denbighshire, Flintshire, Merionethshire and Montgomeryshire affairs 17th-19th cent, incl papers rel to subsidies and taxes from 17th cent, turnpikes, the Flintshire election 1784 and the Flintshire militia 18th-19th cent; papers rel to Anglesey and Flintshire charities 18th-19th cent; Llandwye and Llanenddwyn (Merionethshire) poor law papers 1812-16, with papers rel to Llandwye club 1757-72; papers rel to Whitford (Flintshire) rectory *c*1619-31 and poor law 1826-41; Holywell (Flintshire) hunt records 1707-1827.

Mostyn, Lloyd and Lloyd-Mostyn family corresp and papers 16th-19th cent, incl appointments and commissions 17th-19th cent, papers of Sir Roger Mostyn, 3rd Bt, as Paymaster-General, paymaster of marines and teller of the Exchequer 1704-16, engagement and memoranda books of Sir Thomas Mostyn, 6th Bt,

1822-31 and papers rel to the debts of the 1st and 2nd Barons Mostyn 1853-7; Vaughan family corresp and papers 16th-18th cent, incl diaries and notebooks of William and Evan Lloyd Vaughan of Corsygedol 1749-88; ecclesiastical papers of Dr Hugh Wynn *c*1721-1750; Hough family papers 16th cent, incl papers of William Hough as bailiff of Halton (Cheshire) *c*1554-70 and steward of the estates of Sir Francis Englefield at Stanford-in-the-Vale (Berks) and Wootton Bassett (Wilts) 1562-75; Whitmore and Savage family papers 16th-17th cent; literary, genealogical and historical MSS 16th-19th cent; misc papers 14th-19th cent, incl orders rel to the government of Harlech (Merionethshire) 1612, account book of John Williams as agent to Dr John Gwynn 1572-3, survey and rentals of Crown lands in the commotes of Is Aled and Ceinmeirch (Denbighshire) 16th-17th cent, Gwydir (Carnarvonshire) estate timber account 1685-6 and abstract of Gwydir estate rental 1724.

University of Wales Bangor Library, Department of Manuscripts (Mostyn Collection). Deposited by the 4th and 5th Barons Mostyn 1962, 1969. HMC *Papers of British Politicians 1782-1900*, 1989, pp63, 74. NRA 22953.

[b] Deeds 14th-20th cent, mainly Flintshire 14th-20th cent, Carnarvonshire 15th-20th cent, Denbighshire 16th-20th cent, Merionethshire, Montgomeryshire and Radnorshire 16th-19th cent and Cheshire 15th-19th cent; abstracts and schedules of title 18th-20th cent; wills, settlements, executorship, trust and legal papers, Mostyn, Lloyd and Lloyd-Mostyn 16th-20th cent and Vaughan 17th-18th cent; Savage settlements and Whitmore legal case papers 17th cent; Pryce settlements and case papers 17th-18th cent.

Records of Mostyn and Lloyd-Mostyn family estates in Carnarvonshire, Denbighshire, Flintshire, Merionethshire and Cheshire 17th-20th cent, incl leases, surveys, maps and plans 18th-20th cent, valuations 19th cent, rentals and accounts 17th-19th cent and corresp from 17th cent; papers rel to tithes, enclosure, game and transport 18th-20th cent; records of mining and quarrying 18th-20th cent, Mostyn quay and docks 19th-20th cent and Mostyn estates company 20th cent; Liverpool (Lancs) leases 20th cent; extensive records of the Llandudno estate 19th-20th cent, incl leases, maps, plans and drawings (*c*650), rentals, accounts, vouchers, corresp and mineral papers; papers rel to estates of the Lloyd family in Carnarvonshire, Denbighshire and Merionethshire (Pantglas estate), Flintshire (Pengwern estate), and Montgomeryshire and Radnorshire (Berthlwyd estate) 18th-19th cent; survey of Cheshire and Flintshire estates of William Hough of Leighton 1576.

Mostyn and Gloddaeth building papers 19th-20th cent; misc inventories of Mostyn family houses 19th-20th cent; household papers of the Lloyd family 18th cent, incl Pengwern, Bodfach and Lincoln's Inn (Middlesex); misc papers rel to Flintshire and Merionethshire local affairs 18th-19th cent; Mostyn, Lloyd and Lloyd-Mostyn family corresp and papers 18th-20th cent, incl appointments and commissions 18th cent and accounts of Bell Lloyd of Bodfach and Edward Lloyd of Pengwern 18th cent; genealogical and misc papers 14th-19th cent, incl papers rel to Gibraltar coal 18th cent.

Flintshire Record Office (D/M). Deposited by the 5th Baron Mostyn, some through the Chief Agent, Mostyn Estates Ltd, Llandudno, 1969-90. NRA 17858.

[c] Papers of Edmund Herbert (d1769) of Gray's Inn and Whittlebury (Northants) as agent of the Mostyn family, incl misc Welsh deeds and abstracts 17th-18th cent, Mostyn Hall and London household records 1728-32 and Mostyn family accounts and corresp 1702-68; other papers of or rel to Edmund Herbert, incl marine pay office papers 1702-40 and papers rel to the Swift family 16th-18th cent.

Flintshire Record Office (D/M). Deposited by the Historical Manuscripts Commission 1964. NRA 17858. The provenance of these papers is uncertain but they may derive from the Chancery Masters' Exhibits now held by the Public Record Office.

[d] Mostyn colliery papers 1852-76.

Caernarfon Record Office (XD 8/4/1252-88). Deposited by Messrs Breese, Jones & Casson, solicitors, Portmadog *c*1972. NRA 29828.

[e] Corsygedol and Plas Hen (Carnarvonshire) estate papers 18th-19th cent, incl valuations and accounts.

National Library of Wales (MS 4965). *Handlist of MSS*, ii, p58.

[f] Denbighshire, Flintshire, Merionethshire, Montgomeryshire and Radnorshire deeds and estate papers of the Lloyd (later Lloyd-Mostyn) family 1737-1846.

National Library of Wales. Deposited by Winter Tunstill of Bodfach 1961. *Annual Report 1960-1*, pp61-2.

[g] Welsh literary, genealogical and political MSS from Nannau, Gloddaeth and Corsygedol 13th-18th cent.

National Library of Wales (MSS 3020-76, 21238-54, 21693). Purchased privately 1918 and at Christie's 24 Oct 1974. This collection also includes MSS sold at Christie's 13 July 1920 and acquired subsequently. *Handlist of MSS*, i, pp261-3. HMC *Report on Manuscripts in the Welsh Language*, I (Mostyn MSS), 1898, *passim*. Other MSS sold 1920 and 1974 are now widely dispersed: see HMC *Guide to the Location of Collections*, 1982, p45.

Related Collections: Heathcote-Drummond-Willoughby, Earls of Ancaster, no 48, including Wynn of Gwydir papers 1515-1690; Vaughan of Nannau (University of Wales Bangor Library, Department of Manuscripts, NRA 25758); Mostyn of Talacre (Flintshire Record Office D/MT, NRA 14045); Herbert of Whittlebury (Huntington Library, San Marino, California, see *Guide to British Historical Manuscripts in the Huntington Library*, 1982, pp311-12, and Northamptonshire Record Office ZB 311, NRA 25877), including papers of Edmund Herbert; Swift family papers (London Metropolitan Archives AC.64.043, NRA 41370).

[63] LOWTHER, Earls of Lonsdale

The Lowther family, seated at Lowther in Westmorland by the twelfth century, also held estates in Cumberland by the fourteenth century. These were greatly extended in the seventeenth century by Sir John Lowther (d1637), whose acquisition of the manor of St Bees (Cumberland) laid the foundations of the Whitehaven estate. He also purchased a small estate centred on Marton (Yorkshire, North Riding), but this property later passed to the Ramsden family of Byram (Yorkshire, West Riding). On his death the Lowther estate passed to his eldest son John (created a baronet 1638), whilst Whitehaven descended to his second son Christopher (created a baronet 1642), who also acquired Sockbridge and Hartsop (Westmorland) through his marriage to Frances Lancaster of Sockbridge. A third son, William, purchased an estate in Yorkshire and founded the Lowther family of Swillington. Sir John Lowther of Lowther, second Bt, was created Viscount Lonsdale in 1696. Outlying estates in Yorkshire and County Durham were sold in the 1720s.

On the death without issue of the third Viscount in 1751, the baronetcy and Lowther estates were inherited by his second cousin Sir James Lowther (1736-1802), whose father, Robert Lowther of Maulds Meaburn (Westmorland), Governor of Barbados, had acquired an estate in Barbados through his marriage in 1709 to Joan, widow of Robert Carleton, and had purchased the Duke of Wharton's Westmorland estates in 1730. Sir James Lowther's trustees purchased for him additional Westmorland property and an estate in Cleveland (Yorkshire, North Riding). Sir James Lowther further inherited the estates of the fourth and last Lowther Bt of Whitehaven (d1755), including an estate at Laleham (Middlesex), which had been purchased by the fourth Bt. Having bought Sir Charles Pelham's Workington (Cumberland) property in 1758 and an estate at Haslemere (Surrey) in 1780, Lowther was created Earl of Lonsdale in 1784. Dying without issue in 1802, he left his

Barbados property to his sisters (see Vane, Barons Barnard, no 109), his Cumberland and Westmorland estates to his third cousin Sir William Lowther, Bt, of Swillington (who had purchased Cottesmore in Rutland in 1796), and his Yorkshire property to Sir William's younger brother John Lowther; whilst Laleham was sold. On his inheritance of the Lonsdale estates Sir William Lowther (who was created Earl of Lonsdale in 1807) surrendered his paternal Swillington property to his brother John Lowther in accordance with their father's will. The Lowther and Whitehaven estates were administered separately until the latter was sold in 1956.

Estates in 1883: Westmorland 39,229 acres, Cumberland 28,228 acres, Rutland 493 acres, Lancs 115 acres, total 68,065 acres worth £71,333 a year.

[a] Deeds 12th-20th cent (over 1,000 medieval), mainly Cumberland and Westmorland but incl Yorks 12th-19th cent, Northumberland 12th-16th cent, Norfolk and Suffolk 13th-17th cent, Middlesex (Laleham) 16th-19th cent, Surrey (Haslemere) 17th-19th cent and Rutland (Cottesmore) 1776-1824; deed registers and abstracts of title 16th-18th cent, incl abstracts of deeds rel to Wharton estates in Cumberland and Westmorland c1731; wills, settlements and related papers 16th-20th cent; legal and case papers 16th-20th cent, incl papers rel to title of Wharton manors 17th-19th cent, Laleham 1697-1745 and the estate of Sir Home Popham 1794-1823; manorial records 15th-20th cent, mainly Cumberland and Westmorland but incl Middlesex (Laleham) 1428-1674.

Lowther estate (mainly Westmorland and Cumberland, but some Yorks) records 16th-20th cent, incl leases, surveys and valuations, maps and plans, rentals and accounts, corresp 17th-20th cent, memoranda books 1558-1680, and papers rel to boundaries 1541-20th cent, coal and fisheries 17th-19th cent, the Lowther Linen and Carpet Manufactory 1741-74 and the Hackthorpe tilery 1846-66; Wharton estate extent and valuation 1561-1605; Sockbridge rental and account 1574-1641; rental of Sir Charles Pelham's Cumberland estate 1751-7; Meaburn (Westmorland and Yorks) estate accounts 1676-1788; Whitehaven estate (Cumberland and Westmorland) records 15th-20th cent, incl leases 15th-20th cent, surveys and valuations 17th-20th cent, maps and plans c1700-20th cent, rentals and accounts 1510-20th cent, corresp 17th-20th cent, memoranda books 1661-1766, and salmon fishery and foreshore papers 1553-1892; extensive records of the Whitehaven estate's coal, iron ore and other mining operations 17th-20th cent; Laleham estate papers 1613-1766; Barbados plantation records 1649-1802; Wensleydale rentals and accounts 17th cent; accounts of Lord Lonsdale's agent at Haslemere 1796-9; Cottesmore accounts 1824-43.

Lowther Castle architectural drawings and plans from late 17th cent, incl Lancelot Brown 1763-71, Robert and James Adam 1767-71 and Sir Robert Smirke 1806-34, with household and building accounts 17th-20th cent and inventories 18th-20th cent; Whitehaven Castle architectural drawings 1766-1836, with household and building accounts 17th-20th cent and inventories 1697-20th cent; Meaburn household accounts 17th-18th cent; London household papers 18th-20th cent, incl inventories and a visitors' book 1758-71; Cottesmore inventories and accounts 19th cent; papers rel to the Council of the North 1537-1637, the Vice-Admiralty of Cumberland and Westmorland late 17th-18th cent, and Cumberland and Westmorland lieutenancy and militia from 17th cent; Cumberland shrievalty papers 1572-1663; bonds and receipts for recusancy fines 1632-9; Westmorland tax assessments 1641-1813; Cumberland and Westmorland customs papers 1550-18th cent; papers rel to elections in Cumberland and Westmorland 1695-20th cent and Lancaster 1784-6; Lowther parish records 1827-1903; papers rel to St Bees School 1610-1878, Workington dock and harbour 19th-20th cent, the Lonsdale Battalion 20th cent and the Whitehaven Primrose League 1886-20th cent; register of JPs' warrants and recognisances for Howdenshire (Yorks ER) 1682-8.

Patents and appointments 1643-20th cent; Lowther family papers 16th-20th cent, incl Admiralty papers 1598-18th cent, parliamentary and political papers from 16th cent, corresp c1530-20th cent, personal accounts 16th-19th cent and diaries and general memoranda books 17th-20th cent; Barbados governorship records 1707-20; personal and political papers of the 1st and 2nd Earls of Lonsdale 1770-20th cent; racing papers 1700-20th cent and game, hunting and yachting records 19th-20th cent.

Metcalf Carleton family of Hillbeck and Appleby (Westmorland) papers, incl deeds 1694-1785, wills, etc 1703-90, legal papers 1670-1805, manorial records 1498-1789, estate papers 1633-1792 and family letters 1663-1793, with Appleby, etc (Tufton family) rentals and accounts 1690-1724; papers rel to the Curwen family of Workington, incl rental and bailiffs' accounts for Seaton (Cumberland) 1449-51 and account book of Sir Patricius Curwen 1625-46, and to the Fleming family of Rydal, incl estate accounts 1758-69 and memorabilia late 17th cent; rental 1661 and account books 1664-1701 for the Duke of Somerset's Yorks estates; Denton of Cardew account book 1587-1637 and family pedigrees; letter books and account books of Henry and John Fleming of Whitehaven and Norfolk, Virginia 1771-1817 and of William Wood of Tallentire Hall (Cumberland) 1851-80; letters to the Revd Henry Zouche of Sandal 1787-91; St Bees Priory accounts 1516, rental 1500 and survey 16th cent; papers rel to scholarship endowment at Oriel College, Oxford 16th-17th cent and bursar's daybook of an (unnamed) Oxford college *c*1726-40.

Cumbria Record Office, Carlisle (D/LONS). Deposited by the 7th Earl of Lonsdale 1963 onwards. HMC *Thirteenth Report, App VII*, 1893; *Papers of British Cabinet Ministers 1782-1900*, 1982, p40; *Papers of British Politicians 1782-1900*, 1989, p65. HM Colvin, JM Crook, T Friedman, *Catalogue of Architectural Drawings from Lowther Castle*, 1980. NRA 17777 (partial list).

[b] Agency papers for Westmorland and Cumberland, mainly 19th-20th cent but incl papers rel to baronies of Burgh and Kendal and other Lowther and Wharton manors late 18th-20th cent and case papers from late 17th cent.

Cumbria Record Office, Carlisle (D/RGL). Deposited by Little & Shepherd, solicitors, Penrith 1981. NRA 36596.

[c] Legal corresp and papers late 18th-20th cent; Cumberland manorial and estate papers early 18th-20th cent; mining corresp and papers and election papers 19th-20th cent.

Cumbria Record Office, Carlisle (D/A). Deposited by R Allison, solicitor, Whitehaven 1963. NRA 23766.

[d] Westmorland deeds 16th-19th cent; survey of manor of Kirkby Lonsdale (Westmorland) 1757; rental of manor of Casterton (Westmorland) 1764.

Cumbria Record Office, Kendal (WDX 331). Deposited by the British Records Association through Tullie House Library, Carlisle 1971. County Archivist's Report June-Oct 1971, p7.

[e] Asby Grange and Ravenstonedale (Westmorland) deeds 12th cent-1704; case papers (Lowther *v* Raw) 1733-4; Ravenstonedale manorial records 17th-19th cent and parish will register 1670-1857.

Cumbria Record Office, Kendal (WD/Kilv). Deposited by Fell, Kilvington & Co, solicitors, Kirkby Stephen 1986. NRA 32567.

[f] Westmorland manorial records 16th-20th cent, incl Kirkby Lonsdale court book 1844-1905 and Lupton court books 1598-1902.

Cumbria Record Office, Kendal (WD/PP). Deposited by Pearson & Pearson, solicitors, Kirkby Lonsdale 1963. NRA 40440.

[g] Maulds Meaburn rental 1587.

Cumbria Record Office, Kendal (WD/CAT). Purchased by the Curwen Archives Trust 1991. County Archivist's Report Jan-Mar 1991, p13.

[h] Kendal rental 1734-5.

Cumbria Record Office, Kendal (WD/K 130). Deposited by Kendal Library 1966. County Archivist's Report Aug-Nov 1966, p4.

[i] Lowther estate (Westmorland and Cumberland) rentals 1792, 1846, 1861, with manor call books 19th-20th cent and collectors' books 1861-9; Lake Windermere encroachment books 1893, 1907.

Cumbria Record Office, Kendal (WD/Lons (Acc 87, 268)). Deposited by M Rowling, Kendal 1964. County Archivist's Report Dec 1964, p3.

[j] Account book of Sir James Lowther of Whitehaven 1737-46.

Cumbria Record Office, Whitehaven (DH 31). Transferred from Whitehaven Public Library.

[k] Letters to the 1st Viscount Lonsdale 1687-97.

Yale University, Beinecke Library (Osborn MSS Files, Folders 9294-5). Purchased 1971.

Related collections: Vane, Barons Barnard, no 109; Tufton, Barons Hothfield, no 108; Lowther of Swillington (Denbighshire Record Office DD/L, NRA 19944, and West Yorkshire Archive Service, Leeds Acc 1634, NRA 40558); Barons Muncaster (Cumbria Record Office, Whitehaven D/Pen, D/P, NRA 12093), including papers of the 3rd Viscount Lonsdale as Constable of the Tower of London 1726-7 and as lord lieutenant of Cumberland 1745-6; Ramsden of Byram (West Yorkshire Archive Service, Leeds RA, NRA 7344), including deeds for Marton, etc, letter book of Lady Elizabeth Lowther 1682-9 and volume relating to the 3rd Viscount Lonsdale's appointment as Constable of the Tower 1726; Marton deeds and estate papers (North Yorkshire County Record Office ZFE, NRA 40287), including Lowther family papers 13th-18th cent.

[64] LUMLEY, Earls of Scarbrough

The Lumley family owned land in County Durham by the twelfth century. Its estates, the core of which was at Lumley Castle, situated on the Durham coalfield by the River Wear, were extended in the fifteenth century through the marriage of George, Lord Lumley and the heiress of Roger Thornton, a Newcastle-upon-Tyne merchant. Created (Irish) Viscounts in 1628, the family achieved further eminence when Richard Lumley (d1721) was promoted Earl of Scarbrough in 1690. In the eighteenth century extensive properties were acquired from the Saunderson family.

The Saundersons were merchants and landowners who built up estates in Yorkshire (West Riding) and Lincolnshire through marriage and purchase in the fifteenth and sixteenth centuries. Important acquisitions were made at Saxby

(Lincolnshire) and, in 1549, Sandbeck (Yorkshire, West Riding), a former possession of the Cistercian abbey of Roche. Roche itself was bought in 1627, and in the early eighteenth century Glentworth and Winteringham (Lincolnshire) were inherited from the Wray family. The Lincolnshire estate, which included Reasby and Skegness, was scattered through Lindsey, but that in Yorkshire (including Maltby, Stainton and Stone) was concentrated around Sandbeck. From the eighteenth century nearby Tickhill was leased from the Duchy of Lancaster.

The Saunderson family, created baronets in 1612 and Viscounts Castleton (Irish) in 1627, was extinguished on the death in 1723 of the first and only Earl of Castleton (created 1720). He left his Yorkshire and Lincolnshire estates to Thomas Lumley (1691-1752), second son of his cousin the first Earl of Scarbrough, who adopted the name Lumley-Saunderson, and succeeded his brother as third Earl of Scarbrough in 1739. The County Durham estate, together with an estate at Stansted (Sussex) acquired by the marriage of John, Lord Lumley (d1609) and Jane, daughter and co-heir of the twelfth Earl of Arundel, passed to James Lumley, another son of the first Earl of Scarbrough. On James Lumley's death in 1766 the County Durham estate reverted to the fourth Earl but Stansted descended to Lumley's nephew the second Earl of Halifax.

Owing to an inheritance dispute involving the will of Sir George Savile, eighth Bt (1726-84), of Rufford (Nottinghamshire), the seventh and eighth Earls held the Nottinghamshire and Yorkshire (West Riding) estates of the Savile family between 1832 and 1856 (see Lumley-Savile of Rufford, no 65). When the eighth Earl died unmarried in 1856 the Lumley and Saunderson estates were inherited by a cousin as ninth Earl of Scarbrough, while the Savile estates passed to Henry Savile Lumley (d1881) and afterwards to the first Baron Savile of Rufford (d1896), both natural sons of the eighth Earl.

An urban estate at Warrington (Cheshire) entered the family through the eleventh Earl's mother Constance Ellinor (d1933), eldest granddaughter of John Wilson Patten (1802-92), Baron Winmarleigh. Property in the North Riding of Yorkshire (Thornton, etc) and the East Riding (Scampston), formerly owned by John, Lord Latimer (d1577), descended to his granddaughter Elizabeth, Viscountess Lumley (d1658), widow of Sir William Sandys, and was sold after her death.

Estates in 1883: Lincs 11,270 acres, Yorks WR 8,640 acres, Co Durham 1,788 acres, total 21,698 acres worth £31,597 a year.

[a] Deeds 13th-20th cent, mainly Co Durham, Lincs and Yorks WR, with some for Gloucs,

Northumberland, Sussex, etc; wills, settlements, executorship and trust papers, schedules of title and legal papers 15th-20th cent, Lumley and Saunderson families, incl inquisitions *post mortem* 15th cent-1704 and executorship papers for the 1st Earl of Halifax 1739-41; Yorks WR manorial records 14th-20th cent, mainly Slade Hooton and Austerfield, with records for the honour of Tickhill 1469-18th cent and Mexborough court leet c1662-1731; manorial court records for Yorks NR (Thornton, Sinnington) and ER (Scampston) c1457-1637, Lincs (Saxby, Stainton, Reasby) c1547-64 and manors of Lady Elizabeth Sandys (Hants, Wilts, etc) 1560-1.

Records of the entire Scarbrough estate mainly 18th-20th cent, incl particulars 1899 and letter books 1861-1939, with tithe, enclosure, drainage and railway papers from 17th cent; Yorks WR leases, maps, plans, surveys and valuations, rentals, accounts, corresp and papers 15th-20th cent, incl papers rel to collieries and Tickhill and Doncaster leasehold properties 18th-20th cent; Lincs estate records 14th-20th cent, incl Winteringham maps 1719 and valuations c1780-9, Glentworth particulars 1732, Reasby survey 1743 and Skegness estate papers from 17th cent, with urban development and Pier Company records 19th-20th cent; Co Durham estate papers 15th-20th cent, incl Cold Hesleton map 1730, Lumley rentals mid-18th cent and coal mining records (leases and way-leaves from 1408, plan 1748, accounts from 1674, etc); accounts and corresp for Warrington (Cheshire) estate c1930-53; papers rel to Yorks ER and NR (Thornton, Sinnington) estate mainly 16th-17th cent; other estate papers 16th-20th cent, incl papers for Northumberland and Newcastle-upon-Tyne 18th cent and for Notts 1792-1807, valuation of estates of Baron Sandys 1531-8, rental and sale papers for the Earl of Inchiquin's Irish estate 1737-50, and accounts of the estates of Lord Lumley 1583-1606 and of the earldom of Arundel 1359-60, 1574-7, 1590.

Sandbeck building accounts and papers 18th-20th cent, incl accounts of James Paine c1757-78, architectural papers for Sandbeck chapel (Benjamin Ferry) 1869-70 and landscaping accounts 1771-4; Glentworth architectural drawings and vouchers (James Paine) 1753-5; household inventories 16th-20th cent, mainly Sandbeck 18th-20th cent but incl Lumley Castle 1590, London books 1732 and Rufford House 1787; household accounts and papers, mainly Sandbeck house, chapel and garden 19th-20th cent, with misc records of Sandbeck and other houses from 17th cent, incl Rufford House accounts 1768-1804 and Lumley Castle records 20th cent; papers rel to Lincs affairs 16th-20th cent, incl shrievalty papers (Nicholas Saunderson) 1592-3, 1613-14, election accounts 1758-80, militia papers 1759-63, Glentworth overseers' and churchwardens' vouchers and accounts 1791-1820 and Skegness District Cricket and Lawn Tennis Club minutes 1906-

23; papers rel to Yorks WR affairs 18th-20th cent, incl school records for Maltby 1714-1901 and Stone 1858-20th cent, Maltby overseers' accounts c1843-50 and mission church papers 1910-13, and records of Sandbeck reading room 1865-98, Sandbeck nursing association 1902-12 and the Tickhill Association for the Prosecution of Felons 1816-55; records of Henry Smith's charity, Little Lumley and Chester-le-Street (Co Durham) 1747-76.

Appointments and commissions 15th-19th cent; family accounts, diaries and papers 17th-20th cent, incl inventories of the 1st Earl of Orkney 1736-7 and the 1st Earl of Halifax 1739, estate book of Sir Nicholas Saunderson 1608-22, accounts and papers of Sir Thomas Saunderson c1724-9 and of the 6th Earl of Scarbrough 1793-1815, accounts of Richard Lumley Savile c1789-98 and solicitors' accounts 18th cent; papers of the 10th Earl, incl some rel to Yorks WR yeomanry and territorial forces; diaries of Richard Bassett, agent at Glentworth 1771-1804; household papers of Frederick, Prince of Wales, incl the 3rd Earl's accounts as Treasurer and Receiver-General 1715-51, 1767, with rental and survey of Kew estate 1732, Duchy of Cornwall rental 1716, Duchy of Lancaster court orders 1717-19, naval and military estimates (mainly copies) 1735, 1751, and Port of London Survey Office accounts 1740-50; literary and misc papers from 16th cent, incl Lumley pedigree 1733, game books, and weather records from 1877; deeds 1425-17th cent, ordinances 1425 and rental 1618 for St Katherine's Hospital, Newcastle-upon-Tyne; ministers' accounts c1509 and rental c1540, estates of the Preceptory (Knights Hospitallers) of Willoughton (Lincs); terrier of St Crucis's chantry in Tickhill c1547.

Papers of the Wilson Patten family, incl executorship and trust papers late 19th-20th cent, corresp and papers of Baron Winmarleigh, and diary of Ellinor Wilson Patten 1848-1913.

In private possession. Enquiries to the Earl of Scarbrough, Sandbeck Park, Maltby, nr Rotherham, South Yorkshire. Partially listed by the National Register of Archives c1950-4. The collection includes records transferred to Sandbeck by Messrs Walker, solicitors, Bawtry in 1964. NRA 6155.

[b] Legal and estate papers 18th-20th cent, incl misc manorial papers for Stainton and Slade Hooton 1725-1925, estate maps (Maltby and Slade Hooton) 18th-19th cent and solicitor's day books (Cartwright of Bawtry, Yorks WR) 1837-8, 1843-5.

Sheffield Archives (L.C. 1088-1101). Deposited by Messrs Walker, solicitors, Bawtry 1964. NRA 112.

[c] Skegness estate records 18th-20th cent, mainly for the urban estate late 19th-20th cent,

incl deeds and legal papers, leases, agreements, maps and plans 19th-20th cent, valuations 1775-1802, rentals, accounts, corresp and papers; Skegness churchwardens' papers 1937-48; misc agreements, valuations, estate papers and tithe papers for other Lincs properties (Glentworth, Saxby, Stainton with Reasby, etc) mainly 19th-early 20th cent.

Lincolnshire Archives. Deposited by the 12th Earl of Scarbrough from the Skegness Estate Office 1983. *Archivists' Report 1983-84*, p9.

[d] Corresp and papers of the 10th Earl of Scarbrough rel to the Royal Niger Company and the Niger Company 1887-1932.

Rhodes House Library, Oxford (MSS Afr. s. 85-101*). Deposited by the 11th Earl of Scarbrough 1950, 1957. NRA 24247.

[e] Papers of the 11th Earl of Scarbrough rel to the governorship of Bombay and to Indian affairs 1937-63.

British Library, Oriental and India Office Collections (MSS Eur. F 253). Deposited by the 12th Earl of Scarbrough 1975. NRA 36734.

[f] Family and business corresp and papers of Baron Winmarleigh (1802-92).

Lancashire Record Office (DDSb). Deposited by the 12th Earl of Scarbrough 1986, 1994. NRA 31246.

[g] Legal and financial papers of and rel to the 4th Earl (d1782), incl accounts of work by Lancelot 'Capability' Brown at Sandbeck Park and Roche Abbey 1774-80 and by Henry Holland 1776-81, and accounts, corresp and papers rel to Lumley Colliery c1778-82; family and business corresp and papers of the 5th Earl (d1807), incl London household accounts 1797-1801 and personal accounts and vouchers c1782-1807; misc deeds, agreements and related papers mainly 18th cent; will of the 5th Viscount Castleton 1709; settlements 1654 (Wray family) and 1752 (4th Earl of Scarbrough); Co Durham and Lincs estate rental 1784; appointments, Earl of Castleton and Sir Thomas Saunderson 1703-27.

Public Record Office (C 104/30, C 112/19). NRA 39979.

[h] Portuguese letter book of the 3rd Earl of Scarbrough 1722-3.

Bodleian Library, Oxford (MS Eng. Lett. c. 18.).

[i] Manuscript and printed book collection of John, Lord Lumley (d1609).

British Library, Manuscript Collections (Royal MSS). Purchased by King James I on Lord Lumley's death (see *Catalogue of Royal and Kings Manuscripts in the British Library*, 1921, ppxix, xl-xliv).

[j] Rentals and accounts for Lord Lumley 1532-1608, mainly Co Durham, Northumberland and Yorks estates but incl Hants, Surrey (Nonsuch Palace) and Sussex.

Surrey History Centre (836). Presented by TW Futrille, solicitor, Sunningdale 1972. NRA 3518.

Related collections: Lumley-Savile of Rufford, no 65; Wilson Patten family and estate papers from 17th cent (Cheshire Record Office DWW, NRA 41665, and Warrington Library, NRA 14602); Fitzalan-Howard, Dukes of Norfolk, no 37, including papers relating to the 12th Earl of Arundel's estates.

[65] LUMLEY-SAVILE of Rufford

The Saviles were an established Yorkshire knightly family by 1300. In the late middle ages Thornhill and extensive estates in the West Riding of Yorkshire, concentrated near Dewsbury, were acquired by marriage. Early in the seventeenth century the Rufford Abbey estate, near Mansfield (Nottinghamshire), was acquired through the marriage of Sir George Savile, first Bt, to Mary, daughter of the sixth Earl of Shrewsbury.

Sir George Savile, fourth Bt (1633-95), was created successively Viscount (1668), Earl (1679) and Marquess (1682) of Halifax by Charles II. The peerage became extinct on the death in 1700 of the second Marquess. An estate at Barrowby (Lincolnshire), inherited from the Vernon family in the mid-sixteenth century, appears to have passed to a co-heir of the second Marquess and thence to the Boyle and later the Cavendish families (see Cavendish, Dukes of Devonshire, no 17). The baronetcy and other estates, however, devolved on the second Marquess's cousin Sir John Savile of Lupset (Yorkshire, West Riding), the baronetcy eventually expiring on the death, unmarried, of his descendant Sir George Savile, eighth Bt (1726-84). Savile left his Thornhill and Rufford estates to his nephew Richard Lumley-Saunderson, brother of the fifth Earl of Scarbrough and one of seven sons of his sister Barbara Savile, wife of the fourth Earl (see Lumley, Earls of Scarbrough, no 64). Savile stipulated that, should the nephew in possession of the Savile estates succeed to the earldom of Scarbrough, he should relinquish the Savile property to his next eldest brother. This occurred on the deaths of the fifth and sixth Earls in 1807 and 1832, but the seventh Earl of Scarbrough succeeded in uniting the Savile and Lumley inheritances and passed them to his son, who became eighth Earl in 1835 and held them until he died unmarried in 1856. The Lumley and Saunderson estates then descended to the ninth Earl of Scarbrough, whilst the Savile estates devolved upon Henry Savile Lumley (d1881) and afterwards upon John

Savile-Lumley (1818-96), Baron Savile of Rufford, both natural sons of the eighth Earl. Rufford Abbey was sold in 1938.

Estates in 1883: Notts 17,820 acres, Yorks WR 16,000 acres, total 33,820 acres worth £52,213 a year.

[a] Deeds 12th-19th cent (c1,000 pre-1500), mainly Notts, Yorks and Lincs but with some for Bucks, Derbys, Co Durham, Lancs, Northants, etc, incl Rufford Abbey charters 12th-15th cent; misc schedules 16th-19th cent; wills, settlements and related papers 14th-19th cent, incl the 6th Earl of Shrewsbury 1590-1618, the Cole family of Brancepeth (Co Durham) 1701-29, Sir Brian Broughton 1737-50 and the 6th, 7th and 8th Earls of Scarbrough 1799-1851; inquisitions *post mortem* 16th-17th cent; legal papers 13th-19th cent; manorial court records, Notts (Ollerton, Wellow, etc) c1614-1859 and Yorks WR (Barkisland, Heptonstall, Stainland, Wadsworth, etc) 1273-19th cent; misc manorial records 14th-17th cent, Lancs, Lincs, Northants and Westmorland, incl court rolls for Foulridge (Lancs) 1326, 1338, Barrowby (Lincs) 1386, 1452 and Fotheringhay (Northants) 1555-6.

Yorks WR estate records 14th-19th cent, incl leases, surveys, Hunsworth plan (by Christopher Saxton) 1599 and other maps and plans, rentals, accounts and vouchers, corresp, wood accounts 1700-11, and enclosure and tithe papers from 15th cent; Notts estate records from 14th cent, incl leases, surveys, maps, valuations and rentals from 16th cent, accounts and vouchers from 14th cent, Rufford labour accounts 1731-1861, and Sherwood Forest Book (Rufford Abbey copy) c1500 and related forest papers 17th-19th cent; misc estate papers 14th-19th cent, incl some for Derbys (iron works papers 1643-9, etc), Lancs, Lincs (Barrowby survey 1592, etc) and Northants (Fotheringhay accounts 1665-71, etc); accounts and papers rel to Scarbrough properties in Co Durham and Lincs c1812-56; plans and papers for the proposed re-establishment of Savilestown (Newtown Savile, Co Tyrone) 1757; Rufford household papers 17th-19th cent, incl building accounts by Anthony Salvin 1839-42, inventories 1642-1743 and stable accounts 1659-63; other household papers 17th-19th cent, incl Sandbeck inventory 1832 and accounts for Thornhill 1629-34, London 1723-33, 1747-9, Osberton 1790-1817 and Edwinstowe 1818-34.

Misc papers rel to Notts and Yorks affairs 13th-19th cent, incl shrievalty papers for Notts 1381-2, 1706-7 and Yorks 1486-7, 1584-9, 1629, Agbrigg (Yorks WR) muster roll 1599, Yorks subsidy rolls and papers 1575-6, 1585-91, 1671-3, and Elland (Yorks WR) market charter 1281-2; patents and appointments 17th-20th cent; personal inventories, incl Katherine, Duchess of Suffolk c1580, the 5th, 6th and 7th

Earls of Scarbrough 1807, 1832, 1835 and Francis Ferrand and Mary Foljambe 1800-16; family and personal papers 16th-19th cent, Savile, Lumley and Foljambe, incl political papers of the 7th Bt (d1743) and 8th Bt (d1784), diplomatic and personal papers of the 1st Baron Savile (d1896), papers of Henry Savile (1642-87), and corresp of the 1st and 2nd Marquesses of Halifax, Francis Ferrand and Mary Foljambe 1780-1817 and the 7th and 8th Earls of Scarbrough c1785-1856; accounts of Captain Savile's company 1683-1703; genea-logical and misc papers 16th-19th cent, incl pamphlets on political, theological and other subjects from 17th cent; monastic ordinances (Rufford Abbey) 1481; *valor* of Beds religious houses, mainly Warden, 1534-5 (copy); rentals and accounts of the free chapel of St Mary and the Holy Angels, York 1546, 1584.

Nottinghamshire Archives (DD SR). Transferred to the British Records Association on the sale of Rufford Abbey 1938 and deposited through the Historical Manuscripts Commission in 1957 and later. Further deposits were made by Lord Savile in 1974 and Worksop Library in 1982. HMC *Eleventh Report, App VII*, 1888, pp119-26; *Private Papers of British Diplomats 1782-1900*, 1985, p59. NRA 6119.

[b] Misc Yorks rentals c1572-1704 and accounts 1610-15; particulars of rents and debts due to Sir George Savile 1635-66.

Nottinghamshire Archives (DD SR 233/1-11). Deposited by Lawrence, Graham & Co, solici-tors, London, through the British Record Association 1968. NRA 6119.

[c] Misc Notts deeds and legal, estate and gen-ealogical papers 17th-20th cent, incl misc man-orial records 18th-19th cent and estate maps and plans 20th cent; papers rel to Rufford school 1883-1950.

Nottinghamshire Archives (DD BO). Deposited from Ollerton House by John Baker 1952-3. NRA 6874.

[d] Yorks deeds 16th-20th cent; schedules of deeds 1633, 1686-1713; Scarbrough trust min-utes 1869-82; Heptonstall manor call book 1712-86 and misc Yorks WR manorial papers 1783-4; Yorks WR estate records 16th-20th cent, incl leases 17th-19th cent, leasehold sche-dules 1695, 1898, surveys, maps, particulars and valuations 17th-20th cent, rentals 16th-19th cent, accounts 1625-35, 19th cent, and Emley glebe rent and tithe accounts 1814-49; other papers 17th-20th cent, incl coal mining leases and plans 1871-1928 and drainage papers late 19th cent.

West Yorkshire Archive Service, Kirklees (DD/S). Deposited in Dewsbury Central Library from the Savile Estate Office, Thornhill 1969, with an additional deposit by Lord Savile's London

solicitors 1972, and transferred 1999. *Kirklees Archives 1959-1989*, 1989, p31. NRA 14864.

[e] Deeds 16th-20th cent, mainly Yorks but incl some for Laxton and Bilsthorpe (Notts) 1730-95; schedules (Co Durham, Lincs, Notts and Yorks) 1811, 1835-7; will and probate of the 4th Earl of Scarbrough; family settlements 1739-1801; Thornhill survey by Christopher Saxton 1602 and Yorks WR estate survey c1630; particulars of the Earl of Scarbrough's estates (Co Durham, Lincs, Yorks WR) 1785, 1793, with valuation of Winteringham rectory nd.

In private possession. Enquiries to the Savile Estate Office, Thornhill, Dewsbury, West Yorkshire. NRA 14864.

[f] Yorks WR estate plans 1865-1932.

West Yorkshire Archive Service, Kirklees (KC 179, 180, DD/G). Deposited 1985 from Dewsbury Museum and through the Colne Valley Museum. *Kirklees Archives 1959-1989*, 1989, p31.

[g] Rental and accounts of the Marquess of Halifax's Derbys (Bolderstone) and Yorks (Bradfield, Ecclesfield and Sheffield) estate c1670-90.

Sheffield Archives (MD 149-151). NRA 23246. Purchased 1908, 1911.

[h] Rufford Abbey cartulary 14th-15th cent.

British Library, Manuscript Collections (MS Loan 41). Deposited by Lord Savile 1954.

[i] Wadsworth (Yorks WR) manor maps by Christopher Saxton 1594, 1602.

British Library, Manuscript Collections (Add MS 63751). Formerly at Rufford Abbey. Purchased at Sotheby's, 11 July 1986, lots 362-3.

Related Collections: Lumley, Earls of Scarbrough, no 64; Foljambe of Osberton, no 38, and Hartley of Bucklebury (Berkshire Record Office D/EHy/O47-49, NRA 844), including papers of Sir George Savile, 8th Bt; Cavendish, Dukes of Devonshire, no 17, and Spencer, Earls Spencer, no 97, including papers of the 1st Marquess of Halifax.

[66] LUTTRELL of Dunster

Geoffrey Luttrell of Gamston (Nottinghamshire) married c1200 a daughter of William Paynell of Irnham (Lincolnshire) and East Quantoxhead (Somerset). Gamston and Irnham descended in the senior line of the Luttrell family, which became extinct in the fifteenth century, but East Quantoxhead passed to a junior branch, whose Somerset holdings were later augmented by inheritance and purchase. Andrew Luttrell mar-ried in 1359 Lady Elizabeth Courtenay, who brought lands in Somerset, including Dunster Castle, purchased from the Mohun family, and in Norfolk and Suffolk (later sold). Dunster Priory lands were acquired at the Dissolution. Thomas Luttrell (d1571) married Margaret Hadley, heiress of Withycombe, near Dunster. Francis Luttrell (1659-90) married Mary Tregonwell, but her property in Dorset (Milton Abbas) and Somerset did not descend to the Luttrells.

On the death of Alexander Luttrell in 1737 his estates passed to his daughter, who in 1747 married Henry Fownes, later Fownes Luttrell, of Nethway House, Kingswear (Devon). Their son John Fownes Luttrell married Mary Drewe of Grange (Broadhembury, Devon) in 1782. In 1824 their third son married his cousin Emma Louise Drewe, through whom the Wootton Fitzpaine (Dorset) estate was inherited. In 1867 their son George succeeded his uncle in the Dunster Castle, East Quantoxhead and Kingswear estates.

The Devon and Dorset estates were largely sold by the end of the nineteenth century. More recently Dunster Castle passed to the National Trust, and East Quantoxhead again became the family seat.

Estates in 1883: Somerset 15,374 acres, Devon 154 acres, total 15,528 acres worth £22,000 a year. The 1875 *Return of Owners of Land* gives GF Luttrell 12,732 acres in Somerset, HF Luttrell (decd) 1,852 acres in Devon and (Mrs) EL Luttrell 1,571 acres in Dorset.

[a] Deeds 12th-20th cent (*c*650 medieval), mostly Somerset but incl Devon *c*1200-19th cent, Dorset 16th-19th cent, and a few for Norfolk and Suffolk 14th-16th cent; wills, settlements and related papers 15th-19th cent, Luttrell, Fownes, Drewe, etc; legal and case papers 13th-19th cent, incl inquisitions *post mortem* and papers rel to the forfeiture of the estates late 15th cent; manorial court records, Somerset (Dunster manor and borough, Carhampton, Minehead, etc) 13th-19th cent, Devon (Kingswear, etc) 16th-18th cent and Dorset (Wootton Fitzpaine, etc) 16th-18th cent; records rel to the barony of Dunster 13th-17th cent (incl deeds of homage and grants of wardship) and to the hundred of Carhampton 14th-19th cent.

Somerset estate records 15th-20th cent, incl leases from 16th cent, surveys and valuations, maps and plans, rentals, accounts from early 15th cent, corresp from 18th cent, farm accounts 18th-20th cent, and papers rel to timber, tithes and advowsons, game, water supply, roads and railways, marshland drainage, foreshore and sea defences, Dunster mills, copper mining, and sales; papers rel to Minehead town and harbour 16th-20th cent; Devon (Kingswear, etc) and Dorset (Wootton Fitzpaine, etc) estate records 17th-19th cent, incl surveys, rentals,

accounts, corresp and sale papers; Nethway farm accounts 18th-19th cent; Cornish estate papers 18th cent; papers rel to Dunster Castle 14th-20th cent, incl inventories, papers rel to its restoration 19th cent and household accounts from early 15th cent; Nethway household accounts 18th-early 19th cent.

Somerset coroner's roll 1315-21; papers rel to Somerset shrievalty and county affairs 16th-18th cent, and to Somerset and Minehead elections 17th-19th cent; Dorset shrievalty papers 1691-1716 (Rose family of Wootton Fitzpaine); papers rel to the borough and parish of Dunster 16th-19th cent, and to Timberscombe (Somerset) charity and school 19th cent; Minehead Railway accounts and papers 1863-82; Luttrell family corresp and papers 15th-19th cent, incl estate notes of George Luttrell 16th cent (2 vols) and political papers of John Fownes Luttrell (1752-1816); Fownes family papers 17th-18th cent, incl shipping accounts; papers of or rel to the Kellond family of Painsford (Devon) 17th-18th cent and the Pinson family of Dartmouth (Devon) 18th-19th cent; genealogical and misc papers 16th-20th cent, incl transcripts of Dunster parish deeds and list of Dunster Castle muniments by William Prynne 1650; deeds and papers rel to Bruton Priory (Somerset) 13th-16th cent, incl presentation deeds, and to Dunster Priory 16th cent; Cleeve Abbey (Somerset) ministers' accounts 1536-7; list of Scottish noblemen killed or captured at Homildon Hill 1402.

Somerset Archive and Record Service (DD/L). Deposited by Lt-Colonel GWF Luttrell 1958-88. HMC *First Report, App*, 1870, pp56-7; *Tenth Report, App VI*, 1887, pp72-81; *Papers of British Politicians 1782-1900*, 1989, p39. NRA 6670. (Rentals and accounts for the Wootton Fitzpaine estate 1790-1879 passed to the purchasers of the estate: see Pass of Wootton Fitzpaine, Dorset Record Office D/WFP.)

[67] LYGON, Earls Beauchamp

The Lygon family was established at Madresfield (Worcestershire) in the mid-fifteenth century. Thomas Lygon married Anne, second daughter of the second Baron Beauchamp of Powick (d1503), acquiring through her the Beauchamp Court property in Worcestershire (in Powick, near Madresfield) and land in Gloucestershire (subsequently sold). (For other Beauchamp property see Greville, Earls Brooke and Earls of Warwick, no 45.) Property in Warwickshire (Hall End in Polesworth, etc) was acquired through the marriage of William Lygon to Margaret, daughter of Thomas Corbyn of Hall End and Kingswinford (Staffordshire) in 1688. Margaret Lygon, daughter of William and Margaret and heir to the Worcestershire and Warwickshire estates, married in 1713 Reginald Pyndar of Kempley (Gloucestershire) and Duffield (Derbyshire).

Their son Reginald Pyndar (d1788) succeeded to the Lygon estates on his mother's death in 1736 and took the name of Lygon.

The Worcestershire and Gloucestershire estates (both with adjacent properties in Herefordshire) were extended in the nineteenth century, notably by William Lygon (1747-1816), who was created Earl Beauchamp in 1815. The Derbyshire estate, however, was disposed of by 1800, except for the Duffield tithes, and the Hall End estate was sold in the late nineteenth century. Thomas Pindar (d1813) of Brumby (Lincolnshire) bequeathed his estate to the Hon John Lygon, who changed his name to Pyndar and succeeded his brother as third Earl Beauchamp in 1823.

Estates in 1883: Worcs 10,624 acres, Lincs 2,878 acres, Gloucs 2,429 acres, Warwicks 959 acres, Herefs 744 acres, total 17,634 acres worth £24,941 a year.

[a] Deeds 12th-19th cent (*c*360 medieval), mainly Worcs 13th-19th cent but incl Derbys from 14th cent, Gloucs (Lygon and Pyndar) from 13th cent, Herefs from 15th cent, Staffs (Corbyn) from 14th cent, Warwicks (Beauchamp and Corbyn) from 12th cent and other counties; wills, settlements and related papers, Lygon family 16th-19th cent, incl 2nd Earl Beauchamp decd 1823-1830s, Beauchamp family late 15th cent, Corbyn 16th-17th cent, Pyndar 17th-18th cent and William Jennens decd 1798-9; legal and case papers 16th-19th cent, incl Beauchamp *v* Winn (Lincs estate) *c*1870; manorial court records, Worcs (Bransford, Madresfield, etc) 14th-18th cent and Gloucs (Kempley) 17th-18th cent.

Worcs estate records 14th-20th cent (mainly 18th-20th cent), incl leases 14th-19th cent, surveys and valuations from 1500, maps and plans 18th-20th cent, rentals from 18th cent, estate accounts from 17th cent, farm and tithe accounts 18th-20th cent, and papers mainly 20th cent rel to buildings, sales, etc; Gloucs estate records 17th-20th cent, incl leases, surveys, maps, rentals, accounts and tithe papers; Warwicks estate records 16th-19th cent, incl leases, surveys, rentals and accounts; Derbys estate rentals and accounts 18th cent, with Duffield tithe papers 18th-19th cent; Lincs estate accounts and papers 1863-92; Beauchamp estate accounts 1415-76; Staffs (Corbyn) estate rentals 1509-72; architectural drawings for Madresfield Court (PC Hardwick, Norman Shaw, etc) *c*1864-early 20th cent; Madresfield inventories and household accounts 16th-20th cent (mainly 18th-20th cent).

Papers rel to Worcs affairs 15th-19th cent, incl militia, taxation and shrievalty papers; Worcs election papers 1806-85; Worcester sessions roll 1477; Madresfield parish account book *c*1665-1745; Powick poor rate assessments 1714-97; drawings for Newland (Worcs) church and

almshouses by PC Hardwick 1861-3; Hemlingford hundred (Warwicks) subsidy roll 1566; Derbys shrievalty papers 1683-4; Kempley Hospital terriers, etc 1590-1781; Longney (Gloucs) pool reeves' accounts 1841-1937; commissions, appointments, etc, Lygon 16th-?19th cent and Corbyn 17th cent; Lygon and Pyndar family corresp and papers 17th-20th cent, incl corresp of William Lygon 1688-1720 and Reginald Pyndar 1697-1717, corresp of the 1st Earl Beauchamp 1775-1815, and political and religious corresp of the 6th and 7th Earls late 19th-early 20th cent; Corbyn family corresp 1660-92; pedigree 16th cent, with antiquarian and genealogical papers late 19th cent; Star Chamber accounts 1594-1603; account of expenses, Gentleman Pensioners 1635-6; Great Malvern Priory view of accounts 1453.

In private possession. Not normally open for research. CL Kingsford, *Madresfield Muniments*, pr 1929 (copy in Worcestershire Record Office, Worcester, 970.5:99). NRA 5234 (partial list).

[b] Deeds 13th-20th cent, mainly Worcs, Herefs and Gloucs 14th-20th cent but incl Staffs (Corbyn, etc) 13th-16th cent, Middlesex 18th-20th cent and Lincs 19th-20th cent; will of Sir William Lygon 1618; trust deeds 19th-20th cent; legal papers mainly 18th-20th cent, incl papers rel to Derbys properties and tithes 19th-20th cent, London estates 19th cent, New River Company shares 18th-19th cent, Severn Navigation Bill 1920 and Canadian property 20th cent; manorial court records 16th-20th cent, Worcs (Madresfield, Pixham in Powick, etc) and Gloucs (Dymock and Kempley); misc estate papers 15th-20th cent, incl rental of Lady Beauchamp's manors 1421-2, Lygon *valor c*1535, Pyndar rental (Gloucs, Derbys, etc) 1731-4, Worcs account book 1755, misc Worcs and Gloucs estate papers 18th-19th cent and misc Middlesex (London) estate papers 19th cent; misc local and family papers 17th-20th cent, incl Worcs shrievalty roll 1646-7 and items rel to the Cinque Ports 1918-33 (7th Earl); papers rel to the Comedy Theatre, London 19th-20th cent.

Worcestershire Record Office (Acc 3375, 3464, 5497, 5540). Deposited by Hasties, solicitors, London, through the British Records Association 1960-9. NRA 8108.

[c] Deeds late 16th-late 19th cent, mainly Lincs 16th-19th cent and Derbys 17th-19th cent but incl some for Worcs, Gloucs and Warwicks; misc estate papers 17th-18th cent, incl terrier of Pindar estate in Owston (Lincs) 1682 and map of Duffield estate 1711; list of Haxey (Lincs) charities late 17th cent.

Worcestershire Record Office (Acc 5489). Deposited by Farrer & Co, solicitors, London, through the British Records Association 1969. NRA 3524.

[d] Deeds and legal papers 16th-19th cent, Worcs, Herefs and Gloucs; misc estate and local papers 18th-19th cent, incl Worcs election papers 1831.

Worcestershire Record Office (Acc 5589/19-23, 51-2, 70(i), 168, 174-6). Deposited by Lord & Parker, solicitors, Worcester 1970. NRA 4744.

[e] Legal papers rel to sales of property in Worcs and Gloucs 1894-1903.

Worcestershire Record Office (Acc 4925/75). Deposited by John Stallard & Co, solicitors, Worcester 1967. NRA 10005.

[f] Diplomatic corresp of the 6th Baron Paget 1690-1702 (mainly 1690-1), with some corresp of the 1st Earl of Uxbridge 1709-25.

British Library, Manuscript Collections (Add MS 61830). Acquired 1980 (Sotheby's, 21-22 July, lot 10).

[g] Corresp of the 5th and 6th Earls Beauchamp with Benjamin Disraeli, Earl of Beaconsfield 1859-80, with some papers acquired by the 6th Earl as Disraeli's private secretary 1873.

British Library, Manuscript Collections (Add MS 61892). Acquired 1980 (Sotheby's, 15 Dec, lot 127). HMC *Papers of British Politicians 1782-1900,* 1989, p66.

[h] Account book of Reginald Lygon 1743-52.

National Library of Wales. Given by G W Bright. *Annual Report 1955-6,* p25.

[i] Papers of the 7th Earl Beauchamp as lord lieutenant of Gloucs 1911-20.

Gloucestershire Record Office (D 551). Deposited by the 8th Earl Beauchamp 1950. NRA 11510.

[j] Corresp and papers of the 7th Earl as Governor of New South Wales 1899-1902.

State Library of New South Wales, Mitchell Library (A 3012, 3295, 5016-47, etc). HMC *Private papers of British Colonial Governors 1782-1900,* 1986, p38.

Related collection: Greville, Earls Brooke and Earls of Warwick, no 45.

[68] MANNERS, Dukes of Rutland

The Manners family was established at Etal (Northumberland) by 1232. In 1469 Sir Robert Manners married Eleanor, sister and co-heir of Edmund, eleventh Baron Ros (d1508). The Ros family, originating at Roos in Holderness (Yorkshire, East Riding), had inherited Helmsley (Yorkshire, North Riding) in the late twelfth century and Belvoir Castle and barony (Leicestershire) in the mid-thirteenth. By the late fifteenth century the Ros possessions also included land in north Lincolnshire (Wrawby, Melton Ross, etc), Nottinghamshire (Warsop, Orston, etc), Middlesex (Enfield) and Essex (Walthamstow). Sir George Manners (d1513) succeeded to the barony of Ros on the death c1512 of Isabel Lovell, the second co-heir. His son Thomas Manners (c1492-1543) was created Earl of Rutland in 1525.

The first Earl acquired numerous monastic properties, including Rievaulx Abbey, near Helmsley, Warter Priory in the East Riding, and Belvoir Priory and Croxton Abbey in north-east Leicestershire. In 1547, however, the Etal estate was alienated; on the death of the third Earl of Rutland in 1587 the East Riding estates passed to his daughter Elizabeth, who in 1589 married William Cecil, later second Earl of Exeter; and on the death of the sixth Earl of Rutland in 1632 most of the Helmsley estate, together with the barony of Ros, passed to his daughter Katherine, widow of George Villiers, Duke of Buckingham.

The north Lincolnshire estate passed on the death of the seventh Earl in 1641 to the Tyrwhit family of Kettleby (Lincolnshire), into which his sister Bridget had married. The Belvoir estates, however, passed to a cousin, John Manners of Haddon (Derbyshire), who succeeded as eighth Earl. His grandfather Sir John Manners (d1611), younger brother of the second Earl, had married Dorothy, daughter and co-heir of Sir George Vernon, through whom he had inherited extensive estates in north Derbyshire and elsewhere.

The ninth Earl was created Duke of Rutland in 1703. In 1717 John Manners, later third Duke, married Bridget (d1734), daughter and heir of Robert Sutton, second Baron Lexinton, but the Kelham (Nottinghamshire) estate of this family descended to younger sons of the marriage, who took the name of Manners-Sutton. The Marquess of Granby (1721-70), eldest son of the third Duke, married in 1750 Lady Frances Seymour, sister of, and co-heir to the paternal (Seymour) estates of, the seventh Duke of Somerset (d1750) (see also Percy, Dukes of Northumberland, no 82; Wyndham of Orchard Wyndham, no 118). Lord Granby was a trustee for the Duke's estates in Wiltshire, Cambridgeshire and elsewhere, and on their partition in the late 1770s his heir (who became fourth Duke of Rutland in 1779) received the Cheveley estate in Cambridgeshire and Suffolk, and the Marlborough and Trowbridge estates in Wiltshire. The Cheveley estate was retained until 1892, but Marlborough was sold in 1779 (to the Marquess of Ailesbury) and Trowbridge in 1809.

Between the late seventeenth and the late nineteenth centuries outlying properties in Nottinghamshire and Lincolnshire were sold, but the Belvoir and Haddon estates were consolidated. By 1883 the Belvoir estate comprised nearly 35,000 acres, mainly in Leicestershire but including Granby (Nottinghamshire), Bisbrooke (Rutland) and Woolsthorpe and Ropsley (Lincolnshire, both former Belvoir Priory possessions). Both the Belvoir and the Haddon estates were reduced by sales following the first World War.

Estates in 1883: Leics 30,188 acres, Derbys 27,069 acres, Cambs 6,585 acres, Lincs 2,837 acres, Suffolk 1,591 acres, Notts 1,103 acres, Rutland 764 acres, total 70,137 acres worth £97,486 a year.

[a] Deeds 12th-19th cent, mainly Derbys, Leics, Lincs and Notts but incl Cambs and Suffolk 12th-19th cent, Norfolk 12th-17th cent, Yorks ER and NR 12th-17th cent and lesser quantities for Essex (Wethersfield 13th-17th cent), Northumberland (12th-15th cent), Rutland (Bisbrooke 14th-18th cent), Warwicks (Pillerton, etc 13th-17th cent) and other counties; wills, settlements, trusteeship papers and executorship papers 15th-19th cent, mainly Manners and Vernon but incl accounts of Sir Thomas Lovell as trustee for Lord Ros *c*1488-1523, executorship accounts for the 2nd Baron Lexinton 1723, and accounts, etc, of the Marquess of Granby as trustee for the paternal estates of the 7th Duke of Somerset *c*1750-67; legal papers 13th-20th cent, incl High Peak cartulary 13th-14th cent, bonds from 14th cent, Vernon case papers from *c*1450, records of the purchase of monastic and other lands *c*1514-43 (4 vols), papers rel to the barony of Ros 17th cent, and schedules of muniments, etc 17th-19th cent; manorial records (court rolls and papers, ministers' accounts, etc) 13th-19th cent, mainly Derbys and Leics 13th-19th cent but incl Lincs, Notts and Yorks 14th-17th cent and other counties 13th-19th cent.

Belvoir (Leics and Lincs) estate records early 16th cent-1930s, incl surveys, maps and plans, rentals and accounts, wood accounts 1736-1850, granary accounts 1715-1836 and agent's diaries early 19th cent; Vernon, later Manners (Derbys and Notts) estate records 14th cent-*c*1920, incl surveys, rentals and accounts, lead accounts and case papers early 17th-late 19th cent, Haddon timber accounts 19th cent and Ilkeston (Derbys) lease books early 20th cent; Ros (Yorks ER and NR, Lincs, etc) estate records 14th-18th cent, incl surveys, rentals from 14th cent and accounts mainly early 15th-early 16th cent; Cheveley (Cambs and Suffolk) estate records 1778-1892, incl rentals, general accounts and timber accounts; Walthamstow rentals 1422, 1515-16; Mundford (Norfolk) survey 16th cent; Kelham accounts 1733-63 (1 vol); Petworth (Sussex) estate accounts 1747-9.

Belvoir Castle building accounts, inventories, catalogues, etc 16th-19th cent, incl accounts for rebuilding 1801-30; papers rel to Haddon Hall 16th-20th cent, incl inventories from 16th cent

and papers rel to restoration 1920s; inventories, Helmsley Castle 16th cent, Holywell (London) 1529, Kelham and Averham Park Lodge (Notts) 1723, etc; household accounts from late 14th cent, Ros, Vernon and Manners, incl Belvoir Castle from 1520s; household accounts, Elsings (Enfield, Middlesex) and Holywell (London) early 16th cent, Kelham 1722-3 and London and Petworth (Duke of Somerset) 1743-9; cellar books 18th-20th cent, Belvoir Castle, London houses, Haddon, Cheveley, Longshaw Lodge (Derbys), etc; Belvoir Castle garden labour accounts 1818-1924.

High Peak (Derbys) crown rents 1429-46, *temp* Henry VII; list of the retinue of Sir Thomas Lovell (for military service) 1508; papers rel to Derbys local affairs mainly late 16th-early 17th cent (*temp* Sir John Manners of Haddon), incl muster, subsidy, assize and licensing papers; Lincs muster list 1614; papers rel to Leics militia 1715-1856 and to the Belvoir Castle Volunteers 1803; Bottesford (Leics) hospital accounts 1682; Thorpe Arnold (Leics) overseers' accounts 1698-1702; Grantham (Lincs) poll books and papers rel to freemen 18th-19th cent; Belvoir Hunt corresp and papers 18th-20th cent.

Commissions, appointments, etc from 15th cent, mainly Manners family; Manners family corresp and papers 16th-20th cent, incl papers of the 2nd Earl of Rutland as Warden of the East and Middle Marches of Scotland 1549-51 and President of the Council of the North 1561-3, political and other corresp of the 3rd Earl (d1587), diary of the 7th Earl 1639, letters and papers of Sir John Manners of Haddon late 16th-early 17th cent, accounts of the 3rd Duke as Master of the Horse 1762-6, military papers of the Marquess of Granby 1759-69, corresp and papers of the 4th Duke as Lord Lieutenant of Ireland 1784-7, extensive corresp of the 5th Duke and his wife *c*1790-1857, official and personal corresp and papers of Lord John Manners (later 7th Duke) 1830-1906, and corresp of the 9th Duke and his family 20th cent; personal vouchers 16th-19th cent; Vernon and Ros corresp 15th-16th cent; literary and genealogical papers from 16th cent, incl pedigree rolls (Manners, Ros and Vernon); Belvoir Castle weather records 1858-1939; diary of Lord Berkeley of Stratton 1756-63; autograph letters and papers 16th-19th cent collected by Capt the Hon CH Lindsay, incl political letters 1625-60, papers rel to the French Revolution 1790-6 and letters of Benjamin Disraeli and the 1st Duke of Wellington; further autograph letters purchased by the 9th Duke; calendars, indexes and transcripts of the Belvoir Castle MSS; calendar of documents in Westminster Abbey Treasury *c*1547.

Monastic records 12th-16th cent, incl charters of Belvoir Priory, Byland Abbey, Darley Abbey and Rievaulx Abbey, cartularies of Belvoir Priory and Croxton Abbey (Leics) 13th-16th cent (4 vols and 1 roll), formulary of Croxton Abbey early 16th cent, Belvoir priory court rolls and accounts 13th-early 16th cent, Croxton Abbey inventory 1443-4 and rental early 16th cent, and Rievaulx Abbey inventory *temp* Henry VIII.

In private possession. Not normally available for research. HMC *First Report, App,* 1870, pp10-12; *Rutland I - IV,* 1880-1905.

[b] Greasley Castle (Notts) estate deeds and papers 1596-1687 (13 items), incl survey and valuations; Ilkeston agreements, etc 1598-1650 (16 items); abstract of Belvoir and Haddon accounts 1658.

Nottinghamshire Archives (Fillingham of Syerston papers). Deposited by GA Fillingham 1970. (The Fillingham family were stewards to the fourth and fifth Dukes of Rutland.) NRA 14327.

[c] Misc bonds 1721-62; Derbys estate papers 1721-88, incl Bakewell survey 1757 and land tax papers 1756-68.

Sheffield Archives (Bar D). Deposited by Major Barker 1957. (The Barker family of Bakewell were stewards to the Manners family in the late seventeenth and early eighteenth century.) NRA 6730.

[d] Misc Derbys lead mining papers 1608-1891, incl barmoot court rolls, accounts and legal papers; Bakewell and Over Haddon enclosure minutes 1806-11.

Derbyshire Record Office (D 1289). Deposited 1973-95. (Formerly in the possession of John Wagstaffe, barmaster to the Duke of Rutland until 1882.) NRA 19306.

[e] Newmarket (Suffolk) manorial records 1400-1642, 1779-1932.

Suffolk Record Office, Bury St Edmunds branch (Acc 387/1-44; Acc 1476; Acc 1748). Deposited by WJ and JG Taylor 1952-65. NRA 12988.

[f] Cheveley manorial court books 1736-1849; Ditton Camoys (in Wood Ditton, Cambs) court rolls and papers 1727-1914; misc legal and estate papers late 18th-early 19th cent, incl terrier and map of Cheveley estate 1775.

Cambridgeshire County Record Office, Cambridge (R.54.10.5-9, 12-21, 36, 37). Deposited by WJ Taylor of Newmarket *c*1956. NRA 3503.

Related collections: Cecil, Marquesses of Exeter, no 19, including Roos in Holderness manorial records 1307-1422; Percy, Dukes of Northumberland, no 82, including Seymour legal and estate papers; Seymour, Dukes of Somerset, no 92, including Cheveley estate papers early 18th cent; Wyndham, Barons Leconfield and Egremont, no 117, including East Anglian estate accounts 1732-43;

Wyndham of Orchard Wyndham, no 118, including Wiltshire and Somerset (Seymour) manorial records; Earls of Feversham (North Yorkshire County Record Office, NRA 11230), including Helmsley, etc rentals 1637, 1714-57, transferred from the Belvoir muniments 1802.

[69] MONTAGU, Dukes of Manchester

Henry Montagu (*c*1563-1642), third son of Sir Edward Montagu of Boughton (Northampton-shire) (see Montagu-Douglas-Scott, Dukes of Buccleuch and Queensberry, no 70), acquired Kimbolton (Huntingdonshire) in 1615, and was created Earl of Manchester in 1626. The second Earl (1602-71) married in 1626, as his second wife, Anne Rich (d1642), eldest daughter of the second Earl of Warwick. On the death of the fourth Earl of Warwick in 1673 the Montagu family succeeded to the Leighs estate in Essex (sold to Guy's Hospital *c*1750). The fourth Earl of Manchester (*c*1662-1722) was created Duke of Manchester in 1719. In 1863, following the death of his grandmother Lady Olivia Bernard Sparrow (see below), the seventh Duke (1823-90) inherited estates in County Armagh (Tanderagee, etc), Huntingdonshire (Brampton) and Cambridgeshire. Kimbolton Castle was given up after the Second World War.

Sir John Bernard, 2nd Bt, purchased Brampton Park in 1653. Sir John Bernard (*c*1695-1766) married in 1737 Mary, daughter and heir of Sir Francis St John, Bt (d1756), of Thorpe (Northamptonshire), through whom estates in Northamptonshire (Thorpe), Essex (Kelvedon, etc), Cambridgeshire (Doddington) and County Armagh (Tanderagee, etc) were inherited. (Property in Suffolk (Stoke-by-Clare) and Staffordshire appears to have been sold about 1756.) On the death of Sir Robert Bernard, 5th Bt, in 1789 the Thorpe estate was sold, but the estates in Huntingdonshire, Essex, Cambridge-shire and Ireland passed to Robert Bernard Sparrow. He married Lady Olivia Acheson, daughter of the first Earl of Gosford, and died in 1805, leaving an only daughter, Millicent, who married the sixth Duke of Manchester (1799-1855) and died in 1848.

Estates in 1883: Hunts 13,835 acres, Cambs 1,124 acres, Beds 55 acres, Co Armagh 12,298 acres, total 27,312 acres worth £40,360 a year.

[a] Deeds 13th-20th cent, mainly Hunts but incl Essex (Leighs and Kelvedon estates) 14th-18th cent, Staffs and Suffolk 13th-17th cent, Beds, Cambs, Herts, Northants, etc 13th-19th cent and Co Armagh 19th cent; wills, settle-ments and related trust and executorship papers, Montagu family 17th-20th cent and Bernard, St John and Sparrow families 17th-mid-19th cent; papers rel to the Earl of Warwick decd 1673; legal and case papers 16th-20th cent, incl schedules and abstracts of title, papers rel to ex-monastic properties 16th cent and case papers (Manchester *v* Sparrow) mid-

19th cent; manorial court records 13th-20th cent, incl Essex (Kelvedon, etc) 13th-19th cent, Hunts (Kimbolton, Houghton-cum-Wyton, Little Stukeley, etc) 14th-20th cent and Northants 16th-17th cent.

Hunts (Kimbolton and Brampton) estate records late 16th-mid-20th cent, incl leases 17th-20th cent, surveys from 1593, maps and plans 16th-19th cent, rentals from 16th cent, accounts and vouchers from 17th cent, corresp from 17th cent, letter books 19th-20th cent, and papers rel to enclosure 18th-19th cent, tithes 17th-19th cent, fen drainage 17th-19th cent, brickworks 19th cent, schools 19th cent and St Ives market and fair 17th-20th cent; accounts rel to farms in hand 19th cent-1945; Essex (Kelvedon) estate records 17th-19th cent, incl leases, surveys, maps, rentals, accounts and sale papers, with papers rel to the Leighs estate late 16th-mid-18th cent; Northants (Thorpe) estate records 17th-18th cent, incl survey 1770, maps, rentals, accounts and corresp; misc estate records rel to Cambs (March and Doddington) 17th-19th cent, Beds 18th-19th cent, Staffs and Suffolk early 18th cent and Co Armagh 18th-19th cent; Cornhill (London) rental 1694 (Gregory family); Holborn (Middlesex) building leases 1639-51 (St John); Hyde Park Corner (Middlesex) rental 1782, etc (Bernard); New Zealand accounts and papers 1858-72.

Papers rel to Kimbolton Castle 17th-early 20th cent, incl building accounts 1709, Adam designs 1763-6, inventories 1790-early 20th cent, catalogues of books and paintings 19th cent, visitors' books 1865-1937 and household accounts and vouchers 17th-19th cent (mainly 19th cent); Brampton Park papers 18th-early 20th cent, incl plans, inventories and household accounts; Thorpe Hall inventories and papers 1789-90; London household accounts 19th cent and 1909-11 (Duchess of Devonshire); papers rel to Hunts lieutenancy, militia and elections 17th-19th cent, to Weybridge Forest (Hunts) 17th-19th cent, and to the Manchester Light Horse Volunteers 1859-82; papers rel to Ellington (Hunts) clothing club 1846-50 and Leighs school 1833-55.

Patents, commissions, etc 17th-19th cent; Montagu family papers 17th-20th cent, incl misc political, Civil War and other papers of the 1st and 2nd Earls of Manchester, misc diplomatic corresp of the 1st Duke 1699-1708 and misc corresp and papers of the 4th, 5th and 7th Dukes; misc Court of Augmentations papers of Sir Richard Rich 1530s; Irish Commission papers of Sir Nathaniel Rich (brother of the 2nd Earl of Warwick) early 17th cent; St John papers 17th cent, incl parliamentary diary 1640; Bernard papers 18th cent; corresp and papers of Lady Olivia Bernard Sparrow early 19th cent; genealogical papers 16th-19th cent; misc papers 14th-19th cent, incl Knowle (Warwicks) manorial accounts 1371-2, Westminster Abbey acquisitions roll 1509, Earl of Ormonde *valor*

1510-11 and receivers' accounts 1529-30, map of Thorney Abbey (Cambs) grounds 1609, parliamentary diary 1627-8 and Hunts shrievalty roll 1682-3.

Cambridgeshire County Record Office, Huntingdon (ddM, ddMB, BB, L.39.1-3). Deposited by the 10th Duke of Manchester and others 1948-88, and by Wade-Gery & Brackenbury, solicitors, St Neots 1972-3. *Annual Report 1987*, p16, *1988*, p18. HMC *Papers of British Politicians 1782-1900*, 1989, p72. NRA 902, 2565, 3503. Some documents are damaged and unfit for production. Seven items from Sir Nathaniel Rich's papers relating to John Donne were withdrawn and sold in 1975 (Sotheby's, 24 June, lots 266-7).

[b] Letter book, Park Farm, Kimbolton 1864-7.

Cambridgeshire County Record Office, Huntingdon. Deposited by HJ Baxter 1987. *Annual Report 1987*, p14.

[c] Vouchers, Park Farm, Brampton, etc 1822-50.

Cambridgeshire County Record Office, Huntingdon. Deposited by Kimbolton School 1990. *Annual Report 1990*, p21.

[d] Kimbolton Castle provision books 1859-66.

Cambridgeshire County Record Office, Huntingdon. Deposited by Kimbolton Local History Society 1992. *Annual Report 1992*, p22.

[e] Marshland and West Dereham (Norfolk) estate accounts 1636-44.

Norfolk Record Office. Acquired 1971 (Sotheby's, 14-15 June, lot 1546).

[f] Deeds and wills for the Ballymore (Tanderagee) estate and St John family 1673-1780.

Public Record Office of Northern Ireland (D 2529). Deposited by the Goldsmiths' Company, London, through the British Records Association 1969. *Deputy Keeper's Report 1966-72*, pp105-6.

[g] Co Armagh estate records 17th-20th cent, incl leases from early 18th cent, maps from late 17th cent, rentals 1715-1934, farm and labour accounts 1835-1936, agency corresp 1833-1959, and papers rel to disputes with tenants, schools, Poor Law administration, Irish Land Commission, etc 19th-20th cent; Tanderagee Moral Agency accounts (clothing fund, schools, etc) 1833-78; Tanderagee Castle drainage plan 1904.

Public Record Office of Northern Ireland (D 1248). Deposited by the 10th Duke of Manchester 1961, 1972, and by ED Atkinson & Son, solicitors, Portadown 1986. *Deputy Keeper's*

Report 1960-5, pp135-6, *1966-72*, p159, *1986*, p20.

[h] Co Armagh estate maps 1701-1852.

Public Record Office of Northern Ireland (D 720, 727). Deposited by TGF Paterson, Armagh County Museum 1955. *Deputy Keeper's Report 1954-9*, p82.

[i] Irish Land Commission papers rel to the Manchester estates 1874-1916.

Public Record Office of Northern Ireland (D 935). Deposited by Fisher & Fisher, solicitors, Newry. *Deputy Keeper's Report 1954-9*, p45.

[j] Tanderagee Castle household accounts 1845-55.

Public Record Office of Northern Ireland (D 2862). Transferred from Armagh County Museum. *Deputy Keeper's Report 1966-72*, p38.

[k] Letter book of the 1st Earl of Manchester rel to Customs 1620-1, with accounts and papers 1620-35.

British Library, Manuscript Collections (Add MS 4147). Bequeathed by Dr Thomas Birch 1766.

[l] Corresp and papers of the 2nd Earl of Manchester as Speaker of the House of Lords 1640-7.

British Library, Manuscript Collections (Add MS 34253). Acquired 1892.

[m] Corresp of Lady Olivia Bernard Sparrow 1803-54, incl letters from Hannah More and William Wilberforce.

British Library, Manuscript Collections (Eg MSS 1964-6). Acquired 1865.

[n] Illustrated armorial roll by John Rous (d1491).

British Library, Manuscript Collections (Add MS 48976). Acquired 1955. HMC *First Report, App*, 1870, p13.

[o] Papers of Sir Richard Rich (afterwards 1st Baron Rich) rel to the Court of Augmentations 1535-9.

John Rylands University Library of Manchester. Deposited in the Public Record Office by the 7th Duke of Manchester *c*1881. Withdrawn 1969 and presented to the Library. HMC *Eighth Report, App, part II*, 1881, pp20-6, nos 1-114. The other Rich and Montagu papers described in the *Eighth Report* were sold in 1970 (Sotheby's, 24 Mar, lots 389-421, 23 June, lots 267-8, 21 July, lots 606-10 and 27 Oct, lots 336-67) and subsequently. For the major groups now in public repositories see [p]-[x] below, which follow the order in which they were described in the *Report*. Smaller groups and

individual documents have been widely dispersed.

[p] Irish corresp and papers of Sir Nathaniel Rich *c*1620-7.

National Library of Ireland (MSS 8013-14, 18638-66 *passim*). Purchased 1931, 1970. HMC *Eighth Report, App, part II*, 1881, pp28-31, 50, nos 132, 156, 162, 172-202a, 429; Sotheby's, 24 Oct 1970, lots 354, 355, etc; microfilm in British Library, Manuscript Collections, RP/536. Richard J Hayes, *Manuscript sources for the history of Irish civilisation*, iv, 1965, pp225-6; first supplement, 1979, pp645-6.

[q] Corresp and papers of Sir Nathaniel Rich rel to Bermuda and Virginia mainly 1615-34.

Bermuda Archives. Sold by Sotheby Parke-Burnet, New York 1970 and acquired by the Bermuda National Trust. HMC *Eighth Report, App, part II*, 1881, pp31-50, nos 203-426 *passim*; microfilm in British Library, Manuscript Collections, RP/420. Similar papers *c*1605-24, but rel mainly to Virginia, were acquired at the same sale by the Arents collection for the history of tobacco, New York Public Library (nos 203-410 *passim*; RP/420).

[r] Parliamentary journal Jan-Mar 1629.

House of Lords Record Office. Purchased 1970. HMC *Eighth Report, App, part II*, 1881, p50, no 431; Sotheby's, 24 Mar, lot 411. See also Maurice F Bond, *Guide to the records of parliament*, 1971, p279. Further letters and papers 1613-*c*1671 (*c*25 items) were purchased 1993-4 (Hist. Coll. 67 addnl) and 1997. The Record Office also holds copies of documents in Cambridgeshire County Record Office, Huntingdon and belonging or formerly belonging to Mr RM Willcocks (*Guide*, pp275-6, 284; NRA 20336; and see also Sotheby's, 19 July 1993, lot 340).

[s] Letters and papers of the 4th Earl (later 1st Duke) of Manchester, mainly rel to the lieutenancy of Hunts *c*1689-99.

Cambridgeshire County Record Office, Huntingdon. Purchased 1970. HMC *Eighth Report, App, part II*, 1881, pp66-7, nos 671-81; Sotheby's, 24 Mar 1970, lot 407. Additional (re-sold) items *c*1626-71 were acquired in 1981 (nos 456, etc), 1986 (nos 471-666 *passim*; Sotheby's, 18 Dec 1986, lot 229) and 1989 (no 427). For letters and papers *c*1629-71 deposited by CR Boxworth see Cambridgeshire County Record Office *Annual Report 1986*, p18. The Record Office also holds copies of other documents sold in 1970.

[t] Diplomatic and other corresp and papers of the 1st Duke 1697-1737 (mainly 1697-1708) (17 vols).

Yale University, Beinecke Library (Osborn MSS fo. 37). Purchased 1987. HMC *Eighth Report, App, part II*, 1881, pp67-109, nos 682-98; unsold 1970; Sotheby's, 23-24 July 1987, lot 257. See also *English Manuscript Studies*, i, 1989, p261.

[u] Letters from George Montagu to Horace Walpole (4th Earl of Orford) 1736-70.

British Library, Manuscript Collections (Add MSS 70987-9). Purchased 1992. HMC *Eighth Report, App, part II*, 1881, pp111-20, nos 719-902; unsold 1970; Sotheby's, 23 July 1987, lot 29.

[v] Diary of naval movements 1778-9.

Portsmouth City Museums and Records Service. Purchased 1970. HMC *Eighth Report, App, part II*, 1881, p120, no 909; Sotheby's, 27 Oct 1970, lot 362.

[w] French naval intelligence 1779-82 (1 vol).

Bodleian Library, Oxford (MS Eng. misc. d. 704, Eng. lett. c. 251 ff 45-50). Purchased 1971. HMC *Eighth Report, App, part II*, 1881, p121, no 922; Sotheby's, 27 Oct 1970, lot 366. The library also acquired a manuscript of John Donne at the sale of 23 June 1970 (lot 267; no 593).

[x] Diplomatic and naval intelligence papers of the 4th Duke 1779-88, principally as ambassador to France 1783.

University of Michigan, William L Clements Library, Ann Arbor. Purchased 1970. HMC *Eighth Report, App, part II*, 1881, pp120-39, nos 910-20, 946-1287; Sotheby's, 21 July 1970, lots 606-10, 27 Oct 1970, lots 357-8, 365; microfilm in British Library, Manuscript Collections, RP/517. See also William L Clements Library, *Guide to the Manuscript Collections*, 3rd edn 1978, p83.

Related collection: Earls of Sandwich (Cambridgeshire County Record Office, Huntingdon HINCH, NRA 5472), including papers of the 7th Earl of Sandwich as trustee for the 7th Duke of Manchester's Irish estates 1856-68 (HINCH 3/7/9-28).

[70] **MONTAGU-DOUGLAS-SCOTT, Dukes of Buccleuch and Queensberry**

The Scott family, already settled at Murdieston (Lanarkshire) by the thirteenth century, was an established border family in the later middle ages, with property at Buccleuch (Selkirkshire), Kirkurd (Peeblesshire) and Branxholm (Roxburghshire). Sir Walter Scott (d *c*1469) exchanged Murdieston for further Branxholm property, was granted Eckford (Roxburghshire) and owned Langholm (Dumfriesshire). He acquired Abington (Lanarkshire) and other property of James, Earl of Douglas, who was

attainted in 1455. His descendant Sir Walter Scott (d1611, created Baron Scott 1606) received Liddesdale (Roxburghshire) and other forfeited estates of the fifth Earl of Bothwell in 1594. The first Baron's son was created Earl of Buccleuch in 1619 and his grandson the second Earl (d1651) bought Dalkeith (Midlothian) from the Earl of Morton in 1642. The second Earl was succeeded in turn by his sisters Marie (d1661) and Anna (d1732), who in 1663 married Charles II's son James, Duke of Monmouth (executed 1685), and was created Duchess of Buccleuch and Countess of Dalkeith. She rebuilt Dalkeith Palace, bought Hawick (Roxburghshire) from the first Duke of Queensberry in 1674 and Melrose Abbey (Roxburghshire) from the sixth Earl of Haddington, and extended her estates by further purchases in Selkirkshire and elsewhere. Bowhill (Selkirkshire) was bought by her grandson the second Duke in 1746.

Francis, Earl of Dalkeith, son of the second Duke, married in 1742 Lady Caroline Campbell, eldest daughter and co-heir of the second Duke of Argyll (see Campbell, Dukes of Argyll, no 13). She was created Baroness Greenwich in 1767. From her her son the third Duke (d1812) obtained Caroline Park (Granton, Midlothian), Adderbury (Oxfordshire) and Sudbrook (Surrey), Adderbury being settled on him in 1770 and the other two properties passing to him on her death in 1794. The third Duke sold Adderbury, and Sudbrook was disposed of in 1819.

In 1810 the third Duke further inherited Drumlanrig (Dumfriesshire) and the dukedom of Queensberry from William Douglas, fourth Duke of Queensberry (1725-1810), who had succeeded his cousin the third Duke (d1778) in the extensive Queensberry estates. The Douglas family was settled in Dumfriesshire by 1388, and obtained Hawick (sold 1674, see above) in 1407. It acquired Tibbers (Dumfriesshire) *c*1508-9 and other Dumfriesshire lands, together with Lincluden (Kirkcudbrightshire), during the sixteenth century. William Douglas (d1640), created Baron Douglas and Viscount of Drumlanrig 1628 and Earl of Queensberry 1633, bought the Dumfriesshire estates of Torthorwald in 1622 and Sanquhar (from the first Earl of Dumfries) in 1637. The second Earl extended these estates and the third Earl (d1695), created Marquess 1682 and Duke of Queensberry 1684, built Drumlanrig Castle.

The third Duke of Queensberry inherited Amesbury (Wiltshire) and Middleton Stoney (Oxfordshire, sold 1737-48 to the third Earl of Jersey), with property at Petersham (Surrey), from Henry Boyle, Baron Carleton (d1725). Neidpath (Peeblesshire), purchased by the first Duke of Queensberry, was settled by him on his younger son William, Earl of March (so created 1697), and descended in 1731 to the first Earl's grandson the third Earl, who afterwards succeeded as fourth Duke of Queensberry in 1788 (see above). Neither Amesbury nor Neidpath, however, devolved upon the Duke of Buccleuch in 1810, as the former passed by entail to the first Baron Douglas (d1827, see Douglas-Home, Earls of Home, no 31), who sold it to the Antrobus family, and the latter descended to Francis Charteris-Wemyss-Douglas, sixth Earl of Wemyss. A portion of the Queensberry estates in Dumfriesshire, moreover, appears to have been inherited with the marquessate of Queensberry by Sir Charles Douglas, fifth Bt, of Kelhead (Dumfriesshire), as heir male of the first Earl of Queensberry.

The third Duke of Buccleuch also acquired the extensive English estates of the Montagu family, including Boughton House (Northamptonshire), Montagu House (Whitehall) and a mansion at Richmond (Surrey), by marriage with Elizabeth, daughter and heir of the fourth Earl of Cardigan (also created Duke of Montagu 1766, see Brudenell, Earls of Cardiagan, no 11). Cardigan's wife Mary, younger daughter of John Montagu, second Duke of Montagu (d1749), had inherited the principal Montagu estates and on Cardigan's death in 1790 these descended to the Duchess of Buccleuch. A portion, however, of the Montagu estates (Beaulieu, Hampshire, and Ditton, Buckinghamshire), had passed to the second Duke of Montagu's elder daughter Isabella, wife of Sir Edward Hussey, created Baron Beaulieu 1762 and Earl of Beaulieu 1784. He retained this portion until his death in 1802, when it too devolved upon the wife of the third Duke of Buccleuch.

The Montagu family was established by Sir Edward Montagu (d1556), Chief Justice of King's Bench, who bought numerous Northamptonshire properties, including Boughton (1528), Hemington and Barnwell (1540), Luddington (1544), Armston (1547) and Polebrook (1548). This estate was subsequently extended, for example by the purchase in 1613 of the hundreds of Polebrook, Navisford and Huxloe and in 1748 of the estate of Grafton Underwood, and it included property in Huntingdonshire (Coppingford, etc). Edward Montagu (d1644) was created Baron Montagu of Boughton in 1621. His son the second Baron (d1684) married Anna, daughter of Sir Ralph Winwood (d1617), whose Ditton (Buckinghamshire) estate passed to the Montagu family in 1691. The third Baron (d1709), created Duke of Montagu in 1705, built Boughton House. His marriage to Elizabeth, daughter and co-heir of Thomas Wriothesley, fourth Earl of Southampton (d1667), brought estates at Beaulieu (Hampshire), which had been bought by the first Earl of Southampton in 1538, and Dunchurch (Warwickshire), which had belonged to the fourth Earl's wife, the daughter of Francis Leigh, Baron Dunsmore and Earl of Chichester (d1653). (For the Southampton estates see Leigh, Barons Leigh, no 60; Noel, Earls of

Gainsborough, no 74; Russell, Dukes of Bedford, no 90.)

In 1692 the first Duke married as his second wife Elizabeth Monck (1653-1734), widow of the second Duke of Albemarle, on whose death in 1734 the former Albemarle estates of Clitheroe and Furness (Lancashire) entered the Montagu family. Other Albemarle property, however, was divided among the co-heirs of the first Duke of Albemarle, with much of it passing to the Granville Earls of Bath and some of it from that family to the first Earl Gower (see Sutherland-Leveson-Gower, Dukes of Sutherland, no 101).

When the third Duchess of Buccleuch died in 1827 the Clitheroe estate was divided. One moiety, including Clitheroe castle and honour, was settled on her younger son Henry James Montagu-Scott, Baron Montagu of Boughton (d1845), on whom Beaulieu (Hampshire) and Ditton (Buckinghamshire) were also settled. The other moiety, including the manor of Slaidburn (Yorkshire, West Riding) and the Forest of Bowland, passed to the fifth Duke, who sold it to the Towneley family. On the death of Baron Montagu in 1845, his Montagu estates reverted to the fifth Duke (d1884), who later settled Clitheroe and Beaulieu on his second son Henry John Douglas-Scott-Montagu, created Baron Montagu of Beaulieu in 1885, to whom Ditton also passed on his mother's death in 1895. After the fifth Duke's death, some of the Montagu family papers from Montagu House (Whitehall) were transferred to Palace House, Beaulieu (see HMC *Report on the Manuscripts of Lord Montagu of Beaulieu*, 1900), but the bulk of the Montagu House papers, including those reported on by the Commission between 1899 and 1926 (HMC *Report on the Manuscripts of the Duke of Buccleuch and Queensberry Preserved at Montagu House, Whitehall*, I-III), were removed to Boughton House at the time of the demolition of Montagu House c1925.

Estates in 1883: Dumfriesshire 254,179 acres, Roxburghshire 104,461 acres, Selkirkshire 60,428 acres, Lanarkshire 9,091 acres, Midlothian 3,436 acres, Kirkcudbrightshire 1,000 acres, Peeblesshire 272 acres, Fife 60 acres, Northants 17,965 acres, Warwicks 6,881 acres, Hunts 1,065 acres, Bucks 894 acres, Lancs 369 acres, Surrey 7 acres, total 460,108 acres worth £217,163 a year, exclusive of minerals worth £4,091 a year and Granton Harbour worth £10,601 a year.

[a] Charters and writs 14th-20th cent, mainly Dumfriesshire (Buccleuch and Queensberry estates), Peeblesshire, Roxburghshire and Selkirkshire from 15th cent and Midlothian from 16th cent, incl Melrose (Earls of Haddington) writs 16th-18th cent; inventories of writs, wills, marriage contracts, testamentary, executry and tutory papers 16th-19th cent, incl

executry accounts for the Duchess of Buccleuch 1731-3, commissioners' minutes and papers 17th-19th cent, executorship papers of the 2nd Duchess of Argyll (d1767) and the 2nd Baroness Montagu 1857-60, and tutory papers for the 2nd Marquess of Bute 1803-18; Buccleuch legal and financial papers 16th-20th cent, incl papers relating to the Bothwell estates 16th-17th cent, to the Duke of Monmouth (d1685), and to the Duchess of Buccleuch's disputes with the Earls of Leven and Melville and purchases from John Scott of Harden (Roxburghshire) c1700-27; legal papers rel to the 4th Duke of Queensberry 1774-1823; records of the regality courts of Melrose, Musselburgh (Midlothian) and Eskdale (Dumfriesshire) 1662-1748; Selkirk and Jedburgh (Berwickshire) justiciary court papers 1645.

Peeblesshire, Selkirkshire, Roxburghshire and Dumfriesshire estate records (Buccleuch family estates) 16th-20th cent, incl maps 18th-20th cent, rentals, accounts and vouchers c1630-20th cent, corresp from 18th cent, papers rel to teinds, commonties and woodlands 16th-19th cent, records of coal mining at Byreburnfoot and Canonbie (Dumfriesshire) c1768-97, stock census 1684 and rentals of the 'debateable lands' 1637-55; Bowhill lease book 1836-1914 and accounts c1746-1910; Melrose rentals and accounts 1756-1915; Midlothian (Dalkeith) estate records 17th-20th cent, incl maps and plans 18th-20th cent, rentals, accounts and vouchers c1688-20th cent, corresp from 18th cent, teind books 1706-8, feu duty papers 17th-20th cent, and papers rel to wood sales c1784-1803 and to railways, Firth of Forth mussel fishings and pollution of the North and South Esk rivers 19th-20th cent; Dalkeith mill and farm accounts 18th-19th cent; mining plans and records (Sheriffhall and Cowden quarries) c1671-20th cent; accounts and papers rel to the Midlothian estates of Musselburgh, Inveresk, Caroline Park and Granton 17th-20th cent, incl rentals of Musselburgh and Inveresk 1712 and Caroline Park 1753; Granton brickwork accounts 1842-7 and harbour records 1834-1906; Burntisland (Fife) pier and ferry papers mid-19th cent; Inchkeith (Fife) island plan 1804; accounts of the Duchess of Buccleuch's English properties 1696-1701; rental of the entire Buccleuch estate in Scotland 1766.

Dumfriesshire (Drumlanrig, former Queensberry) estate records mainly 1810-20th cent, with Drumlanrig and Sanquhar rental 1710 and misc estate papers from c1772; Wanlockhead (Dumfriesshire) lead mining records 1766-1900, incl bar lead books 1811-23; papers rel to Wark Common (Northumberland) enclosure 1796-7 (former property of the 2nd Duke of Argyll); accounts and papers rel to Adderbury (Oxon) and Surrey estates c1759-95; papers rel to Montagu family estates late 18th-mid-19th cent, incl corresp rel to Beaulieu (Hants) 1845-53.

Architectual plans, building papers and inventories for Dalkeith 17th-20th cent, incl accounts of repairs c1701-19 and work by William Adam c1741-2, report by John and Robert Adam 1752, building journal 1829-31, household inventory 1652 and inventory of muniments 1695; plans, inventories and papers for Drumlanrig 1738-1840, Caroline Park 1738-1835, Sudbrook 1794-1814 and Adderbury c1678-1786, incl accounts of work at Adderbury by Lancelot 'Capability' Brown 1785; inventories and accounts for East Park (Smeaton, Midlothian) and Hawick 18th cent and London (South Audley Street) 1812-16 (purchased from the Marquess of Bute 1812); misc inventories 17th-20th cent, incl Newark (Selkirkshire) 1632-4, Langholm 1812-19 and Cawston (Warwicks) 1861; household accounts and vouchers for the family's principal residences in Scotland and England (Dalkeith, Bowhill, Edinburgh, London, etc) mainly c1769-1921, with some earlier accounts from 17th cent, incl Dalkeith accounts 1651-2, Edinburgh and Canongate accounts and vouchers c1629-45 and accounts of the English households of the Duchess of Buccleuch 1701-6 and the 2nd Duke 1728-50; household accounts of the 1st Earl of Buccleuch in Holland 1631 and of the 2nd Duchess of Argyll (d1767); Nuneaton (Warwicks) and Hinckley (Leics) household accounts of Lady Charlotte Scott 1817-22; Cannes and Bad Gastein household accounts 1867-71.

Midlothian and Roxburghshire militia and yeomanry papers 18th-19th cent, incl records of the South Fencible and Buccleuch Fencible regiments c1775-1800, the Edinburgh County Milita c1794-1879 and the North British Militia, Edinburgh Regiment c1798-1812; Dumfriesshire militia papers c1798-1819; papers rel to Dumfriesshire, Midlothian, Roxburghshire and Selkirkshire lieutenancy, politics, elections and affairs 17th-19th cent, incl Roxburghshire election papers 1831-3 and Hawick turnpike papers mid-18th cent; papers rel to the Free Church of Scotland in Dumfriesshire and Roxburghshire c1845-51 and to episcopal chapels and churches at Drumlanrig, Galashiels, Jedburgh, Langholm, Melrose and Selkirk 19th-20th cent, incl building vouchers for the Melrose and Selkirk chapels 1848-70; Hawick St Cuthbert's and Dalkeith St Mary's school and chapel records c1841-1942; Dalkeith heritors and kirk sessions records 18th-20th cent; minutes of Dalkeith justice court 1804-16 and society of special constables 1830-6; Dalkeith statute labour and workhouse records 1816-49; papers rel to Dalkeith customs and markets 1832-1915, Trinity College, Glenalmond (Perthshire) 1830-88 and the Prince Albert Memorial, Edinburgh 1861-76; minutes of the Honest Country Club (a society of Borders gentlemen) 1711-16; Buccleuch Hunt records c1802-1957.

Appointments, commissions and personal inventories 16th-19th cent, incl patent of the dukedom of Greenwich 1719 and inventories of Sir Walter Scott 1577 and the 3rd Duke of Buccleuch 1761; family and personal accounts and papers 17th-20th cent, incl papers of the Duke of Lauderdale (d1682), the Duke of Monmouth 1661-85 (with a muster roll of Monmouth's troop of Horse Guards 1679), Baroness Greenwich (d1794), Anna, Duchess of Buccleuch (d1732), Francis, Earl of Dalkeith 1746-9, Major Walter Scott of Datchet (Bucks) c1750-1825, the 3rd and 5th Dukes, and Louisa, Duchess of Buccleuch (d1912); accounts of the Earl of Buccleuch's Regiment 1644; papers rel to peerage elections c1787-1847, Douglas Heron & Co (Ayr), bankers, 1770-93, the Roxburghe Club and Royal Company of Archers 19th cent, and Queen Victoria's visit to Dalkeith 1842; letterbook of the 2nd Duke of Argyll 1715-16; letters of Sir Walter Scott 1807-32, and of the antiquaries JW Pycroft 1860-84 and Sir William Fraser (d1898); papers collected by the antiquary James Anderson (d1728); papers of William Gartshore MP (d1806) rel to the political patronage of Launceston (Cornwall); records of game c1810-1928 and of the yacht *Flower of Yarrow* 1830-41; misc papers 16th-20th cent, incl memoranda books of David Scrymgeour of Cartmore c1676-88, valuation of royal revenue in Scotland 1670 and a military order book (Dettingen campaign) 1743.

National Archives of Scotland (GD 224). Deposited from Dalkeith Palace by the 8th and 9th Dukes of Buccleuch 1967-76. HMC *Papers of British Cabinet Ministers 1782-1900*, 1982, p42; *Papers of British Politicians 1782-1900*, 1989, pp72, 93. NRA 34806. The collection includes records deposited from Bowhill Estate Office 1974 and papers transferred from the Edinburgh solicitors Strathern & Blair, WS (GD 224/1122-8) and Tods, Murray & Jamieson, WS (GD 224/1130, formerly GD 237/68-71). Papers relating to the Montagu family and estates were mainly withdrawn in 1971 (see [m] below).

[b] Melrose Abbey charters 1124-1625, with related papers 13th-19th cent.

National Archives of Scotland (GD 55). Deposited by the 8th Duke of Buccleuch from Dalkeith Palace 1952. *Keeper's Report 1952*, p5. Cosmo Innes, *Liber Sancte Marie de Melros. Munimenta Vetustiora Monasterii Cisterciensis de Melros* (Bannatyne Club, 1837). NRA 30352.

[c] Chamberlain's and receiver's accounts (Buccleuch estates) 1744-54, with tutory accounts of Caroline, Countess of Dalkeith, for the 3rd Duke 1750-5.

National Archives of Scotland (CS 96/3157-66).

[d] Commissioners', receivers' and executry accounts (4th Duke of Queensberry: Queensberry and March estates) 1808-18.

National Archives of Scotland (CS 96/2427-32).

[e] Charters and writs c1190-18th cent, mainly Dumfriesshire, Kirkcudbrightshire and Lanarkshire, with some for Roxburghshire (Hawick) 16th-17th cent, Midlothian (Canongate, etc) 16th-18th cent, and Fife (Aberdour) and Kinross-shire (Loch Leven) c1669-73, etc; bonds of manrent c1510-1601; misc deeds for English counties (Queensberry estates) and inventories of writs (Buccleuch and Queensberry estates) 17th-18th cent; wills, marriage contracts and testamentary and related papers 15th-18th cent, Douglas family; legal and curatory papers and bonds, discharges and financial papers 16th-18th cent, Douglas family, incl legal papers rel to Canongate mid-18th cent; legal and financial papers of the Dukes of Buccleuch late-18th-20th cent, incl papers rel to Dumfriesshire mines 19th-20th cent; papers rel to the 2nd Earl of Queensberry's losses in the Civil War c1655-62; New Delgarno (Dumfriesshire) regality court records 1730-46.

Queensberry (Dumfriesshire, etc) estate records 16th-20th cent, incl tacks 16th-early 19th cent, maps and plans 18th-20th cent (extensive), rentals, accounts and vouchers c1619-1837 (mainly pre-1790), victual rent books c1748-80 and corresp 17th-19th cent; commissioners' sederunt books and papers and tenants' petitions 18th-20th cent; papers rel to marches and commonties 17th-18th cent and to Dumfriesshire (Kirkmahoe, etc) and Kirkcudbrightshire teinds and churches 16th-18th cent; Drumlanrig home farm valuations and shooting leases 20th cent; Wanlockhead (Dumfriesshire) lead mining records c1712-81; Byreburnfoot (Dumfriesshire) colliery accounts 1730; accounts of the Duke of Buccleuch's overseer of works in Peeblesshire, Roxburghshire and Selkirkshire 1810-22, with misc Selkirkshire and Roxburghshire tacks of teinds 17th-18th cent and estate papers 18th-19th cent; accounts of the estates of the earldom of March 1734-9; rental of the 1st Marquess of Annandale's estates 1672-98; misc Middleton Stoney (Oxon) estate papers 17th-18th cent, incl rental 1615 and wood book 1654-5.

Drumlanrig house and garden records 17th-19th cent, incl architectural plans, drawings and building papers c1618-22 and 1697-19th cent, household inventories c1694-1882, and accounts and vouchers mainly 17th-18th cent; Sanquhar town house building vouchers 1735-9; misc architectural plans and drawings 18th-19th cent, incl some for Montagu Bridge (Dalkeith) 1791-3, Dalkeith Palace 1830-1 and Caroline Park and Branxholm 1835-6; misc household inventories 17th-20th cent, incl inventories for Sanquhar Castle 1694-9, Canongate c1707-54 and Dalkeith Palace 1769-1931; misc household papers 17th-19th cent, incl household accounts for Sanquhar Castle and London 1694-8, Edinburgh, Holyrood and Canongate c1689-1723, and Naples 1838-9; architectural plans, Morton (Dumfriesshire) church 1840; papers rel to Dumfriesshire affairs 16th-19th cent, incl respites and papers rel to the Borders 16th-17th cent and election accounts 1734; Dumfriesshire, Annandale and Eskdale valuation books 1653-67 and cess roll 1687; corresp rel to Dumfries county house and gaol 1801-2; Friendly Mining Society (Wanlockhead) papers 1721-57.

Patents and commissions 16th-20th cent, Queensberry and Buccleuch families; Douglas family inventories, accounts, corresp and papers 16th-18th cent, incl inventories of Sir William Douglas 1513-15 and the 2nd Duke of Queensberry 1712, accounts and journals of continental travel 1654-93, and official and political corresp and papers of the 1st and 2nd Dukes of Queensberry; Buccleuch family papers 18th-20th cent, incl letters of the British and French royal families and the 4th Duke of Queensberry c1775-1816, and Drumlanrig game books 1845-77; papers of the Duke of Montagu rel to the Prince of Wales and Prince Frederick 1776; corresp of Baroness Greenwich rel to Sudbrook 1783-6; family papers of Henry Hyde, 2nd Earl of Rochester and 4th Earl of Clarendon 16th-18th cent, incl accounts 1713-20; papers of the Dukes of Argyll 1677-1721, with papers rel to Roubiliac's monument for the 2nd Duke in Westminster Abbey 1745; literary and misc papers 16th-19th cent, incl protocol books 16th cent, journal of the Jacobite rising 1746, Lord Chatham's narrative of the Walcheren expedition 1809, and papers rel to the Queensberry family and Scottish music collected by CK Sharpe.

In private possession. Access restricted. Enquiries to the National Register of Archives (Scotland) (NRA(S) 1, 1275). HMC *Fifteenth Report, App VIII*, 1897; *Drumlanrig Castle*, 1903; *Sixteenth Report*, 1904, pp117-22; *Papers of British Politicians 1782-1900*, 1989, pp72, 93; *Guide to the Location of Collections*, 1982, p8. NRA 6184. The collection includes papers transferred from Strathern & Blair, WS, family papers (2 volumes) formerly in the possession of CK Sharpe and presented by the 5th Earl of Rosebery 1897, and further manuscript volumes owned by CK Sharpe c1827 and subsequently acquired by the Dukes of Buccleuch. Also included are estate accounts and papers mainly c1696-1769 (49 bundles, nos 1526-75) purchased from a dealer on behalf of the third Marquess of Bute in 1897 (see Stuart, later Crichton-Stuart, Earls and later Marquesses of Bute, no 100) but returned to the ninth Duke of Buccleuch in 1981.

[f] Accounts of William Stewart of Shambellie as chamberlain to the 1st and 2nd Dukes of Queensberry 1693-1719.

Dumfries and Galloway Archives (GD 37, NRA(S) 3535). Deposited 1987. NRA 11018.

[g] Drumlanrig rentals 1660-95.

Dumfries and Galloway Archives (GGD 146). *Holding Guide and Source List*, 1992, p19A.

[h] Drumlanrig estate and household account book 1736-63; Wanlockhead lead mining journals 1755-1811.

Hornel Library, Kirkcudbright (NRA(S) 0118). NRA 10173.

[i] Scottish estate plans (Buccleuch estates) 1810; misc Roxburghshire rentals and papers 1688-1724, with accounts and memoranda 1808-19 and journal of Roxburghshire and Selkirkshire mineral observations 1816; Dalkeith stock and wages book 1810-29; architectural plans and drawings 18th-20th cent, many by William Burn (d1870), incl some for Bowhill from c1812, Caroline Park 18th cent-1834, Dalkeith Palace c1701-1883, Montagu House (by Anthony Salvin) 1829 and St Nicholas's church, Dalkeith 1847; papers rel to Henry Scott, 4th Earl of Delorain (d1807); corresp of the 3rd, 4th and 5th Dukes of Buccleuch; literary and misc papers 16th-19th cent, incl letters and annotated proofs of works by Sir Walter Scott (d1832), literary MSS of James Hogg (d1835) and Thomas Campbell (d1844), papers rel to James VI and the Octavians 1596 and to the proposed union of England and Scotland 1670, survey of Scottish ecclesiastical benefices 1658, and printed maps, pamphlets and books.

In private possession. Access restricted. Enquiries to the National Register of Archives (Scotland) (NRA(S) 1, 1275). NRA 6184.

[j] Court papers, Amesbury manors and hundred 1768-1814; Amesbury and Urchfont (Wilts) estate records 1711-1824, incl rentals and accounts 1711-1816, vouchers, corresp, and sales papers; Amesbury household inventory 1786.

Wiltshire and Swindon Record Office (776/1117-25). Deposited by Messrs Parker, Bullen, solicitors, Salisbury 1965. NRA 40205.

[k] Amesbury (Wilts) estate plans, accounts, vouchers, corresp and papers c1778-1810, incl papers rel to sales c1800-10; Amesbury Abbey household inventory 1779 and accounts c1779-87; corresp and papers rel to the Amesbury turnpike and volunteers 1778-1810; misc papers 17th-19th cent, incl appointment of the 4th Duke of Queensberry as deputy lieutenant of Wilts 1780 and draft deed rel to the Dunchurch (Warwicks) estate of the 5th Duke of Buccleuch 1860.

Wiltshire and Swindon Record Office (WRO 377). Deposited by Nicholl, Manisty & Co, solicitors,

London, through the British Records Association (BRA 969) 1967. NRA 7073.

[l] Misc letters of the 3rd Duke and Duchess of Queensberry rel to Amesbury Abbey gardens 1722-77.

Wiltshire and Swindon Record Office. Transferred from the Salisbury and South Wiltshire Museum 1952. NRA 699.

[m] Official and political corresp and papers of Charles Townshend (d1767), Chancellor of the Exchequer (and second husband of Caroline, Countess of Dalkeith), incl papers rel to North America, the West Indies, the East India Company and Harwich (Essex) borough 1761-7.

University of Michigan, William L Clements Library, Ann Arbor. Purchased from the 9th Duke of Buccleuch 1976. Formerly amongst the records at Bowhill and those deposited in the Scottish Record Office from Dalkeith Palace. *Guide to the Manuscript Collections of the William L Clements Library,* 1978, pp134-90. NRA 6184, 34806.

[n] Deeds 12th-19th cent, mainly Northants, with some for Essex, Lancs and Yorks 17th-18th cent, London 17th-19th cent and Surrey 18th-19th cent; executorship and trust papers 17th-20th cent, Brudenell, Monck, Montagu and Montagu-Douglas-Scott families, incl the 1st Duke of Montagu 1711-14, the 2nd Duke 1749, the 4th Earl of Cardigan 1790-2, the Duchess of Buccleuch 1827-30, the 4th Duke of Buccleuch c1819-33, and Countess Granville 1725; legal and financial papers 17th-19th cent, incl copies of Montagu wills and settlements and papers rel to the Monck and Montagu inheritances; manorial records, Kettering (Northants) 1825-1925 and Ulverston (Lancs) 1740-53.

English estate stewards' papers 18th-20th cent, incl rentals, accounts and vouchers 1707-1881, corresp c1787-1883, and letter books 1898-1914; Boughton and Barnwell (Northants and Hunts) estate records 17th-20th cent, incl abstract of Montagu leases c1750, maps and plans 18th-20th cent, particulars and rentals 17th-19th cent, accounts, vouchers, corresp and papers 18th-20th cent, and records of estate labour, small holdings, cottages and allotments 19th-20th cent; records of Boughton home farm 1858-1936 and other farms 1866-1904; Warwicks estate survey 1722-5 and accounts, vouchers, corresp and papers c1847-20th cent; Furness (Lancs) surveys and ministers' accounts 1537-1696, rental 1767 and papers mid-19th-early 20th cent, with transcripts of estate accounts from the Middle Ages to c1696 (43 vols); Clitheroe (Lancs) estate accounts 1767, 1778, c1843-82; Forest of Bowland (Lancs) valuation 1764; misc Bucks and Hants estate papers 18th-19th cent, incl Bucks accounts 1786-96, c1850-70 and Beaulieu (Hants) par-

ticulars 1767 and accounts 1847-66; Surrey estate plans and papers 18th-19th cent, incl survey 1765; misc estate papers 17th-20th cent, incl London (Montagu) estate accounts 1669-81, 1724 and Orange Street (St Martin-in-the-Fields, Middlesex) accounts 1820; survey of the Surrey and Sussex lands of Lady Cordell Herveye 1616.

Architectural plans and drawings 17th-19th cent, Boughton, Clitheroe, London houses (Privy Garden, Dover Street), etc; misc Boughton household inventories and papers 17th-20th cent, incl building accounts 1700; Barnwell household inventory or account 1683; building accounts for Montagu House 1698-1706 and Privy Garden 1731-43; London house inventories 18th-19th cent, mainly Montagu House but incl Cockpit 1709-10 and Grosvenor Square 1776-8; catalogue of Montagu House pictures 1898; misc London household accounts and papers 1669-early 19th cent, mainly Montagu House; misc Ditton household papers 18th-19th cent, incl inventory 1709 and accounts 1885-95; Richmond household inventories and vouchers c1772-1832; Blackheath household vouchers 1789-90 and garden papers 1767; Beaulieu inventory 1828; Edinburgh and Dalkeith household vouchers 1804-8.

Weekley Hospital (Northants) ledger 1780-1820 and rule book 1614; Stamford and Kettering turnpike account book 1867; Boughton horticultural show records 1869-70; papers rel to Richmond (Surrey) schools and charities 19th cent; patents and appointments, Montagu family 18th cent; Montagu and Montagu-Douglas-Scott family accounts and papers 17th-19th cent, incl corresp of the 1st Duke of Montagu with Lord Arlington 1668-78 (2 vols), military plans and papers of the 2nd Duke of Montagu, and official and personal papers of the 4th Earl of Cardigan and Duke of Montagu 1742-90; Monck family papers 17th cent, incl corresp of the 2nd Duke of Albemarle; antiquarian papers of Gervase Holles (d1675) and Sir Frescheville Holles 1614-67; Boughton game records 1822-1907; heraldic, genealogical, literary and misc papers from 15th cent, incl Peterborough Abbey register of George Fraunceys 1404, Wriothesley Garter book c1488 and collection of printed music books.

In private possession. Access restricted. Enquiries to the County Archivist, Northamptonshire Record Office. HMC *Report on the Manuscripts of the Duke of Buccleuch and Queensberry at Montagu House, Whitehall,* 1899-1926. The collection includes papers withdrawn from the Scottish Record Office 1971 (see [a] above). A further Peterborough Abbey register by George Fraunceys is British Library MS Cotton Faustina B iii (see GRC Davis, *Medieval Cartularies of Great Britain,* 1958, pp87-8, no 765).

[o] Deeds 13th-20th cent, mainly Northants, Bucks, Hunts, Lancs and Warwicks, with some for Beds, Leics, Middlesex, Oxon, Staffs, etc; Montagu family settlements, trust papers and mortgages 16th-early 19th cent; legal and financial papers 14th-20th cent, mainly from 16th cent, incl inquisitions *post mortem* 16th-17th cent, papers rel to franchises, forests (Rockingham Forest and Geddington Brand) and rights of common, etc 16th-19th cent, and papers rel to the 2nd Duke of Albemarle's debts 1700 and the sale of Southampton Buildings (Middlesex) 1727-30; extensive manorial records, Northants (Barnwell, Brigstock, Geddington, Gloucester honour, etc) and Hunts (Coppingford, etc) 13th-19th cent, Norfolk (Foxley) 13th-16th cent, and Bucks (Chalvey, Datchet, Ditton, etc) and Warwicks (Church Lawford and Newbold-on-Avon) 14th-19th cent; Northants (Huxloe, Navisford and Polebrook) and Warwicks (Knightlow) hundred records 15th-19th cent; misc Lancs (Dalton in Furness, etc) manorial records 16th-18th cent; Colworth (Beds) manorial terriers, rentals and accounts *c*1413-1547.

English estate stewards' accounts and vouchers *c*1788-1912, incl accounts with Messrs Hoare 1788-1815 and with the Dowager Duchess of Buccleuch 1805-27; Boughton and Barnwell (Northants and Hunts) estate records 16th-20th cent, incl maps 19th-20th cent, particulars and surveys from 16th cent, valuations 1814, rentals, accounts and vouchers 1690-1917, labour accounts 1794-1813, stewards' corresp 1692-1795, and papers rel to enclosures 18th-19th cent and woods and tithes 16th-19th cent; records of Boughton and Barnwell drainage 1833-94 and farms and crops 1826-94; Warwicks estate records 17th-20th cent, incl leases from 1680, Dunchurch survey 1701, rentals, accounts and vouchers 1720-1918, corresp 1711-85, wood accounts 1723-39, drainage and farm accounts 1880-91, and enclosure and tithe papers 18th-19th cent; Lancs estate papers 17th-20th cent, incl Muchland leases 1711-65 and survey 1649, misc plans 18th cent, Furness mineral leases 19th cent, Furness and Clitheroe valuations and rentals 1813-14, Furness accounts and vouchers 1741-1899 and corresp 1752-90, and Clitheroe accounts 1868-80 and corresp 1727-91; Bucks estate papers 17th-19th cent, incl surveys 1604-5, accounts and vouchers 1721-1895 and corresp 1775-87; Beaulieu (Hants) particulars 1832; misc Foxley (Norfolk) estate papers 16th-17th cent, incl valuation 1606 and wood sale accounts 1586; estate accounts for Orange Street (St Martin-in-the-Fields, Middlesex) 1787-1810, Norton Disney (Lincs) and Grindon (Staffs) 1702-8, and Deene (Northants) 1783; Richmond (Surrey) and Montagu House (London) household vouchers 1809-28; Ditton (Bucks) household bills 1807.

Official, political and family corresp and papers of the Montagu family (mainly the 1st and 2nd Barons and the 1st and 2nd Dukes) *c*1483-1758 (18 vols), incl papers rel to Northants affairs; bank accounts, 5th Duke of Buccleuch 1859-80; inventory of goods of the 4th Earl of Cardigan 1763; corresp and papers of Sir Ralph Winwood 1564-1628 (11 vols) and of the Duke of Shrewsbury 1674-1708 (17 vols); misc papers, incl collected proclamations 17th cent.

Northamptonshire Record Office (1933/25, 1936/31, 1941/10, 1965/212, 1977/23). Deposited by the 7th, 8th and 9th Dukes of Buccleuch from Boughton 1933-77, except for the 1941 deposit which was received from the family's London solicitors. Beaulieu estate papers deposited in 1977 were transferred to Palace House, Beaulieu. HMC *Report on the Manuscripts of the Duke of Buccleuch and Queensberry at Montagu House, Whitehall*, 1899-1926. *Summary Guide to the Northamptonshire Record Office*, 1954, p12. NRA 4039, 23059 (partial lists). Misc items rel to the Northamptonshire Yeomanry Corps 1797-1800 were presented by the 8th Duke of Buccleuch 1939 (1939/25, NRA 4039).

[p] Barnwell (Northants) estate survey 1823.

Northamptonshire Record Office. Purchased at Bloomsbury Book Auction's sale 12 Jan 1995.

[q] Dunchurch, Knightlow and Newnham Regis (Warwicks) manorial court records 1716-21.

Northamptonshire Record Office (QCR). Deposited with other records by the Clerk to Northamptonshire County Council 1962 (1962/98). NRA 4039.

[r] Warwicks (Dunchurch, etc) deeds 14th-20th cent; Dunchurch manor court rolls 1716-20, with court papers for Dunchurch, Newnham Regis and Thurlaston 1666-1736; misc estate papers 17th-20th cent.

Warwickshire County Record Office (CR 2105, CR 2874). Deposited by A Maynard Taylor through the British Records Association 1981 and by Kidd Rapinet, solicitors, London 1991. NRA 34185.

[s] Account books of Marc Antonie of Colworth (Beds) as steward of the Dukes of Montagu 1706-24.

Bedfordshire and Luton Archives and Record Service (X 800). Deposited by the National Trust, through the British Records Association (BRA 2524) 1992. NRA 7125.

[t] Papers of William Folkes (d1773), of King's Lynn (Norfolk) and London, as agent of the Dukes of Montagu.

Norfolk Record Office. Deposited by the Norfolk Record Society 1975. NRA 4635.

[u] Manorial records, liberty of Furness and manors of Dalton in Furness, Plain Furness, Egton with Newland, Hawkshead and Ulverston

1740-1938, incl perambulation maps 1856-77, with Pennington in Furness court book 1823-71; Furness estate records mainly 19th-20th cent, incl leases, maps, plans, rentals, accounts, vouchers, letter books and corresp, with steward's papers 1743-59; mineral working leases, plans, accounts, reports and papers 18th-20th cent; wreck book 1821-1918; papers rel to Furness charities, churches (Lindal, Dalton in Furness, etc), schools (Askam, Ulverston, etc) and local affairs 18th-20th cent; misc deeds and legal and other papers 17th-20th cent.

Cumbria Record Office, Barrow (BD/BUC). Deposited 1976 and 1978 by the Boughton Estates Company (Kettering and Weekley), to which the records had been transferred from the agent's premises at Tytup Hall, Dalton in Furness, in 1968. NRA 32574.

[v] Misc Furness deeds, abstracts and legal papers mainly 19th-20th cent; manorial court records, liberty of Furness and manors of Dalton in Furness, Plain Furness, Egton with Newland, Hawkshead and Ulverston c1633-20th cent; misc leases, accounts, estate papers, etc 16th-20th cent; papers rel to the Furness manors of Muchland and Torver (leased from the Crown by the Dukes of Montagu and their heirs c1739-1804).

Cumbria Record Office, Barrow (BD/HJ). Deposited by Hart, Jackson & Sons, solicitors, Ulverston 1977-8. NRA 32581.

[w] Official accounts and papers of the 1st and 2nd Dukes of Montagu as Masters of the Great Wardrobe 1660-1749.

Royal Archives, Windsor Castle. Presented by the 7th Duke of Buccleuch 1917. Enquiries to the Registrar, Royal Archives, Windsor Castle, Berkshire.

[x] Survey and map of Clitheroe honour 1809-10.

British Library, Manuscript Collections (Add MS 64817). Purchased from JH Rendall 1987.

[y] *Valida Consolatio* of Sydney Montagu (son of Sir Edward Montagu of Boughton) 1613.

British Library, Manuscript Collections (Add MS 28560). Acquired 1871.

[z] Surveys of Sir Edward Montagu's lands in Beds (Hoo and Pertenhall), Hunts (Folkesworth) and Northants (Farndon, Weekley) 1550-6.

British Library, Manuscript Collections (Add MS 29611). Acquired 1874.

[aa] Diary of the 1st Duke of Montagu as ambassador to France.

Yale University, Beinecke Library (Osborn MSS fb 191). NRA 18661.

Related collections: Brudenell, Earls of Cardigan, no 11; Campbell, Dukes of Argyll, no 13; Douglas-Home, Earls of Home, no 31; Sutherland-Leveson-Gower, Dukes of Sutherland, no 101; Earls of Leven and Melville (National Archives of Scotland GD 26, NRA 29368), including Buccleuch curatory, legal and estate papers c1614-1707; Barons Polwarth (National Archives of Scotland GD 157, NRA 32440), including curatory, tutory and executry papers for the 2nd Earl of Buccleuch and his sisters Marie and Anna; Clerk of Penicuik (National Archives of Scotland GD 18, NRA 29182), including correspondence of Sir John Clerk as commissioner for the Queensberry and March estates 1726-55; Barons Montagu of Beaulieu (in private possession, NRA 4880 and see HMC *Guide to the Location of Collections*, 1982, p44), including Hants and Bucks deeds 15th-20th cent, Beaulieu and Datchet (Bucks) manorial records 17th-20th cent, Beaulieu, Ditton and Datchet estate rentals, accounts and papers 16th-20th cent, and bound volumes from Montagu House, with other Montagu family papers 16th-20th cent; Clitheroe honour and estate records 14th-20th cent (Lancashire Record Office DDHCl, NRA 40716, with Clitheroe estate company papers deposited from Beaulieu 1975); Dukes of Albemarle (Public Record Office C 107/25-9, 61-2 and C 116/2-8, 163-71, 174, 183-8, NRA 39973), including Furness, Clitheroe and Forest of Bowland estate papers 17th cent.

[71] MURRAY, later STEWART-MURRAY, Dukes of Atholl

The Murray family was settled at Tullibardine (Perthshire) in the thirteenth century and extended its Perthshire estates in the later middle ages, acquiring property at Easter Gask, Polgour and elsewhere. John Murray (d1613), created Earl of Tullibardine 1606, was granted Balquhidder (Perthshire) in 1587. The second Earl (d1627), married a daughter and co-heir of John Stewart, fifth Earl of Atholl (d1595). Their son John Murray (d1642) was created Earl of Atholl in 1629 and secured a royal grant of the Perthshire estates of the earldom of Atholl, centred on Blair Atholl and Dunkeld, the Balvenie (Banffshire) property of the fifth Earl of Atholl having been sold in 1610. The earldom and estates of Tullibardine, however, were settled on a brother of the second Earl of Tullibardine. They were subsequently inherited on the fourth Earl's death in 1670 by his cousin John Murray, second Earl of Atholl (d1703), created Marquess of Atholl 1676, whose son the second Marquess (d1724) was promoted Duke of Atholl in 1703.

The second Duke inherited the tenth Earl of Derby's estates in the Isle of Man, together with the sovereignty of the island and the barony of Strange (see Stanley, Earls of Derby, no 99).

On his death in 1764 he was succeeded as third Duke by his nephew John Murray (d1774), the son of the Jacobite Lord George Murray (d1760), who owned property at Glencarse and Strowan (Perthshire). In 1765 the third Duke alienated the sovereignty of Man to the Crown, investing the proceeds in further Perthshire property. The remaining Isle of Man possessions were sold by his son the fourth Duke (d1830) shortly before his death. The Tullibardine estate was exchanged by the fourth Duke for Balnaguard, a property of the Drummond of Strathallan family near Dunkeld. The seventh Duke, who succeeded in 1864, adopted the surname Stewart-Murray.

Lord William Murray (d1726), younger son of the first Marquess, was granted the Jacobite title of Earl of Nairn and Viscount Stanley, having acquired Mukkersy (Perthshire) by marriage with the Nairn family. His son and heir John, Lord Nairn, was attainted in 1746.

General Lord John Murray (1711-87), a younger son of the first Duke, acquired the Banner Cross (Derbyshire) estate through marriage. His daughter and heir married Lt-General William Foxlowe (d1818), who took the surname Murray. From him the estate passed to his sister, who had married William Bagshawe in 1798, and thence to their descendants.

Estates in 1883: Perthshire 201,640 acres worth £42,030 a year.

[a] Charters, writs and titles c1180-19th cent, mainly Perthshire; inventories of writs and abstracts of title 17th-19th cent; wills, marriage contracts, executry papers and trust papers 18th-20th cent, incl records of the Atholl trust 1830-63, the Dunkeld bishopric trust 1821-81 and the Manx trust 1830-5; legal papers 15th-20th cent, incl some rel to the Isle of Man and the Earls of Derby and to the Robertson family of Lude (Perthshire) 17th-19th cent; bonds, discharges and financial papers 16th-19th cent.

Perthshire estate records 17th-20th cent (extensive), incl tacks 19th-20th cent, maps and plans from 18th cent, rentals, accounts and vouchers from 17th cent, letter books from 18th cent and papers rel to tileries and drainage mid-19th cent; papers rel to minerals 18th-19th cent, incl Blairington coal, lead and silver papers c1718-1842, and to roads, ferries and waterways 18th-19th cent, schools 19th cent, Dunkeld bridge 19th cent and railways 19th-20th cent; records of forestry and timber 17th-20th cent, Tay salmon fishings 1782-1930, incl rental 1820, and game 19th-20th cent; Lude estate papers, incl rentals 1879; papers rel to Banner Cross estate late 18th-mid-19th cent; rentals and papers rel to the estates of Lord Nairn and Stanley c1756-9; Blair Castle and Dunkeld architectural papers 18th-20th cent, incl Blair Castle plans 1736 and Dunkeld Palace drawings 1829-30; extensive Blair and Dunkeld house-

hold records 17th-20th cent, mainly from 18th cent, incl accounts and vouchers for building and repairs, inventories, and household and cellar accounts; inventories, accounts and papers rel to London house and other Scottish residences 18th-20th cent, incl papers rel to London house building 1769-73; inventory of Derby House (?London) ? c1736.

Papers rel to Perthshire elections and politics 18th-20th cent, incl lieutenancy letter book 1804; records of Perthshire militia, fencibles and yeomanry c1794-1825; papers rel to the Perthshire Prisoners of War Association c1914-18; papers rel to Dunkeld ecclesiastical, parochial and cathedral affairs 18th-20th cent; Dunkeld Curling Club records c1846-1950; Royal Manx Fencibles records 1802-8; appointments and commissions 15th-20th cent; family accounts and papers 16th-20th cent, incl papers of the 1st Marquess as lieutenant in Argyll and Tarbet 1684-5, the 1st Duke as Lord Privy Seal c1733-5, the 2nd, 3rd, 4th, 6th and 7th-10th Dukes and the 6th and 8th Duchesses; papers rel to the Jacobite risings of 1715 and 1745 and the Murray family of Ochtertyre 1672-1745; papers of Lord George Murray (d1760), the Duke of Rannoch (d1746) and Sir George Herbert Murray (civil servant, d1936); misc papers of the 7th Earl of Derby (d1651); Crimean War papers of Lord James Murray 1854-5; records of the 42nd (Black Watch), 71st and 78th regiments of foot and 3rd Regiment of Foot Guards c1757-94; records of the Atholl Highlanders 1839-1980; papers rel to the Scots Fusilier Guards mid-19th cent, to HMS *Atholl* 1816-32 and to the brig *Larch* 1818-29; papers rel to the Robertson family of Lude c1791-1801; literary and misc papers 17th-20th cent, incl papers rel to pipe music and Gaelic literature, MS narrative of James Murray of Glencarse 1698-1708 and journal of John Drummond of Megginch 1858-81; Isle of Man travel journal 1779.

In private possession. Enquiries to the National Register of Archives (Scotland) (NRA(S) 234, 980). HMC *Seventh Report, App*, 1879, pp703-16; *Twelfth Report, App, Part VIII*, 1891, pp1-75; *Papers of British Politicians 1782-1900*, 1989, p74. NRA 11000, 19071. The collection includes papers deposited by the Edinburgh solicitors Tods, Murray & Jamieson at the Scottish Record Office (GD 237) in 1958 and subsequently transferred.

[b] Atholl estate accounts 1818-49, letterbooks 1818-68 and report 1844-8.

National Library of Scotland (Dep 301/23-82). Deposited by Tods, Murray & Jamieson, WS, Edinburgh 1979. NRA 29083.

[c] Estate accounts and report 1845-6.

National Archives of Scotland (CS 96/1074).

[d] Dunkeld bridge building journal 1803-6, with accounts of bridge income and expenditure 1808-67.

National Archives of Scotland (CS 96/562-3).

[e] Misc family corresp 1691-8; corresp rel to the rising of 1745-6.

National Library of Scotland (MSS 5136-8). Purchased with papers of the Erskine Murray family 1939. HMC *Fourth Report, App*, 1874, pp521-8; *Guide to the Location of Collections*, 1982, p21. The letters may have passed into the possession of James Erskine, Lord Barjarg, on his appointment as sheriff-depute of Perthshire in 1748.

[f] Papers of the 1st Duke rel to his dispute with James Murray of Dowally 1709-19; Atholl peerage papers 1761-82.

Edinburgh University Library, Special Collections Department (MSS La.Add.13.13/17-36). Bequeathed by the antiquary David Laing (1793-1878). *Index to Manuscripts*, 1964, i, p60.

[g] Corresp of the 2nd Duke rel to the rising of 1745-6.

Edinburgh University Library, Special Collections Department (MSS Dc.1.37). *Index to Manuscripts*, 1964, i, p60.

[h] Regimental records of the Scottish Horse (raised by the 8th Duke 1900), with military corresp and papers of the 8th Duke *c*1900-18.

In private possession. Enquiries to the National Register of Archives (Scotland) (NRA(S) 2007). NRA 23009.

[i] Corresp and papers of the 8th Duke and Duchess rel to the Scottish National War Memorial and Museum *c*1917-58.

National Library of Scotland (Acc 4714). Deposited 1969, having been on temporary loan since 1961. NRA 26176.

[j] Papers of the 8th Duchess rel to Indian self-government *c*1928-35.

British Library, Oriental and India Office Collections (MSS Eur.D 903). Deposited by Grizel, Lady Warner 1978. NRA 27472.

[k] Legal and financial papers 17th-19th cent, incl some rel to the revestment act 1765; papers rel to the Manx estate and Manx affairs *c*1736-1831, incl agents' accounts and corresp, tenants' petitions 1790-1, valuation papers *c*1820-8, and papers rel to tithes, mines, minerals and smuggling; records of the Manx fencibles and volunteers 1793-1813; records of the 2nd Royal Veteran Company 1822-4; accounts of the 4th Duke's commissioners *c*1785-1824; papers of the 4th Duke as governor of the Isle of Man *c*1793-1830; misc papers 16th-19th

cent, incl Savile Row (Westminster) lease 1736, St James's Square (Westminster) inventory and valuation 1831 and MS history and description of the Isle of Man *c*1764-74.

Manx National Heritage Library (Acc 9707). Deposited by the 9th Duke of Atholl from Blair Castle 1954. NRA 41467.

Related Collections: Stanley, Earls of Derby, no 99; Muir Mackenzie of Delvine (National Library of Scotland MSS 1101-1530), including Atholl factory papers 1750-1, 1772-8 and legal and other papers 1685-1821 (MSS 1238-9, 1403-9, 1415, 1529); Adam of Blair Adam (in private possession, NRA 9954, NRA(S) 1454), including Atholl trust papers 1830; Bagshawe of Ford (John Rylands University Library of Manchester, NRA 10462), including papers of Lord John Murray (d1787) and Lt-General William Murray (d1818), Banner Cross estate and household papers, military papers and Black Watch regimental records mainly 18th cent; Robertson of Lude (National Archives of Scotland GD 132, NRA 32025); Murray of Ochtertyre (National Library of Scotland Acc 6026, NRA 20932); Castle Rushen papers (Manx National Heritage Library Acc 9782), including papers rel to the Dukes of Atholls' property and affairs mainly 18th cent.

[72] MURRAY, Earls of Mansfield

Sir Andrew Murray, second son of Sir William Murray (d *c*1459) of Tullibardine (Perthshire), was granted Crown leases of Letter Bannachty in Strathearn (Perthshire) from 1491 and a feu of these lands in 1510. Arngask (Fife, Kinross-shire and Perthshire) and Balvaird and Kippo (Fife) were brought by his wife Margaret Barclay, granddaughter and heir of James Barclay of Kippo and heir of Henry de Freslay of Arngask and Fargy. Sir David Murray, second son of Sir Andrew Murray (d1572) of Balvaird, was created Lord Scone 1604 and Viscount Stormont 1621, the site and lands of the dissolved monastery of Scone (Perthshire) having been granted him following the fall of the third Earl of Gowrie (d1600). In 1624 he inherited the estates of his nephew Sir Andrew Murray of Balvaird and Arngask. Following his death in 1631, the first Viscount was succeeded through special entail in turn by Sir Mungo Murray (d1642) of Drumcairn (Fife), James Murray, second Earl of Annandale (d1658), and David Murray, second Baron Balvaird and fourth Viscount Stormont. The fourth Viscount (d1668) acquired property by marriage with the widow of the second Earl of Annandale. This comprised the ancestral Dumfriesshire estates of the Murray Earls of Annandale (Cockpool, Comlongon, etc) and a portion of the extensive acquisitions of the first Earl of Annadale (d1640, so created 1624) in Dumfriesshire (Lochmaben, etc) and County Donegal, the latter soon alienated. (Other property of the first

Earl in Fife, East Lothian and elsewhere, however, was sold and did not pass to the fourth Viscount.)

The seventh Viscount (d1796) succeeded to the estates and titles of his uncle William Murray (1705-93), Lord Chief Justice, created Earl of Mansfield 1776, who had purchased Kenwood (Middlesex) from the third Earl of Bute in 1754 and also acquired property in Cheshire (Anderton) and Derbyshire (Bradbourne). Schaw Park in Alloa (Clackmannanshire) was bought by the seventh Viscount and second Earl from his brother-in-law the tenth Baron Cathcart in 1799. Later Perthshire acquisitions included the former Graham estate of Lynedoch and the Drummond-Stewart estate of Logiealmond. Colston Bassett (Nottinghamshire) was acquired by the third Earl in 1838, but was apparently sold soon afterwards. Properties in Merionethshire and Montgomeryshire, including an estate purchased in 1797 from Lord Cawdor, were also disposed of before 1883. Kenwood was sold 1920-5 and Schaw Park in 1922.

Estates in 1883: Perthshire 31,197 acres, Dumfriesshire 14,342 acres, Clackmannanshire 1,705 acres, Fife 795 acres, Middlesex 539 acres, Derbyshire 250 acres, Cheshire 224 acres, Cumberland 22 acres, total 49,074 acres worth £42,968 a year, exclusive of Clackmannanshire minerals worth £1,886 a year.

[a] Charters, writs and titles c1260-19th cent, mainly Perthshire 13th-19th cent, Fife 14th-19th cent, Dumfriesshire 15th-19th cent and Clackmannanshire 16th-18th cent; deeds for English estates 16th-19th cent, mainly Middlesex 16th-19th cent, Cheshire 18th-19th cent and Derbys, Essex and Notts 19th cent, with misc deeds rel to the first Earl of Annandale's properties in Northumberland, Surrey and Co Donegal 17th cent; Scone Abbey cartulary 1538-62; inventories of writs and abstracts of title 16th-20th cent; wills, settlements, trust and executry papers 16th-20th cent, incl executry papers of the 1st and 2nd Earls c1793-1808; legal papers 16th-19th cent, incl papers rel to Highgate Archway Co c1822-47; barony court minutes for Sauchie (Clackmannanshire) 1717-20 and Lochmaben (Dumfriesshire) 1846-59.

Estate records for Perthshire, Clackmannanshire, Dumfriesshire and Fife 17th-20th cent, incl tacks 17th-20th cent, surveys, maps, plans, particulars and valuations 18th-20th cent, rentals, accounts and vouchers 17th-20th cent, corresp and memoranda 18th-20th cent and letter books 19th-20th cent; papers rel to teinds 17th-20th cent, timber 18th-20th cent, commonalty divisions 18th cent, fishing and game 19th-20th cent, roads 18th-19th cent and railways 19th cent; papers rel to minerals 18th-20th cent, incl Sauchie (Clackmannanshire) colliery accounts 1749-51 and papers rel to New Sauchie colliery 19th cent; London and Middlesex estate records 18th-20th cent, incl leases 18th-19th cent, particulars 18th cent, maps, plans and rentals 18th-20th cent, accounts 19th cent and vouchers, memoranda and corresp 18th-19th cent; papers rel to Middlesex roads 18th cent and to railways and tithes 19th cent, with papers rel to the lease of Kenwood (Middlesex) to Grand Duke Michael of Russia 1909-15; misc Cheshire and Derbys estate papers 18th-20th cent, incl some rel to Anderton salt works c1758-1860; misc Welsh estate maps, plans and accounts 18th-19th cent; misc papers rel to the Gosfield Hall (Essex) estate (mortgaged to the Earls of Mansfield and sold 1854) c1837-54.

Scone building papers 17th-19th cent, incl estimate by James Playfair 1790, plans by George Saunders 1802 and plans, accounts and corresp rel to work by William Atkinson c1803-28; Kenwood building papers 18th-19th cent, incl accounts and vouchers rel to work by Robert and James Adam 1764-79 and George Saunders 1793-6; Comlongon building accounts and plans 18th-20th cent; household inventories 17th-20th cent, incl Scone and Comlongon 17th-20th cent, Balvaird (Fife) 1698 and Kenwood 1831-1922; household accounts 17th-20th cent, incl Scone 17th-20th cent, Balvaird 1659-60, Kenwood 18th-20th cent, Vienna 1766-7 and Paris 1776, 1819; red book for Kenwood by Humphry Repton 1793; papers rel to proposed landscape improvements at Scone by John Loudon 1803 and to John Flaxman's monument to the first Earl in Westminster Abbey c1793-6; papers rel to local affairs in Clackmannanshire, Dumfriesshire and Perthshire from 17th cent, incl some rel to the Clackmannanshire troop of yeomanry cavalry c1820-5, the poor in Dumfriesshire and Perthshire c1829-39, the Black Watch Association 20th cent and the Perthshire Home Guard 1942; papers rel to Middlesex local affairs from 18th cent, incl East Middlesex Militia papers c1798-1803 and papers rel to Highgate School and Chapel c1821-38.

Appointments, patents, commissions and family corresp and papers 16th-20th cent, incl accounts of the 1st Viscount Stormont as Comptroller 1603-5, with letters to him from James I c1592-1623, account book of Katherine, Countess of Erroll 1678-88, judicial notebooks of the 1st Earl of Mansfield c1757-86, extensive diplomatic and political papers of the 2nd Earl 1756-96 and political papers of the 3rd Earl c1812-40; genealogical MSS 18th-19th cent; Scone Abbey rentals 14th-15th cent; deeds rel to Viscount Boyne's Co Louth estate 1765-71.

In private possession. Enquiries to the National Register of Archives (Scotland) (NRA(S) 776). NRA 10988. HMC *Papers of British Cabinet Ministers 1782-1900*, 1982, pp43-4; *Papers of British Politicians 1782-1900*, 1989, pp74-5.

[b] Perthshire writs 19th-20th cent; inventories and registers of title 16th-20th cent; legal papers rel to Tay and Solway salmon fishings 19th cent; misc Dumfriesshire, Fife and Perthshire estate records from 17th cent, incl tack book 1661-5 and misc rentals and accounts 17th-20th cent; Schaw Park estate papers 18th-20th cent, incl plans 19th cent, sale particulars 1922 and papers rel to mineral extraction 19th-20th cent; Kenwood drainage plan *c*1900; Scone Abbey rental 1465.

In private possession. Enquiries to the National Register of Archives (Scotland) (NRA(S) 776). NRA 10988.

[c] Inventory of writs, 1st Viscount Stormont (d1631).

Edinburgh University Library, Special Collections Department (MSS La.III.327²). *Index to Manuscripts*, 1964, ii, p564.

[d] Misc corresp of the 4th Viscount Stormont (d1668).

Edinburgh University Library, Special Collections Department (MSS La.II.66). *Index to Manuscripts*, 1964, ii, p564.

[e] Kenwood household accounts 1785-93, 1801-2, 1807-8, with Isle of Wight bills 1794; corresp of the 2nd Earl 1781-8.

Iveagh Bequest, Kenwood. Acquired by the Iveagh Bequest 1927, with further papers donated by Mrs D Hall-Christie 1954 and found in the roof at Kenwood 1962. NRA 10988.

[f] Kenwood estate map 1794.

London Metropolitan Archives. Accessions List July-Dec 1978, p25.

[g] Kenwood library catalogue 1802.

Camden Local Studies and Archives Centre. Guide, 1989, p58.

[73] NEVILLE, Barons Braybrooke

Thomas Audley (d1544), Lord Chancellor and founder of Magdalene College, Cambridge, was created Baron Audley in 1538 and granted the Walden Abbey estate in Saffron Walden (Essex). His daughter and sole heir, Margaret, married as her second husband, Thomas Howard, fourth Duke of Norfolk. Thomas Howard (1561-1626), the eldest son of this marriage, who was created Baron Howard (of Walden) in 1597 and Earl of Suffolk in 1603, inherited the estate and built Audley End 1603-16. He married a daughter and co-heir of Sir Henry Knyvett of Charlton (Wiltshire), whose Wiltshire inheritance was settled on their younger son, created Earl of Berkshire 1626, the elder inheriting the earldom of Suffolk. The fifth Earl of Suffolk (d1709) married the widow of Sir John

Maynard, but her Gunnersbury (Middlesex) and other estates passed at her death to the Hobart family (see Kerr, Marquesses of Lothian, no 58). The mansion of Audley End, though not the estate, was sold to Charles II in 1669 but reconveyed to the fifth Earl in 1701.

On the death of the tenth Earl in 1745 the earldom of Suffolk devolved upon his cousin the fourth Earl of Berkshire, but the title to his estates passed to his heirs general, the descendants of the two daughters of the third Earl of Suffolk The estate was divided in 1753, when one portion was received by the Countess of Portsmouth (d1762) and Anne Whitwell (d1770), both daughters of the second Baron Griffin of Braybrooke, and the other portion by George Hervey, second Earl of Bristol. The first portion was subsequently united in the possession of John Griffin Griffin, Anne Whitwell's son, created fourth Baron Howard 1784 and Baron Braybrooke 1788, who also inherited property in Northamptonshire from his Griffin ancestors. On Braybrooke's death in 1797 he was succeeded in his barony of Braybooke (but not of Howard) and his estates by his cousin Richard Aldworth Neville (1750-1825), who adopted the surname Griffin.

Neville inherited from his father, Richard Neville Aldworth Neville (d1793), the Aldworth family estate at Stanlake (Berkshire), including Ruscombe, Hurst and Frogmore House (New Windsor). He also inherited the Neville family estate at Billingbear Park (Berkshire), with property in Wargrave, Warfield and elsewhere, including Ashridge hundred (Wiltshire until 1844), which had passed to Richard Neville Aldworth Neville in 1762 from the Countess of Portsmouth, widow of his maternal uncle Henry Neville alias Grey. (Grey's father had married a sister of the fourth and last Baron Grey of Wark (d1702), but no Grey property appears to have devolved to her or her Neville descendants.)

In 1814 the second Baron Braybrooke purchased Lord Bristol's portion of the Audley End estate (Littlebury). During the nineteenth century the adjacent Heydon estate in Great and Little Chishall (Essex, Cambridgeshire after 1895) was acquired and Chrishall (Essex) bought from the Buckworth-Herne-Soame family. By the end of the nineteenth century the Braybrooke (Northamptonshire) and Wargrave estates had been sold, and Audley End was sold to the Ministry of Works in 1948. The Braybrooke archive includes papers of the Cornwallis family acquired by the marriage in 1819 of the third Baron Braybrooke to Jane, eldest daughter and co-heir of the second Marquess Cornwallis (d1823).

Estates in 1883: Essex 9,820 acres, Berkshire 3,691 acres, total 13,511 acres worth £18,173 a year.

[a] Deeds 14th-20th cent, mainly Essex, with some for Northumberland and Sussex (Grey

family) 14th-18th cent and Northants (Griffin family) 17th-18th cent; wills and settlements 18th-19th cent, incl administration papers for the will of the 3rd Baron Grey of Wark (d1701); trust and executorship papers 19th cent, incl Sir Stephen Glynne 1819-28 (son-in-law of the 2nd Baron Braybrooke), the Earl of Portsmouth 1825-43 and the Cornwallis family 1822-56; legal papers 16th-19th cent, incl registers of Suffolk (Cornwallis) deeds *c*1584, schedules of deeds 1650, 1754 (Countess of Portsmouth), and papers rel to the Audley End estate partition 1745-50, JG Griffin's claim to the barony of Howard 1784, the Littlebury (Essex) estate 1822-81, and Suffolk lighthouses; financial papers 18th-19th cent, Howard and Neville families; manorial records 13th-18th cent, mainly Essex, incl Brook Walden court rolls 1285-1746 and accounts for the Earl of Suffolk's Cambs, Essex, Herts and Suffolk manors 1580-1643.

Audley End estate records 16th-19th cent, incl maps, plans, particulars, surveys and valuations 18th-19th cent, sequestration rental 1645-6, rentals and accounts 16th-19th cent, extensive vouchers 18th-19th cent, and corresp 17th-19th cent, with papers rel to timber, herds, stock, game and farms 18th-19th cent; Billingbear (Berks) estate records 18th-19 cent, incl valuations, accounts and corresp; Heydon (Essex) estate rentals and accounts 19th-20th cent; Hawarden (Flintshire) estate rental and corresp 19th cent, Glynne family; Suffolk (Cornwallis) estate and household accounts and corresp 17th-19th cent; Audley End household records 18th-19th cent, incl building accounts from 1763, bills and corresp of Robert Adam 1762-8, and inventories, household accounts and tradesmen's accounts; inventories and accounts for Chillingham Castle (Northumberland) and Uppark (Sussex) 17th-18th cent, Grey family; papers rel to Essex and Berks local affairs 17th-20th cent, incl plans of Harwich and Thames defences 1795-7, and lieutenancy papers of the 1st Baron Braybrooke 1795-6 and the 3rd Viscount Maynard 1861-4; Saffron Walden churchwardens' accounts 1439-90 and poor law papers 1832; charity accounts and papers 18th-19th cent; Haveringland (Norfolk) parish register 1560-1631 and churchwardens' accounts 1602-13; papers rel to Magdalene College, Cambridge 1687-8.

Appointments and commissions 17th-19th cent, Griffin and Neville families; family papers 16th-20th cent, Howard, Grey, Griffin, Whitwell, Neville, Aldworth and Glynne families, incl papers rel to the debts of the 2nd Earl of Suffolk 1640-6 and the 7th Earl 1721-7, papers of Sir Edward Griffin and his son Edward as Treasurers of the Chamber 1600-85, corresp of the 2nd Baron Grey as governor of Barbados 1700-6, papers of the 1st and 2nd Barons Braybrooke, papers of the 3rd Baron rel to his *History of Audley End*, and corresp and accounts of RNA Neville 1739-93; corresp of the

Cornwallis and Bacon families 1613-44 and the nonconformist divine William Greenhill 1622-30; genealogical, topographical and misc papers, incl cartulary of Eye priory *c*1260, compotus of Walden Abbey pittancer 1409-10, precedent book of Richard Heyward *c*1575 and typescript catalogues of manuscripts at Audley End 1881-*c*1952.

Essex Record Office (D/DBy). Deposited by the 9th and 10th Barons Braybrooke 1947 with additions 1948, 1983 and 1992. HMC *Eighth Report, App I*, 1881, pp277-96; *Guide to the Location of Collections*, 1982, p6. *Guide to Essex Record Office*, 1969, pp119-22. NRA 6803. Grey family papers were returned from Berkshire Record Office 1954 and other papers transferred from Cambridge University Library 1966. Braybrooke (Northamptonshire) enclosure papers 1779-90 were transferred to Northamptonshire Record Office 1953 (1953/36a).

[b] Essex manorial records 14th-20th cent, incl Walden 1660-1886 and Littlebury 1607-1884.

Essex Record Office (D/DAd). Deposited by Adams & Land, solicitors, Saffron Walden 1946. NRA 5391.

[c] Essex estate maps and papers 18th-19th cent.

Essex Record Office (D/DQy). Purchased from Nockolds & Sons, estate agents, Saffron Walden 1949-50. NRA 6036.

[d] Audley End estate papers late 18th-early 20th cent, incl maps, day book, cash book and gamekeeper's book; Audley End household papers 19th cent, incl cellar, kitchen and wages accounts 1845-97; family corresp and papers 17th-20th cent, Aldworth, Griffin, Howard, Neville and Whitwell, incl account books of Dr Charles Aldworth of Magdalen College, Oxford 1692-1781, personal and Berks estate account books of RNA Neville 1763-93, corresp of the Calandrini family 1625-76, and corresp of the Countess of Portsmouth rel to her claim to Audley End 1745-60; accounts, corresp and papers of the 2nd, 3rd, 4th, and 6th Barons 19th-20th cent; genealogical and archaeological papers 18th-19th cent.

Essex Record Office (D/DBy). Deposited by the Department of the Environment 1978-9, 1983. NRA 6803.

[e] Deeds 16th-19th cent, mainly Berks, Oxon and Wilts (Billingbear and Stanlake estates), with some for Hants (Grey family); register of Berks and Oxon (Aldworth family) deeds 1556-1683; abstracts of title 1551-1700; wills and settlements 14th-18th cent, Aldworth, Grey and Neville; executorship and trust papers, Sir Jonathan Trelawney 1604-10, Richard Aldworth 1680 and Elizabeth Aldworth 1745; papers rel to the sequestration of Richard Aldworth's estates 1650-6; legal and financial papers 16th-19th cent, incl some rel to the barony of

Abergavenny 16th-18th cent, Richard Aldworth's duel case 1721-34 and disputes between Sir Henry Neville and the tenants of Warfield (Berks) 1577-1641; manorial records 14th-18th cent, mainly Berks, incl Billingbear accounts 1400-1555; Ashridge (Wilts) hundred court rolls 1621-1754; Berks estate (Neville and Aldworth families) maps, plans, surveys, particulars, rentals, accounts and papers 17th-20th cent, with corresp rel to the former Neville estates in Berks and Yorks ER 1598-1608; Billingbear and Frogmore household inventories and accounts 18th-19th cent.

Papers rel to Berks lieutenancy and local affairs 16th-19th cent, incl some rel to Windsor Forest 1550-1817, New Windsor and Wokingham boroughs 1562-1786, and Berks elections 1711-1820; appointments and commissions 16th-18th cent; Aldworth and Neville family papers 17th-18th cent, incl New River Company and other papers of Sir Henry Neville c1600-14, corresp of Richard and Henry Neville 1640-97, papers of RNA Neville (parliamentary notebook 1747-66, etc), and papers of the Jalabert family of Geneva 18th cent; misc genealogical and historical papers of the 3rd Baron Braybrooke; Faringdon (Berks) tithe composition deed 1221.

Berkshire Record Office (D/EN). Deposited by the 9th Baron Braybrooke in Essex Record Office 1947 and transferred 1948, with further transfers 1953-4, 1987. *Guide to Berkshire Record Office*, 1952, pp70-1. NRA 431, 6803.

[f] Manorial records 17th-20th cent, mainly Berks (Wargrave, Hinton Pippard, etc); misc estate papers, incl Warfield tithe map 1905 and Berks enclosure papers 19th cent.

Berkshire Record Office (D/EN). Deposited by Langton & Passmore, solicitors, London, through the British Records Association 1964. NRA 431.

[g] Berks deeds 18th cent; Hurst (Berks) manorial court records 17th-20th cent.

Berkshire Record Office (D/EN). Deposited by Blandy & Blandy, solicitors, Reading on the instructions of the 9th Baron Braybrooke 1950-4. NRA 431.

[h] Berks and Wilts (until 1844) manorial and estate papers 18th-19th cent, incl Billingbear estate maps, Hurst tillage book c1840 and Newenham Lakes (Warfield) quit rentals 1835-96.

Berkshire Record Office (D/EZ9). Acquired from Nockolds & Co, estate agents, Saffron Walden 1954. NRA 431.

[i] Personal corresp of the 2nd Baron Braybrooke 1780-1825.

Berkshire Record Office (D/EZ6). Purchased at Sotheby's 1950 (27 Feb, lot 250). NRA 431.

[j] Misc deeds for the 1st Earl of Portsmouth's Hants estate 1669-1763; case papers 1749-61; rental of Essex and Cambs estates of JG Whitwell, later 1st Baron Braybrooke c1749.

Hampshire Record Office (7M48). Formerly at Audley End. Transferred from Essex Record Office 1948. NRA 8807.

[k] Personal and official papers of the Neville and Aldworth families 16th-19th cent, incl Sir Henry Neville as ambassador to France 1594-1608, Richard and William Aldworth as exchequer auditors 1611-1705, and RNA Neville as Under-Secretary of State and diplomat 1748-63; deeds, legal papers and accounts rel to the Neville family's office of provost-marshal general, Jamaica 1758-1834.

Public Record Office (PRO 30/50). Transferred from Essex Record Office and Cambridge University Library 1948, 1987. HMC *Eighth Report, App I*, 1881, pp277-96. NRA 6803, 23642.

[l] Official corresp and papers of the 1st Marquess Cornwallis 1780-1802, with family papers 1614-1854.

Public Record Office (PRO 30/11). Deposited by the 5th Baron Braybrooke 1880 and the 9th Baron 1947, with transfers from Essex Record Office 1948-87. HMC *Eighth Report, App I*, 1881, pp277-96; *Private Papers of British Diplomats 1782-1900*, 1985, p15; *Papers of British Cabinet Ministers 1782-1900*, 1982, p14. NRA 6803, 8658.

[m] Manorial, estate, official and family papers 14th-18th cent (Yorks, Norfolk, Suffolk, Essex, etc), Cornwallis and Neville families.

Suffolk Record Office, Ipswich branch (HA 411). Part of the Cornwallis archive acquired by the 3rd Baron Braybrooke through marriage in 1819, bought by the 2nd Earl of Iveagh from a London bookseller 1931 and purchased by the Record Office 1987. NRA 4134.

[n] Walden Abbey survey 1399-1400; household book of the Duke of York 1662-73; accounts of the debts of the 2nd Earl of Suffolk 1640-6; journal of the 1st Marquess Cornwallis; papers of the 6th Baron Braybrooke rel to Cambridge University 1856-61.

Cambridge University Library (Add 7090-7110; Doc 3810-12, 3896-8). Deposited by the 9th Baron Braybrooke 1947. *Summary Guide to accessions of Western manuscripts since 1867*, 1966.

[o] Archaeological papers of the 4th Baron Braybrooke 1839-92.

Cambridge University Museum of Archaeology and Anthropology (GO 2/2-4). Purchased from the 9th Baron Braybrooke 1947. NRA 39203.

[p] Norfolk deeds 16th-18th cent, Grey family; legal papers and corresp rel to lighthouses in Norfolk and Suffolk 1726-1836.

Guildhall Library (MS 30145-48). Formerly at Audley End. Transferred from Essex Record Office to the Corporation of Trinity House 1948, and later to the Guildhall Library 1992. NRA 6803.

[q] Walden Abbey cartulary c1387.

British Library, Manuscript Collections (Harleian MS 3697). Known to have been in the possession of the Earl of Suffolk 1640.

[r] Corresp, official papers and collections of the 1st and 2nd Earls of Suffolk 1604-36.

Bodleian Library, Oxford (MSS Carte 121, 123). Presented by Thomas Carte c1753.

Related collections: Barons Griffin of Braybrooke (Northamptonshire Record Office Acc 1949/ 121); Marquesses of Bristol (Suffolk Record Office, Bury St Edmunds branch HA 507, NRA 6892), including Essex deeds, family settlements, and legal and estate papers 18th cent; Glynne-Gladstone MSS (St Deiniols Library, Hawarden, NRA 14174), including papers of the 2nd and 3rd Barons Braybrooke (MSS 50-4, 2312, 2357).

[74] NOEL, Earls of Gainsborough

The Noel family was settled in Staffordshire in the Middle Ages. Andrew (d1563), third son of James Noel of Hilcote (Staffordshire), acquired property in Staffordshire (Perry Barr, later sold), Leicestershire (Old Dalby, or Dalby-on-the-Wolds, sold 1617) and Rutland (Brooke) in the 1540s. His son Sir Andrew Noel (d1607) settled at Brooke, and married a daughter of Sir James Harington of Exton (Rutland). Sir Edward Noel (d1643), son of Sir Andrew, acquired Ridlington (Rutland), on the sale of the Harington estates by the second Baron Harington (d1614) and his heirs, and was created Baron Noel of Ridlington in 1617. Exton itself was acquired by Sir Baptist Hicks (d1629), who had amassed a large fortune in trade in London and had already acquired various country estates, including Chipping Campden (Gloucestershire) in 1609. He was created Viscount Campden in 1628, and following his death in 1629 his estates were divided principally between his daughters and co-heirs, Julian, who had married Edward Noel in 1605, and Elizabeth Morrison of Cassiobury (Essex) (see Capell, Earls of Essex, no 16). The Noel share of the Hicks inheritance was the Exton and Whitwell estate (Rutland), the Chipping Campden estate, and other property including the manor of Hampstead (Middlesex) (sold in 1707) and Campden House, Kensington (Middlesex) (sold in 1708). Lord Noel also succeeded his father-in-law as second Viscount Campden.

The third Viscount Campden (1612-82) married in 1639 Hester, second daughter of the second Baron Wotton, through whom the Valle Crucis (Denbighshire) estate was inherited. (It was sold in 1663 to Sir John Wynn, fifth Bt: see Williams Wynn of Wynnstay, no 115.) Their son the fourth Viscount (1641-89) married in 1661 Elizabeth Wriothesley, elder daughter of the fourth Earl of Southampton, and was created Earl of Gainsborough in 1682. She brought the Titchfield (Hampshire) estate, but following the second Earl of Gainsborough's death in 1690 that property passed to his daughters, who married respectively the first Duke of Portland and the second Duke of Beaufort (see Cavendish-Bentinck, Dukes of Portland, no 18; Somerset, Dukes of Beaufort, no 96; and, for other estates of the fourth Earl of Southampton, Leigh, Barons Leigh, no 60, and Montagu-Douglas-Scott, Dukes of Buccleuch and Queensberry, no 70). The Exton and Chipping Campden estates and the earldom of Gainsborough, however, were inherited in 1690 by the second Earl's cousin, Baptist Noel, of North Luffenham (Rutland) and Cottesmore (Rutland: a property inherited from the Croke, Heath and Fanshawe families: see also Verney, Barons Willoughby de Broke, no 111).

The sixth Earl of Gainsborough inherited the Walcot (Northamptonshire), Castle Bytham (Lincolnshire) and Kinnoulton (Nottinghamshire) properties from a cousin, Thomas Noel of Walcot (d1788). On the sixth Earl's death in 1798 his estates were divided. The Walcot properties passed to CH Nevile, who took the name of Noel; but the Exton and Chipping Campden estates passed to Gerard Noel Edwards, later Sir GN Noel, second Bt (1759-1838), son of Gerard Anne Edwards (d1773) of Welham Grove (Leicestershire) by Jane (d1811), sister of the fifth and sixth Earls of Gainsborough. GN Edwards had inherited from his father various properties in Leicestershire (Welham, etc), London and Middlesex (Islington, Kensington, etc), Kent (Dartford, etc), and Ireland, but these were all sold between 1805 and 1840. He had married in 1780 Diana, daughter of the first Baron Barham (d1813), who succeeded her father in the barony and the Barham Court estate near Maidstone (Kent). On her death in 1823 she was in turn succeeded in the Barham estate and peerage by her son Charles Noel (d1866). He further inherited the Gainsborough estates from his father in 1838 and was created Earl of Gainsborough in 1841.

Campden House (Chipping Campden) was destroyed in the Civil War. After Exton Hall was severely damaged by fire in 1810 Barham Court became the principal seat until the sale of the Kent estate in 1845-6, but a new house at Exton was completed in the early 1850s. The Gloucestershire estate was sold and the Rutland estate reduced in the 1920s.

Estates in 1883: Rutland 15,076 acres, Gloucs 3,170 acres, Leics 159 acres, Lincs 89 acres, Warwicks 68 acres, Northants 6 acres, total 18,568 acres worth £28,991 a year.

[a] Deeds 12th-20th cent (*c*310 medieval), mainly Rutland and Leics 12th-19th cent and Gloucs 15th-20th cent but incl Kent 16th-19th cent, London and Middlesex 13th-20th cent, other English counties 13th-19th cent, Wales 15th-17th cent and Ireland 17th-18th cent; wills, settlements and related trust and executorship papers 16th-20th cent, mainly Noel, Hicks and Edwards families, incl trust and executorship papers for Sir GN Noel, 2nd Bt *c*1801-57; legal and case papers 15th-20th cent, incl schedules and abstracts of title, sale papers early 19th cent, Valle Crucis evidences 15th cent and volume rel to the Duke of Buckingham's (later Finch) estates in Rutland 17th cent; manorial court records, Rutland (Exton, etc) 14th-18th cent, Leics (Pickwell) 1391-1662, Gloucs (mainly Chipping Campden) 1544-67 and Denbighshire (Valle Crucis) 1536-96.

Estate records (all estates) mainly 18th-early 20th cent, incl valuations 1799, 1813, rentals and accounts, memoranda and corresp; Exton (Rutland, Leics, Lincs) estate records mainly 17th-20th cent, incl leases and agreements, surveys and valuations, maps, rentals and accounts, stewards' and agents' corresp and papers, wood accounts 1620, 18th-19th cent, granary and livestock accounts 18th-20th cent, brick and lime accounts 18th-19th cent, labour records 18th-20th cent, and papers rel to enclosure, tithes, improvements, ironstone mining 19th-20th cent and sales; Chipping Campden estate records 17th-early 20th cent, incl leases, agreements, valuations, maps and plans, rentals and accounts mainly from 18th cent, wood accounts 1795-1882, quarrying accounts 1895-1922, and papers rel to railways, improvements, allotments and sales; Welham estate records 18th-19th cent, incl rentals and accounts; misc records rel to other Edwards properties in Kent, London, Middlesex and Ireland 18th-mid-19th cent; Barham estate records *c*1803-48, incl valuations, accounts and sale papers; leases of Hicks Hall, Clerkenwell 1630 and Campden House, Kensington (with inventory) 1684; misc estate records 16th-19th cent, incl rental of Edward Wotton's Denbighshire estates 1587 and papers rel to property in Stamford and Bath early 19th cent; papers rel to Thomas Noel's estates in Northants, Rutland, Lincs and Notts 17th-late 18th cent.

Papers rel to Exton Old Hall and New Hall 18th-20th cent, incl drawings for New Hall 19th cent, inventories and household accounts; papers rel to Campden House (Gloucs) 1834-81 and to London houses (Gainsborough House (Cavendish Square), etc) 19th cent; vouchers for Ketton Hall (Rutland) (Lady Jane Edwards) early 19th cent and Walcot (Thomas Noel) 1759-65; papers rel to Rutland affairs 16th-20th

cent, incl lieutenancy and militia 17th-19th cent, shrievalty and commission of the peace 16th-19th cent, elections 1710-1847, and schools and charities 17th-20th cent; papers rel to Exton parish 19th-20th cent; papers rel to Gloucs politics 1763-1843; Chipping Campden borough charter 1605 and hospital foundation deed 1635; recusancy papers 1591-3; misc political papers late 18th-early 19th cent, mainly rel to Sir GN Noel; Pinley (Warwicks) charity papers 17th-19th cent; patents, grants of arms, etc 17th-20th cent; Noel family papers 17th-20th cent, incl corresp, diaries, accounts, banking and other papers of Sir GN Noel, religious papers mainly 19th-20th cent and hunting papers late 18th cent; papers of Thomas Blore (1764-1818), solicitor and antiquary, incl some rel to Derbys and the Gell family (of Hopton, Derbys); papers of Richard Westbrook Baker (d1859), agent and agriculturist, incl papers rel to Rutland allotments, agricultural society and friendly society; misc literary and other papers mainly 18th-19th cent; accounts and valuation rel to the diocese of Lincoln early 16th cent (3 vols); Rutland (Manton, etc) chantry certificates 1548-9.

Leicestershire Record Office (DE 3214). Deposited by the 5th Earl of Gainsborough 1987-91. Some recusancy papers of Sir Andrew Noel 1591-3 were purchased in 1988 (Sotheby's, 15 Dec, lot 135). Closed to research while cataloguing is in progress. NRA 41841 (summary list).

[b] Papers rel to sales of properties in Rutland 1925-6.

Leicestershire Record Office (DE 3177/36-44). Deposited by Fowler & Co, solicitors, Oakham 1987. NRA 30447.

[c] Rutland and Stamford deeds 17th-19th cent; trust deeds, mortgages and related papers 19th cent, incl papers rel to the New River Company 1824-83.

Leicestershire Record Office (DE 2459). Deposited by Bridges, Sawtell & Adams, solicitors, London, through the British Records Association 1983. NRA 26147.

[d] Pickwell maps 1616, 1736.

Leicestershire Record Office (89-91/30). Deposited in Leicester Museum by Frere, Cholmeley & Co, through the British Records Society 1931, and later transferred to the record office.

[e] Misc Rutland deeds, trust papers and legal papers 17th-19th cent: manorial court papers, Exton 1722-31 and Langham (Rutland) 1731-3; misc estate papers 18th-19th cent, incl survey of Pickwell 1765 and Irish rentals 1777, 1791-2; Noel and Edwards family corresp mainly 1740-20th cent, incl letters to Lady Jane Edwards, Sir GN Noel and the Hon BW Noel; misc Noel and Edwards family papers 17th-20th cent, incl

account book of Lady Campden 1663-75, vouchers of Lady Jane Edwards 1775-1827, genealogical papers 19th-20th cent and papers rel to *Some records and letters of the Noel family* by Emilia F Noel (granddaughter of the Hon BW Noel) 1910; papers of Sir Baptist Hicks as a JP for Middlesex 1613, 1615 (2 items).

Leicestershire Record Office (DE 1797). Deposited in Cambridgeshire Record Office by the British Records Association 1953 and transferred 1983. NRA 26147.

[f] Gloucs (Chipping Campden estate) deeds 1707-1881 (44 items).

Gloucestershire Record Office (D 329). Deposited by Frere, Cholmeley & Co, solicitors, London, through the British Records Association 1952. *Handlist*, 3rd edn 1995, p204.

[g] Noel and Edwards family corresp and papers 1757-1945, incl further letters to Lady Jane Edwards, Sir GN Noel and the Hon BW Noel, accounts, journals, and further papers of Emilia F Noel; travel journal of Margaret Middleton (later Lady Barham) 1763-7.

In private possession. Enquiries to the Historical Manuscripts Commission. NRA 19513.

[h] Naval and other corresp and papers of the 1st Baron Barham principally as 1st Lord of the Admiralty 1805-6.

National Maritime Museum (MID). Acquired 1966-94, mainly from the 5th Earl of Gainsborough 1977, 1994. NRA 315, 30121.

[i] Commonplace book of the 1st Viscount Campden.

In private possession. NRA 6393.

Related collections: Cavendish-Bentinck, Dukes of Portland, no 18, including papers relating to the 1st and 2nd Earls of Gainsborough and the Titchfield estates (Hampshire Record Office 5M53, NRA 8800); Agnew of Lochnaw (National Archives of Scotland GD 154, NRA 33903), including journals and diaries of Lady Barham 1819-29 (GD 154/779, 835).

[75] OGILVIE-GRANT, Earls of Seafield

By the early sixteenth century the Grant family had considerable estates in Morayshire (Mulben, Freuchie) and Inverness-shire (Inverallan, Urquhart). The family subsequently consolidated its possessions from Freuchie (afterwards Castle Grant) throughout the Spey valley by purchase and exchange. The lordship of Strathspey was acquired from the bishop of Moray in the mid-sixteenth century, Abernethy and Cromdale (Inverness-shire) were bought in the early seventeenth century, and in 1694 the Grant lands received the status of a regality. Sir

James Grant (d1747) married Anne, heiress of Sir Humphrey Colquhoun, fifth Bt, of Luss (Dunbartonshire) and at Colquhoun's death in 1718 acquired his lands and baronetcy, on condition that they should never be held by the laird of Grant. On inheriting the Grant estates from his elder brother Alexander Grant in 1719, Sir James, whilst retaining the baronetcy, relinquished his Colquhoun inheritance to his second son James (d1786), who adopted the name Colquhoun. In 1763 Sir James Grant, eighth Bt, married Jean, only daughter of Alexander Duff of Hatton (Aberdeenshire) and his wife Anne, daughter of the first Earl Fife. The entailed Duff estates (Balquholly, Hatton and Knockleith) were inherited by Duff's brother and the unentailed estates sold by trustees in the late eighteenth century, though Lady Anne Duff retained Balquholly Lodge until her death in 1805.

Sir Walter Ogilvy of Deskford and Findlater (Banffshire) was made Baron Ogilvy of Deskford in 1610. His son James Ogilvy (d1652), created Earl of Findlater 1638, was succeeded by his son-in-law Sir Patrick Ogilvy (d1659) of Inchmartine (Perthshire), who, however, sold Inchmartine in 1650 to the Earl of Leven. Both Ogilvys were descended from Walter Ogilvy of Auchterhouse (Forfarshire) (see Ogilvy, Earls of Airlie, no 76). James Ogilvy (d1730), son of the third Earl of Findlater, became Earl of Seafield in 1701 and inherited the earldom of Findlater in 1711. The Seafield estates, including Cullen (Banffshire) and Deskford, were built up mainly in the Banffshire coastal lowlands from the fifteenth century. They were united into the barony of Ogilvy in 1510. A major acquisition was the barony of Boyne (Banffshire), with lands in Fordyce and Portsoy, bought from the Ogilvys of Boyne in 1709. On his death in 1811, the estates and earldom of the fourth Earl of Seafield passed to his cousin, Sir Lewis Alexander Grant (d1840), ninth Bt, of Castle Grant, whose brother Francis William Ogilvy-Grant (d1853) succeeded him as sixth Earl. (The spelling Ogilvie-Grant was adopted by the eleventh Earl of Seafield.)

Estates in 1883: Inverness-shire 160,224 acres, Morayshire 96,760 acres, Banffshire 48,946 acres, total 305,930 acres worth £78,227 a year.

[a] Writs, Banffshire 14th-19th cent, Inverness-shire and Morayshire 12th-19th cent; inventories of writs 17th-18th cent; wills, settlements, executry and curatory papers 15th-19th cent, Grant and Ogilvy families; minutes of the trustees of Sir John Houston 1722-4 and related executry papers; legal and financial papers from 15th cent, incl papers rel to the sack of Cullen House 1746-53 and to boundary disputes with the Duke of Gordon mid-18th cent; Ogilvy and Strathisla (Banffshire) barony court records 1707-43; records of Strathspey justice court and the barony courts of Abernethy, Cromdale,

Grant and Urquhart 1601-83, with records of
Inverness-shire barony court 1722-40 and
Strathspey barony court 1764-92; Kilravock
(Nairnshire) barony court minutes 1628.

Banffshire, Inverness-shire and Morayshire
estate records 15th-20th cent, incl tacks, surveys
and maps, particulars and valuations, rentals,
accounts, vouchers and corresp, with papers rel
to teinds 17th-19th cent; accounts and vouchers
for home farms at Cullen 18th-20th cent and
Castle Grant 19th-20th cent; records of
Strathspey woodlands and sawmills 18th-20th
cent; papers rel to Strathspey and Inverness-
shire roads 1622-1796; Keith (Banffshire) stone
quarry accounts 1880-1901; Portknockie
(Banffshire) harbour extension accounts 1862;
other estate papers 15th-20th cent, incl some rel
to linen manufacture 1743-55, to forfeited
estates 18th cent, to development at Grantown
late 18th cent and at Cullen new town 1821-3,
and to church building at Rathven (Banffshire)
1793-1803 and at Urquhart (Inverness-shire)
1835-8; Nairnshire estate papers 1784-95,
Ogilvie family; papers rel to Sir James Grant's
Mile End (Middlesex) property 1770-91; valuation of the Duke of Gordon's Inverness-shire
lands 1691; corresp and papers of Thomas
Charles Bruce rel to the Earl of Elgin's estates
1853-7.

Papers of James Playfair (1755-94) and letters
and accounts c1765-81 of James and Robert
Adam rel to building at Cullen House; Banff
Castle building accounts 1749-52; papers rel to
building at Moy House (Morayshire) 1761-2;
plans and elevations 18th-20th cent, Cullen
House, Castle Grant, Moy House, Elgin, etc;
household inventories, accounts and papers
16th-20th cent, mainly Cullen House and
Castle Grant, incl catalogue of books at Cullen
House 1708, Cullen garden papers 18th cent,
and Castle Grant library catalogue and borrow-
ing book 1695-1744; misc household inventories
17th-20th cent, incl Dunphail (Morayshire)
1658, Moy House 1770 and Banff Castle 1780.

Papers rel to Banffshire, Inverness-shire and
Morayshire elections 17th-19th cent, incl
Banffshire freeholders' rolls 1779-99 and
Morayshire freeholders' minutes 1787; official
papers of William Syme, bailie of Banff and
sheriff of Banffshire 1663-1731; Inverness-shire
lieutenancy papers 18th-19th cent, incl corresp
of Sir James Grant, 8th Bt and the 6th Earl of
Seafield as lords lieutenant 1794-1852 and minutes of the justices of peace and commissioners
of supply 1779, 1788; records of the Cromdale
Volunteers and Militia 1792-1813, the 1st
Regiment of Fencible Highlanders 1793-1809
and the 97th (Inverness-shire) Regiment c1794-
7; rolls of the Dunphail (Morayshire) militia
company 1671 and the Grantown Strathspey
Volunteers 1797; turnpike records (Cullen,
Deskford, etc) 1804-67; Duthil (Inverness-shire)
kirk session records 1719-71 and Knockando
(Morayshire) heritors' minute book 1883-1928;

accounts of Speyside Orphan Hospital 1795,
Castle Grant Clothing Club 1877-1911 and the
Ian Charles Hospital, Grantown 1885-1921;
records of Walter Ogilvy of Redhythe's
Mortification (school and college bursaries for
residents of Fordyce, Banffshire) 1678-20th
cent.

Patents and commissions, Ogilvy and Grant
families 17th-19th cent; inventories 16th-19th
cent, incl James Grant of Freuchie 16th cent
and the 5th Baron Banff 1727; Ogilvy and
Grant family and political papers 16th-19th
cent, incl papers rel to the Grants' conduct in
the risings of 1715 and 1745, political papers of
the 1st and 2nd Earls of Seafield, papers of the
5th and 6th Earls and of Sir James Grant, 8th
Bt, and letters of the 12th Baron Lovat 1714-46
and Charles Grant, Vicomte de Vaux c1781-
1800 to the Grant family; papers rel to Colonel
Alexander Grant's Regiment of Foot 1705-19;
military accounts of Major George Grant 1716-
56; East Indian journal of Lt John Grant 1748-
50; naval papers of Captain Charles Cathcart
Grant of Coathall 1757-71; antiquarian papers
of William Lorimer 18th cent; papers of John
Grant, minister of Elgin 1724-1801 and letters
of Henry MacKenzie (1745-1831), author;
journal and waste book 1757 of James Grant
and journal 1759 of Duncan Grant, merchants
of Aberdeen; literary, genealogical and misc
papers 16th-19th cent, incl minutes of the
Commissioners of Estates of the Kingdom of
Scotland 1689 and parliamentary journal 1738-
40.

Duff family of Hatton Castle papers 14th-19th
cent, incl Aberdeenshire writs 14th-18th cent,
settlements, legal papers and tacks 16th-19th
cent, Balquholly (Aberdeenshire) barony court
minutes 1710-11, rentals and accounts for
Balquholly and Craigston (Aberdeenshire)
1673-1753, accounts of work by James, John
and Robert Adam 1755-6, letters of Lady Anne
Duff 1783-1802 and Aberdeenshire freeholders'
roll 1751; misc legal and Dunbartonshire estate
papers 1603-1783 (Colquhoun of Luss), incl
tacks, rentals and accounts 1709-38.

National Archives of Scotland (GD 248).
Deposited by the Countess of Seafield and the
13th Earl of Seafield 1956-70. HMC *Third
Report, App*, 1872, pp403-4; *Fourteenth Report,
App III*, 1894, pp191-238. NRA 32594.

[b] Writs 15th-20th cent, mainly Banffshire and
Morayshire, with some for Aberdeenshire;
inventories of writs 19th-20th cent; marriage
contract of Sir Lewis Grant and Lady Margaret
Ogilvie 1735; legal and misc papers 17th-20th
cent, incl Rothes (Morayshire) teind papers
1758-1813.

National Archives of Scotland (GD 248).
Deposited by Brodie, Cuthbertson & Watson,
solicitors, Edinburgh 1968. NRA 32594.

[c] Executry papers 1811-58, Ogilvie-Grant family; minutes and papers of the Countess of Seafield's trustees 1911-53; papers rel to salmon fishings in the River Spey 1849-1950; family papers of the Stuart family, Barons Blantyre 19th cent, incl letters of Lt-Colonel James Stuart from the Crimea 1854-6.

National Archives of Scotland (GD 424). Deposited by Eric Cuthbertson, WS 1985. NRA 32594.

[d] Legal and estate corresp and papers 1856-1940.

National Archives of Scotland (GD 296/169-87). Deposited by Innes & McKay, solicitors, Inverness 1974-6. NRA 19358.

[e] Cullen estate book 1764-93.

National Archives of Scotland (GD 1/804). Purchased 1977. *Keeper's Report 1977*, p17.

[f] Account book of cereal liveries to tenants at Castle Grant 1783.

National Library of Scotland (Acc 6020). Purchased 1973-4. *Annual Report 1973-4*, p49.

[g] Cullen household account book 1707-24.

University of Guelph Archival and Special Collections, Ontario (XS1 MS A 107). Presented by Phyllis Jefferson 1985. NRA 31936.

[h] Political papers of the 1st Earl of Seafield.

Edinburgh University Library, Special Collections Department (Laing MSS). HMC *Report on the Laing Manuscripts Preserved in the University of Edinburgh*, ii, 1925, pp8-135.

Related collections: Colquhoun of Luss (Glasgow City Archives, NRA 12270); Duff of Meldrum and Hatton (Aberdeen University Library, Department of Special Collections and Archives MS 2778, NRA 10138; in private possession, enquiries to the National Register of Archives (Scotland) NRA(S) 75, 2442, NRA 10138).

[76] OGILVY, Earls of Airlie

Sir Walter Ogilvy (d1440), High Treasurer of Scotland 1425-31, was a younger son of Walter Ogilvy (d1391) of Auchterhouse (Forfarshire), a descendant of the Earls of Angus, and an ancestor of the Earls of Seafield (see Ogilvie-Grant, Earls of Seafield, no 75). He acquired Lintrathen (Forfarshire) by marriage with Isabel Durward c1401 and other lands by a second marriage. He also purchased lands in Forfarshire, including Airlie in 1431, and in Perthshire. His grandson James was created Baron Ogilvy in 1491. James, fifth Baron Ogilvy (d1606), purchased much property, including Glenisla (Forfarshire). His grandson, created

Earl of Airlie in 1639, bought the Forfarshire estates of Cortachy, Clova and Glenprosen in 1625 from Sir David Ogilvy of Inverquharity and also acquired the barony and lands of Alyth (Perthshire) in 1623. His son the second Earl (d1703) bought the barony of Coupar (Forfarshire and Perthshire) in 1669 from the widow of James, Lord Coupar, and his grandson the third Earl (d1717) bought Auchterhouse (Forfarshire) with the proceeds of the sale of Glenprosen.

The Perthshire estate of Cluny came into the family on the marriage in 1722 of John Ogilvy, titular Earl of Airlie (d1761), with Margaret, heiress of David Ogilvy of Cluny. It was sold in 1892. Keltie (Perthshire), gained on the marriage in 1812 of the fourth Earl (d1849) and Clementina, heiress of Gavin Drummond, was sold in 1837. Estates in Banffshire, including the harbour, lands and fishings of Banff, were bought by the first Earl. Some Banffshire property was alienated in 1699 but the bulk was sold about 1778 by David, Lord Ogilvy, who devoted the proceeds to the re-acquisition of Glenprosen. Although the earldom came under attainder from 1716 to 1826, the family estates were not forfeited during the eighteenth century.

Estates in 1883: Forfarshire 65,228 acres, Perthshire 4,647 acres, total 69,875 acres worth £28,592 a year.

[a] Writs, mainly Forfarshire and Perthshire 12th-20th cent, with some for Banffshire 1522-1711, Fife 1467-1799, etc; inventories of title 16th-19th cent, incl Arbroath Abbey 17th cent; wills, settlements and executry papers 1464-1886; legal and case papers 15th-19th cent; Balbegno (Kincardineshire) barony court book 1693-1803, with Arbroath (Forfarshire) regality court records 1681-1739, vassal rolls of the regality of Brechin (Forfarshire) 1727, 1747 and minute book of the regality of Coupar 1731-46.

Forfarshire and Perthshire estate records 15th-20th cent, incl tacks from 1481, maps, plans and particulars 18th-20th cent, valuations 17th-19th cent, rentals, accounts, vouchers and corresp 16th-20th cent, and papers rel to teinds 15th-20th cent, enclosure 1787-1859 and drainage 1846-61; Perthshire slate quarrying papers 18th-19th cent and Auchterhouse (Forfarshire) quarry accounts 1832-5; Keltie (Perthshire) estate accounts and papers 1803-55; Banffshire estate papers 16th-19th cent, incl tacks (estate and fishings) 1630-1857 and rentals 17th-19th cent, with valuation of Banff burgh 1652; papers rel to losses under the Commonwealth 1645-80; misc estate papers 16th-19th cent, incl rentals of Bargany (Ayrshire) 1645-6, Airth (Stirlingshire) 1648-68 and the estates of the second Earl of Perth 1655 and Sir John Ogilvy of Inverquharity 1780, with rental and accounts of the Arbroath Abbey estates 1593-4 and accounts of the Earl of Airlie as bailie of the regality of Coupar 1699-1707; Ferry Pen (Jamaica) estate papers 1812-73; household plans 19th-20th cent, inventories 17th-20th cent and accounts and papers 1621-1954, mainly for Cortachy (Forfarshire), but incl inventories for households at Banff 17th cent, Cluny 1803, 1810 and Keltie 1826, etc; household accounts of the Drummond family of Keltie (Perthshire) 1817-20.

Election accounts and papers 1830-60, mainly Forfar borough and Forfarshire, with some for Perth and Perthshire; Forfarshire and Kincardineshire militia and lieutenancy papers 17th-19th cent, incl corresp rel to Chartist disturbances in Forfarshire 1839; papers rel to Forfarshire and Perthshire roads, bridges and railways 17th-19th cent, schools 1668-1887 and church building 1700-1874; rent valuation rolls of the shire of Forfar 1649-53, 1682; Alyth (Perthshire) market papers 1788-1840; Glenisla (Forfarshire) poor rate papers 1840-61; accounts of Thomas Ogilvy, provost of Banff 1673; records of the 1st Battalion, 4th Regiment Breadalbane Fencibles 1793-1824.

Patents and commissions 15th-19th cent; family accounts, corresp and papers 16th-20th cent, incl civil war papers 1637-84, personal inventories 17th-20th cent, corresp of the 2nd Earl, papers of the 4th and 6th Earls, and papers of William Ogilvy of Loyal, MP 1820-70; corresp, accounts and papers of the Drummond family of Keltie late 18th-mid 19th cent, incl papers of Major Mark Drummond 1815-25 and trustees' accounts of William Drummond 1843-4; papers of the Home family of Polwarth 1557-1613, mainly rel to the keepership of Tantallon Castle (E Lothian), incl castle inventory and accounts 1592; personal corresp of James McNicoll, factor to the Earls of Airlie 1792-1827; records of the Earl of Airlie's Troop of Horse c1639-88 and misc papers rel to Ogilvy's Regiment 1753-80, incl accounts 1755-9; literary, genealogical and misc papers 16th-20th cent, incl accounts of the household expenses of Queen Anne of Denmark 1597, 1601.

National Archives of Scotland (GD 16). Deposited by the 7th Earl of Airlie 1945, with additions by Skene, Edwards & Garson, WS, Edinburgh 1962 and Lady Helen Nutting 1964. HMC *Second Report, App*, 1874, pp186-8. NRA 29181.

[b] Misc tacks, legal papers, accounts and family papers 1670-1820.

National Archives of Scotland (GD 240). Deposited by Bruce & Kerr, WS, Edinburgh 1963. NRA 34966.

[c] Misc family corresp of David, Lord Ogilvy c1745-65.

Edinburgh University Library, Special Collections Department (La.II.502). *Index to Manuscripts*, II, 1964, p284.

[d] Corresp and papers of the 6th Earl, incl some rel to the Boer War; diaries and corresp of Mabell, Countess of Airlie (d1955).

British Library, Manuscript Collections (Add MSS 52418-9). Presented by Lady Helen Nutting 1958, 1963. The Countess of Airlie's diaries, deposited 1958, are closed to research until 2008.

[e] Family corresp and papers of the Lamb family, Viscounts Melbourne c1780-1864, incl letters of Lord Palmerston.

British Library, Manuscript Collections (Add MSS 45446-56, 45911). These papers passed on Lady Palmerston's death to her daughter, Viscountess Jocelyn, whose granddaughter Mabell, Countess of Airlie presented them 1940, 1944.

Related Collections: Ogilvy of Inverquharity (National Archives of Scotland GD 205; National Library of Scotland Acc 5012, NRA 29130); Earls of Marchmont (National Archives of Scotland GD 158, NRA 8151), including further Home of Polwarth papers.

[77] ORDE-POWLETT, Barons Bolton

The fortunes of the Paulet (or Powlett) family were established by the soldier Sir John Paulet (fl c1497-1501), who married Constance, heiress of Thomas, Baron St John of Basing (d1428) and acquired his property at Basing (Hampshire) and elsewhere. His son, the statesman William Paulet (d1572), created Marquess of Winchester 1551, received extensive grants of monastic land in Hampshire, Wiltshire and elsewhere, including the priory of the Austin Friars in London. His son, the second Marquess, received Dorset lands (Sherborne Castle, Hooke, etc) formerly belonging to the Duke of Somerset (d1551) and acquired property in Cornwall, Devon, Dorset, Somerset and Wiltshire by marriage to Elizabeth, daughter and co-heir of the second Baron Willoughby de Broke (d1521). (For other Willoughby estates, inherited by the grandaughter of the second Baron Willoughby de Broke, see Greville, Earls Brooke and Earls of Warwick, no 45; Verney, Barons Willoughby de Broke, no 111.) Further Hampshire estates (Kingsclere, Nether Wallop, Frobury, Hackwood, etc) were purchased in the sixteenth century. Basing House was demolished in the Civil War and Hackwood became the family seat.

The northern estates of the Paulet family were acquired through the marriage in 1654 of the sixth Marquess of Winchester (created Duke of Bolton 1689) to Mary Scrope, daughter of the eleventh Baron Scrope (created Earl of Sunderland 1627). She was heiress to her father's Bolton Castle (Yorkshire, North Riding) estate, part of the extensive property acquired by the Scrope family in the north of England in the late middle ages. (Further Scrope estates passed to two other daughters of the Earl of Sunderland).

By a settlement of 1763 the fifth Duke of Bolton provided that his estates in Hampshire (centred on Hackwood) and in the North Riding of Yorkshire (Bolton Castle) should pass to his illegitimate daughter Jean Powlett, who inherited them on the death of the sixth and last Duke of Bolton in 1794. In 1778 she had married the politician Thomas Orde (1740-1807), younger son of John Orde of Morpeth and East Orde (Northumberland), who adopted the additional surname Powlett in 1795 and was created Baron Bolton in 1797. Their son the second Baron sold considerable Hampshire property in the early nineteenth century, the purchasers including Alexander Baring (later Baron Ashburton) and the second Marquess of Buckingham, and Bolton Hall near Leyburn (Yorkshire, North Riding) became the family seat. The remaining Hampshire property was alienated in 1936, when Baron (later Viscount) Camrose bought Hackwood, and in 1946, when Basing was sold.

The Cornwall, Devon, Dorset and Wiltshire estates of the sixth Duke of Bolton, who died without male issue, passed at his death to his daughters and their husbands. By an act of Parliament in 1863 they were divided between their descendants the seventh Earl of Sandwich and the fourth Duke of Cleveland (see Vane, Barons Barnard, no 109) and were largely sold between 1880 and 1919.

Estates in 1883: Yorks NR 15,413 acres, Hants 13,808 acres, total 29,221 acres worth £27,552 a year.

[a] Deeds 13th-20th cent (*c*650 medieval), mainly Yorks NR but incl some for other Scrope family estates 13th-17th cent; Middleham (Yorks NR) lordship deeds 17th-18th cent; abstracts of title and schedules of deeds mainly 18th-19th cent; wills, settlements, executorship and trust papers 16th-19th cent, Scrope, Powlett and Orde-Powlett families; legal and financial papers 16th-20th cent, Powlett and Orde-Powlett; manorial records 16th-19th cent, mainly Yorks NR (Bolton, etc), with some for Notts and Co Durham; Yorks NR estate records 16th-20th cent, incl maps, surveys, valuations, rentals, accounts and corresp, with papers rel to boundaries and enclosure 17th-20th cent and tithes 19th cent; records of Yorks NR quarries and lead mining 17th-19th cent, incl deeds, leases, accounts and corresp; rentals, Notts estates of the Scrope family 16th cent.

Bolton Hall (Yorks NR) building plans and accounts 19th-20th cent and household inventories 18th-19th cent; records rel to Yorks Hussars and Volunteers 19th cent, incl muster rolls and corresp; patents and appointments

16th-19th cent, mainly Orde-Powlett family but incl some for the Powlett family; family and political papers 17th-20th cent, Powlett and Orde-Powlett families, incl letters of the sixth Marquess of Winchester 1686-7, continental tour diaries of Thomas Orde 1772, 1774, official and political papers of the 1st Baron Bolton, and papers of the 4th and 5th Barons Bolton.

North Yorkshire County Record Office (ZBO). Mainly purchased from the 7th Baron Bolton 1982. The papers of the 4th and 5th Barons were deposited 1993. The collection includes Yorkshire estate papers and papers of the 1st Baron Bolton transferred to Bolton Hall from Hampshire Record Office in 1958. See *Guide to North Yorkshire County Record Office*, No 1, 1986 and Supplements 1989, 1995. HMC *Bulletin of the National Register of Archives 10*, 1959, pp8-11; *Papers of British Politicians 1782-1900*, 1989, p79. NRA 8638.

[b] Account roll of John, Lord Scrope 1535-6.

North Yorkshire County Record Office (Z100). Deposited by HJ Willis 1962.

[c] Deeds 14th-19th cent, mainly Hants, but incl some for Cornwall, Devon and Dorset (Powlett) 16th-17th cent, and Bucks (Scrope) 17th cent; settlements and legal papers 17th-19th cent, Powlett and Orde-Powlett; manorial records, Hants 16th-19th cent (incl Old Basing 1547-1684), Wilts 14th-17th cent (incl Edington 1376-96) and Cornwall, Devon and Dorset 16th-18th cent (incl Ludgvanleaze, Cornwall *c*1660-1730); Hants estate records 17th-20th cent, incl leases 17th-19th cent and maps, plans, surveys, valuations, rentals, accounts and corresp 18th-20th cent; leases for Powlett estates in Devon, Dorset, Wilts and Middlesex (Grosvenor Square) 17th-18th cent; Hackwood Park and Basing House records 17th-20th cent, incl plans, inventories and papers rel to staff and gardens; records of the Duke of Bolton's charity 17th-20th cent; patents and appointments 16th-19th cent, mainly Powlett family, incl some of the 1st Baron Bolton; memoranda of the 1st Duke of Bolton as lord lieutenant of Hants and Warden of the New Forest 1672-99; papers rel to Hants and Isle of Wight militia *c*1794-1807.

Hampshire Record Office (22M58, 11M49 Addnl). Formerly at Bolton Hall and purchased from the 7th Baron Bolton 1982. The collection includes Hampshire estate papers and papers of the first Baron Bolton transferred from Bolton Hall in 1958. NRA 16.

[d] Deeds 16th-20th cent, mainly Hants but incl some for Devon and Wilts 17th-18th cent; abstracts of title 18th-19th cent; wills and settlements 17th-20th cent, Powlett and Orde-Powlett; steward's accounts for recovery of forfeited estates 1651-4; manorial records 17th-

19th cent, Hants (incl contract books for Hants manors 1761-96), Cornwall 17th-18th cent, Devon 18th cent (incl Bigbury and Brixham), Dorset 17th-18th cent (incl Powerstock) and Wilts 18th cent (incl Edington), with a few for Somerset; Hants estate records 17th-20th cent, incl leases, maps, plans and surveys 18th-19th cent, accounts and vouchers 18th-20th cent, letter books 1863-1920, and game and stock books 19th-20th cent; papers rel to Hants timber 18th-19th cent, Hackwood brick kiln 19th cent and cottages and allotments 19th-20th cent; Dorset estate particulars and accounts late 18th cent; Edington (Wilts) estate accounts 1720-46; Hackwood Park building accounts 19th-20th cent, inventories 18th-19th cent, and house and garden accounts 19th-20th cent; Old Basing House visitor's book 1899-1910; letter books and papers of the 1st Baron Bolton rel to Hants and Isle of Wight affairs 1794-1807.

Hampshire Record Office (11M49, 10M57, 23M72). Deposited by the 5th and 6th Barons Bolton in Basingstoke Museum 1936, 1946, transferred to Hampshire Record Office 1949, 1957, 1972, and purchased by Hampshire Record Office from the 7th Baron Bolton 1982. NRA 16, 8807, 37523.

[e] Deeds 17th-18th cent, mainly Basing (Hants) abstracts of title 1763-1816; Hants manorial records 18th-19th cent, incl Nether Wallop court books 1755-1851; Hackwood (Hants) estate records 17th-20th cent, incl maps 1683, 1798, stock valuations 18th cent, rentals mid-19th cent-1916, accounts 1662-1765, and game and park keepers' books late 19th cent; Hackwood Park building accounts, workmen's and tradesmen's accounts, bills of fare, cellar book and cash book 1807-48.

Hampshire Record Office. Deposited by the trustees of the late Viscount Camrose from Hackwood Park 1998. See HMC *Bulletin of the National Register of Archives 9*, 1957, p20. NRA 5671. Hackwood architectural drawings 18th cent (3 items) were purchased from Hackwood Park in 1998.

[f] Testamentary and executorship papers of the 2nd Baroness Bolton c1860-1905.

Hampshire Record Office (50M63/B7). Deposited by Lamb, Brooks & Bullock, Solicitors, Odiham 1963. NRA 41331.

[g] Official papers of the 1st Baron Bolton, secretary to the Lord Lieutenant of Ireland 1784-7.

National Library of Ireland (MSS 15800-15978, 16326, 16349-74). Purchased from the 7th Baron Bolton 1969. NRA 8638.

[h] Official papers of the 1st Baron Bolton rel to appointments in Ireland 1784-92.

House of Lords Record Office (Hist Coll III). Borrowed by the 1st Baron Ashbourne from his son-in-law the 5th Baron Bolton for his *Pitt: some chapters of his life and times* (1898). Deposited by the 3rd Baron Ashbourne 1972. NRA 18808.

[i] Draft of proposals for education in Ireland by Thomas Orde-Powlett 1787.

Bodleian Library, Oxford (MSS Top. Ireland d. 2-3). Given by H Raynbird 1920.

[j] Austin Friars (London) particular c1625.

Guildhall Library (MS 6238). Purchased 1950. See *Bulletin of the Institute of Historical Research XXIV*, 1951, p112.

Related collections: Vane, Barons Barnard, no 109; Earls of Sandwich (Dorset Record Office D 45, NRA 5472), including Bolton (Powlett) manorial and estate records for Cornwall, Devon, Dorset, Hants and Wilts 18th-20th cent.

[78] **OSBORNE, Dukes of Leeds**

Sir Edward Osborne (d1592), Lord Mayor of London, acquired the Kiveton estate at Harthill (Yorkshire, West Riding) by marriage to the daughter and heir of Sir William Hewitt. He also owned Parsloes (Essex). His grandson Sir Edward Osborne (created a baronet 1620) bought further Yorkshire property but sold Parsloes in 1619. Sir Thomas Osborne, second Bt (d1712), the statesman, was created Earl of Danby 1674, Marquess of Carmarthen 1689 and Duke of Leeds 1694. His additions to the family estates included the manor of Wakefield (Yorkshire, West Riding). The lordship of Conisborough (Yorkshire, West Riding), formerly owned by the Coke family of Longford (Derbyshire), was acquired in the mid-eighteenth century. The second Duke (d1729) married in 1682 Bridget, daughter and heir of Sir Thomas Hyde, second Bt, of Aldbury (Hertfordshire). The marriage brought Hertfordshire estates (Aldbury, sold 1736 to the first Duke of Bridgewater, Tring, sold 1758, and North Mimms, sold 1799), with Wingrave (Buckinghamshire, sold 1776) and property in Dorset (sold before 1692).

The Hornby Castle (Yorkshire, North Riding) estate entered the family in 1784 on the death of Amelia, *suo jure* Baroness Darcy and Baroness Conyers. She was the wife of Francis Osborne (d1799), Marquess of Carmarthen (5th Duke of Leeds 1789) and daughter and heir of the fourth Earl of Holdernesse (d1778). The Hornby Castle estate had descended in the Darcy family, Barons Darcy and Barons Conyers (created Earls of Holdernesse 1682), since its acquisition through the marriage of Thomas Darcy (d1605) and Elizabeth, daughter and co-heir of John, Baron Conyers (d1557). From 1811, when Kiveton was demolished, it was the main seat of the Dukes of Leeds, although Mar Lodge (Aberdeenshire) was also acquired as a family residence in the nineteenth century.

In 1785, on the death of the second Baron Godolphin of Helston, cousin and heir of the second Earl of Godolphin (d1766), the entailed Godolphin family estates descended to the Marquess of Carmarthen through his mother Mary, daughter of the second Earl and his wife Henrietta, *suo jure* Duchess of Marlborough. These consisted principally of Cornish estates near Helston, where the Godolphin family had been established since the middle ages, and the Scilly Isles (on lease from the Crown since the reign of Elizabeth I), with property in St James's Place (Middlesex), a Cambridgeshire estate (Gog Magog Hills in Stapleford, apparently bought by the second Earl of Godolphin from Sir William Halton in 1734) and property in Suffolk (Newmarket, purchased by the second Earl 1730-44). Also inherited was the Baylies estate in Stoke Poges (Buckinghamshire) bought in 1718 by Henry Godolphin (d1738, brother of the first Earl, and father of the second Baron), together with Farnham Royal, bought by the second Baron from the Earl of Leicester in 1752 (see Coke, Earls of Leicester, no 23). The Buckinghamshire and Cambridgeshire estates were later settled on Francis Godolphin Osborne, second son of the fifth Duke of Leeds, created Baron Godolphin of Farnham Royal 1832, whose son the second Baron succeeded his cousin as eighth Duke in 1859. (The Cambridgeshire estate was sold in 1885.) The Godolphin estate of Abertanat (Shropshire), with property in Denbighshire (Tanyllwyn) and Montgomeryshire (Broniarth), did not descend to the Marquess of Carmarthen but to Margaret Ormsby, the second Baron Godolphin's niece, and thence to the Ormsby Gore family, Barons Harlech.

The sixth Duke (d1838) bequeathed unentailed property in Yorkshire (North and West Ridings), including the manors of Wakefield and Conisborough and lands in Wales (Yorkshire, West Riding), with a mansion in St James's Square, to his son-in-law Sackville Lane-Fox (d1874), third son of James Lane-Fox of Bramham (Yorkshire, West Riding). In 1859, on the seventh Duke's death, Lane-Fox also succeeded to the baronies of Conyers and Darcy. This inheritance passed to his son Sackville George Lane-Fox (d1888), whose elder daughter, Marcia Lane-Fox (afterwards Baroness Fauconberge and Conyers), married the fourth Earl of Yarborough in 1886, subsequently bringing former Osborne property to that family (see Anderson-Pelham, Earls of Yarborough, no 1).

Extensive papers of the Dukes of Leeds were sold in 1868-9 and the remainder were dispersed on the sale of Hornby Castle in 1930. Certain Godolphin family papers passed to the Wentworth-Fitzwilliam family through the marriage of the second Baron Godolphin of Helston to his second wife Anne (d1805), daughter of the second Earl Fitzwilliam (see Wentworth-Fitzwilliam of Milton, no 114).

Estates in 1883: Yorks NR and WR 14,772 acres, Cornwall 5,911 acres, Bucks 3,117 acres, Cambs 436 acres, Middlesex 1 acre, total 24,237 acres worth £33,881 a year.

[a] Deeds 12th-19th cent (c1,000 medieval), mainly Yorks NR and WR but incl some for Beds, Bucks, Cambs, Carnarvonshire, Denbighshire, Essex, Herts, London, Middlesex (St James's Place), Montgomeryshire, Notts, Salop and Surrey; abstracts of title 16th-19th cent; wills, settlements and executorship papers 17th-19th cent, incl executorship accounts of Peregrine, Duke of Leeds 1734 and executorship papers for the 3rd Earl of Sunderland (d1722); legal papers and financial papers 17th-19th cent, incl St James's Market case papers 1781 and papers rel to the 4th Duke's bankruptcy c1742-5; Yorks NR and WR manorial court records 14th-19th cent, mainly Conisborough 1339-1693, Harthill 16th cent, Hornby 1703-1819 and Wales (Yorks WR) 16th-17th cent.

Yorks NR and WR leases, maps, surveys, valuations, rentals, accounts, vouchers and other estate records 16th-19th cent, incl survey of Sir William Hewitt's estates 1564, Harthill plan 1605, Todwick (Yorks WR) chantry estate rental 1544, Conisborough particulars 1747, Wakefield rentals and accounts 18th-19th cent, and steward's accounts 1678-1744; papers rel to Yorks farms, woods and enclosures and to Barnsley (Yorks WR) coal mining mainly 18th cent, with Yorks WR colliery accounts 1719-41; Yorks tithe papers 17th-19th cent (Barnsley, Conisborough, etc); Hatfield Chase (Yorks WR) rental and papers c1636; fee farm rentals and accounts (Lincs, Notts and Yorks) 17th-19th cent; papers rel to estates in Cornwall and the Scilly Isles 18th-19th cent, and to London and Middlesex 18th cent, incl St James's Street building leases 1701 and St James's Market rentals and accounts c1777-83; Cambs leases and estate papers mainly 17th-18th cent; misc papers for estates in Bucks, Dorset, Herts, Lincs, Norfolk (incl E Dereham survey 1648), Notts (incl Kingston rental 1745-6), Oxon, Suffolk and Surrey 14th-18th cent; Invereshie (Inverness-shire) estate papers mid-19th cent; Abertanat (Salop, Denbighshire and Montgomeryshire) estate accounts 1716-66, with Denbighshire rental 17th cent; particulars and papers rel to Godolphin Edwards's estate c1784; papers rel to the 1st Baron Lexinton's estate 17th cent.

Records of building at Kiveton and Hornby Castle 17th-19th cent, incl Kiveton agreement and accounts c1694-1704 and AWN Pugin's drawings for Hornby Castle 1847; Kiveton and Hornby Castle household inventories and papers 17th-19th cent, incl inventories for

Kiveton 1668, 1726-8 and Hornby Castle 1778, and Kiveton accounts and vouchers from 1691; catalogue of the books of the dramatist William Congreve in the Duke of Leeds's library 18th cent; misc household records 17th-19th cent, incl Wallingford House (Westminster) accounts 1676-7, Holborn (Middlesex) and Wimbledon (Surrey) household accounts 1702-15, Syon Hill (Middlesex) library catalogue 1760 and sale papers 1783-4 (Earl of Holdernesse), Grosvenor Square (Middlesex) household papers 1775, and Mar Lodge household accounts and vouchers 1815-52.

Papers rel to Yorks affairs 17th-19th cent, incl muster rolls 1688, corresp rel to River Don navigation 1731, Scarborough (Yorks NR) election accounts 1735, papers rel to Yorks NR volunteers, militia and yeomanry 1803, and Halifax (Yorks WR) gaol accounts 1813-19; misc patents and appointments 17th-19th cent; family papers 1589-19th cent, mainly Osborne family, incl letters of Sir Edward Osborne 1640-7, Treasury and other accounts of the 1st Duke, foreign travel accounts and diaries 1733-92, corresp of the 4th Earl of Holdernesse 1775, papers of the 3rd and 5th Dukes, and family corresp of the 7th Duke (d1859) and of Lord and Lady Wellesley c1820-53, with letters of the Duke of Wellington to Colonel Hervey 1817; papers of and rel to the 2nd Duke and Duchess of Beaufort c1702-12; literary and misc papers 15th-19th cent, incl parliamentary diaries 1673-5 and pamphlets and sermons 17th-18th cent.

West Yorkshire Archive Service, Yorkshire Archaeological Society, Leeds (DD 5). Deposited by the 11th Duke of Leeds 1930. NRA 12923. Sotheby's Hornby Castle library sale, 2-4 June 1930, included William Congreve's library, which had passed on his death in 1729 to Henrietta, Duchess of Marlborough, and thence to her daughter the Duchess of Leeds (P Beal, *Index of English Literary Manuscripts, vol 2, part 1*, 1987, pp140-1). For some of the few MSS in the sale see [u] below. For further papers of the 5th Duke see HMC *Papers of British Cabinet Ministers 1782-1900*, 1982, p45, HMC *Private Papers of British Diplomats 1782-1900*, 1985, p51, and [n]-[p] below.

[b] Misc deeds, wills, settlements, legal and trust papers, leases and other papers rel to the Bucks, Cambs, Cornwall, Middlesex and Yorks estates 18th-20th cent.

West Yorkshire Archive Service, Yorkshire Archaeological Society, Leeds (DD 192). Deposited by Bircham & Co, solicitors, London, through the British Records Association 1980. NRA 12923.

[c] Trust, legal and financial papers 19th-20th cent, incl papers rel to the Bishop of Exeter's Cornish leaseholds 1807-49 and to the 1st Marquess of Cholmondeley's will 1840; deeds and papers rel to estates in Bucks 1799-20th

cent and Cornwall 1760-1859, incl Penryn manor map 1788; misc Yorks estate corresp 1834-53; papers rel to the Chesterfield Canal c1770-1805 and the enclosure of Lindrick Common (Yorks WR) c1880-1907.

West Yorkshire Archive Service, Yorkshire Archaeological Society, Leeds (DD 225). Deposited by Bolton & Lowe, solicitors, London, through the British Records Association 1988-9. NRA 12923.

[d] Manorial records 1792-1896, Harthill, Todwick and N and S Anston.

Sheffield Archives (SC 575-81). Deposited by Wake Smith & Co, solicitors, Sheffield 1970. NRA 41262.

[e] Surveys and rentals, Yorks NR and WR 1805-6; rentals and accounts, Kiveton estate (Yorks WR) 1765-1808; misc papers.

Sheffield Archives (5/F). Deposited by Mrs Pashley of Chesterfield in Derbyshire Record Office and transferred 1974. NRA 21603.

[f] Hornby estate plans 1762.

Rotherham Metropolitan Borough Archives. Deposited 1987.

[g] Hornby extent 1823.

Leeds University, Brotherton Library (MS 424). Purchased 1978. NRA 25809.

[h] Legal papers 17th-19th cent, Godolphin family, incl some rel to Helford River oysterage, the Scilly Isles, and Abertanat (Salop) estate boundaries, with misc deeds; court book, Cornish manors (Godolphin, Penventon, Tresowes, etc) c1707; Cornwall estate records 16th-19th cent, incl lease book 1740-53, surveys, valuations and particulars c1661-1803, rentals, accounts and vouchers 16th-19th cent, corresp 1803-49, and papers rel to copper and tin mining 18th cent; corresp and papers rel to the Scilly Isles 16th-19th cent, incl rentals and accounts 1710-1800; Helston borough papers mid-18th cent, incl church building accounts 1757-9; appointments (Godolphin family) 18th cent; Scilly Isles governorship papers 1636-1806, incl garrison accounts 1675-6; family and misc papers 17th-18th cent, incl some rel to the Frampton family of Moreton (Dorset) early 18th cent and to repairs at Tanyllwyn (Denbighshire) 1763.

Cornwall Record Office (DDGO). Deposited by the 11th Duke of Leeds in the Yorkshire Archaeological Society 1930 and transferred 1967-72. NRA 27107.

[i] Cornish deeds 1704-1934 and abstracts of title 20th cent; Cornish estate records 18th-20th cent, incl leases (with related surveys and corresp), lease book 1766-85, manorial plans 1786-

91, and surveys, rentals, accounts, papers and mining setts 18th-19th cent.

Cornwall Record Office (DDRH/1426-2293). Deposited by Ratcliffe & Henderson, solicitors, Helston 1959. NRA 37648.

[j] Penryn deed 1806; Helston plan 1788.

Cornwall Record Office. Presented by P Bolitho 1965. NRA 5235.

[k] Cornish legal and estate papers c1619-1859, mainly leases (incl Helston market and Helford River anchorage, keelage and oysterage) and related lease books.

Royal Institution of Cornwall (P/14-24). Deposited by the 11th Duke of Leeds in Yorkshire Archaeological Society and transferred 1930. NRA 37909.

[l] Bucks deeds, settlements and legal papers 16th-19th cent, incl abstracts of title 17th-18th cent; Bucks (Farnham Royal, Quainton and Wexham) manorial records 14th-20th, incl Quainton terrier 1347-8 and account rolls 1356-1427; Bucks estate papers 15th-19th cent, incl leases 16th-18th cent, Farnham Royal survey 1629 and map 1801-2, accounts and vouchers 15th-17th cent, c1749-87, Upton enclosure award 1821 and Stoke Poges tithe papers 17th cent; accounts of work at Baylies House 1726-35; Eton College accounts 1679-81; inventory of goods of Dr Cradock, Provost of Eton 1695; misc papers, incl accounts of Mrs Godolphin 1748-53.

Buckinghamshire Record Office. Deposited by the 11th Duke of Leeds 1930-7, except for some miscellaneous items received subsequently through Bristol Record Office. NRA 35794.

[m] Bucks estate map 1824.

Buckinghamshire Record Office. (Ma 198/1.R). Purchased 1949.

[n] Legal papers rel to the marriage of the 2nd Duke; misc Yorks manorial suit rolls and papers (Osborne family) 1744-1825; terrier of Yorks WR estate of Sir Edward Osborne 1634; rentals and steward's accounts (Hyde estates in Bucks and Herts) 1687-95; rental and accounts, estates of the 1st Duke c1700-03; political, official and other papers of the 1st, 3rd, 5th and 7th Dukes of Leeds and the 4th Earl of Holderness; literary and misc papers 17th-19th cent, Osborne family, incl catalogues of libraries of the Dukes of Leeds 1686-1850 and inventory of the household of the 1st Earl of Plymouth c1678; papers rel to the Essex branch of the Darcy family 15th-17th cent, incl wills, inquisitions *post mortem* and valuation 1558 and register book 1575 for the Essex and Suffolk lands of the 2nd Baron Darcy of Chiche; antiquarian papers rel to Yorks families of Darcy and Conyers 17th cent.

British Library, Manuscript Collections (Eg MSS 3324-3508, Eg Ch 2290-2300). Deposited on loan by the 11th Duke of Leeds 1930 and purchased 1947. HMC *Eleventh Report, App VII*, 1888, pp1-58. The reported MS treatise by Dean Colet and the Roman de la Rose were not purchased but remain on loan (Loan MS 55/1-2). The British Library acquired further family papers from the collections of JE Hodgkin 1914 (Add MS 38849, ff115-327), Alfred Morrison 1917 (Add MS 39757, ff90-105) and John Webster (see below, [q]), but other items from these collections have been dispersed to the National Library of Scotland (MS 3420), the Carl H Pforzheimer Library, New York (MSS 137-9) and elsewhere: see HMC *Guide to the Location of Collections*, 1982, pp31, 36, 45, 64. Further papers of the 1st Duke of Leeds were purchased at Phillips's, 24 Oct 1985, lot 538 (Add MS 63650).

[o] Political and misc papers of the 5th Duke.

British Library, Manuscript Collections (Add MSS 27914-18, 28570). Purchased 1868, 1871 following the sales of family papers at Sotheby's, 11 July 1868 and 5 Apr 1869.

[p] Official and political papers of the 1st Duke of Leeds and the 1st Earl of Godolphin; legal papers rel to the marriage of the 2nd Duke 1675-1703; political papers of the 5th Duke; Yorks NR lieutenancy corresp of the 6th Duke 1831-7; business accounts and papers and family corresp 17th-18th cent, Godolphin and Osborne families; literary and misc papers.

British Library, Manuscript Collections (Add MSS 28040-95). Purchased at Sotheby's, 5 Apr 1869.

[q] Letters to the 1st Earl of Godolphin from Lord Seafield 1703-8.

British Library, Manuscript Collections (Add MS 34180). Purchased from the collection of John Webster at Sotheby's 1892. HMC *Guide to the Location of Collections*, 1982, p64.

[r] Diaries and papers of the 12th Duke (d1964).

British Library, Manuscript Collections (Eg MSS 3822-62D). Purchased at Quaritch's 1989.

[s] Official accounts and papers of the 1st Duke of Leeds as Lord High Treasurer and Treasurer of the Navy; misc estate accounts 1681-1717, Osborne family; household accounts, Wallingford House (Westminster) 1667.

Public Record Office (PRO 30/32). Deposited by the 10th Duke of Leeds 1905 and purchased 1929. NRA 8655.

[t] Treasury, naval, popish plot and other papers of the 1st Duke, incl Yorks militia papers c1670-80, with misc family and literary papers.

LIVERPOOL UNIVERSITY LIBRARY

Yale University, Beinecke Library (Osborn MSS 6, Danby Papers). Purchased from the collection of George Moffatt (who had acquired certain manuscripts owned by John Webster), Sotheby's, 27 Oct 1959, lot 384. NRA 20036. The locations of other family papers in this sale have not been traced (lots 350, 368, 383, 426-9, 432-34, 441, 446, 487).

[u] Medical and culinary recipe books late 17th-early-18th cent, Osborne family.

Wellcome Institute for the History of Medicine (MSS 1804, 2990, 3724, 4054-5). Purchased at Sotheby's Hornby Castle library sale 2-4 June 1930, lots 161-4, 403. The whereabouts of miscellaneous literary and music manuscripts included in this sale are not known.

[v] Kiveton and Thorpe Salvin (Yorks WR) household inventory 1727.

Victoria and Albert Museum, National Art Library (MS.L. 1983/11). Purchased 1983. NRA 38891.

[w] Osborne family corresp 1673-1722.

In private possession. Enquiries to the Historical Manuscripts Commission. NRA 26617.

[x] Political and family corresp and papers of the 1st Duke.

Untraced. Formerly in the possession of the Earls of Lindsey at Uffington, Lincolnshire. HMC *Fourteenth Report, App IX,* 1895, pp367-457; *Supplementary Report on the Manuscripts of the Late Montagu Bertie, Twelfth Earl of Lindsey,* 1942, pp1-69; *Guide to the Location of Collections,* 1982, p39.

[y] Scarborough election corresp of the 4th Duke 1735-9.

Untraced. NRA 7143.

[z] Journal of the 1st Duke of Leeds rel to the battle of La Hogue 1692.

In private possession. Enquiries to the County Archivist, Staffordshire and Stoke on Trent Archive Service. NRA 6393.

Related collections: Anderson-Pelham, Earls of Yarborough, no 1; Wentworth-Fitzwilliam of Milton, no 114; Barons Harlech (National Library of Wales, NRA 11471), including Abertanat estate papers and Godolphin family correspondence; Temple-Gore-Langton of Newton Park (Somerset Archive and Record Service DD/GL, NRA 781), including Newmarket (Suffolk) deeds and papers of the Godolphin family 17th-18th cent.

[79] PAGET, Marquesses of Anglesey

Sir William Paget (*c*1509-1563), statesman and diplomat, was created Baron Paget in 1549. Between about 1544 and 1554 he acquired extensive estates in Staffordshire (including Burton-upon-Trent, formerly belonging to Burton Abbey, and Beaudesert, formerly belonging to the bishops of Coventry and Lichfield), Derbyshire (Littleover, a Burton Abbey property), Middlesex (West Drayton, Harmondsworth), Buckinghamshire (Iver, Great Marlow) and Leicestershire.

The fifth Baron married in 1602 Lettice, daughter and co-heir of Henry Knollys, through whom estates in Berkshire (Stanford-in-the-Vale, sold 1715) and Warwickshire (Nuneaton, sold 1765) passed to the Paget family. The seventh Baron (counted by GEC, *The Complete Peerage,* as the eighth) was created Earl of Uxbridge in 1714. He married in 1686 Mary Catesby of Whiston (Northamptonshire), but the Whiston estate, together with unsettled estates in Anglesey, Carnarvonshire and Staffordshire, passed on Lord Uxbridge's death in 1743 to his kinsman Sir William Irby, second Bt, later first Baron Boston. On the death of the second Earl of Uxbridge in 1769 the Paget barony and estates were inherited by Sir Henry Bayly, third Bt, of Plas Newydd (Anglesey), who was created Earl of Uxbridge in 1784. The second Earl was created Marquess of Anglesey in 1815.

Sir Edward Bayly, first Bt, grandfather of Sir Henry Bayly and grandson of Lewis Bayly, Bishop of Bangor (d1631), had inherited in 1715 estates in Wales (Anglesey, Carnarvonshire, etc) and Ireland (the Cooley and Omeath estates in County Louth, four townlands in the Newry area of County Down and property in Galway town) from his cousin Nicholas Bagenal. (The major part of the Newry estate, however, passed to the Needham family, Viscounts and later Earls of Kilmorey.) In addition to the Paget and Bayly estates Lord Paget also succeeded in 1780 to part of the extensive Dorset and Somerset estates (Stalbridge, Milborne Port, etc) of Peter Walter (d1752).

Sales of property in Buckinghamshire and Middlesex (Iver and West Drayton) in the late eighteenth century were followed by the disposal of a major portion of the Walter estates (Milborne Port, etc) in 1825, and Stalbridge (to Lord Grosvenor, see Grosvenor, Dukes of Westminster, no 46), Harmondsworth and the Irish estates in the 1850s. Most of the Staffordshire estates were sold in the twentieth century, and in 1935 Beaudesert was demolished, Plas Newydd becoming the principal seat.

Estates in 1883: Staffs 17,441 acres, Derbys 1,559 acres, Dorset 1,117 acres, Anglesey 9,620 acres, total 29,737 acres worth £110,598 a year.

[a] Deeds 10th-19th cent, incl Staffs (Burton-upon-Trent, etc) 10th-19th cent, Derbys 13th-16th cent, Bucks and Middlesex 14th-18th cent and Warwicks 16th-18th cent; settlements and related papers 16th-19th cent, mainly Paget, incl 1st Marquess decd 1854-60; legal and case papers 16th-19th cent, incl copies of Burton Abbey leases early 16th cent; bonds and other financial papers 15th-19th cent; manorial court records, Staffs (Cannock and Rugeley, Burton-upon-Trent, Haywood, Longdon, etc) 14th-19th cent, Derbys (Littleover, Weston-on-Trent, etc) 14th-17th cent, Middlesex and Bucks (Iver, etc) 15th-18th cent and other counties 15th-19th cent.

General estate accounts and papers 16th-19th cent; Staff and Derbys (Beaudesert, Burton-upon-Trent, etc) estate records 16th-19th cent, incl leases and tenancy papers (extensive), surveys and valuations, maps and plans from 18th cent, rentals, accounts and vouchers, corresp, and papers rel to enclosure, tithes, mining and collieries, ironworks 16th-18th cent, railways, and Trent fishery and navigation; Berks, Bucks and Middlesex estate papers 16th-19th cent, incl surveys, rentals, accounts, corresp and papers; Dorset and Somerset rentals, accounts and estate papers mainly late 18th-mid-19th cent; misc papers rel to estates in Leics (Misterton) 1548-52, Oxon 18th cent, Surrey (Surbiton) early 19th cent and Warwicks (Nuneaton) 17th-18th cent; misc rentals, accounts and papers rel to estates in Wales (Anglesey, etc) and Ireland (Cos Louth and Down) 18th-19th cent.

Papers rel to Beaudesert mid-16th-early 20th cent, incl building papers, architectural drawings from late 18th cent, inventories, household accounts and papers rel to the gardens and farm; papers rel to Burton and Longdon Hall late 16th cent, Drayton House (Middlesex) 16th-18th cent, and Uxbridge House (London) and Plas Newydd (Anglesey) 18th-19th cent; papers rel to establishments of the 1st Marquess of Anglesey at Surbiton, Cowes and Dublin c1800-34; papers rel to Staffs lieutenancy and militia 16th-19th cent, N Staffs election 1832, Rugeley (Staffs) Fair tolls 1780s, 1810-19 and Burton-upon-Trent grammar school 1746-52; Paget family commissions and appointments 18th-19th cent; official and military papers 17th-19th cent; personal and family papers, Paget 16th-19th cent, incl the 1st, 3rd, 5th and 6th Barons Paget, 2nd Earl of Uxbridge (d1769), 1st Earl of Uxbridge (second creation) and 1st Marquess of Anglesey; Bayly family papers 18th cent.

Burton Abbey muniments 1004-1545, incl foundation and confirmation charters, licences, grants, case documents, formulary late 13th cent, constitutions early 14th cent, leases, *valor* 1545 and accounts 14th-15th cent; bishopric of Coventry and Lichfield records 15th cent-1542, incl cartulary fragment and estate and house-hold accounts; Hulton chantry cartulary 13th-14th cent; rental of St George's chantry in Lichfield Cathedral ?15th cent; Farewell Nunnery extents and rentals 14th cent; Burton peculiar probate records 1578-97; misc papers 15th-19th cent, incl Armitage (Staffs) brick-works accounts and papers 1808-18 and Shugborough, etc (Staffs) cricketing records 1859-64.

Staffordshire and Stoke on Trent Archive Service, Staffordshire Record Office (D 603, D 603/A/ADD, D(W) 1734, D 4793). Deposited by the 7th Marquess of Anglesey 1959-c1993, with earlier deeds and papers deposited in the William Salt Library, Stafford (D(W) 1734) and Burton-upon-Trent Public Library (D 603/A/ADD) and subsequently transferred to the record office. Staffordshire Record Society, *Collections for a history of Staffordshire* 1937 (Burton Abbey deeds as calendared by IH Jeayes). NRA 10.

[b] Legal and case papers 18th-20th cent, incl Cannock Chase case papers 19th cent-1903; Cannock and Rugeley, Haywood and Longdon manorial records 18th-20th cent; misc estate papers 16th-19th cent, mainly Staffs, incl leases, lease books, maps, and bailiffs' accounts (Staffs and Derbys) 1577-8; 1st Baron Paget, commission 1554.

Staffordshire and Stoke on Trent Archive Service, Staffordshire Record Office (D(W) 1511, D 4648). Deposited by Gardner & Co, solicitors, Rugeley in the William Salt Library, Stafford 1933-47 (WSL 86-91/33, 298/35, 95/41, 112/41 *passim*, 7/42, 40/45, 41/45, 47/45, 71/45, 60/47, 61/47) and subsequently transferred to the record office, with additional manorial records deposited in the record office by Gardner, Champion, solicitors, Rugeley 1987. NRA 10, 3516, 41388.

[c] Staffs deeds 18th-20th cent; trust deeds, mortgages and related legal and financial papers 19th-20th cent, incl papers rel to sales; misc Staffs estate papers 19th-20th cent, incl leases, schedules of Beaudesert and Burton leaseholds c1905, and colliery leases and papers; account of Harmondsworth householders c1740; Beaudesert architectural drawings 1911.

Staffordshire and Stoke on Trent Archive Service, Staffordshire Record Office (D 1282, 3000). Deposited by Farrer & Co, solicitors, London 1972, 1975. NRA 10.

[d] Trust and legal papers 19th-20th cent, incl papers rel to Staffs and Derbys estates and to sales (Beaudesert Hall, etc).

Staffordshire and Stoke on Trent Archive Service, Staffordshire Record Office (D 894). Deposited by Lucas & Wyllys, solicitors, Great Yarmouth through the Yarmouth Borough Archivist 1967. NRA 41389.

[e] Staffs estate maps, plans and related papers 1789-1929.

Staffordshire and Stoke on Trent Archive Service, Staffordshire Record Office (D(W) 1821). Deposited by WF Clark & Son, Aldridge in the William Salt Library, Stafford and subsequently transferred to the record office. NRA 3515.

[f] Settlements and related trust and legal papers 19th-20th cent; particulars of Burton-upon-Trent chief rents 1781-1926; Staffs estate papers 19th-20th cent, incl Burton leases and related papers, mining leases and papers, and accounts for settled estate 1885-1948.

Staffordshire and Stoke on Trent Archive Service, Staffordshire Record Office (D 3078). Deposited by Strutt & Parker, land agents, Lewes on behalf of the 7th Marquess of Anglesey 1976. NRA 10.

[g] Burton Abbey deeds and extracts 10th-15th cent (10 items).

William Salt Library, Stafford (84/1-10/41). Presented by RH Landor, descendant of a Paget agent. NRA 10.

[h] Manorial court records for Cannock and Rugeley, Haywood and Longdon mainly 1778-1831.

Staffordshire and Stoke on Trent Archive Service, Lichfield Record Office (D(W) 1851, D(W) 3222). Deposited by Hinckley & Birch, solicitors, Lichfield in the William Salt Library, Stafford; subsequently transferred to Staffordshire Record Office and then to Lichfield Record Office. NRA 8864.

[i] Burton-upon-Trent Abbey cartulary 13th cent.

British Library, Manuscript Collections (MS Loan 30). Deposited by the 7th Marquess of Anglesey. GRC Davis, *Medieval Cartularies of Great Britain*, 1958, p13.

[j] Paget and Bayly family corresp and papers 17th-20th cent, incl the 5th Baron Paget 1640-60, the Bayly family 18th cent, the 1st Earl of Uxbridge late 18th-early 19th cent, official, political, military and family corresp of the 1st Marquess of Anglesey, papers of Lord William Paget (1803-73) and Lord Queenborough (1861-1949), and extensive papers of the 6th and 7th Marquesses.

In private possession. Access restricted. Enquiries to the Archivist, Department of Manuscripts, University of Wales Bangor Library. HMC *Papers of British Cabinet Ministers 1782-1900*, 1982, p46.

[k] Deeds, Middlesex 13th-18th cent and Bucks 16th-18th cent; settlements and related documents 16th-18th cent; legal papers 13th-18th cent, incl case papers rel to Harmondsworth

13th cent; manorial records, Middlesex (West Drayton, Harmondsworth, etc) 15th-18th cent and Bucks (Iver) 16th-18th cent; Middlesex and Bucks estate records 15th-18th cent, incl leases, surveys, rentals, accounts and corresp; London and Drayton inventories and household accounts mid-16th-late 18th cent; misc commissions and official papers, Paget family 16th-18th cent.

London Metropolitan Archives (Acc 446). Deposited by the 7th Marquess of Anglesey in Middlesex Record Office 1952. NRA 2595.

[l] Bucks deeds (Iver, Great Marlow, etc) 13th-18th cent; legal papers 16th-18th cent; Bucks manorial records (Iver, etc) 14th-19th cent; Bucks estate papers 15th-18th cent, incl leases 1597-1601, surveys of Great Marlow 1546, 1745, Iver maps *c*1760, rentals 1447-1655 and timber, etc accounts 1567-86; bailiffs' accounts for all Paget estates 1556; household and personal vouchers 1746-53 (Upton Court, etc); commission of the Hon Henry Paget as deputy-lieutenant for Bucks 1702.

Buckinghamshire Record Office (AR 31/57, 24/87, 16/89). Deposited in Buckinghamshire Archaeological Society 1954 and transferred to the record office 1987, with additional deposits in the record office 1957, 1989. HMC *Accessions to Repositories 1954*, pp35-6. Buckinghamshire Record Office *Annual Report 1987*, p10, *1989*, p12.

[m] General account book of the 5th Baron Paget 1649-52, incl London and Marlow establishments.

Buckinghamshire Record Office (D/X 728). Purchased from Henry Bristow Ltd, Ringwood 1981. NRA 3576.

[n] Dorset and Somerset deeds and legal papers 1746-1815.

Dorset Record Office (D 591). Deposited by Withers, Nicholl, Manisty & Co, solicitors, London, through the British Records Association 1977. NRA 7828.

[o] Dorset, Somerset and Wilts deeds and leases 1640-1935; Dorset, etc estate records 1640-1873, incl rentals 1784-1854, accounts and related papers 1780-1873, corresp 1799-1854 and sale particulars 1825; household vouchers (Stalbridge, Weymouth) late 18th cent; Milborne Port (Somerset), etc election accounts and papers late 18th cent-1831; commission of the Earl of Uxbridge as deputy-lieutenant for Dorset 1796.

Dorset Record Office (D 20, D/ANG). Deposited by the 7th Marquess of Anglesey 1956, 1991. HMC *Accessions to Repositories 1991*, p28. NRA 8984.

[p] Temple Combe (Somerset) manorial court book 1802-50; Dorset and Somerset estate papers 1825-1910, incl rentals, letter book 1850-60 and sale particulars 1825, 1849.

Dorset Record Office (D/CRL). Deposited by Chislett & Rawlence, land agents, Wimborne Minster 1989-90. NRA 34750. (For a valuation of the Stalbridge estate 1840 see Dorset Record Office C/1531 DD BT, NRA 20479.)

[q] Anglesey and Carnarvonshire deeds and legal papers 17th-20th cent; misc trust deeds and papers 16th-19th cent, Bagenal, Bayly and Paget; misc Staffs manorial papers (Cannock, etc) 1823-55; Welsh estate records 17th-20th cent (mainly from mid-18th cent), incl leases from 17th cent, tenancy papers 19th-20th cent, valuations 19th cent, maps, plans, rentals and accounts 18th-20th cent, corresp, letter books, memoranda, reports, and papers rel to schools, charities, minerals and sales; records rel to the Mona copper mine (Anglesey) 1762-1878, incl contracts, royalty accounts, smelting papers, marketing papers and agency corresp and papers; misc estate rentals, etc rel to Staffs and Derbys 1789-1872, Dorset 1781-1854 and Ireland 1833-46.

Papers rel to Plas Newydd 18th-20th cent, incl accounts for alterations 1783-6, architectural drawings mainly 20th cent, inventories 19th-20th cent, and household accounts and vouchers 18th-20th cent; Plas Newydd home farm accounts and papers 19th-20th cent; schedule of Uxbridge House muniment room 1839; corresp and papers rel to Anglesey lieutenancy, militia, magistracy and vice-admiralty 1762-1855, to Anglesey and Carnarvonshire county and borough politics 1784-1868, to roads, bridges and railways 1765-1864, and to local affairs in Anglesey, Carnarvon and Bangor late 18th-20th cent; patents and commissions 18th-20th cent; Bayly and Paget family corresp and papers 18th-19th cent, incl Irish estate corresp of Sir Nicholas Bayly c1737-82 and political, local and patronage corresp of the 1st Earl of Uxbridge and 1st Marquess of Anglesey c1783-1854; Anglesey and Carnarvonshire pedigrees 17th-18th cent; military, naval and other maps and plans.

University of Wales Bangor Library, Department of Manuscripts (Plas Newydd MSS, Mona Mine MSS). Deposited by the 7th Marquess of Anglesey 1946-84. NRA 30502.

[r] Settlements and related papers 1783-1930, Paget family.

University of Wales Bangor Library, Department of Manuscripts (Bangor MSS 37139-37203). Deposited through the British Records Association. NRA 30502.

[s] Maps, plans, sale particulars and related papers concerning the Anglesey estates and copper mines 1821-1975, incl book of reference c1857-8.

University of Wales Bangor Library, Department of Manuscripts (Bangor MSS 31584-31685 *passim*). Deposited by Peckover, Burrill & Owen, land agents, Bangor c1982. NRA 30502.

[t] Legal and estate papers rel to the Anglesey and Carnarvonshire properties 1743-1857 (mainly OA Poole as legal agent early 19th cent), incl case papers, papers rel to purchases, sales and exchanges, leases 1799-1829, valuations 1805-13 and rental 1823.

Caernarfon Record Office (X/Poole/2046-2552). Deposited by Messrs Poole, solicitors, Caernarfon. NRA 37581.

[u] Misc Paget estate papers 1779-1864 (39 items), incl corresp 1830-5 and accounts 1828-41.

Caernarfon Record Office (M/1010). Deposited 1966. NRA 29346.

[v] Deeds, Cos Louth, Down and Galway 17th-19th cent; legal and case papers 1716-1841; Irish estate records 17th-19th cent, Cos Louth (Omeath, etc), Down (Crobane, etc) and Galway (Galway town), incl leases, surveys, maps, rentals, accounts, agents' corresp, and papers 18th-19th cent rel to Louth Infirmary, Omeath school and the living of Kilkeel (Co Down); rentals for whole Bagenal estate in Ireland 1688-1714; Irish estate corresp 18th-mid-19th cent, Bayly and Paget families; corresp and papers of the 1st Marquess of Anglesey as Lord Lieutenant of Ireland 1828-9, 1830-3.

Public Record Office of Northern Ireland (D 619). Deposited by the 7th Marquess of Anglesey 1953-82. NRA 10.

[w] Beaudesert estate and household account book 1611-12.

Folger Shakespeare Library, Washington, DC (563.1). Purchased 1912. Seymour De Ricci and WJ Wilson, *Census of Medieval and Renaissance Manuscripts in the United States and Canada*, 1935, repr 1961, i, p327.

[x] Plas Newydd rentals early 18th cent (2); Co Louth rentals 1727-32.

National Library of Wales (Panton collection 30/10-11a, 18-21). Collected by Paul Panton (1727-97) of Plas Gwyn (Anglesey) or his son Paul Panton junior. NRA 28740.

[y] Diplomatic corresp of the 6th Baron Paget 1681-1707 (mainly 1688-1705).

London University, School of Oriental and African Studies Library. Deposited by the 7th Marquess of Anglesey 1964. NRA 10.

[z] Regimental papers of the 1st Marquess of Anglesey as Colonel of the 7th Light Dragoons (7th Hussars) 1771-1817.

National Army Museum (6806/43, 8211/123). Presented by the 7th Marquess of Anglesey 1968, with two volumes subsequently purchased. NRA 20796.

[aa] Misc corresp of the 1st Marquess 1830 (59 items).

Duke University, William R Perkins Library, Durham, North Carolina (MS 4024). Acquired 1972. *Guide to the Catalogued Collections*, 1986, p417.

[bb] Misc corresp and papers of the 1st Earl Holland c1630-49, incl letters to him from Queen Henrietta Maria and a letter from him to his daughter Lady Paget.

Untraced. Sold at Phillips's, 16 June 1983, lots 499-506.

Related collection: Barons Boston (University of Wales Bangor Library, Department of Manuscripts, Lligwy MSS, NRA 8487, 41003), including Paget legal and estate papers 1626-1771; Irby (previously Paget) legal papers 1672-1815 (Staffordshire and Stoke on Trent Archive Service, Staffordshire Record Office D 418/M, NRA 3515); Earls of Verulam (Hertfordshire Record Office, NRA 7246), including Stalbridge estate papers mainly 18th cent; Lygon, Earls Beauchamp, no 67, including further papers of the 6th Baron Paget.

[80] PELHAM, Earls of Chichester

The Pelham family was settled in East Sussex from the fourteenth century, and between the fourteenth and late sixteenth centuries acquired extensive lands there, including Laughton (where Laughton Place was the principal seat until Halland was built in the 1590s), Waldron, Burwash, Bivelham (in Mayfield) and the rapes of Pevensey and Hastings. Sir Thomas Pelham was created a baronet in 1611. Sir John Pelham, third Bt (d1703), married Lucy Sidney, daughter of the second Earl of Leicester. Sir Thomas Pelham, fourth Bt (d1712), married in 1686 Lady Grace Holles, daughter of the third Earl of Clare, and was created Baron Pelham in 1706.

The second Baron Pelham (1693-1768) succeeded to the Holles estates of his uncle the Duke of Newcastle in 1711 (see Pelham-Clinton, later Pelham-Clinton-Hope, Dukes of Newcastle, no 81), and was himself created Duke of Newcastle in 1715. He divided the Pelham estates in Sussex between himself and his brother Henry Pelham (d1754). The properties that passed to Henry Pelham, including Ifield (a former Holles estate), Laughton Place, Burwash and Bivelham, were left to his daughters as co-heirs, and later partitioned and partly

sold, but on the death of the Duke of Newcastle in 1768 the remaining Sussex estates in his possession, including Laughton and the rape of Hastings, passed to his cousin and heir male Thomas Pelham of Stanmer (Sussex) (1728-1805).

Thomas Pelham (who also inherited the personal and political papers of the Duke of Newcastle, kept during his lifetime at Claremont (Surrey)) was the grandson of Henry Pelham of Lewes (brother of the first Baron Pelham), who had acquired Stanmer c1716 and built a house there in the 1720s. He and his successors built up an extensive estate in East Sussex, and after 1768 Stanmer continued to be the principal seat, Halland being converted to a farmhouse. Thomas Pelham succeeded the Duke of Newcastle as second Baron Pelham (of the 1762 creation), and was created Earl of Chichester in 1801. In 1804, on the death of Frances Pelham, he inherited the unsold remainder of Henry Pelham's Sussex properties.

Estates in 1883: Sussex 16,232 acres worth £13,650 a year.

[a] Deeds 12th-19th cent, mainly Sussex but incl some for Dorset 17th-18th cent, Kent 14th-17th cent, Lincs 16th-17th cent, Notts and Yorks 17th-mid-18th cent and Ireland 17th cent; list of Pelham deeds 1280-1764; schedule of deeds at Newcastle House (London) 1714; Pelham family wills 1450-1729; trusteeship and executorship accounts and papers 18th cent, incl 1st Duke of Newcastle and Cardonell (later Frankland) family; misc legal papers 16th-early 19th cent, mainly Pelham; Sussex manorial court records 14th-early 19th cent, incl Burwash, Laughton, hundred of Shiplake and rape of Hastings; court book of South Malling College (Sussex) 1333-1562; honour of Nottingham and Sherwood Forest presentments c1535; Sussex estate records 14th-18th cent, incl rentals, estate and farm accounts, and ironworks accounts 1628-1716; Dorset and Wilts accounts 1754-74; Notts rent accounts 1737-68; Clare Market (Middlesex) estate accounts 1764-81; Claremont farm accounts 1758-69; building accounts of the 1st Duke 1714-20; 1st Duke decd, valuations of furniture 1768-9; household accounts, Laughton, Halland, etc 17th-early 19th cent, incl Twickenham Park (Duchess of Newcastle) 1769-76 and 1st Earl of Chichester 1774-1802.

Papers rel to Sussex affairs 1581-1814, incl county poll book 1734, and to Notts affairs 1701-68, mainly of the 1st Duke as lord lieutenant; commissions, appointments, etc 14th-early 19th cent, mainly Pelham family, incl indulgences, etc 1412-75; Pelham family corresp, accounts and papers 16th-early 19th cent, incl official, personal and family corresp of the 1st and 2nd Earls of Chichester; misc Holles papers 16th-17th cent; extensive official, political, personal and family corresp and papers of the 1st

Duke of Newcastle mostly 1697-1768; Sidney family papers 16th-17th cent, incl corresp of the 1st Earl of Romney 1674-91; misc records 14th-early 19th cent, incl inventory of Queen's robes early 15th cent, ordinances of war 15th cent, Arlington (Sussex) churchwardens' accounts 1456-79, inventories of Leicester House 1644, 1677, and papers rel to biographies of the 1st Duke of Newcastle by the 2nd Earl of Chichester and Archdeacon Coxe early 19th cent.

British Library, Manuscript Collections (Add Ch 28655-6, 29259-32739, 33198, 34940, 36450-2; Add MSS 32645E, 32679-33201, 33320-44, 33441-3, 33617-31, 36586-7). Presented by the 4th Earl of Chichester 1886-90, 1901. HMC *Papers of British Cabinet Ministers 1782-1900*, 1982, pp47-8.

[b] Ledger of Henrietta, Duchess of Newcastle and Lord Pelham 1775-6.

British Library, Manuscript Collections (Add MS 62926). Purchased 1983. (For similar ledgers 1761-74 see Add MSS 33325-36.)

[c] Family corresp and papers 1738-1922, incl letters to the Duke of Newcastle 1757-68, Sussex election expenses 1768, 1784, and Seaford (Sussex) election corresp of the 2nd Earl of Chichester 1812.

British Library, Manuscript Collections (Add MS 64813). Purchased 1987 (Phillips's, 17 Sept, lot 488.)

[d] Sussex deeds 15th-early 19th cent, Laughton and Stanmer estates, with legal papers (abstracts of title, etc) 17th-18th cent and mort-gages by the 1st Duke of Newcastle; Pelham family wills and settlements 17th-18th cent; Sussex leases early 19th cent; misc papers 18th-early 19th cent.

East Sussex Record Office (SAS/P *passim*). Given to Sussex Archaelogical Society by the 4th Earl of Chichester c1886 and transferred to the record office 1982. EHW Dunkin, 'A calendar of the deeds and other documents in the pos-session of the Sussex Archaelogical Society', *Sussex Arch Coll* XXXVII, 1890, pp39-108.

[e] Sussex deeds 14th-19th cent, mainly Stanmer estate; Pelham wills, settlements and related deeds 1620-1778; legal and case papers 16th-18th cent; Sussex manorial court records (Ewhurst, etc) 14th-18th cent; hundred of Shiplake presentments 1770-85; misc leases 18th cent; Walstead (Sussex) rental 1666; Pelham family corresp and papers mainly 1737-1824, incl letters to the Duke of Newcastle 1760-8 and papers of the 1st and 2nd Earls of Chichester rel to legal and estate matters, Sussex militia and politics, ecclesiastical affairs, etc; Stanmer rough marriage register 1754-62, with banns and licences 1741-1809.

East Sussex Record Office (SAS/A). Purchased by Sussex Archaelogical Society from Mrs H Saxby of Lewes 1894. Mostly transferred to the record office 1982. NRA 10264.

[f] Stanmer estate maps 1776-c1850; drawings for Stanmer Park c1840-1930.

East Sussex Record Office (Acc 3714). Deposited by the trustees of the Earl of Chichester with Sussex Archaelogical Society 1954, and trans-ferred to the record office 1982. NRA 6751.

[g] Stanmer estate accounts 1769-1950, letter book 1907-20 and files 20th cent; farm accounts 1852-1905; Stanmer church building accounts 1722-c1730, 1838-9; Falmer national school cash book 1875-87; Stanmer household accounts and papers 1809-1904, with inven-tories, etc (Stanmer ?) 1712-70; game books 1862-1905.

East Sussex Record Office (Acc 4600). Deposited by the 9th Earl of Chichester through Brighton Reference Library 1986. NRA 6751.

[h] Sussex deeds 18th-20th cent; trust deeds and papers 1801-1950; Falmer manorial papers 1637-1776; Stanmer estate papers 1923-57, incl sale papers.

East Sussex Record Office (Acc 4765, 6797). Deposited by the 9th Earl of Chichester through Adam & Remers, solicitors, Lewes 1986, with an additional deposit of twentieth-century legal papers 1996. NRA 6751.

[i] Sussex deeds (Laughton and Stanmer estates) 16th-20th cent; Pelham wills and settle-ments 1712-1913, with trust accounts and cor-resp 1866-1933; legal papers mainly 19th cent, incl abstracts and schedules; misc Sussex man-orial records 14th-19th cent, incl Laughton extent 1325 and rape of Hastings rentals 1788-1803; Yorks fee farm rents (manor of Kippax (Yorks WR), etc) 1828; Sussex estate records 18th-mid-20th cent, incl leases, agreements, maps and plans, particular 1861, rentals, accounts and corresp mainly 20th cent, Laughton enclosure papers c1813-18 and papers rel to sales 19th-20th cent; papers rel to chur-ches and tithes 1774-1901; Stanmer inventories, etc c1886-1950; Stanmer overseers' accounts 1849-67; Stanmer and Falmer Men's Club accounts 1924-50; misc personal and family papers 19th-20th cent.

East Sussex Record Office (CHR 1-30; Acc 1091 (BMW C21); Acc 1482). Deposited by Markby, Stewart & Wadesons, solicitors, London, through the British Records Association 1955-62 and by Strutt & Parker, estate agents 1961-93. NRA 6751, 37657.

[j] Sussex manorial records (Laughton, South Malling, Lindfield, etc) 16th-20th cent, incl maps 17th-19th cent, rentals 19th cent, leases and enfranchisements, and steward's papers.

East Sussex Record Office (Acc 2327/1). Deposited by Blaker, Son & Young, solicitors, Lewes 1960. NRA 37772. (A Falmer court book 1628-41 and some maps and reference books early 19th cent were retained by the firm.)

[k] Sussex manorial court records ?17th-20th cent, with records rel to the rape of Hastings 1569-1809.

East Sussex Record Office (SAS/RA/64, 69-75; Acc 2300). Deposited with Sussex Archaeological Society 1938 and subsequently. NRA 5244 (partial list).

[l] Papers of John Collier of Hastings (1685-1760) as agent and steward for Newcastle and Pelham estates and manors c1733-64, incl Stanmer estate rentals 1745 and accounts c1735-63, and corresp with Henry Pelham, the Duke of Newcastle and others.

East Sussex Record Office (Sayer MSS 81-251, 369-590). Deposited by RC Sayer 1965. NRA 28259.

[m] Laughton estate accounts 1769-89.

East Sussex Record Office (AMS 2132-3). Given by the 4th Earl of Chichester to his agent Frederick Jones, and by him to Lord Wolseley in 1926. Subsequently deposited in Hove Library and transferred to the record office. NRA 7797.

[n] Pelham estate maps 1792, 1799 and accounts 1750-83.

East Sussex Record Office (SAS/Acc 1100/1/18, 57, 177; FIG 82, 710). From the antiquarian papers of William Figg of Lewes. Transferred to the record office 1982.

[o] Stanmer household account book 1897-1905.

East Sussex Record Office (Acc 2854). Deposited with the Historical Manuscripts Commission by Lady Studholme and transferred to the record office 1982. NRA 5956. (For further papers deposited by Lady Studholme see Acc 4098.)

[p] Misc Sussex deeds and legal papers 18th-19th cent; Laughton quit rents 1721-60; misc Sussex estate papers 18th-19th cent, incl agreements, survey of farm in Seaford 1764, map of Halland Farm early 19th cent, rentals c1750-1804, Stanmer estate accounts 1757, 1765-6, Laughton, etc estate accounts 1764-7 and Stanmer enclosure book of reference 1770; papers rel to building work at Stanmer 1721-8, 1771-3 and to repair of Halland House (as a farm house) 1769; inventories of books 1928 and fixtures 1940, Stanmer Park.

East Sussex Record Office (Norris Collection 22). Collected by the late NES Norris and deposited

by the National Trust, through the British Records Association 1991-2. NRA 37850.

[q] Deeds rel to the honour, castle and rape of Hastings 1429-1840 (18 items); rape of Hastings cottage and castleguard rental 1731-41.

East Sussex Record Office (Acc 7010). Transferred from Hastings Museum (to which the deeds had been given by the 4th Earl of Chichester) 1996. NRA 1153.

[r] Rape of Hastings cottage and castleguard rental 1717-25.

East Sussex Record Office (AMS 5735/53). Formerly in the collection of Sir Thomas Phillipps. Transferred from Worthing Library.

Related Collections: Pelham-Clinton, later Pelham-Clinton-Hope, Dukes of Newcastle, no 81; Sidney, Barons De L'Isle and Dudley, later Viscounts De L'Isle, no 95; Papillon (formerly Cressett-Pelham) of Crowhurst (East Sussex Record Office Acc 6588).

[81] PELHAM-CLINTON, later PELHAM-CLINTON-HOPE, Dukes of Newcastle

Sir William Holles, Lord Mayor of London 1539-40, bought property in Middlesex (London, St Clement Danes) from c1532, and purchased Haughton (Nottinghamshire) in 1541. These estates were extended particularly by John Holles of Haughton (1564-1637), who was created Earl of Clare in 1624. The family also acquired estates in Lincolnshire (Irby-on-Humber, etc), but these were later sold. Denzil Holles, younger brother of the second Earl of Clare, acquired the Ifield (Sussex) estate, and was created Baron Holles of Ifield in 1661: his lands were inherited by the fourth Earl of Clare in 1694.

John Holles, fourth Earl (1662-1711), married in 1690 Margaret Cavendish, daughter and co-heir of the second Duke of Newcastle, who died in 1691 (see Cavendish-Bentinck, Dukes of Portland, no 18). He was himself created Duke of Newcastle in 1694. At his death most of the Cavendish (Newcastle) estates passed to his daughter, but the Holles estates, together with the Cavendish properties of Nottingham Castle and Clumber Park (Nottinghamshire), passed to his nephew Thomas Pelham (later Pelham-Holles), second Baron Pelham of Laughton (see Pelham, Earls of Chichester, no 80), who was created Duke of Newcastle in 1715.

This Duke of Newcastle, the well-known statesman, held both the Pelham estates in Sussex and the Holles estates, and also acquired Claremont in Surrey. Outlying Holles estates, however, in Derbyshire, Dorset, Hertfordshire, Kent and Wiltshire were sold to meet debts, and he made over estates in both

Nottinghamshire and Sussex to his brother Henry Pelham (d1754, First Lord of the Treasury 1743-54). The Duke reacquired the Nottinghamshire properties in 1761, but Henry Pelham's other estates (lands in Sussex and the Esher Place estate in Surrey which he had purchased in 1729) were left to his daughters and co-heirs and dispersed by sale (see also below).

On the death of the Duke of Newcastle in 1768 Claremont was sold, and the remaining Sussex estates passed to his cousin and heir male Thomas Pelham of Stanmer (Sussex) (see Pelham, Earls of Chichester, no 80), but the Nottinghamshire, Yorkshire and Middlesex (Holles) estates passed to his nephew Henry Clinton, ninth Earl of Lincoln (1720-94), who also succeeded under a special remainder as second Duke of Newcastle-under-Line.

The old Lincolnshire estates of the Clinton Earls of Lincoln had been alienated following the death of the fourth Earl in 1692 (see Fortescue, Earls Fortescue, no 39), but the ninth Earl had succeeded in 1730 to other Lincolnshire estates (Baumber, Brinkhill, etc) acquired by his family since 1700, together with property in the Bedford Level (Whittlesey (Cambridgeshire), etc) and Surrey (Oatlands in Weybridge). In 1744 he married Catherine, elder daughter and co-heir of Henry Pelham (d1754) (see above), through whom he inherited a share of Pelham's Sussex estates (sold, however, between 1767 and 1772) and most of his personal papers. The Bedford Level estates were sold before 1768, the Lincolnshire estates between c1776 and 1789, and Oatlands (to the Duke of York) in 1788-9, but after his succession to the Newcastle estates the second Duke extended the Nottinghamshire properties, making Clumber Park his principal seat, and also added to the Aldborough and Boroughbridge estate in the West Riding of Yorkshire, first acquired in the early eighteenth century. Between 1794 and 1806 the trustees for the fourth Duke, a minor, continued the expansion of the Nottinghamshire estates but disposed of the Clare Market (Middlesex) property.

The fourth Duke (1785-1851) married in 1807 Georgiana Miller Mundy, heir to further Nottinghamshire property (West Leake, etc). The Worksop Manor estate was purchased from the Duke of Norfolk in 1839 (see Fitzalan-Howard, Dukes of Norfolk, no 37), but largely re-sold in 1890. The Yorkshire estates were mostly sold in the 1830s. Hafod (Cardiganshire) was acquired in 1835 but sold (apart from its celebrated library) ten years later. In 1861 the sixth Duke (1834-79) married Henrietta, daughter of Thomas Hope of Deepdene (Surrey) and heir to estates in Surrey, Gloucestershire, Warwickshire and County Monaghan (Castleblayney). These descended to a younger son, Lord Francis Pelham-Clinton, who took the additional name of Hope on

coming of age in 1887 and eventually succeeded his brother as eighth Duke in 1928. (The Gloucestershire properties were sold in 1911.) Clumber was given up shortly before the Second World War. In the 1950s the ninth Duke settled in Wiltshire, acquiring the former Fane estate of Boyton, but papers relating to that and other properties in the south of England acquired after 1945 are not dealt with in this entry.

Estates in 1883: Duke of Newcastle: Notts 34,467 acres, Derbys 827 acres, Yorks WR 237 acres, Lincs 16 acres, total 35,547 acres worth £74,547 a year; Mrs Hope of Deepdene: Surrey 3,931 acres, Gloucs 4,893 acres, Warwicks 1,249 acres, Co Monaghan 11,700 acres, total 21,773 acres worth £22,138 a year.

[a] Deeds, mainly Notts 12th-20th cent, but incl Lincs (Irby-on-Humber, etc) 14th-18th cent, Middlesex (St Giles-in-the-Fields, St Clement Danes, Newcastle House (Lincoln's Inn Fields) and Arlington St) 14th-19th cent, Surrey (Hope family) 15th-20th cent and Yorks WR 16th-early 19th cent; wills, settlements and trust and executorship papers late 15th-20th cent, Holles, Cavendish, Pelham, Pelham-Clinton and Hope, incl trusteeship accounts 1689-93 and papers of John Gally Knight during the 4th Duke's minority 1794-1806; trusteeship papers for the Whetham family of Kirklington (Notts) and related families (connected with the wife of the 4th Duke) c1646-1811; legal papers 16th-20th cent, incl papers rel to Lincs, Bedford Level, Middlesex, Notts, Surrey and Yorks estates; manorial court records, Notts 14th-20th cent, incl Gamston, Maplebeck, Newark and bailiwick of Bassetlaw, and Surrey (Brockham and E Betchworth) 16th-20th cent.

Notts estate records 15th-20th cent, incl leases from 17th cent, Haughton surveys 15th and 16th cent, other Notts surveys and valuations 16th-early 20th cent, maps and plans 17th-20th cent, rentals and accounts from 16th cent, wood accounts 1876-81, enclosure awards 18th-19th cent, farm accounts 19th cent, cultivation books 1878-1924, reports on churches on the estate 1813, 1853, papers rel to Brinsley and Shireoaks collieries 18th-19th cent, and papers rel to Nottingham Castle and Park 19th-20th cent; Middlesex estate papers 14th-early 19th cent, mainly 1610 onwards, incl rentals, accounts, and papers rel to the sale of Clare Market and construction of Newcastle Street late 18th cent; Yorks rentals, accounts, corresp and papers 17th-early 19th cent, incl sale papers 1830s; Clinton estate (Lincs and Bedford Level) accounts and papers 18th cent; misc Ifield and other Sussex estate papers c1741-68; Surrey (Oatlands) estate accounts and vouchers 1763-88; Surrey (Deepdene) estate papers 19th-20th cent, incl leases, maps and corresp; Co Monaghan rentals 1929-36; misc estate papers 17th-19th cent, incl papers rel to Cavendish (later Cavendish-Bentinck) estates 1699-1760 (1 vol), survey of Welsh (Cardigan, etc) estates c1792 and map of the Boyton estate 1873; papers rel to Clumber House 18th cent-1913, incl building vouchers c1763-80, inventories and library catalogues; Clumber visitors' book 1890-1928; papers rel to the building and furnishing of Oatlands mainly 1755-8; financial papers rel to the Arlington St house 1775-8; inventory of Nottingham Castle 1783; papers rel to Clumber and Haughton parks early 19th cent; papers rel to Deepdene and Castleblayney 19th-20th cent; misc household accounts 18th-19th cent.

Bassetlaw subsidy roll 1593; election papers (Notts, Newark, Boroughbridge, etc) 1790-1865; Surrey shrievalty roll (Thomas Hope) 1828-9; appointments, commissions, etc 16th-20th cent; Pelham-Clinton family papers 18th-early 20th cent, incl papers of the 2nd, 4th, 5th and 7th Dukes; Holles papers late 16th-early 18th cent, incl letter books 1591-1637 (2 vols); Clinton papers 1703-66, incl papers of the 7th Earl of Lincoln as Paymaster-General; political and other corresp of Henry Pelham 1725-54; misc Wriothesley and Rachel, Lady Russell corresp c1608-1706; pedigrees and genealogical papers 17th-20th cent, with purchased and other misc items 15th-19th cent; accounts of James Needham as Surveyor-General and Clerk of the King's Works 1535-42; account book of Edward Carne, Teller of the Exchequer 1626-7.

Nottingham University Library, Department of Manuscripts and Special Collections (Ne). Deposited by the trustees of the will of the 7th Duke of Newcastle 1955, with an additional deposit 1966, and allocated to the Library, having been accepted for the nation in lieu of tax, 1981. Additional deposits were made by the Newcastle Trustees in 1990 and 1998 (Ne 5, Ne 6). HMC *Third Report, App*, 1872, pp221-3; *Papers of British Cabinet Ministers 1782-1900*, 1982, p48; *Papers of British Politicians 1782-1900*, 1989, p82. NRA 7411 (partial list).

[b] Executorship and trusteeship accounts, vouchers and papers, 2nd Duke of Newcastle decd 1781-1809.

Nottingham University Library, Department of Manuscripts and Special Collections (NL). Deposited by Lee, Bolton & Lee, solicitors, London, through the British Records Association 1971. NRA 7411.

[c] Misc papers rel to the Byfleet (Surrey) estate 1718-1828; misc appointments and personal papers of the Hon Henry Pelham 1714-50.

Nottingham University Library, Department of Manuscripts and Special Collections (Acc 666). Deposited by Farrer & Co, solicitors, London, through the British Records Association 1986.

[d] Accounts and papers of Henry Walter and his executor as collectors and receivers-general

for the Notts (Haughton, etc) estates 1656-96, incl rental 1665-6 and accounts 1669-86.

Nottingham University Library, Department of Manuscripts and Special Collections (NS). Purchased 1972 (Sotheby's, 24 Oct, lots 385-6). NRA 19801.

[e] Worksop estate papers c1825-1904 (mainly 1860s: agency papers of Joel Haslam), incl maps late 19th cent, rental 1839, corresp, and sale particulars 1890, 1892.

Nottingham University Library, Department of Manuscripts and Special Collections (Acc 672). Purchased from Deighton Bell & Co, Cambridge 1986.

[f] Abstracts of title, mortgages, etc rel to the Worksop manor 1649-1850; misc Worksop estate leases 1856-73; Notts (Clumber, etc) rentals 1771-7, with papers rel to Walesby and Haughton tithes 18th-19th cent, and to Worksop rectory and Shireoaks chapel 19th cent; railway papers 19th cent.

Nottinghamshire Archives (DD HO). Deposited by Hodding & Wordsworth, solicitors, Worksop 1953. NRA 6875.

[g] Newark manorial records 1583-1895, incl court books 1583-1665 and suit rolls 1695-1776; Balderton (Notts) estate map 1819.

Nottinghamshire Archives (DD T 122, BN/1/R). Deposited by Tallents & Co, solicitors, Newark 1965. NRA 5838.

[h] Misc Newark, etc estate papers c1802-25, incl rental 1806 and election papers 1791-1812, with papers of ES Godfrey as clerk of the peace for Notts.

Nottinghamshire Archives (CP 5/2/1-59, 5/6/225-51). NRA 11878.

[i] Letters mainly from the 4th Duke to John Chambers, agent for the Nottingham estate 1825-30.

Derbyshire Record Office (D 885 M/B 1-34). Deposited 1970. NRA 15429.

[j] Misc Worksop estate papers 1862-86, incl further agency corresp of Joel Haslam.

West Yorkshire Archive Service, Yorkshire Archaeological Society, Leeds (MD 380). NRA 3525.

[k] Papers rel to the sale of the Worksop Manor estate, mainly 1886-92 but incl a valuation c1857.

Hull University, Brynmor Jones Library (DX/103). Given by NI Secker 1975. NRA 10731.

[l] Accounts for the Hon Henry Pelham's Sussex estates 1731-54 (3 vols), with rental 1761, particulars and summary of partition [1767].

East Sussex Record Office (SAS/FB 112-117). Deposited by Farrer & Co, solicitors, London, through the British Records Association 1942. NRA 10702.

[m] Misc Deepdene estate records 20th cent, incl rentals and accounts 1910-26 and letter book 1924-41; Deepdene game book 1891-4.

Surrey History Centre (2226). Deposited by JC Hawkes 1978. NRA 25870.

[n] Misc estate records 19th-early 20th cent, mainly Surrey but with some for Gloucs and Warwicks, incl lease book (all estates) *c*1858-1913, Surrey agreements and tenancy papers 1872-1907, accounts 1888-1918, Surrey timber papers 1900-13 and misc Gloucs estate papers 1871-1901.

Surrey History Centre (2971). Formerly in the Deepdene estate office. Deposited by R Arthur of Dorking 1984. NRA 40841.

[o] Gloucs (Hope estate) terriers and maps 1748-1821.

Gloucestershire Record Office (D 363). Presented to Gloucestershire County Council by Harman Bros, land agents, London 1914.

[p] Castleblayney estate maps and valuations 1762, *c*1830-60 and rentals 1768, 1828-1938; elevation of Temple House, Castleblayney *c*1854; Co Antrim (Lord Blayney) deeds and rental 17th-19th cent.

Public Record Office of Northern Ireland (D 1421). Deposited by Dr R Pritchard *c*1960-5. *Deputy Keeper's Report 1960-65*, p156.

[q] Castleblayney rental 1878-9 (Miss Anne Hope) and cash books 1931-43 (8th Duke of Newcastle).

Public Record Office of Northern Ireland (D 1406). Deposited by John Corrigan, solicitor, Castleblayney *c*1960-5. *Deputy Keeper's Report 1960-65*, p73.

[r] Clare Market rentals 1780-93.

Public Record Office (C 109/85, Duke of Newcastle *v* Brudenell).

[s] Building account for Arlington House, Arlington St, London 1740-54.

British Architectural Library (PEL/1). Given by Farrer & Co, solicitors, London, through the British Records Association 1941. NRA 34275.

[t] Commonplace book of the 2nd Earl of Clare *c*1629-32.

Yale University, Beinecke Library (Osborn MSS b.32). From the library of the 4th Duke of Newcastle. Purchased 1956 (Emily Driscoll catalogue 16, no 240). NRA 18661.

[u] Corresp of the Hon Henry Pelham rel mainly to Cornish borough politics 1746-54.

Royal Institution of Cornwall (BRA A.437). Given by Farrer & Co, solicitors, London, through the British Records Association 1942. NRA 38757.

[v] Political, personal and family corresp and papers of the 5th Duke of Newcastle 1822-64, with trusteeship corresp and papers of WE Gladstone *c*1849-85 and estate accounts 1862-74.

St Deiniol's Library, Hawarden (Glynne-Gladstone MSS 2927-3028). Deposited by Sir William Gladstone, Bt 1968. CJ Williams, *Handlist of the Glynne-Gladstone MSS in St Deiniol's Library, Hawarden*, List and Index Society, special series vol 24, 1990. NRA 14174.

[w] Letters to the 5th Duke from WE Gladstone 1832-63.

British Library, Manuscript Collections (Add MSS 44262-3). Acquired from the Gladstone Trustees 1935.

[x] Naval MSS 17th-18th cent, collected by the 4th Duke.

National Maritime Museum (CLU). Acquired from the Clumber House library by Sir James Caird 1938 (Sotheby's, 14-16 Feb, lots 1236-7, 1250-7). *Guide to the Manuscripts in the National Maritime Museum*, vol 2, 1980, pp86-7.

Related collections: Pelham, Earls of Chichester, no 80; Cavendish-Bentinck, Dukes of Portland, no 18; Earl Sydney (papers dispersed by sales), including correspondence of Henry Pelham relating to Jamaica and the Netherlands 1740s (National Library of Jamaica; Yale University, Beinecke Library, Osborn MSS 48); Watson of Rockingham (Northamptonshire Record Office, NRA 25867), including papers relating to Henry Pelham's estates (Lady Sondes a co-heir) mainly 1728-87, and a rental of the Duke of Newcastle's Dorset estate 1732-45; Barons Monson (Lincolnshire Archives MON, *Archivists' Report 3*, 1951-2, p30), including trusteeship papers 1738-69 (Duke of Newcastle's debts).

[82] PERCY, Dukes of Northumberland

The Percy family was established in the North Riding of Yorkshire (Topcliffe, etc) and elsewhere in the eleventh century. Petworth (Sussex) was acquired *c*1150, and Leconfield (Yorkshire, East Riding) *c*1240. Henry, first Lord Percy, purchased the barony of Alnwick (Northumberland) in 1309, and his son had a grant of the reversion of Warkworth (Northumberland) in 1329.

The fourth Lord Percy was created Earl of Northumberland in 1377. In 1386 he married Maud, widow of Gilbert Umfraville, Earl of Angus, and sister of Lord Lucy of Egremont, through whom estates in Northumberland (Prudhoe, *ex* Umfraville), Cumberland (Cockermouth, Egremont, Allerdale), the East Riding of Yorkshire (Wressell) and elsewhere came to the Percy family. The third Earl (1421-61) married Eleanor Poynings, who brought properties in the west of England and Wales descending from the Poynings, Fitzpaine and Bryan families, including Haselbury Bryan (Dorset), Stogursey (Somerset) and Laugharne (Carmarthenshire).

The sixth Earl made over his estates to the Crown shortly before he died in 1537, but they were mostly restored to his nephew and successor in 1557. The eighth earl married *c*1562 a daughter and co-heir of John Neville, Lord Latimer, bringing the estate of Burton Latimer (Northamptonshire) and other valuable properties into the family. The ninth Earl (1564-1632) acquired the freehold of Syon and Isleworth (Middlesex) in 1603-4, to which other Middlesex properties (East Bedfont and Hatton) were added from 1656. The tenth Earl (1602-68) acquired Northumberland House in the Strand (London) at the time of his marriage to Elizabeth, daughter of the second Earl of Suffolk, in 1642.

Some outlying properties were sold in the late seventeenth century, but the principal Percy estates (Petworth, etc in Sussex, Alnwick, Warkworth, Prudhoe, etc in Northumberland, Leconfield and Wressell in the East Riding of Yorkshire, Topcliffe and Catton in the North Riding, Spofforth and Tadcaster in the West Riding, Cockermouth, Egremont, etc in Cumberland, Syon in Middlesex and Northumberland House) passed on the death of the eleventh Earl in 1670 to his daughter Elizabeth, who in 1682 married Charles Seymour, sixth Duke of Somerset (d1748). On the death of their son the seventh Duke in 1750 the dukedom passed to the male heir (see Seymour, Dukes of Somerset, no 92), but the Seymour and Percy estates were divided. The Seymour estates were inherited by co-heirs (see Manners, Dukes of Rutland, no 68, Wyndham of Orchard Wyndham, no 118). Of the Percy estates, those in Cumberland, Yorkshire and Sussex passed to a nephew of the seventh Duke, Sir Charles Wyndham (see Wyndham, Barons Leconfield, no 117). The Northumberland and Middlesex estates, however, passed to the seventh Duke's daughter Elizabeth, who in 1740 had married Sir Hugh Smithson, fourth Bt. The Smithson family had estates in the North Riding of Yorkshire (Stanwick, etc), County Durham (Darlington), Middlesex (Tottenham) and London. Sir Hugh Smithson succeeded by special remainder to the Earldom of Northumberland and was created Duke of Northumberland in 1766.

The Werrington (Devon and Cornwall) estate was purchased in 1775 and sold in 1864. On the death of the fourth Duke without issue in 1865 he was succeeded by his cousin the second Earl of Beverley (whose father, second son of the first Duke, had been created Earl of Beverley in 1790: the family had property at Airmyn, in the West Riding of Yorkshire, derived from the Smithsons, and the parliamentary borough of Bere Alston in Devon). The sixth Duke (1810-99) married in 1845 Louisa, daughter and co-heir of Henry Drummond of Albury (Surrey).

Estates in 1883: Duke of Northumberland: Northumberland 181,616 acres, Surrey 3,765 acres, Middlesex 882 acres, Co Durham 134 acres, total 186,397 acres worth £176,048 a year; Dowager Duchess: Yorks NR 5,683 acres (the Stanwick estate) worth £8,320 a year.

[a] Deeds for Northumberland 12th-20th cent, Middlesex (Syon and Westminster estates) 16th-19th cent and Surrey 16th-20th cent; deeds for Smithson estates in Middlesex (Tottenham) and London 16th-20th cent; deeds for Percy estates in Yorks ER, NR and WR, Cumberland and Sussex 13th-18th cent, and for other alienated estates (Percy, Poynings, Latimer, etc) in various counties 13th-17th cent; deeds for Seymour properties (Somerset, Wilts, etc) 13th-18th cent; general deeds, grants, acts, etc rel to the acquisition, forfeiture and restoration of estates 14th-17th cent; inquisitions, licences, etc mainly 16th-17th cent; abstracts, schedules, etc 14th-19th cent, incl Percy cartulary 14th cent; settlements and wills mainly 15th-19th cent, Percy, Seymour and Smithson; mortgages, bonds, grants of annuity, etc 17th-19th cent; legal and case papers 14th-20th cent, mainly 16th cent onwards, incl papers from London solicitors 19th-20th cent; manorial court records, Northumberland 15th-20th cent, incl Alnwick manor, borough and barony and Wark manor, borough and barony, and other counties 13th-18th cent, incl Devon (Slapton) 15th-16th cent, Dorset (Haselbury Bryan) 16th cent, Lincs 14th-16th cent, Somerset (Cary Fitzpaine, Isle Abbots, etc) 15th-18th cent, Wilts (Pewsey, Trowbridge, etc) 14th-18th cent and Yorks (Catton, Pocklington, Topcliffe, etc) 15th-17th cent.

General estate records (Northumberland, Cumberland, Yorks ER and NR, Sussex, Dorset, Somerset, Wilts, etc) late 15th-mid-18th cent, incl valuations, surveys, rentals and accounts; appointments of receivers, commissioners, stewards, etc 16th-19th cent; Northumberland estate records 15th-20th cent, incl leases and related papers from late 16th cent, lease registers from 1615, agreements from *c*1800, surveys and rentals from 15th cent, maps and plans from late 16th cent, corresp from late 16th cent, petitions from tenants, and letters and papers rel to mines, quarries, collieries, enclosure, boundaries, woods and forests, mills, fisheries, water supply and schools; Thirston (Northumberland) glass clay accounts 1695-1719, 1767, 1777; Middlesex (Syon and Westminster) estate records 15th-20th cent, incl leases, surveys and valuations, maps from 1607, rentals, accounts and enclosure papers; Devon and Cornwall estate records c1770-1865, incl leases, valuations, plans, rentals, accounts, corresp and papers; Surrey estate records early 18th-20th cent, incl surveys, maps, accounts and misc papers; Yorks NR (Stanwick estate) and Co Durham estate records 17th-20th cent, incl maps and plans 18th-19th cent, valuations 18th-19th cent, rentals and accounts from 1690s and corresp and papers mainly 19th-20th cent; misc Tottenham, Bere Alston and Airmyn estate records 16th-19th cent; Sussex, Cumberland and Yorks estate records mainly 16th-mid-18th cent, incl leases, surveys, maps, rentals, accounts and papers; misc Seymour estate papers mid-16th-mid-18th cent, incl papers rel to Marlborough (Wilts); misc records rel to former Percy estates in Cornwall, Devon, Dorset, Lincs, Norfolk, Somerset and elsewhere 14th-18th cent; papers rel to estates in South Wales 15th-early 18th cent, incl leases, rentals and accounts, and to the Thomond estates in Ireland c1606-1706.

Drawings, accounts and papers rel to Alnwick Castle 17th-19th cent, incl restoration 19th cent, Syon House 17th-19th cent, incl Adam drawings, Northumberland House (London) 17th-19th cent, Werrington House 18th-19th cent and Stanwick Hall (building papers 1839-46); inventories, catalogues, etc late 16th-19th cent, incl Alnwick from 18th cent, Syon from 1592 and Northumberland House 18th-19th cent; household accounts 16th-20th cent, incl general accounts 1564-1686, etc, Syon House and garden from 17th cent, Alnwick Castle, Northumberland House 17th-19th cent and Werrington 18th-19th cent; misc Petworth inventories, accounts and papers 1592-mid-18th cent; Wressell Castle (Yorks ER) repair account 1602-3; household accounts for Striguil (Monmouthshire) 14th cent and Snape (Yorks NR) 1496-8; inventories for Carew (Pembrokeshire) 1601 and Somerhill (Kent) 1646, Earls of Essex; papers rel to local affairs 13th-20th cent, incl Northumberland shrievalty roll 1427-8, Northumberland lieutenancy, militia and vice-admiralty papers mainly 18th-19th cent, papers rel to Middlesex militia and volunteers, and election papers for Northumberland, Middlesex, Devon and Cornwall 18th-19th cent.

Patents, grants, commissions, etc, Percy 16th-20th cent and Seymour 17th cent; Percy family papers 14th-20th cent, incl accounts and corresp of the 9th Earl of Northumberland, Admiralty and other papers of the 10th Earl, papers of the 1st Duke as Lord Lieutenant of Ireland 1763-5, political and military papers of the 2nd Duke, and papers of the 3rd Duke as Lord Lieutenant of Ireland 1828-31; estate corresp of the Percy family from late 16th cent; papers of the Earls of Beverley early 19th cent; papers of the 2nd Baron Seymour of Trowbridge (d1665) and of the 5th, 6th and 7th Dukes of Somerset 1673-1750; letter book of the 1st Earl of Hertford as lord lieutenant of Wilts and Somerset 1604-6; Fitzjames family of Leweston (Dorset) (ancestors of Frances Thynne, wife of the 7th Duke of Somerset), papers 17th cent; political and religious corresp and papers of Henry Drummond 1809-60; papers of Sir John Perrott (d1592, Lord Deputy of Ireland) and his son Sir Thomas Perrott (first husband of Dorothy Devereux, later wife of the 9th Earl of Northumberland); notebook of Thomas Thynne, Viscount Weymouth c1667-74; papers rel to the Earl of Bedford's estates (Covent Garden, Thorney, etc) ?17th cent; pedigrees and genealogical papers; other papers 14th-19th cent, incl Tynemouth Priory (Northumberland) register 14th cent, Exeter archdeaconry court book 1537-40, commonplace book of Sir Robert Catlin (d1574), Star Chamber papers early 17th cent, book of privy seals delivered to Sir John Swinnerton 1611-12, diplomatic letter book of Sir Isaac Wake 1631-2, Breda letter book of Henry Coventry 1667, collections of Bishop Percy of Dromore 18th cent, letters of the 2nd Duke of Northumberland to the 1st Viscount Exmouth and Lord Strangford early 19th cent, collections rel to the history of Northumberland, and literary and liturgical MSS.

In private possession. Enquiries to the Archivist, Alnwick Castle, Northumberland. Intending readers should consult the *Guide to Searchers* (copy available at the Commission). Uncatalogued papers and papers less than one hundred years old are not available for research. HMC *Third Report, App*, 1872, pp45-125; *Sixth Report, App*, 1877, pp221-33; *Papers of British Cabinet Ministers 1782-1900*, 1982, pp48-9; *Papers of British Politicians 1782-1900*, 1989, p83. NRA 836 (partial lists).

[b] Maps of Northumberland estates c1766-late 19th cent, with valuations and other papers; Rothbury (Northumberland) rentals 1720.

Keep and Black Gate Museum, Newcastle-upon-Tyne (Society of Antiquaries of Newcastle-upon-Tyne, Bell collection, incl papers of John Thompson, John Bell and Thomas Bell, surveyors). NRA 7878.

[c] Further Northumberland estate maps by John and Thomas Bell 19th cent.

Northumberland Record Office (ZGI). Deposited by Sir William Gibson 1960. NRA 7878.

[d] Agency papers 19th cent, mainly Alnwick, Alnmouth and Warkworth (Northumberland), incl draft maps, valuations and corresp, with schedule of vacant farms on the Northumberland estates 1847-76.

Northumberland Record Office (Bell collection, ZHE). Deposited by WP Hedley. NRA 7878.

[e] Collections for the history of Northumberland by John and Thomas Bell (*c*214 vols).

Northumberland Record Office. Purchased by the 4th Duke of Northumberland after Thomas Bell's death in 1860. Deposited by the 10th Duke in Newcastle University Library 1964 and transferred to the record office 1968.

[f] Tynemouth agent's corresp 1831-69.

Tyne and Wear Archives Service (Acc 2561). HMC *Accessions to Repositories 1991*.

[g] Manorial records, Isleworth Syon 1279-1937, East Bedfont with Hatton 1381-1936.

London Metropolitan Archives (Acc/1379). Deposited from Syon House by the 10th Duke of Northumberland 1977. NRA 41249.

[h] Westminster estate terrier 1828; rentals and accounts, Middlesex estates 1773-1880.

Hounslow Library Service. NRA 13857.

[i] Surrey manorial records (Albury, Haldersh, Weston Gumshalve) *c*1390-1932.

Surrey History Centre (1322). Deposited from Syon House by Earl Percy 1977.

[j] Marriage settlement, Lord Lovaine and Louisa Drummond 1845.

Surrey History Centre (1568). Deposited by Boodle, Hatfield, solicitors, London 1988. NRA 29445.

[k] Plan of Airmyn estate 1815.

West Yorkshire Archives Service, Yorkshire Archaeological Society, Leeds (MS 662). *Guide*, 1985, p75.

[l] Garthorpe (Lincs: Earl of Beverley) deeds and abstracts 1614-19th cent and maps 1783, 1822.

Lincolnshire Archives (Misc Dep 530). HMC *Accessions to Repositories 1989*.

[m] Household and personal vouchers of Charlotte, Duchess of Northumberland 1856-65.

Bodleian Library, Oxford (MS Johnson e. 1).

[n] Corresp and papers of the Seymour family, Barons Seymour of Trowbridge, with some papers of the Earls and Marquesses of Hertford, mainly 17th cent.

British Library, Manuscript Collections (Add MS 32324). Part of the collection of Thomas Percy, Bishop of Dromore.

[o] Letter books of Henry Coventry as Secretary of State 1672-80 (9 vols); copies of papers rel to the Board of Trade 1660-2 and to the East India Company 1667-9.

British Library, Manuscript Collections (Add MSS 25115-25). Presented by the 4th Duke of Northumberland 1863.

[p] Letter book of Frances, Duchess of Somerset (wife of the 7th Duke).

Birmingham University Information Services, Special Collections Department (13/i/20). NRA 32504.

[q] Sherborne missal *c*1400.

British Library, Manuscript Collections (Add MS 74236). Deposited by the 10th Duke of Northumberland. Accepted for the nation in lieu of tax and allocated to the Library 1998. HMC *Third Report, App*, 1872, p112.

Related collections: Wyndham, Barons Leconfield and Egremont, no 117; Manners, Dukes of Rutland, no 68, and Wyndham of Orchard Wyndham, no 118, including further estate papers 17th-mid-18th cent relating to the Seymour family, Barons Seymour of Trowbridge and the 5th-7th Dukes of Somerset; Slingsby of Scriven (West Yorkshire Archive Service, Yorkshire Archaeological Society, Leeds DD 211, NRA 12891), including a Northumberland, etc rental 1599; Peel of Bryn-y-Pys (Flintshire Record Office D/BP, NRA 26972), including papers of Charlotte, Duchess of Northumberland *c*1825-66.

[83] PETRE, Barons Petre

Sir William Petre, principal Secretary of State 1543-66, and his son John (1549-1613), created Baron Petre 1603, acquired extensive estates in Essex and Devon, including much former monastic property and Crown lands such as the former de Bohun manor of Writtle (Essex). The Essex estate, centred on Ingatestone Hall and Thorndon Hall (bought from the Mordaunt family in the sixteenth century), was retained, with property at Asheldham and Dengie being added in the 1830s, but the Devon, Somerset, and Gloucestershire properties, administered as the 'western estate', were sold *c*1780-1826.

Estates in Lancashire (Dunkenhalgh) and the East Riding of Yorkshire (Selby Abbey) were acquired through the marriage in 1712 of the seventh Baron and Catherine Walmesley (d1788), sister and eventual heir of Francis Walmesley of Dunkenhalgh. The Selby Abbey estate was disposed of in the mid-nineteenth century, while the Dunkenhalgh estate passed to the descendants of George William Petre, brother of the tenth Baron (1763-1809).

Estates in 1883: Essex 19,085 acres worth £22,595 a year.

[a] Essex deeds 12th-20th cent, mainly pre-1700, with misc deeds for other counties incl South Brent (Devon) charter 962; wills, settlements, executorship and trust papers 15th-20th cent, incl some for families of Clifford of Irnham (Lincs), Heneage of Hainton (Lincs) and Howard of Buckenham (Norfolk) 18th-19th cent; inquisitions *post mortem* for the 2nd Baron Petre (d1637); legal papers 15th-19th cent, incl register of deeds and surveys c1565-1602, sequestration papers c1645-57, recusancy papers from 17th cent and papers rel to the Radcliffe family, Earls of Derwentwater c1680-1740; extensive Essex manorial records 13th-20th cent, incl Ingatestone 1279-1937 (with other Barking Abbey lands 1470-1540), Writtle 1379-1938 (with other Bohun, later Buckingham, lands 1421-1522), Rayleigh honour 1373 and Waltham Abbey manors 1456.

Essex estate records 15th-20th cent, incl leases, lease books, surveys, maps, rentals and valuations 16th-19th cent, agents' accounts from 18th cent, estate sale and purchase accounts 1766-92, other accounts from 15th cent, and papers rel to tithes 17th-19th cent, enclosures and Billericay fairs and markets 18th-19th cent, and railways 19th-20th cent; valuations, accounts and papers for western and other Petre estates 16th-19th cent, incl Whittlesey (Cambs) valuation c1725, Lancs and Yorks rentals and accounts 1792-1800, Chertsey (Surrey) farm accounts 1802-19 and Devon estate corresp 1810-22; estate papers for the Heneage family of Hainton 1740-91 and Clifford family of Irnham 19th cent (incl rentals and accounts 1849-91); Buckenham estate accounts 1801-14; Yorks ER estate accounts (Charles Stourton Walmesley) 1741-2; rental of the Craven estate (Earl of Thanet) 1820.

House building records 17th-19th cent and household inventories and accounts 16th-19th cent, mainly Thorndon, Ingatestone and London; Thorndon Chapel rule book 1741; Howard of Buckenham and Heneage of Hainton household papers c1721-84; plans for the Duke of Norfolk's Worksop (Notts) house and garden c1737-8; Essex subsidy book 1587-1625 and Essex taxation and shrievalty papers of the 1st Baron Petre 1576-92; tax records, Writtle 1490-1667 and West Horndon c1512; Essex and Writtle forest papers 17th cent, with estreat roll 1458; records rel to Chelmsford Grammar School 1386-1678 and Ingatestone almhouses 1563-1897; other papers rel to Essex affairs from 15th cent, incl accounts of the Treasurer for Charitable Uses (Eastern Division) 1686-8, turnpike papers 18th-19th cent and Ingatestone parish accounts 1813-14; Woburn Park (Surrey) and Northwood Park (Isle of Wight) schools accounts 1877-85; papers rel to the Oxford colleges of All Souls

1557-94, Exeter 1565-1830 and Wadham 1604-15.

Personal inventories of John, Lord Mordaunt 1562, 1571 and Thomas, Earl of Sussex 1583; appointments, commissions, financial, family and religious papers 16th-19th cent, Petre family; papers of Sir William Petre (d1572), incl law books and papers rel to dissolved religious houses; papers of Alexander Geddes (1737-1802), biblical critic, of Canon CT Kuypers (Lord Petre's archivist) c1910-38 and of Henry William Clifford 1844-58; misc Radcliffe family papers 17th-18th cent, incl letters of the 3rd Earl of Derwentwater (executed 1716); genealogical and misc papers 15th-20th cent, incl Thoby Priory (Essex) decimary c1350, Wilts hundreds estreat roll 1471 and MS 'Answer' of the English regulars to the Bishop of Chalcedon 1629.

Essex Record Office (D/DP). Deposited by the 17th Baron Petre and through Collyer, Bristow & Co, solicitors 1938-85, by Miss M Petre 1956, and by P F Coverdale 1955. *Guide to the Essex Record Office*, 1969, pp 99-108. NRA 23544.

[b] Misc Essex deeds and papers 1597-1848, incl will of Lady Mary Petre of Bellhouse 1747 and Ingatestone household accounts 1713-1819.

Essex Record Office (D/DZf). Some of these items were transferred from Lancashire Record Office 1940-52 and some deposited on permanent loan from the Petre of Dunkenhalgh collection in Lancashire Record Office 1954.

[c] Deeds 12th-early 19th cent, mainly Devon (South Brent and Axminster estates) but incl some for Somerset; misc legal and trust papers 16th-19th cent; manorial records 1353-1685, mostly Devon (South Brent, Churchstow, Kingsbridge, etc), with a few for Somerset 16th cent; leases, lease books, surveys, maps, valuations, rentals, accounts and misc estate papers 16th-19th cent, mainly Devon but incl leases, surveys and accounts for all the western estates 16th-18th cent; Shute (Devon) household inventories 16th cent; rental and accounts of Montacute Priory 1537-8; Athelney Priory rental and copy deeds late 15th cent (1 vol).

Devon Record Office (123 M). Deposited by the 17th Baron Petre 1953. A few leases were deposited later by the British Records Association (1437 M). NRA 9466.

[d] Estate records 12th-18th cent, mainly for the former Westminster Abbey manors of Todenham (Gloucs) and Sutton-under-Brailes (Warwicks), incl deeds 12th cent-1785, court rolls 1469-1774, map 1592-3, rentals, extents and surveys 13th-18th cent, account rolls 1723-1497 and misc legal and estate papers 16th-18th cent.

Gloucestershire Record Office (D 1099). Deposited by the 17th Baron Petre 1954, 1957. NRA 7002.

[e] Petre estate accounts 1639-40.

Cambridge University Library (Ee. III. 27). *Catalogue of Manuscripts*, 1980, II, p80.

[f] Deeds for Selby abbey, manor and town 12th-19th cent; survey, rentals and extents of Selby Abbey lands 1320-1, with Selby *cum membris* rentals 1617-9, 1727-8, Hillam (Yorks ER) accounts 1551-2 and wills and inventories of Selby residents 1636-1715.

British Library, Manuscript Collections (Add MSS 36579-82, Add Ch 45798-961). Purchased from Messrs Quaritch 1901.

[g] Manorial records for Selby *cum membris* 1377-1727, incl accounts of fines 1614-20; Monk Fryston (Yorks ER) rental 15th cent and accounts 1393-4; Selby Abbey timber accounts 1466-72 and domestic accounts 1362-1531, incl pittancer 1362 and bursar 1398-9; misc deeds and papers 12th-19th cent.

Hull University, Brynmor Jones Library (Se). Transferred 1993 on permanent loan from Westminster Diocesan Archives, which has no record of provenance or date of acquisition. NRA 35699.

[h] Account book of the 2nd Baron Petre 1597-1610.

Folger Shakespeare Library, Washington DC. Bought from Maggs 1928. S De Ricci and W J Wilson, *Census of Medieval and Renaissance Manuscripts in the United States and Canada*, repr 1961, i, p425.

[i] Accounts and papers of the 9th Baron Petre 1791-1800.

Public Record Office (E 192/19-20). NRA 30827.

[j] Corresp and papers of the 13th Baron Petre 1872-82.

Downside Abbey Archives. HMC *Papers of British Churchmen 1780-1940*, 1987, p61. NRA 19936.

Related collections: Axminster and South Brent deeds and papers 13th-19th cent, with papers of later owners *c*1826-1914 (Devon Record Office D 517, D 1466, 3841M, 4371M/E 1-2, DD 6800-7938, CR 716-881 and 49/26 (BRA 767), NRA 1563); Petre of Dunkenhalgh (Lancashire Record Office DDPE, NRA 6100); papers of Maude DM Petre (d1942) (British Library, Manuscript Collections Add MSS 44927-31, 45361-2, 45744-5, 52367-82); Earls of Londesborough (Hull University, Brynmor Jones Library DDLO, NRA 7254), including Selby Abbey monastic and estate papers.

[84] PIERREPONT, Earls Manvers

The Pierrepont family owned Holme Pierrepont in south Nottinghamshire by the early fourteenth century, and had acquired interests in Derbyshire by the fifteenth century. Sir Robert Pierrepont (1584-1643) married in 1601 Gertrude, granddaughter and eventual heir of Sir William Rayner of Orton Longueville (Huntingdonshire). He was created Earl of Kingston-upon-Hull in 1628, and acquired extensive estates in north Nottinghamshire (Thoresby, Laxton, etc), Derbyshire (Beighton, Calow, Oldcotes and Heath, from the Cavendish (Earls of Devonshire) and Foljambe families), Lincolnshire (Newball, Hagworthingham, Crowle, Hemingby, Langton-by-Wragby) and Yorkshire (Adwick upon Dearne and Wothersome in the West Riding, and Ingleby Arncliffe in the North Riding). On the death of the first Earl of Kingston in 1643 he was succeeded in the Holme Pierrepont and Orton Longueville estates by his eldest son Henry, who was created Marquess of Dorchester in 1645. Most of the first Earl's purchased estates, however, were settled on his second son William Pierrepont of Tong Castle (Shropshire) and later of Thoresby (d1679), who had married a daughter and co-heir of Sir Thomas Harris of Tong. William Pierrepont's eldest son Robert Pierrepont inherited the Thoresby and Lincolnshire estates, and also acquired the West Dean (Wiltshire and Hampshire) estate through his wife Elizabeth, daughter and heir of Sir John Evelyn (d1684), but the Derbyshire, Yorkshire and Shropshire properties were again left to younger sons.

The Marquess of Dorchester died without male issue in 1680, when he was succeeded as third Earl of Kingston by his great-nephew Robert Pierrepont, son of Robert and Elizabeth of Thoresby, thus re-uniting the Thoresby and Holme Pierrepont estates. The third Earl died in 1682, being succeeded in turn by his brother William as fourth Earl and, in 1690, by another brother Evelyn (c1665-1726) as fifth Earl. The fifth Earl inherited the Holme Pierrepont, Thoresby, Lincolnshire, Huntingdonshire and Wiltshire estates at his accession. He sold Orton Longueville in 1706, but inherited the Beighton and Adwick estates on the death of Samuel Pierrepont of Oldcotes in 1707, and the Shropshire and other Yorkshire estates (Ingleby Arncliffe, Rothwell (West Riding), etc), together with an estate at Hanslope (Buckinghamshire), on the death of his uncle Baron Pierrepont of Hanslape, in 1715. He was created Duke of Kingston-upon-Hull in 1715, and was succeeded in 1726 by his grandson Evelyn (1711-73), son of William Pierrepont (1692-1713) by Rachel, natural daughter and heir of John Hall of Bradford-on-Avon (Wiltshire) and Bath (Somerset).

During the eighteenth century the Yorkshire estates (except Adwick) were disposed of, as were Hanslope in 1763, Tong in 1764 and West Dean after 1773. The second Duke developed his Bath property, but this was sold in the early nineteenth century. The Lincolnshire, Derbyshire and Wiltshire (Bradford-on-Avon) estates, however, were not substantially reduced until the early twentieth century. In 1788, following the death of the second Duke's widow, his estates were inherited by his nephew Philip Medows, later Pierrepont (1737-1816), who was created Viscount Newark in 1796 and Earl Manvers in 1806.

The earlier deeds for the Holme Pierrepont estates have for the most part been lost. (For a fifteenth-century cartulary, however, see Cavendish-Bentinck, Dukes of Portland, no 18 [ll].) The medieval deeds and account rolls in the archive are mainly unconnected with Pierrepont properties, and may have been acquired by a member of the family at a later date. Some family papers may have been destroyed in a fire at Thoresby Hall in 1745.

Estates in 1883: Notts 26,771 acres, Lincs 5,010 acres, Derbys 3,729 acres, Wilts 1,500 acres, Yorks WR 1,026 acres, total 38,036 acres worth £51,649 a year, exclusive of mines and tithes.

[a] Deeds for Pierrepont properties in Notts, Derbys, Lincs, Wilts and Yorks WR late 12th or early 13th-19th cent (c200 medieval); deeds for Bucks and Hunts 13th-18th cent, and for Salop and Somerset 14th-18th cent (c100 medieval); deeds for other counties (many not Pierrepont family) 12th-18th cent (c300 medieval), incl Berks, Gloucs, Herefs, Herts, Kent, London, Middlesex, Northants, Oxon and Staffs; Pierrepont wills, settlements and related executorship and trust papers 16th-19th cent, incl minutes, accounts and papers for the minority of the 2nd Duke of Kingston 1726-35; trust papers, Hall family 16th-17th cent and Harris family 1611-20; legal and case papers 16th-19th cent, incl copies and inventories of deeds; manorial court records 14th-19th cent, Derbys, Lincs, Notts and Wilts, incl Beighton (Derbys), Bassingthorpe and Crowle (Lincs), Car Colston, Laxton, Orston, etc (Notts) and Bradford-on-Avon, etc (Wilts); manorial court rolls for other counties 14th-early 17th cent, many not Pierrepont family, incl Bucks (Beaconsfield, etc) and Herts (Royston, etc) 14th-15th cent, Kent (Bidborough, etc) 14th-early 17th cent, Staffs (Walsall) 1388-1460, Surrey (Charlwood, etc) 14th-16th cent, Warwicks (Aston, etc) 14th-15th cent, Worcs (Beoley, etc) and Yorks 14th-16th cent; Salford (Lancs) hundred roll 1556-7; Bedminster hundred (Somerset) account roll 1418-20.

Notts, Derbys, Lincs and Yorks estate records mainly 17th-mid 19th cent, incl surveys, rentals, accounts, Beighton colliery accounts 1815-25 and Yorks WR (Monk Bretton) timber valuation 1775; misc estate records (surveys, rentals, etc) for Hunts (Orton Longueville) 16th-17th cent,

Somerset and Wilts (Bath, Bradford-on-Avon, etc) 16th-early 19th cent, and Bucks (Hanslope) and Salop (Tong) mainly 17th-18th cent; misc estate accounts and other records 13th-15th cent, not Pierrepont family, incl Haslebury Bryan (Dorset: Poynings) accounts 1438-9, Poynings lands in Norfolk and Suffolk (copies of deeds 1269-1352), estates of the Mortimer Earls of March (Herefs, etc) 14th-15th cent, Earls of Warwick receivers' accounts (Warwicks, etc) 1396-1436, estates of the De La Pole Earls of Suffolk (Essex, Norfolk and Suffolk) 1403-54, and estates of the Dukes of York 1411-53; account of Sir Robert Smirke for Manvers house in Portman Square (London) 1827; Thoresby Park household accounts 1788-1859; Tong Castle inventories 1726-46; inventories of plate, etc 1726-55 (2nd Duke); Orton Longueville inventories 1568, 1576; shrievalty papers, Notts, Salop and Wilts 17th cent; papers rel to Sherwood Forest (Notts) 17th-18th cent; Trowbridge (Wilts) rate roll 1708-9.

Pierrepont patents, commissions, etc 17th-18th cent; commonplace books, Sir William Rayner late 16th cent and Hon William Pierrepont 17th cent; papers of the 1st Duke of Kingston as Lord Privy Seal 1715-25; accounts for the 2nd Duke's regiment of horse 1745-50; misc and literary papers 14th-19th cent; household accounts, 4th Earl of March 1393-4 and 3rd Duke of York *temp* Henry VI; Forest of Dean (Gloucs) amercement roll 1604-5; Cardiganshire and Carmarthenshire receipt rolls 1387-8.

British Library, Manuscript Collections (Eg Ch 2301-8836, Eg MSS 3516-3660). Acquired from Thoresby Park 1942 and incorporated 1948. HMC *Ninth Report, App, Part II*, 1884, pp375-9.

[b] Beaconsfield, etc deeds 13th-18th cent; Laxton (Notts) survey and terrier 1635.

Bodleian Library, Oxford (MSS Ch. Bucks. 882-1318, Derbys. 55-6, Gloucs. 168, Kent 433, Northants. 49, Somerset 70; MS Maps c. 5, 19 (1); MSS Top. Notts. c. 2). Acquired from Thoresby Park 1942.

[c] Misc Derbys, Lincs, Notts, Wilts and Yorks deeds 17th-20th cent (mainly 19th-20th cent); settlements and trust papers, mainly Pierrepont 18th-20th cent, incl accounts 1726-34 (minority of 2nd Duke) and accounts and papers 1926-40 (5th Earl); legal papers mainly 19th-20th cent; manorial court records and related papers, Notts (Laxton, etc) 17th-20th cent, Derbys (Calow and Oldcotes) 18th-19th cent and Lincs (Crowle) 16th-20th cent.

Notts (Thoresby and Holme Pierrepont), Derbys and Lincs estate records 17th-20th cent (extensive), incl surveys and valuations, maps, rentals, accounts, corresp, and papers rel to enclosure, tithes, timber and sales; Yorks estate records 17th-20th cent, mainly Adwick upon Dearne from early 18th cent but incl Wothersome and Ingleby Arncliffe rentals and accounts late 17th-mid-18th cent and Rothwell, etc rentals and accounts c1723-45; Notts, Derbys and Yorks colliery accounts and papers 18th-20th cent; rentals, accounts, etc rel to Hanslope c1703-63, Tong c1715-64 and West Dean, etc late 17th-mid-18th cent; Wilts and Somerset (*ex* Hall family) estate records 18th-early 20th cent, incl papers rel to the Abbey Baths at Bath 1759-1814; survey of the Duke of Newcastle's estates 1676, with Welbeck rental 1703; misc English and Welsh estate accounts 14th-16th cent, not Pierrepont family, incl Ellingham Parva (Norfolk) 1342-55, Shere and Vachery (Surrey) 1351-2, 1362-3, 1441-3, Norwich bishopric estates in Norfolk and Suffolk 1519-20, 1524-5 and Talgarth and Dinas Castle (Breconshire) 1359-61.

Papers rel to Thoresby Park 18th-20th cent, incl drawings c1808 and accounts 1766-72 for house by John Carr of York, drawings and accounts for house by Anthony Salvin 1864-75, inventories and household accounts; household accounts, Morton House 1660-6 and Hanslope, Arlington St (London), etc 18th cent; Budby, Perlethorpe and Edwinstowe (Notts) parochial records 18th-20th cent; Edwinstowe Co-operative Society account book 1895-1913; Rufford Hunt records 1902-35; misc Pierrepont family papers 18th-20th cent, incl personal accounts of the 2nd Duke 1733-68 and game books 1861-1914; papers of the Franquetot family, Counts and Dukes de Coigny 15th-19th cent (inherited by the wife of the 3rd Earl); misc papers c1400-20th cent, incl London household accounts of Thomas Mortimer c1400, Exmoor forest accounts c1400 and letter book of Sir William Gifford as governor of Greenwich Hospital 1711 (reused as an estate account book).

Nottingham University Library, Department of Manuscripts and Special Collections (Ma). Given by the 6th Earl Manvers 1948 and deposited by the Manvers Trustees 1958-93. HMC *Accessions to Repositories 1985, 1986, 1989, 1993.* NRA 3707 (partial list).

[d] Notts manorial court records (Edwinstowe, Holme Pierrepont, Orston, etc) 16th-20th cent; leases of Edwinstowe tithes 1816-84.

Nottinghamshire Archives (DDT). Deposited by Tallents & Co, solicitors, Newark 1951-65. NRA 5838.

[e] Crowle manorial court records 1310-1949.

Lincolnshire Archives (Crowle Manor). Deposited by Tallents & Co, solicitors, Newark 1951-2. NRA 20508.

[f] Deeds and papers rel to Hants estate (Broughton, etc) 1676-1752, with abstracts of title rel to Notts and other estates.

Public Record Office (C 107/161, Kingston *v* Shute).

[g] Drawings and papers rel to Thoresby Park, lake and grounds 1740-72.

British Architectural Library. Acquired 1969. NRA 13619.

Related Collections: Cavendish-Bentinck, Dukes of Portland, no18; Barons Monson (Lincolnshire Archives MON and in private possession, NRA 7153 and Lincolnshire *Archivists' Report 3*, 1951-2, pp29-30), including Kingston trusteeship papers 1725-45.

[85] PLEYDELL-BOUVERIE, Earls of Radnor

The Des Bouveries (afterwards Bouverie) family was settled in Kent in the sixteenth century and bought Folkestone (Kent) from Sir Basil Dixwell in 1697. Sir William Des Bouveries, son of the eminent Turkey merchant Sir Edward Des Bouveries (d1694), was created a baronet in 1714, his son Sir Jacob Des Bouveries raised to the peerage as Viscount Folkestone in 1747, and his grandson William (1725-76) created Earl of Radnor in 1765. Property in London (mainly Whitefriars) was acquired in the late seventeenth century and an estate at Southampton Buildings, Holborn (Middlesex) bought from the second Duke of Montagu in 1734.

Extensive estates in Wiltshire were acquired from the late seventeenth century, including Longford Castle near Salisbury from the second Baron Coleraine. Property formerly belonging to Sir Giles Hungerford was purchased in 1718 from the second Baron Lexinton, to whom it had passed through his marriage to Hungerford's daughter, Mary (d1703). This included Corsham, Coulston and Stanton St Quintin (Wiltshire) and Pucklechurch (Gloucestershire). By the marriage of the second Earl (1750-1828) to Anne, daughter and heir of Anthony Duncombe (d1763), Baron Feversham of Downton (Wiltshire), further Wiltshire estates (Downton, Urchfort, etc) were acquired, together with property, subsequently disposed of, in other counties. The Wiltshire properties were extended by piecemeal purchases in the eighteenth and nineteenth centuries.

Estates in Berkshire (Coleshill, Shrivenham and Watchfield), Gloucestershire (Duntisborne Abbots, Ampney Crucis) and Wiltshire (Lyneham, etc) passed to the second Earl in 1768 from his maternal grandfather Sir Mark-Stuart Pleydell, who had inherited Pleydell family property from his grandfather Thomas Pleydell of Shrivenham and the Coleshill estate from his grandmother Mary Pleydell, heiress of Sir Henry Pratt (who had purchased Coleshill in 1626). A Barbados sugar plantation and an estate in Ermington (Devon), inherited by Sir Mark-Stuart Pleydell's wife Mary from Colonel Robert Steuart, were apparently sold in the late eighteenth century.

In 1889 the Coleshill (Berkshire) estate, which had previously descended with the other family property, devolved upon Duncombe Pleydell-Bouverie, brother of the fifth Earl; it was sold at the end of the Second World War. The Delapré Abbey (Northamptonshire) estate, acquired with property in East and West Ham (Essex) by the first Viscount Folkestone's marriage to Mary, heir of Bartholomew Clarke (died 1746), descended to a younger brother of the first Earl. (The records of the Hungerford family of Farleigh Hungerford (Somerset) included in the collection are thought to have passed to the Earl of Radnor through the St John-Mildmay family of Dogmersfield (Hampshire), the third Earl having married Anne St John-Mildmay in 1814.)

Estates in 1883: Wilts 17,000 acres, Berks 4,334 acres, Kent 3,266 acres, Gloucs 270 acres, total 24,870 acres worth £42,900 a year. (The metropolitan property is excluded.)

[a] Deeds 13th-20th cent, incl Wilts 15th-20th cent, Gloucs and Middlesex 16th-19th cent, Essex 14th-17th cent, Hants 1270, 1597-1674 and Kent 19th cent, with some for Devon, Dorset, Northants, etc; schedules of deeds and abstracts of title 17th-20th cent; wills, settlements, executorship and trust papers 17th-20th cent, Bouverie, Duncombe and Mildmay families, with trust papers of the Holman family of Weston Favell (Northants) 1659-1711, the 8th Baron Napier 1764-1824 and Anna, Lady Methuen 1858-60; legal and financial papers 16th-19th cent, incl register of Berks land tax assessments 1791; Wilts manorial and hundred records 14th-20th cent, incl Alderbury, Coombe Bissett and Downton manor and hundred; misc Pucklechurch manorial records 16th-17th cent.

Wilts and Gloucs estate records 16th-20th cent, incl leases (Wilts from 16th cent, Gloucs 18th-19th cent), maps, plans, valuations, surveys, rentals, accounts and vouchers, Downton estate diary c1681-94 and mill repair accounts 1707-29, papers rel to Alderbury and Downton water meadows c1665-1809, and accounts for surveying and map making 1809-14; Longford farm valuations 1753-1828 and accounts 1891-1900; records of Downton Home Industries 1908-25; Coleshill estate accounts c1737-1838; Whitefriars and Holborn estate papers 17th-20th cent, incl leases, plans 1668, 1730, particulars 1695 and accounts c1698-1751, 1890-1938; Folkestone estate papers 18th-20th cent, incl leases; receipts for East and West Ham 16th cent; accounts and papers for the former estates of Lord Feversham in Bucks, Hunts, Leics, etc c1744-19th cent; Coulsdon (Surrey) plan 19th cent and Hambledon (Surrey) field book 1763; rent book, Holman family of Weston Favell

(Northants) 1704; volume of steward's instructions for the Sherborne (Dorset) estate of Sir Joseph Ashe 1672; papers rel to Yorks property of Launcelot Blackburn, Archbishop of York 1739-59.

Misc Longford household papers 19th-20th cent, incl vouchers 1820-30 and wages accounts 1890-1930; London household inventories and accounts 1807-29; Ivychurch House (Alderbury) plan 17th cent; architectural drawing for Coleshill 18th cent; Wilts election papers 1660-1834, mainly for Downton; papers rel to the recordership of Salisbury 1736-1829; misc Berks and Wilts quarter sessions papers 1786-1813; Downton parochial papers 17th-19th cent, incl churchwardens' accounts 1735-8 and church restoration papers 1817-19; papers rel to Downton and Lyneham schools 16th-19th cent and to Corsham charity school and almshouses 17th-19th cent; cash book, band of the 4th Wilts Regiment (Territorial Army) 1909-15.

Family papers 17th-20th cent, incl personal and mercantile account books (Bouverie family) c1638-early 18th cent, personal accounts of Anne, Countess of Radnor (d1829), family corresp of the 3rd Earl c1830 and letters of Frederick Pleydell-Bouverie, canon of Salisbury 1805-10; diaries of the 1st Baron Skelmersdale 1806-7; Pleydell pedigree book 18th cent; Hungerford family muniments 13th-17th cent, incl deeds (Berks, Somerset, Wilts, etc) from 13th cent, cartularies 1470, 16th cent and misc manorial records 16th-17th cent.

Wiltshire and Swindon Record Office (WRO 490, 1946). Deposited by the 8th Earl of Radnor 1972-87. HMC *Fifteenth Report, App X*, 1899, pp161-72; *Papers of British Politicians 1782-1900*, 1989, p85. NRA 17343.

[b] Executorship and trust papers late 19th cent-1930; Folkestone hundred court records 1784; Wilts and Gloucs estate papers 17th-20th cent, incl schedules, plans and valuations, with Downton memoranda books 17th-18th cent and Longford farm accounts c1929-47; Folkestone estate records 17th-20th cent, incl leases 1863-20th cent, maps 1782, 1798, surveys 1698-9, 1785 and letter book 1697-1716; London estate accounts 1732; drawings and papers rel to Longford Castle building 18th-20th cent, incl accounts 1792-1811 and architectural papers of Daniel Alexander, James Wyatt and Anthony Salvin; misc Longford household papers 18th-20th cent, incl cellar accounts 1769-77; plan of Longford park c1760-70; Coleshill household inventories 1869, 1874-5; wages accounts, Longford Castle, Coleshill and London 1869; architectural drawings and papers for Britford (Wilts) church 1765-6 and the restoration of the Hungerford Chapel in Salisbury Cathedral 1778; patents and appointments 17th-20th cent; valuation, personal estate of Sir William Des Bouveries 1717; family and business papers 17th-20th cent, incl corresp and papers of the

2nd Earl, diaries of the 3rd Earl 1839-63 and papers of the 6th and 7th Earls and Lady Radnor (d1929); Hungerford family letters 16th-17th cent; Clarke family papers mid-18th cent; genealogical and misc papers 17th-20th cent, incl Longford Castle history 17th cent, and fish and game books from 1841.

In private possession. Enquiries to Wiltshire and Swindon Record Office. HMC *Fifteenth Report, App X*, 1899, pp161-72; *Papers of British Politicians 1782-1900*, 1989, p84. NRA 38433.

[c] Downton manor and hundred court records 1496-1732; court books for Corston manor 1792-1833 and Lavington Dauntsey and Rectory manors 1800-77.

Wiltshire and Swindon Record Office (WRO 893). Purchased from Messrs Hofmann & Freeman 1973. NRA 17343.

[d] Surveys of the Earl of Radnor's estates 18th cent, 1810, *c*1820.

Wiltshire and Swindon Record Office (WRO 335/ 184, 1553/40,45). Deposited with other items in the Wiltshire Archaeological Society collections from 1946-7. NRA 1335.

[e] Copy charters for Salisbury *temp* James I-Anne, copied for 2nd Earl (1 vol), with related papers.

Wiltshire and Swindon Record Office. Presented by the 7th Earl to Salisbury Muniment Room 1959 and transferred 1982. HMC *Accessions to Repositories 1959.*

[f] Deeds 16th-19th cent, mainly Berks, Gloucs and Wilts but incl some for Devon, London and Middlesex, etc; legal and trust papers 17th-19th cent, incl executors' accounts for Sir Mark-Stuart Pleydell 1768-77 and trust papers for Colonel Robert Steuart early 18th cent; manorial records, Coleshill 1534-1818, Great and Little Coxwell (Berks) 1606-1914, and Duntisborne Abbots and Leer (Gloucs) 1746-65; leases and agreements, Berks, Gloucs and Wilts 17th-19th cent; extensive Berks and north Wilts estate records 17th-20th cent, incl terriers and maps 18th-20th cent, surveys, particulars, rentals, accounts and vouchers 17th-20th cent, timber and labour accounts from 1795, tax books 1703-61 and misc tithe papers (Great Coxwell, etc) 18th-19th cent; misc Gloucs estate papers 18th-19th cent, incl rental 1701 and Pucklechurch rentals and accounts 1840-68; misc Kent estate records 18th-19th cent, incl Sandgate surveyors' bills 1827-35 and Folkestone estate papers 1856-64; London rental 1675 and Holborn (Middlesex) estate papers 1841-58; papers rel to Ermington (Devon) and Barbados *c*1696-1739.

Coleshill house and garden plans 19th cent, with papers rel to alterations *c*1743-90 and house and stables building vouchers 1822-41;

Coleshill household inventories 1833-6, 1851, house and garden accounts and vouchers 18th-19th cent, and cellar books 1803-14; inventory of Longford and London plate 1836; papers rel to local affairs 17th-19th cent, incl Coleshill churchwardens' accounts 1658-77 and papers rel to Berks quarter sessions 1818-59, elections at Cricklade 1794, 1818 and New Sarum 1818, and Berks, Oxon and Wilts turnpikes late 18th-mid 19th cent; Hythe (Kent) election corresp 1838; misc patents and commissions 17th-19th cent; family accounts and papers 18th-19th cent, incl legal bills 1822-45 and accounts of charitable payments 1777-1865; papers of the 2nd and 3rd Earls; misc papers 18th-19th cent.

Berkshire Record Office (Acc 315, 337, 1167; D/ EPb). Deposited from Coleshill by Miss Kathleen Pleydell-Bouverie 1951, 1965 and by the National Trust 1951, 1992. HMC *Papers of British Politicians 1782-1900*, 1989, pp24-5. NRA 5476. Access to the records deposited in 1992 is restricted until they have been conserved and catalogued.

[g] Berks deeds 18th-19th cent; accounts of Coleshill building work 1814-15; Berks lieutenancy papers of the 2nd Earl 1794-1815; misc papers 18th-19th cent, incl Shrivenham plans *c*1810.

Berkshire Record Office (Acc 1578; D/ERa). Deposited by the 8th Earl of Radnor through Wiltshire Record Office 1971. HMC *Papers of British Politicians 1782-1900*, 1989, p84. NRA 5476.

[h] Survey book of Sir Mark-Stuart Pleydell's estates 1753.

Berkshire Record Office (D/EPb). Presented by George M Whiley Ltd, Ruislip, through the British Records Association 1963. NRA 5476.

[i] Marriage settlement 1883, Duncombe Pleydell-Bouverie, with related trust and other deeds 1883-1945.

Berkshire Record Office (D/EX 658). Deposited by Pettit & Westlake, solicitors, London 1982. NRA 5476.

[j] Kent deeds 1280-19th cent; misc deeds 16th-19th cent, mainly Wilts 1643-1773; wills, settlements and related papers 15th-18th cent, Herdson, Dixwell, Read, Lushington and Bouverie families, incl inquisitions *post mortem* for John Herdson 1622, 1626; executors' accounts 1760-1808, Baron Feversham, with accounts of fee farm rents 1789; legal papers 16th-18th cent, mainly rel to Folkestone barony and hundred; records of manors in Folkestone barony (Ackhanger, Folkestone, Terlingham, etc) and of Folkestone hundred 1402-19th cent; Bourne in Bishopsbourne (Kent) manorial accounts 1324-1425; Kent estate records 15th cent-1900, incl leases 1609-1844, maps 1625-98, terrier of Sir Basil Dixwell's estates 1636,

Folkestone survey c1810, particulars and rentals from 15th cent, accounts and vouchers from 18th cent, cash book 1717-54, letter book 1716-22, corresp 16th-19th cent and railway papers 1841-84; Southampton Buildings valuation 1734; Essex and London estate accounts 1690-1718; accounts of Sir Philip Boteler's estates in Gloucs and Herefs 1765-70; legal accounts of Sir Basil Dixwell c1631; accounts of St John's Hospital, Canterbury 1450-1; accounts 1410, rental 1509 and inventory and survey 1528-9 for the preceptory of Swingfield (Kent); misc papers 15th-19th cent, incl copies of Folkestone Priory charters c1425 (4) and catalogue of Folkestone (Radnor) muniments 1840.

Centre for Kentish Studies (U 270). Deposited by the 7th Earl of Radnor through Smith-Woolley & Co, surveyors and land agents, Folkestone 1950-3. NRA 4712. Eleven Kent deeds 18th-19th cent were transferred from Wiltshire Record Office in 1970 (Acc 1530, U 270 addnl).

[k] Misc Folkestone deeds and papers 1825-1935.

Centre for Kentish Studies (U 2982). Deposited by Boodle Hatfield, solicitors, London, through the British Records Association 1990. NRA 38490.

[l] Corresp of the 3rd Earl rel to his bill for the abolition of subscription to the Thirty-nine Articles at Oxford University 1834-5.

Pusey House Library, Oxford (RAD). Presented by EO Pleydell-Bouverie 1908. HMC *Papers of British Politicians 1782-1900*, 1989, p85. NRA 30608.

[m] Misc letters and papers of the 1st-5th Earls of Radnor 18th-19th cent (c32 items).

Wigan Archives Service (D/DZ EHC/Acc 1589). Presented 1972.

Related collections: Hungerford of Farleigh Hungerford estate surveys c1580-1613 (Wiltshire and Swindon Record Office WRO 442, NRA 17343), cartulary c1475 (Somerset Archive and Record Service DD/SAS/H348, NRA 28398) and deeds and papers 13th-18th cent (British Library, Manuscript Collections, Add Ch 40028-40140).

[86] POLE CAREW, later CAREW POLE, of Antony

The Carew family of Antony (Cornwall), created baronets 1641, was founded by Alexander Carew (d1492), fourth son of Sir Nicholas Carew of Carew Castle (Pembrokeshire), and had estates in east Cornwall at Torpoint, Sheviock (bought 1554), Saltash, and elsewhere, and in Devon (Drewsteignton) by the end of the

sixteenth century. The fifth Bt (d1744) married the daughter and heir of the fourth Earl of Coventry (d1719), whose estates, however, descended to a male cousin. After the death of the sixth Bt without issue in 1748, the Antony inheritance passed to his widow (d1766) and the baronetcy, shortly afterwards extinguished, to a cousin. The estates devolved briefly upon John Carew (d1771) of Camerton (Somerset), nephew of Thomas Carew (d1766) of Crowcombe (Somerset), before descending to Reginald Pole (d1835) of Stoke Damarel (Devon), a great-grandson of the third Bt, who adopted the surname Carew in 1772. The east Cornwall property was extended and concentrated around Antony, most of the property nearer Plymouth (Notter, Saltash, etc) and in Devon being alienated in the late eighteenth and early nineteenth century.

The Pole family was settled in Devon by the sixteenth century, and subsequently built up an estate centred on Shute (acquired from Sir William Petre in 1561), near Colyton. Further Devon property (Sidbury, etc) was gained by the marriage of Sir William Pole (d1635) to Mary, daughter and co-heir of Sir William Perriam. Their son Sir John Pole was created a baronet in 1628. Other property was acquired in Dorset (Broadwinsor, etc) and in Somerset, but was evidently disposed of before 1800. On the death of the eleventh Bt in 1926 the Pole baronetcy and estates were inherited by John Gawen Pole Carew of Antony, who took the surname Carew Pole. Shute House was given up before the Second World War, the muniments being transferred to Antony House, and the remaining property alienated by 1956.

The Buller family was established at Shillingham (Cornwall) by 1600. In the seventeenth century Sir Richard Buller acquired estates in London, Shropshire and Montgomeryshire, later sold, by marriage to Alice, co-heir of Sir John Hayward; King's Nympton (Devon) was bought c1667; and property in the Isle of Thanet (Kent), Banwell (Somerset) and Isleham (Cambridgeshire) was added through a marriage with the Maynard family. West Cornwall estates were gained by the marriage of Francis Buller to the daughter and heir of Ezekiel Grosse of Golden. John, younger son of Francis Buller, acquired Morval in east Cornwall through his marriage to the heiress of John Coode, and extended his Cornish property by another marriage, to the heiress of Walter Langdon of Keverel. In 1707 the estates of the Shillingham branch of the Buller family devolved upon the Morval line. James Buller, son of John Buller of Morval and Shillingham (d1751), married Elizabeth, co-heir to the Devon and Cornwall estates of William Gould of Downes, near Crediton (Devon). He settled the Shillingham and Gould family estates on his son by his first marriage, who founded the Buller family of Downes, and the Morval inheritance, with the Maynard estates and the

Devon (King's Nympton) property (sold in the late-eighteenth and nineteenth century), on his son by a second marriage. After the death of JF Buller in 1890 Morval passed to his sister Charlotte (wife of HM Tremayne), but another sister, Frances (widow of WH Pole Carew) removed many of the Buller muniments to Antony House.

Estates in 1883: Pole Carew of Antony: Cornwall 4,288 acres worth £6,401 a year; Pole of Shute: Devon 5,846 acres worth £7,416 a year, with Berks property valued at £370 a year.

[a] Carew deeds, Cornwall 13th-20th cent, Devon and Somerset 14th-18th cent, with misc deeds (Herts, Northants, etc) 16th-17th cent; Pole deeds, Devon 13th-19th cent, Dorset 13th-18th cent, with misc Somerset deeds 16th-17th cent; Buller deeds, Cornwall (Morval and Shillingham) 13th-19th cent, with misc deeds for Devon (King's Nympton) 14th-18th cent, Kent (Isle of Thanet) and Somerset (Banwell) 16th-18th cent, and Montgomeryshire and Salop 14th-17th cent; wills, settlements, testamentary and executorship papers 15th-20th cent, Carew, Pole, Pole Carew, Buller and Grosse families, incl executorship papers for Sir Richard Bampfylde 1727-47 and Reginald Pole (d1769); legal papers 16th-20th cent, Carew, Pole, Pole Carew and Buller families, incl abstracts of title and papers rel to rights of wreck at Sheviock 18th-19th cent; Cornwall (E and W Antony, Sheviock, etc) and Devon (Drewsteignton, Riddlecombe, etc) manorial records (Carew family) 15th-19th cent; manorial records (Pole family), Devon (Whitford, Colyton, etc) 15th-19th cent, incl Colyton hundred 16th-18th cent, and Dorset (Broadwinsor) 15th-18th cent; Cornwall manorial records (Buller family) 15th-18th cent, incl Morval and Shillingham.

Antony estate records 15th-20th cent, incl leases and tenancy papers from 15th cent, maps, plans and surveys 17th-20th cent, rentals, accounts and vouchers 15th-20th cent, corresp 17th-20th cent, and papers rel to woods from 17th cent, farms 18th-20th cent, Antony passage and Torpoint ferry 18th-20th cent, and tithes from 16th cent; Devon (Carew family) estate papers 15th-18th cent, incl Drewsteignton surveys and rentals 17th-18th cent; misc papers for Pyncombe and Carew family estates in Devon and Somerst mainly 17th-18th cent, incl South Petherton (Somerset) survey mid-18th cent; Devon and Dorset (Pole family) estate records 16th-20th cent, incl lease books 17th-19th cent, maps and plans 18th-20th cent, and valuations, surveys, rentals and accounts 16th-20th cent; Cornwall estate records (Buller family), mainly E Cornwall 15th-18th cent, incl leases and tenancy papers, surveys, rentals, and misc accounts, corresp, and papers rel to tithes 15th-18th cent; misc papers rel to other Buller estates 16th-18th cent, incl surveys of Devon and Kent estates 17th-18th cent, Cambs estate map

c1700, Street Marshall (Montgomeryshire) survey 16th cent and Banwell survey and papers 1712; survey book, Devon lands of Henry Grey, Duke of Suffolk and Peter Carew 1554; valuation of Cornish estate of Francis Godolphin 1615; account book of Sir Charles Cocks for the division of Dumbleton, Houlton and Leigh with Powick (Worcs) 1779.

Agreements, specifications, plans and papers for work at Antony House 1692-20th cent, incl red book 1792 and letters of Humphry Repton; Antony house and library inventories 18th-20th cent and household and garden accounts 17th-20th cent, incl furnishing accounts 1662 and house and cellar accounts c1743-1850; inventories of Pole Carew households at New Cavendish Street and Berkeley Square c1791-1835 and of the Sunninghill (Berks) household of the Hon John Yorke 1801; misc Shute household records 18th-20th cent; inventories and accounts of Buller households at Morval and Haine 1716-82; Downes household accounts c1739-64; Chelsea household accounts 1720-1.

Papers rel to Cornish affairs 16th-20th cent, Carew, Pole Carew, Grosse and Buller families, incl shrievalty accounts 1636, accounts of county stock (western division) 1639-41, election papers 18th-19th cent, E Cornwall Yeomanry Cavalry records c1797-1827, related militia and yeomanry papers late 18th-19th cent, papers rel to tin mining 18th cent (? James Buller as deputy warden of the Stannaries), and accounts and papers rel to the keepership of Trematon castle and park 1594-1692; Antony parish records 16th-20th cent, incl churchwardens' papers 1593-1787, poor rate books 1717-87 and school building accounts 1766-9; papers rel to Torpoint chapel 18th-19th cent, and to Morval parish, Saltash borough and Erth Barton charity 17th-18th cent; papers rel to Devon affairs from 17th cent (Pole family), incl shrievalty papers 17th-20th cent, magistracy papers 18th-19th cent, militia papers 1759-67 and records of the Dragoon Fusiliers (E Devon Troop) 1794-1805; Cornwall, Plymouth and Devon ship money papers c1636-7; Somerset shrievalty accounts (Sir John Carew) 1633-4; Taunton (Somerset) election bills 1754.

Patents and commissions 17th-20th cent, Carew, Pole, Pole Carew and Buller families; Carew, Pole and Pole Carew family accounts and papers 16th-20th cent, incl extensive corresp and papers of Reginald Pole Carew (d1835), papers of Richard Carew as commissioner of prizes at Plymouth 1689-91, corresp of John Carew of Camerton 1728-50, records of W Indian business interests of George Carew 1731-3 and antiquarian papers of Sir William Pole c1600; Grosse family and business papers 16th-17th cent; Buller family papers 16th-19th cent, incl extensive 17th cent corresp, Hayward family letterbook 1627-48, parliamentary notebook of Thomas Wise MP 1640, and foreign travel accounts (Lemon family) 1768; literary, genealogical and misc papers 16th-20th cent, incl civil war and commonwealth pamphlets collected by the Pole family and catalogue of the Hon John Yorke's books 1798.

Legal, estate and family papers of the Earls of Coventry 17th-18th cent, incl rentals, surveys and accounts (Gloucs, Lincs, Worcs, etc), Droitwich (Worcs) boileries papers 1671-1715, Edgeware (Middlesex) accounts 1638, 1700-15, inventories of Croome Court 1712 and the 4th Earl 1719, catalogue of pictures brought from Croome Court to Antony 18th cent, Worcs militia corresp 1715 and family corresp *c*1700-50; Hele legal and family papers 17th cent, incl wills and settlement of Sir Samuel Hele 1671-5 and Cornwall and Devon estate surveys, rentals, vouchers and papers 1623-85.

In private possession. Enquiries to the County Archivist, Cornwall Record Office. HMC *Papers of British Politicians 1782-1900*, 1989, p85. NRA 5960.

[b] Papers rel to Antony estate sales 1920-7, incl surveyor's notebook.

Cornwall Record Office (DDBY/18-21). Deposited in Plymouth City Library by Body, Son & Fleury, chartered surveyors, Plymouth 1962 and transferred to the record office 1968. NRA 30436.

[c] Torpoint leases 19th-20th cent.

Cornwall Record Office (AD 829). Purchased from Torpoint Heritage Centre 1987-8.

[d] Estate and personal accounts of Sir Courtenay Pole 1658-72 and Sir William Pole 1715-23.

Devon Record Office (235M). Deposited by WG Hoskins 1955. NRA 4613.

[e] Estate and personal accounts of Sir Courtenay Pole 1650-8.

Devon Record Office (237M). Deposited by Mrs C Smith 1955. NRA 4613.

Related collections: Buller of Morval (Cornwall Record Office DDBU, NRA 29663), including deeds for Cornwall (Morval and Shillington) 14th-19th cent, Devon 17th-19th cent and other counties 16th-18th cent, wills, settlements and legal papers 16th-19th cent, estate records for Cornwall (Morval and Shillington) 15th-20th cent and for Devon and other counties 16th-19th cent, household papers from 1638, papers relating to Cornish and local affairs 17th-19th cent, and Buller and Grosse family papers 16th-19th cent; Buller (Cornwall) deeds and miscellaneous papers 14th-18th cent, with Grosse and Lemon (of Carclew) family papers 17th-18th cent (Royal Institution of Cornwall, Henderson Collection, NRA 1166); Buller of Downes (Cornwall Record Office DDBU, NRA

29663 and DDWH 3453-4678, NRA 2687; Devon Record Office 2065M, NRA 16965); farming records of Edrica de la Pole (d1946), incl Shute farm acounts 1887-93 (Plymouth and West Devon Area Record Office 1306, NRA 4157); Earls of Coventry (in private possession, NRA 3843); Carew of Crowcombe (Somerset Archive and Record Service DD/TB, NRA 41076; Pembrokeshire Record Office, Haverfordwest DD/CAR, NRA 23930), including papers of the Carew family of Camerton; Carew of Barley (Cornwall Record Office DD.CF 3087-108, 4105-112, NRA 21923), including trust papers for Sir John Carew, 3rd Bt (d1692).

[87] RAMSAY, Earls of Dalhousie

By the sixteenth century the Ramsay family was established in Midlothian (at Carrington, Cockpen and Dalhousie), and had property in Fife (Carnock and Clatty), Berwickshire (Foulden) and East Lothian. William Ramsay (d1672) was created Earl of Dalhousie in 1633, and further property (for example at Melrose (Roxburghshire) and in Fife) was acquired in the seventeenth century. Of these family estates, only those in Midlothian appear to have been retained by the nineteenth century. West Lothian property entered the Ramsay family through the marriage in 1767 of the eighth Earl of Dalhousie and Elizabeth Glen, niece and heiress of James Glen of Longcroft (West Lothian), but was sold in the early nineteenth century. The tenth Earl (1812-60) was created Marquess in 1849 but on his death without male issue the marquessate lapsed, while the earldom and Midlothian estates passed to his cousin Fox Maule, second Baron Panmure (see below).

The fortunes of the Maule family were established by Patrick Maule (1585-1661) of Panmure (Forfarshire), a favourite of James I and Charles I, who was raised to the peerage as Earl of Panmure in 1646 and acquired extensive estates in Forfarshire (Arbroath, Brechin, Downie, Navar) and Kincardineshire (Balmakelly), with Collyweston (Northamptonshire) and Eltham Park (Kent). The second Earl bought Belhelvie (Aberdeenshire) from Patrick, Earl of Kinghorne, in 1663-4, and the third and fourth Earls extended the Forfarshire holdings, purchasing Kelly (from the Irvine family of Drum (Aberdeenshire) in 1679), Edzell and Glenesk (from the Lindsay family of Edzell *c*1703) and other properties. The fourth Earl's estates were forfeited owing to his Jacobitism and sold in 1719 to the York Building Company, the mansions of Panmure House and Brechin Castle, however, being leased by the Countess of Panmure, who also bought Inverkeilor (Forfarshire) in 1724. The Forfarshire estates were subsequently re-purchased in 1764 by William Maule, son and heir of the antiquarian Harry Maule of Kelly and nephew of the fourth Earl. William Maule was created Earl of Panmure in the Irish peerage in 1743 but died without issue in 1782, when he was succeeded in the Forfarshire estates by his nephew the eighth Earl of Dalhousie. From him they passed to his second son William Ramsay (1771-1852), who took the name of Maule and was created Baron Panmure in 1831. Fox Maule, second Baron Panmure, succeeded his cousin as eleventh Earl of Dalhousie in 1860.

Colstoun (East Lothian) was acquired through the marriage of the ninth Earl (1770-1838) to Christian, daughter and heir of Charles Broun of Colstoun. It devolved in 1860 upon the Marquess of Dalhousie's daughter Lady Susan Georgiana Broun-Ramsay, who married firstly the Hon Robert Bourke (created Baron Connemara in 1887) and secondly Lt-Colonel William Hamilton Briggs. On her death in 1898 Colstoun descended to her great-niece Lady Edith Broun-Lindsay, who also inherited the Ayrshire estate (Wellwood, sold in 1925) of her father Lt-Colonel John George Alexander Baird (d1917).

Estates in 1883: Forfarshire 136,602 acres, Midlothian 1,419 acres, total 138,021 acres worth £58,603 a year, exclusive of £250 mine rental.

[a] Writs, Forfarshire 13th-20th cent, Midlothian 14th-20th cent, Aberdeenshire 14th-18th cent, W Lothian 15th-19th cent and Fife 15th-18th cent; misc writs for Berwickshire, Kincardineshire, Roxburghshire, etc 13th-19th cent; inventories of writs and title 17th-19th cent; wills, testamentary papers, settlements, executry papers and trust papers 16th-19th cent, Maule and Ramsay families; executry papers for Brigadier-General John Forbes 1759-74; legal papers, mainly Maule family, and bonds, discharges and financial papers, Maule and Ramsay families, 15th-20th cent, incl papers rel to the re-purchase of the Panmure estates 1764; minutes, court of the lordship of Brechin and Navar 1674-6 and Inverquharity (Forfarshire) baron court 1667-87.

Forfarshire estate records 16th-20th cent, incl tacks, maps, plans, valuations and rentals from 16th cent, factory accounts and vouchers from 1619, grieves' accounts from 1649, corresp from 18th cent, papers rel to Carmyllie quarries 1806-15 and to deer, fishings and grouse 1865-1966, with Balmakelly (Kincardineshire) estate papers 17th-18th cent; Midlothian estate records 16th-20th cent, incl tacks from 1781, rentals and factory accounts and vouchers from 1715 and coal works accounts 1758-66, with E Lothian (Colstoun) rentals 1802-6 and accounts 1847-8; W Lothian (Longcroft) tacks, rentals, accounts and estate papers c1662-1827; estate records for Belhelvie (Aberdeenshire) 1634-1780, incl tacks, rentals and factory accounts and vouchers; papers rel to teinds, heritors, stipends, and churches, mainly Forfarshire and Midlothian 16th-19th cent and Belhelvie 17th cent; misc Collyweston (Northants) and Eltham (Kent) estate papers 1605-60, incl Collyweston survey and valuation 1605 and Eltham accounts 1631-43; records of the Earls of Strathmore and Kinghorne 16th-18th cent, incl Forfarshire rentals and accounts mid-17th cent; records rel to other Forfarshire estates and families 15th-18th cent, incl rentals for Inverquharity 1630, Balnamoon 1704-7, the Earl of Northesk 1723 and Lord Balmerino c1661-7, with rental c1617 and estate accounts 1715 of the Earl of Southesk; earldom of Mar rental 1694.

Panmure and Brechin household records 17th-19th cent, incl plans and drawings from 18th cent, building accounts and papers c1664-early 18th cent, inventories 17th-19th cent, notebook rel to Brechin and Balishen glassworks 1649, and household accounts and vouchers 17th-18th cent, mainly Panmure; papers rel to Dalhousie Castle household and gardens 16th-20th cent, incl accounts of works 1784-6 and inventory of pictures 1829; other household records 17th-19th cent, incl Canongate plan 1772, inventories and accounts for Kelly and Balischen 17th-18th cent and Ardestie (Forfarshire) and Edinburgh inventories c1703-24, with misc accounts of households at London and Bath, etc 17th-18th cent and plan of the Villa Panmure (Cannes) 1868; architectural drawings, Monikie and Monifieth (Forfarshire) churches 1812; inventory, Earl of Kinghorne's chamber at the college of St Andrews 1655; Forfarshire shrievalty accounts 1632-3; papers rel to Forfarshire elections, freeholders, yeomanry, militia and volunteers and to the burghs of Arbroath, Brechin, Dundee and Montrose 17th-19th cent, incl Arbroath town accounts 1632-45, 1766-70, rental and accounts of Brechin Maison Dieu c1657-68, 1706, Dundee town accounts late 17th cent-1705 and Montrose rental 1656; register of the synod of Lothian and Tweeddale 1643-54.

Patents, commissions and licences 16th-19th cent, Maule and Ramsay families; Maule and Ramsay family and legal accounts from 17th cent and family papers from 16th cent, incl papers rel to Covenanting and Jacobitism 17th-19th cent and journals of Dr Blair's continental travel with the 4th Earl of Panmure 1717-18; corresp and papers of the 1st Earl of Panmure (1585-1661); corresp of Margaret, Countess of Panmure, and Harry Maule of Kelly 1678-1734; military accounts of the Earl of Panmure 1742-8; extensive papers of the 9th Earl and Marquess of Dalhousie; political papers of the 11th Earl and naval papers of the 12th Earl; corresp of Alexander Maclean, the 9th Earl's agent 1816-37; papers of Brigadier-General John Forbes 1746-59 and James Glen, governor of South Carolina 1743-56, with Glen of Longcroft family papers 18th cent; records of the Royal North British Dragoons 1748-57; return of the Earl of Panmure's Regiment of Foot 1715; literary and misc papers 16th-20th cent, incl misc Panmure music books 17th-19th cent and Robert Maule's history of the family of Panmure 1611; antiquarian papers and collections of Harry Maule, incl monastic charters c1127-1552 (Holyrood, North Berwick and Inchaffray abbeys), cartulary of the church of St Giles, Edinburgh 14th-16th cent, registers of the priory of St Andrews 1144-1438 and Brechin bishopric c1165-1513, and Arbroath Abbey rental 1531.

National Archives of Scotland (GD 45). Deposited by the 16th Earl of Dalhousie 1951-91. HMC *First Report, App*, 1870, pp117-19; *Second Report, App*, 1871, p186; *Papers of British Cabinet Ministers 1782-1900*, 1982, pp6, 41; *Private Papers of British Colonial Governors 1782-1900*, 1986, p50. NRA 17164. The collection includes papers deposited in 1962 by Brodie, Cuthbertson & Watson, WS, Edinburgh *(Keeper's Report 1962,* pp14-15, GD 247). Further literary and misc papers 16th-18th cent, with Forfarshire estate papers 1882-3, remain in private possession: enquiries to the National Register of Archives (Scotland) (NRA(S) 2655, 3164; NRA 17164, 19459).

[b] Misc estate papers 1839-48.

National Archives of Scotland (GD 1/637). Purchased 1972.

[c] Misc barony of Panmure writs and legal papers 18th-19th cent.

National Archives of Scotland (GD 240). Deposited by Bruce & Kerr, WS, Edinburgh 1963. NRA 34966.

[d] Dalhousie and Panmure estate plans mainly 19th cent.

National Archives of Scotland (RHP 6044-61). Deposited by Dundas & Wilson, CS, Edinburgh c1967.

[e] Panmure music books 17th-19th cent.

National Library of Scotland (MSS 9447-76). Purchased 1957, 1979, having been deposited by the 16th Earl of Dalhousie in 1957.

[f] Naval journals of the 12th and 13th Earls of Dalhousie 1866-71.

Cambridge University Library (Add 9278-9). Purchased 1994 (Sotheby's, 13 Dec, lots 280-1).

Related collections: Broun-Lindsay of Colstoun (in private possession, NRA 11621, NRA(S) 2383), including E, Mid and W Lothian writs from 13th cent, wills, settlements, legal and related papers, Broun, Glen and Ramsay families 16th-19th cent, Colstoun estate and household papers 17th-20th cent, Midlothian (Dalhousie) estate and household papers early-mid-19th cent, W Lothian estate papers c1698-1813, and Broun and Ramsay family papers

17th-19th cent (9th Earl and Marquess of Dalhousie, etc); American papers of James Glen 1738-77 (University of South Carolina Library NUC MS 76-1382, acquired from Lady Broun-Lindsay, Sotheby's, 15 Oct 1974, lot 524, NRA 39094); American papers of Brigadier-General John Forbes (1710-59) (University of Virginia Library NUC MS 77-1216, also acquired from Lady Broun-Lindsay, Sotheby's, 15 Oct 1974, lot 525).

[88] RAWDON-HASTINGS, later ABNEY-HASTINGS, Marquesses of Hastings and Earls of Loudon

Settled in Norfolk in the thirteenth century, the Hastings family had extensive lands in Yorkshire, Leicestershire and elsewhere by the mid-fifteenth century. William Hastings (?1430-1483), created Baron Hastings in 1461, received large grants of forfeited estates, including Ashby-de-la-Zouch, Loughborough and Castle Donington in north-west Leicestershire, where Ashby Castle and, after the Civil War, Donington Park became the principal seat. Edward Hastings, second Baron Hastings (1466-1507), married Mary Hungerford, Baroness Hungerford, Botreaux and Moleyns. A number of Hungerford and Botreaux deeds remain in the collection, although most of the estates were confirmed to the male line of the Hungerford family in the sixteenth century. The third Baron Hastings was created Earl of Huntingdon in 1529. Outlying Hastings estates were later alienated, and by the early nineteenth century the Hastings properties were confined mainly to Leicestershire and adjacent parts of Derbyshire. The seventh Earl (1650-1701) had acquired through his first wife the Ledston estate in the West Riding of Yorkshire, but this later passed through female heirs to the Wheler family.

In 1752 Elizabeth, only daughter of the ninth Earl of Huntingdon, married Sir John Rawdon, third Bt (1720-93), created Earl of Moira in 1762. Although originating in Yorkshire and inheriting property in Cheshire, the Rawdon family had been settled since the seventeenth century in Ireland, where it had estates in County Down, Dublin and elsewhere. Francis Rawdon-Hastings (1754-1826), second Earl of Moira, succeeded his mother in the Hastings estates in 1808 and was created Marquess of Hastings in 1817. In 1804 he had married Flora, Countess of Loudon, heiress of the Loudon Castle and Rowallan estates in Ayrshire. The second Marquess of Hastings inherited the Loudon estates on the death of his mother in 1840.

The Campbell family was settled at Loudon from the Middle Ages. Sir Hugh Campbell (d1622) was created Baron Loudon, and was succeeded by his granddaughter Margaret, whose husband Sir John Campbell of Lawers

(Perthshire) was created Earl of Loudon in 1633. On the death of the fourth Earl in 1782 he was succeeded by his cousin James Mure Campbell of Lawers, whose mother had been heiress of the Mure family of Rowallan.

The Irish estates were sold mostly around 1800, and the Leicestershire estates reduced by sales in the early nineteenth century. On the death of the fourth Marquess in 1868 he was succeeded by his sister Edith, Countess of Loudon (1838-74), who in 1858 had married Charles Frederick Clifton (1822-95, created Baron Donington 1880). In 1859 they took the name of Abney-Hastings on inheriting the Willesley (Derbyshire, later Leicestershire) property of Sir Charles Abney-Hastings, second Bt.

Estates in 1883 (Earl of Loudon and Baron Donington): Ayrshire 18,638 acres, Leics 10,174 acres, Derbys 2,750 acres, Yorks WR 1,348 acres, total 32,910 acres worth £39,977 a year, exclusive of £2,259 for Ayrshire minerals.

[a] Hastings deeds 12th-19th cent (many medieval, incl Repton and Calke priory charters), mainly Derbys and Leics but also Notts, Northants and Yorks ER, NR and WR; deeds for other counties mainly 13th-17th cent, incl Berks, Bucks, Cornwall, Devon, Somerset and Wilts (Hungerford and Botreaux lands); Irish deeds (Co Down, etc) 17th-18th cent; wills, settlements and trust and executorship papers, Hastings and related families from 14th cent and Rawdon from 17th cent, incl executorships of the 3rd and 4th Earls of Huntingdon late 16th-early 17th cent and inquisitions *post mortem* 14th-17th cent; legal and case papers 14th-19th cent; bonds 13th-16th cent; Leics manorial records 14th-19th cent, incl Ashby-de-la-Zouch 15th-18th cent and Loughborough 14th-early 19th cent; manorial records mainly 14th-17th cent, Derbys (Melbourne, etc), Bucks, Cornwall, Somerset, Yorks WR and other counties; rolls or accounts for hundreds of Framland (Leics) 15th cent-1809 and Somerton (Somerset) 1349-1574, honours of Leicester 1399-1400 and Winchester Fee (Leics) 1417-1561, and rape of Hastings (Sussex) 1429-76.

Leics and Derbys estate records 14th-19th cent, incl surveys, maps and plans, rentals and accounts, and papers rel to enclosure 18th-early 19th cent, land tax 1636-1798, fee farm rents 1744-1800, canals, roads and rivers 18th-19th cent, sales 16th-19th cent, collieries 1606-1890, woods, and Ivanhoe Baths c1813-24; estate records rel to other counties 13th-early 19th cent, incl general rentals and receivers' accounts, Cornwall and Hants (Botreaux) accounts early 15th cent, Lincs accounts 1472-8, Somerset (Aller, etc) rentals, etc 15th-18th cent, Notts estate (East Leake, etc) papers 1527-1804, papers rel to Puddletown (Dorset) advowson 1581-1790, Bucks receivers' accounts 1583-8, Northants (Zouche) rental 1587, survey of Ripley (Hants) c1600, Yorks WR (Ledsham,

etc) papers mainly 18th cent and Ettington (Warwicks) papers 18th cent; Norfolk rentals (estates of Lady Elizabeth Hastings) 1722-6; Irish estate papers late 16th-early 19th cent, mainly Rawdon (Co Down, Dublin, etc) but incl Hastings estates in Cos Fermanagh and Tyrone 17th cent and the Duke of Albemarle's estate in Co Wexford 1660-70; Florida estate papers of the Earl of Moira c1763-8.

Papers rel to buildings and their contents 1596-1870, incl Ashby-de-la-Zouch plans c1600, etc, Donington Park building and landscaping papers 18th cent-1808, Ledston Hall inventories 1759-90 and Loudon Castle inventories 1860, 1868; household accounts and vouchers from 16th cent, incl Ashby and Donington gardens and stables and London house; Staunton Harold (Leics)(Shirley family) inventories 1657, 1723-6; papers rel to Leics and Rutland forests 1203-early 19th cent, Leics and Rutland county affairs early 17th cent, city and corporation of Leicester 16th-early 19th cent, Ashby and Donington parishes c1550-1636 (overseers' and churchwardens' accounts, non-consecutive), Repton School and Etwall Hospital (Derbys) 16th-early 19th cent, and Stoke Poges Hospital (Bucks) 15th-18th cent.

Patents, commissions, pardons, grants of livery, summons to parliament, etc from 15th cent; Hastings family corresp and papers 15th-early 19th cent, incl letter book of Sir William Hastings 1477, personal accounts and vouchers from 16th cent, papers of the 3rd Earl of Huntingdon as Lord President of the Council in the North 1572-95, Virginia Company papers of the 5th Earl 1610-25, Civil War and other papers of Henry Hastings, Baron Loughborough (d1667), papers of the 7th Earl as Captain of the Gentlemen Pensioners 1682-8, misc American and other papers of the 1st Marquess c1781-1822, and papers of General Sir Charles Hastings early 19th cent; Rawdon family papers 1583-1751, mainly Irish, with papers of Sir James Graham (Governor of Drogheda), the Duke of Albemarle, John Bramhall (Archbishop of Armagh) and Sir John Davies (Irish Attorney-General, father-in-law of the 6th Earl) 17th cent; misc Shirley family accounts 17th cent; Campbell (Earls of Loudon) family corresp and papers 1510-1839, incl military and political corresp of the 3rd and 4th Earls 18th cent, Mure of Rowallan papers 17th cent and papers of the Marquis de Vaudreuil as governor of Louisiana 1740-53; genealogical papers 15th-19th cent, incl collections by Sir William Dugdale 1677 and Hastings genealogical roll c1540; literary and misc papers 13th-19th cent, incl Leics rental (Knights Templar) c1250 (14th cent copy), roll rel to estates of the Earl of Winchester (d1264)(14th cent copy), rental of Sir Nicholas Montgomery's Derbys and Staffs lands 1481-7, earldom of Salisbury estate papers early 16th cent and book of Devon knights' fees 1635.

Huntington Library, San Marino, California. Acquired 1923 from Sotheby's through the agency of Sir Joseph Duveen (Loudon papers) and 1927 from the Countess of Loudon through Maggs Bros, with an additional purchase from Lady Edith Maclaren 1977. *Guide to British Historical Manuscripts in the Huntington Library*, 1982, pp78-144. Maggs Bros, *The Huntingdon Papers*, parts I-VI, 1926. Kim Watson, ed, *Henry E Huntington Library Hastings Manuscripts*, List and Index Society Special Series vol 22, 1987. HMC *Hastings I-IV* (HMC 78), 1928-47; *Papers of British Cabinet Ministers 1782-1900*, 1982, p53. NRA 10029.

[b] Leics and Derbys deeds 14th-20th cent (mainly post-medieval); trust and legal papers 19th-20th cent, incl schedules and abstracts of title; Leics and Derbys estate papers 18th-20th cent (mainly 1802 onwards), incl surveys and valuations, maps and plans from 1735, rentals, accounts, papers rel to coal and clay extraction 19th-20th cent and papers rel to sales early 20th cent; Rawdon (Yorks WR) rental 1844-9; Donington House inventories and catalogues 1828-57; letters patent 1871.

Leicestershire Record Office (DE 421, 500). Deposited by Crane & Walton, solicitors, Ashby-de-la-Zouch 1960, 1963. NRA 41276.

[c] Schedule of deeds 1757; Melbourne manorial court records 1561-1707, with chief rent book 1839-1902; Leics and Derbys estate records 1771-1925, incl valuations, maps and plans, rentals, accounts, papers rel to minerals 19th-early 20th cent and agency corresp and papers of JG Shields 1920s-30s; misc personal papers of the 1st Baron Donington 1853-95.

Leicestershire Record Office (DE 362, 658). Deposited by JG Shields, Castle Donington 1959, 1966. HMC *Accessions to Repositories 1959*, p22.

[d] Leics and Derbys deeds 1581-1824.

Leicestershire Record Office (DE 2905). Deposited by the Countess of Loudon 1985. *Annual Report 1985.*

[e] Copies of Leics and Derbys surveys, enclosure awards, etc 18th cent (1 vol); maps of estates sold in 1808 (1 folder); estate account 1705-27.

Leicestershire Record Office (13 D 40). Rescued from salvage and deposited in Leicester Museum by Leicestershire Archaeological Society 1940. NRA 21821.

[f] Survey of the Earl and Countess of Huntingdon's estates c1596; Hastings family corresp mainly 1685-1748, incl corresp of Selina, Countess of Huntingdon.

Leicestershire Record Office (14 D 32). Deposited in Leicester Museum by HD Fisher 1932. NRA 6082.

[g] Deeds (mainly Leics) 16th-19th cent; case papers 1722-51; misc family corresp 1670-1805, incl letters to Selina, Countess of Huntingdon.

Leicestershire Record Office (DE 23/1). Acquired from B Halliday 1948. NRA 6263.

[h] Derbys and Leics deeds and legal papers 17th-20th cent, incl purchases and leases of mineral rights; trust and executorship deeds and papers 19th-20th cent, Hastings and Abney-Hastings; Hastings (Sussex) rape and castle leases 1513-1868.

Derbyshire Record Office (D 1336). Deposited by Crane & Walton, solicitors, Ashby-de-la-Zouch 1974. NRA 41437.

[i] Abney-Hastings trust and executorship papers and misc leases mainly 1829-65.

Derbyshire Record Office (D 2496Z). Deposited by Lawrence, Graham & Co, solicitors, London, through the British Records Association 1982. NRA 8918.

[j] Ayrshire (Loudon and Rowallan) deeds and legal papers 14th-20th cent; Ayrshire estate papers 17th-20th cent, incl tacks, rentals, accounts, corresp and papers; misc household and family papers 18th-19th cent, incl Loudon Castle inventory 1851.

Dick Institute, Kilmarnock. Deposited by the 7th Baron De Freyne (son-in-law of Edith, Countess of Loudon) 1983. NRA 18854.

[k] Ayrshire (Loudon) deeds c1210-18th cent (39 items).

Glasgow City Archives (TD 826). Deposited by Andrew Floyer-Acland 1983. (In possession of the Earl of Loudon 1907.) *Annual Report 1983*, p2.

[l] Misc legal papers 18th cent.

National Archives of Scotland (GD 253/141-2). Deposited by D & JH Campbell, solicitors, Edinburgh 1951. NRA 13863.

[m] Misc Irish papers mainly of the Hastings family 1555-1714, incl papers of the 5th and 7th Earls of Huntingdon and Sir John Davies.

Bodleian Library, Oxford (MS Carte 76-78, 103, 117, 228, 234). Given to Thomas Carte by the 9th Earl of Huntingdon. *Summary Catalogue of Western Manuscripts*, vol 3, 1895, pp114-48 *passim.*

[n] Methodist and other corresp of Selina, Countess of Huntingdon 1727-91 (c3,500 items); estate accounts 1760, 1777.

Westminster and Cheshunt Colleges Library, Cambridge. NRA 12352. Letters from her to her husband and son 1732-46, nd (84 items) are in the Methodist Archives and History Center, Drew University, Madison, New Jersey (see Wanda W Smith, *Selina Hastings, Countess of Huntingdon* (exhibition catalogue), Bridwell Library, Perkins School of Theology, Southern Methodist University, Dallas, Texas, 1997). NRA 42014.

[o] Papers of and concerning the 1st Marquess of Hastings and his family mainly 1818-27.

British Library, Oriental and India Office Collections (Macnabb papers, MSS Eur F 206). From the papers of JM Macnabb and Robert Wilson, Hastings's private secretaries. NRA 10746.

[p] Private journal of the 1st Marquess 1813-14.

Duke University, William R Perkins Library, Durham, North Carolina. Purchased 1963. *Guide*, 1980, p240.

[q] Military and other papers of the 4th Earl of Loudon 1739-76.

British Library, Manuscript Collections (Add MSS 44063-84). Acquired through the Friends of the National Libraries 1935.

[r] Papers of the 4th Earl of Loudon 1741-8, 1773 and nd, with notebooks 1750-3, 1764-5.

National Library of Scotland (MSS 2520, 5728-9). Acquired 1937, 1953.

[s] Further papers of the 4th Earl 1755-74.

Loudon Academy, Galston, Ayrshire. Enquiries to the National Register of Archives (Scotland) (NRA(S) 628). NRA 15342.

[t] Misc literary and other papers, incl Donington Park library catalogue 1834.

Untraced. Purchased by Sir Thomas Phillipps from the library of the 4th Marquess of Hastings 29 Dec 1868. (Phillipps MSS 21468-86, 21969-72.)

[u] Parliamentary journal of the 5th Earl of Huntingdon *c*1610.

Folger Shakespeare Library, Washington DC. Purchased 1926. Seymour De Ricci and WJ Wilson, *Census of Medieval and Renaissance Manuscripts in the United States and Canada*, 1935, repr 1961, i, p418.

Related collections: Boyle, Earls of Glasgow, no 9, including Rowallan estate accounts 1743-5; Fitzalan-Howard, Dukes of Norfolk, no 37, including Donington trusteeship and estate papers late 19th-early 20th cent; Shirley, Earls Ferrers, no 93; Stuart, later Crichton-Stuart,

Earls and later Marquesses of Bute, no 100, including extensive Rawdon-Hastings and Loudon papers; Earls of Granard (in private possession, NRA 32660), including Rawdon deeds, estate papers and family papers late 16th-early 19th cent and Hastings genealogical papers; Wheler of Ledston (Yorks) and Otterden (Kent)(West Yorkshire Archive Service, Leeds Acc 1024, 2886, 3444, NRA 9003), including Ledston estate and legal papers early 18th cent; correspondence of Hamilton and Lady Charlotte Fitzgerald, with letters to her mother the Countess of Moira (J and F Anderson Collection, National Archives of Scotland GD 297/1-27, NRA 35600).

[89] ROBINSON, Marquesses of Ripon

William Robinson (d1616), lord mayor of York in 1581, acquired estates in and near York (Clifton and Rawcliffe, North Riding) and at Newby (near Topcliffe, North Riding). Sir William Robinson, fourth Bt (d1770), of Newby Park, sold the reversion of the Clifton estate to his uncle Thomas Robinson, first Baron Grantham (d1770), a younger son of Sir William Robinson, first Bt (d1736). Following the death of the fourth Bt without issue, the third Baron Grantham (1781-1859) succeeded to the remaining unsold estates of the senior Robinson line, including Newby and Dishforth (North Riding) and property in Wensleydale (Askrigg, etc, North Riding). He also inherited Newby Hall (near Ripon, West Riding) and other estates of the Weddell family (see Vyner of Gautby and Newby, no 112); and in 1833 succeeded to the Wrest Park estates as second Earl De Grey (see De Grey, Barons Lucas, no 28).

On Lord De Grey's death in 1859 the De Grey estates passed to his elder daughter Ann, Baroness Lucas, who married the sixth Earl Cowper (see Cowper, Earls Cowper, no 25), and the Newby Hall estate to his younger daughter Lady Mary Vyner (see Vyner of Gautby and Newby, no 112). Of the Robinson properties, however, the Askrigg and Clifton estates passed to the Cowper and Vyner families, but the Newby Park estate passed to Lord De Grey's nephew George Robinson, second Earl and first Marquess of Ripon (1827-1909).

Frederick Robinson (1782-1859), younger brother of the second Earl De Grey and Prime Minister 1827-8, was created Viscount Goderich in 1827 and Earl of Ripon in 1833. In 1814 he married Sarah, only daughter of the fourth Earl of Buckinghamshire (d1816), through whom he succeeded to the Nocton (Lincolnshire) estate inherited by the third Earl from the Ellis family. In 1845, on the death of Elizabeth Lawrence, he further succeeded to the West Riding estates of her grandfather William Aislabie (d1781), including Studley Royal, inherited through Aislabie's mother from the

Mallory family, and the adjoining Fountains Abbey estate, purchased in 1767.

Following the death of the second Marquess of Ripon in 1923 the Studley Royal and Fountains Abbey estate was acquired by his cousin Clare George Vyner, younger son of Lady Alwyne Compton-Vyner (see Vyner of Gautby and Newby, no 112).

Estates in 1883: Yorks NR and WR 14,668 acres, Lincs 7,102 acres, total 21,770 acres worth £29,126 a year.

[a] Deeds 12th-19th cent, mainly Yorks WR and NR (Aislabie and Robinson), incl many Fountains Abbey charters, with a few for Lincs, Norfolk and other counties; wills, settlements and related papers late 16th-19th cent, mainly Aislabie, Lawrence and Robinson but incl Ellis and Hobart (Lincs estate) 1676-1830 and Brownlow and Cecil (Lincs estate, later Aislabie) early 18th cent; legal papers 17th-19th cent, incl schedules and abstracts of title; manorial court records, Yorks WR and NR 15th-20th cent, incl Fountains and Hutton Conyers (NR); roll for Earl of Derby's courts (? in Lancs) 1498-9; Studley Royal (mainly WR) estate records 16th-20th cent, incl agreements 19th-20th cent, surveys of ex-Fountains Abbey lands 16th cent, other surveys and valuations 17th-19th cent, maps and plans 1600-20th cent, rentals and accounts 16th-20th cent, corresp and papers 17th-20th cent, and enclosure and tithe papers 18th-19th cent; Robinson (Yorks NR) estate rentals, accounts and other papers 17th-19th cent, mainly Newby (near Topcliffe) and Clifton estates; Lincs (Gosberton and Surfleet: Aislabie, ex Brownlow) estate papers c1702-1818, with Brownlow trust rental 1702-4; Ripon (Yorks WR) prebendal and collegiate rentals c1380, 1724-1814; Lincs (Nocton and Dunston) valuation 1845 and vouchers late 19th cent; account book for Sir Thomas Gresham's estates 1574-5.

Studley Royal inventory 1924, library catalogues c1870, early 20th cent, and household accounts 18th-19th cent; Newby garden inventory 1835; ? Aislabie household account c1610; York shrievalty account (Sir William Robinson) 1637-8; papers rel to Ripon borough and elections 17th-19th cent; misc local and parochial papers 17th-20th cent; commissions and appointments, Aislabie and Robinson 17th-19th cent; Robinson family corresp and papers c1685-1771, incl some official papers of the 1st and 2nd Barons Grantham; misc Aislabie corresp and papers 18th cent; diaries of Lady Amabel Yorke 1769-1827; papers of Sir John Mallory rel to Skipton Castle 1639-45; literary, heraldic and other MSS 16th-19th cent; Fountains Abbey foundation charters, cartularies and other records 12th-early 16th cent.

West Yorkshire Archive Service, Leeds (VR). Deposited 1958-79 and purchased by Leeds Archives Department 1981. HMC *Papers of British Cabinet Ministers 1782-1900*, 1982, p55. NRA 6160. For library MSS reported on in 1876-7 (HMC *Fifth Report, App*, 1876, p294; *Sixth Report, App*, 1877, pp243-50) see HMC *Guide to the Location of Collections*, 1982, p53.

[b] Misc Mallory, Aislabie and Robinson papers 17th cent-1925, incl will of the Marchioness of Ripon (d1917) and related papers, and indexes to Studley Royal muniments 1814, 1885.

West Yorkshire Archive Service, Leeds (Acc 2938). Deposited by Gregory, Rowcliffe & Co, solicitors, London, through the British Records Association 1986. NRA 5836.

[c] Deeds for Yorks WR (Studley Royal and Grantley Hall estates) 16th-20th cent and Yorks NR (Rainton, etc) 19th cent; settlements, trust deeds and legal papers 19th-20th cent, Robinson and Vyner families; misc leases, agreements and maps 20th cent; letters patent, John Aislabie 1737/8.

West Yorkshire Archive Service, Leeds (Acc 3639). Deposited by Birch Cullimore & Co in Cheshire Record Office and transferred to Leeds 1992. NRA 41228.

[d] Kirkby Malzeard (Yorks WR) manorial court records 17th-19th cent, with map 1600.

West Yorkshire Archive Service, Leeds (Bostock MSS). Deposited by G Bostock 1968. Formerly Vyner of Studley Royal MSS VR 4276, 5314-41, 5343-6, 5442, 5537. NRA 39454.

[e] Papers of the Fountains Abbey Settlers' Society 1934-8.

West Yorkshire Archive Service, Leeds (Acc 3869). Deposited by the National Trust 1994.

[f] Maps of Robinson (Yorks NR) estates by John Humphries of Ripon late 18th-early 19th cent.

North Yorkshire County Record Office (ZM1). From Barron & Barron, York. NRA 12864.

[g] Corresp and papers of the 1st Earl and 1st Marquess of Ripon, with a few earlier family letters from 1704.

British Library, Manuscript Collections (Add MSS 40862-80, 43510-43644). Presented by the executors of the second Marquess 1923. HMC *Papers of British Cabinet Ministers 1782-1900*, 1982, pp54-5; *Private Papers of British Diplomats 1782-1900*, 1985, p56; *Private Papers of British Colonial Governors*, 1986, p51.

[h] Political and other corresp of the 1st Marquess 1855-1907.

Duke University, William R Perkins Library, Durham, North Carolina. Purchased 1973. *Guide*, 1980, pp473-4.

[i] Game books of the 2nd Marquess 1871-1923.

Untraced. Sold at Sotheby's, Billingshurst, 12 Mar 1986, lot 123.

[j] Fountains Abbey library MSS 12th-15th cent.

British Library, Manuscript Collections (Add MSS 62129-32B). Formerly Vyner of Studley Royal MSS 6107-9, 6120, having been acquired with Studley Royal and from the Ingilby of Ripley collection (see also Ingilby of Ripley, no 56). Purchased 1981.

Related collections: Vyner of Newby and Gautby, no 112; De Grey, Barons Lucas, no 28; Earls of Buckinghamshire (Buckinghamshire Record Office D/MH, NRA 1), including papers of the 4th Earl of Buckinghamshire and the Robinson family presented to the 7th Earl of Buckinghamshire by the executors of the 1st Marquess of Ripon 1910.

[90] RUSSELL, Dukes of Bedford

Stephen Russell (d1438), of a Dorset family, owned land at Maiden Newton and elsewhere, and acquired Berwick (Dorset) through his wife. (Kingston Russell, an older family possession, was alienated but re-acquired c1560.) Sir John Russell (1485-1555), courtier, soldier and diplomat, married in 1526 Anne, daughter of Sir Guy Sapcote, through whom the Chenies (Buckinghamshire) and Thornhaugh (Northamptonshire) estates were inherited. He received large grants from the Crown, including lands of Tavistock Abbey and other property in Devon and Cornwall in 1540-50, the reversion of Woburn Abbey (Bedfordshire) in 1547, Thorney Abbey (Cambridgeshire), and the Covent Garden estate (Middlesex) (following the attainder of the Duke of Somerset) in 1552. He was created Earl of Bedford in 1550.

The Thornhaugh estate passed to the first Baron Russell (d1613), fourth son of the second Earl of Bedford. Lord Russell also acquired Shingay (Cambridgeshire) by marriage. The second Baron Russell succeeded his cousin as fourth Earl of Bedford in 1627. Thornhaugh then descended with the earldom of Bedford, but Shingay passed to a younger son, created Earl of Orford in 1697.

The fifth Earl of Bedford (1613-1700) was created Duke of Bedford in 1694. His eldest son William, Lord Russell (1639-83), married in 1669 Lady Rachel Wriothesley, daughter and co-heir of the fourth Earl of Southampton, through whom the Bloomsbury (Middlesex) estate and land in Hampshire (Stratton, Micheldever, etc) came to the Russell family. (See also, for other Southampton co-heirs, Montagu-Douglas-Scott, Dukes of Buccleuch and Queensberry, no 70, and Noel, Earls of

Gainsborough, no 74). The second Duke (1680-1711) married in 1695 Elizabeth Howland, who brought property in Surrey (Streatham, Wandsworth, Lambeth and Rotherhithe), Essex, Suffolk and elsewhere. These properties were sold after her death in 1724, apart from the Surrey estates, which were disposed of between about 1790 and 1816.

In the eighteenth and early nineteenth centuries the Bedfordshire and Tavistock estates were increased by purchase, the Bedfordshire estates notably by Oakley (1737), lands in Houghton Conquest, etc (1738, from the Earl of Ailesbury), Gostwick, etc (1774, from the Duke of Marlborough) and Ampthill and Houghton Conquest (1842, from Lord Holland's devisees), and the Tavistock estates partly by land in Cornwall later sold. The Hampshire estate was sold to the Baring family in 1800, to help meet the fifth Duke's liabilities. The Thornhaugh estate was sold in 1904 (to the seventh Earl Fitzwilliam), the Thorney estate in 1910, Covent Garden in 1917-18, and Chenies and most of the Tavistock estate by the late 1960s.

Estates in 1883: Beds 32,269 acres, Devon 22,607 acres, Cambs 18,800 acres, Northants 3,414 acres, Dorset 3,412 acres, Bucks 3,036 acres, Hunts 1,334 acres, Cornwall 1,231 acres, Hants 148 acres, Herts 83 acres, Lincs 1 acre, total 86,335 acres worth £141,793 a year. (The metropolitan property is excluded.)

[a] Deeds 12th-20th cent, mainly Beds but incl Bucks and Herts ?12th-20th cent, Cambs 16th-20th cent, Northants and Hunts 13th-20th cent, and other counties 13th-18th cent; legal and trust papers from 16th cent (mainly 18th-19th cent), incl executorship papers for the 1st Earl of Upper Ossory 1758-70; Beds manorial records 14th-19th cent, incl honour of Ampthill; manorial records for other counties 13th-early 18th cent, incl Chenies 14th-17th cent, Thornhaugh 15th-17th cent, Thorney 16th-17th cent, and Easton Bavent, etc (Suffolk) 13th-17th cent.

Records of Beds estates (Woburn estates, incl adjacent parishes in Bucks, and Bedford or N Beds estates) 16th-20th cent (extensive), incl leases and tenancy agreements, surveys and valuations mainly from 18th cent, maps and plans from 17th cent, rentals, accounts and vouchers from 17th cent, estate corresp 1590-20th cent (mainly of Woburn stewards from mid-18th cent), letters from Woburn to London agents c1828-56, letter books 19th cent, stewards' papers 18th-mid-20th cent, reports and memoranda, records of stock and cropping, wood accounts 1737-1910, records of farms in hand late 18th cent-early 20th cent, and papers rel to tithes, enclosure, timber, buildings and repairs, game, purchases and sales, and schools; papers rel to Husborne Crawley (Beds) kilns 1801-67, Woburn labourers' Penny-a-Week Club 1838-1921 and Eversholt (Beds) charity estate 1844-68; Ampthill (Ashburnham) survey, valuation and related papers *c*1723-4, with Ampthill (Fitzpatrick) estate papers *c*1737-1812.

Bucks and Herts (Chenies) estate records 16th-mid-20th cent (some with Beds estate records from 1810), incl leases from 1613, surveys and maps from 18th cent, rentals and accounts from 16th cent (mainly 1711 onwards), wood accounts from 1727, labour accounts 1844-1934, and Chesham (Bucks) tithe accounts 1752-92; records of Hitchin (Herts) leasehold estate 17th-18th cent, incl tithe accounts 1729-90; Cambs (Thorney) estate records 16th-early 20th cent, incl leases, surveys 16th-18th cent, maps 17th-19th cent, rentals and accounts from 1651, vouchers from 1654, corresp 18th-19th cent, and papers rel to floods, North Level drainage, farms in hand, etc; estate papers for Helgay and Southrey (Norfolk) 1759-92 and Dry Drayton (Cambs) 17th-late 18th cent; Shingay vouchers 1705-8; Northants and Hunts (Thornhaugh and Wansford (Northants) and Stibbington and Sibson (Hunts)) estate records late 16th-early 20th cent (with Thorney estate records from 1871), incl surveys from 16th cent, maps from 17th cent, rentals and accounts, stewards' corresp and memoranda from 18th cent and wood accounts from 17th cent; Wansford turnpike papers *c*1750-71 and wharf accounts and papers 1756-60; Hants leases 1600-1791; Suffolk leases, rentals, etc *c*1637-1705.

Woburn Abbey building accounts 1748-62 (work by Henry Flitcroft) and 1784-94, with drawings 19th-20th cent and surveyor of works's papers 1897-1929; papers rel to park and gardens mainly 19th cent, incl landscaping by Humphry Repton 1804-9; Woburn inventory 1703, and household accounts and vouchers 17th-20th cent; vouchers for London house, Endsleigh (Devon), etc early 20th cent; Chenies inventory 1585; drawings for Houghton House (Beds) 1793; Oakley House (Beds) building accounts and household vouchers 18th cent; papers rel to Woburn peculiar 18th cent; election papers, Beds and Bedford 1688-1857, Hunts 1826 and Cambs 1831; papers rel to Beds militia and yeomanry 17th-20th cent, to magistracy and county meetings 18th cent, and to Corporation of Bedford *c*1741-52.

Bedfordshire and Luton Archives and Record Service. Deposited at various dates since 1964. *Guide to the Russell estate collections for Bedfordshire and Devon to 1910*, 1966. NRA 10492, 17140.

[b] Cambs (Thorney) estate records late 16th-early 20th cent, incl tenancy registers 1696-1875, surveys and valuations, maps, and steward's letter books and papers 1755-1888; papers 19th-20th cent rel to drainage and navigation, turnpikes, Thorney parish and school, etc; survey and lot book of Great Level 1630-7; misc

Northants and Hunts estate papers 18th-19th cent, incl papers rel to woods 1762-1862 and map of Thornhaugh 1808; letter book 1829-33 and commonplace book 1804-50 of Tycho Wing, surveyor and Bedford agent.

Cambridgeshire County Record Office, Cambridge. Deposited by the North Level Internal Drainage Board, Thorney 1976-7. County Archivist's *Annual Report 1976*, p14; *1977*, pp16-17.

[c] Hants deeds 14th-18th cent; Micheldever (Hants) manorial court papers 1691-1778; Hants (Micheldever, Stratton, etc) estate records mainly 17th-18th cent, incl expired leases 1662-1782, surveys and valuations 1677-1785, maps 18th cent, rentals and accounts 1655-1802, stewards' papers, and papers rel to woods, enclosure, tithes, buildings, farms in hand, lime-burning and sale of the estate 1800; papers rel to the New Forest mainly 1746-73, incl accounts and corresp; papers rel to Stratton Park 18th cent, incl papers rel to alterations by Henry Holland 1789-91, inventories 1737, 1755, and accounts for household and park 1755-90.

Hampshire Record Office. Transferred from Bedfordshire Record Office 1989. NRA 17140 (partial list).

[d] Deeds, Devon and Cornwall 12th-20th cent, Dorset 14th-19th cent; settlements and trust deeds 1606-1732; legal papers 15th-20th cent, incl abstracts of title, schedules, draft conveyances and related papers; manorial records, Devon (Bishop Clyst, Hurdwick, Plymstock, St Thomas, Werrington, etc) 14th-20th cent, Cornwall 13th-19th cent and Dorset 16th-18th cent.

Devon and Cornwall estate records 14th-20th cent, incl leases from 14th cent (numerous from mid-16th cent), lease registers 1730-1918, surveys 16th-19th cent, maps and plans 18th-19th cent, rentals and accounts 15th-20th cent, vouchers 18th-early 20th cent, letters to Tavistock and London agents 18th-19th cent, and papers rel to timber and wood sales 1557-1865, individual farms 1743-1872, enclosure 19th cent, mining (copper, etc) 18th-19th cent, Tamar fisheries 19th-20th cent, markets, railways, purchases and sales; papers rel to Tavistock affairs 16th-20th cent, incl cloth production 1741-56 (accounts, 2 vols), market 16th-20th cent, canal 1803-76 and turnpike trust 1819-35; plans and papers rel to the development of Bedford Circus (site of former Bedford House), Exeter 1773-1840; Dorset estate records 16th-20th cent (many with Devon and Cornwall estate records), incl leases from 16th cent, surveys from 1578, rentals and accounts late 17th cent-1913, vouchers 1868-1906, annual reports 1867-1901, papers rel to woodlands 1779, 1870-1905 and enclosure papers 16th-17th cent; Hants estate survey 1677.

Drawing of Bedford House, Exeter 1755; Endsleigh Cottage building papers 1810-18, household vouchers 19th cent and game book 1841-55; Devon shrievalty roll 1397; Cornwall muster book 1558-9; Devon militia papers mainly 1758-70 (4th Duke as lord lieutenant); election papers 17th-19th cent, mainly Okehampton and Tavistock (Devon) and Camelford and Newport (Cornwall) late 18th cent; Tavistock Abbey cartulary 13th cent and misc documents 15th-16th cent; estreat roll of monastic lands in Devon 1439-1517; list of French prisoners at Tavistock 1759.

Devon Record Office (L 1258, T 1258, W 1258). Deposited from the Bedford Office, London, Tavistock estate office and Woburn Abbey 1963-89. *Guide to the Russell estate collections for Bedfordshire and Devon to 1910*, 1966. NRA 9813.

[e] Dorset estate rentals 1867-1911.

Dorset Record Office. Deposited 1989. *Annual Report 1989*, p15.

[f] Deeds, Middlesex (Covent Garden) 16th-20th cent and Surrey (Streatham, Rotherhithe, etc) 16th-19th cent; Howland family wills and settlements 17th-early 18th cent; legal papers, Covent Garden estate 17th-20th cent and Surrey estates 17th-early 19th cent; misc Tooting Bec (Surrey) manorial accounts 16th cent; Covent Garden estate records 16th-20th cent, incl leases, tenancy agreements and related papers 16th-20th cent, surveys and valuations 17th-18th cent, maps and plans 18th-20th cent, rentals and accounts 1594-19th cent, sale papers 1913-46 and misc corresp and papers from late 16th cent (mainly 18th and late 19th-early 20th cent); building papers 1635-20th cent, incl contracts, specifications, plans and drawings; accounts and papers rel to Covent Garden market c1724-1918, Covent Garden and Drury Lane theatres 1739-1940, and St Paul's church and parish 1631-1938; Surrey (Streatham and Rotherhithe) estate records 17th-early 19th cent, incl leases and lease registers, surveys and valuations, maps and plans, building agreements 18th cent, corresp late 17th-early 19th cent, and accounts and papers rel to Rotherhithe docks mainly 1745-63; particular of Downe (in Wandsworth) 1717; papers rel to Cheam and Ewell (Surrey) estate mid-18th cent; building and household accounts for Bedford House (Strand) 1657-94; inventories and accounts for Streatham Manor House 18th cent.

London Metropolitan Archives (E/BER). Deposited at various dates from 1968. NRA 28054. (For Tooting Bec court rolls *temp* Richard II-1689 see the deposit by the Metropolitan Board of Works (M95/BEC).)

[g] Deeds, wills, trust deeds and legal papers 1598-1927, mainly rel to the Howland and

Russell families and the Streatham estate 18th-early 19th cent; Streatham estate and household vouchers 1705-26 (incl a few for Rotherhithe, Wandsworth and Bloomsbury), 1752-68; estate corresp 1720-65, incl letters to Streatham and London agents; misc papers, incl Howland shrievalty papers (Surrey and Sussex) 17th cent and personal corresp of Edward Theobald (Streatham steward) 1726-35.

Lambeth Archives Department (IV/35). Deposited 1965 on the winding up of the Streatham Antiquarian Society, to which the papers had been given by the 11th Duke of Bedford. NRA 24823.

[h] Estate vouchers c1660-1760 (31 boxes), incl some letters and market reports.

British Library of Political and Economic Science (COLL MISC 147). NRA 29736.

[i] Deeds of alienated properties 16th-20th cent, mainly Beds, Middlesex and London; deed registers c1755-1972; wills, settlements and related trusteeship and executorship papers 18th-20th cent, incl Marlborough trusteeship papers of the 4th Duke c1740-70 and executorship papers for the 4th and later Dukes; solicitors' papers 19th-20th cent; St Giles-in-the-Fields (Middlesex) manorial court books 1742-1844.

General estate records 17th-20th cent, incl abstracts of leases mainly from 1737, rentals and accounts mainly from c1700, annual reports 1815-99, 1964-88, head agents' corresp 18th-19th cent and head office files 20th cent; Beds and Bucks estate records (Woburn, Bedford and Chenies) mainly 19th-20th cent, incl survey 1823-4, maps and plans, rentals from 1803, accounts from 1850, summaries of schools on the Woburn estate 1864-77 and estate papers from 1910 (extensive); Middlesex (Bloomsbury and Covent Garden) estate records 17th-20th cent (mainly from c1728), incl Bloomsbury leases from 17th cent, Bloomsbury and Covent Garden lease registers from 1805, contract books 1730-54 and letting and proposal books 1738-1972, misc Bloomsbury surveys and plans, Bloomsbury rentals and accounts 1728-1970, Bloomsbury and Covent Garden steward's reports 1869-1924, and extensive Bloomsbury estate papers from 1740s; misc papers for other estates 18th-20th cent, incl London and Surrey 18th cent, Thorney and Wansford c1838-1902, and Devon, Cornwall and Dorset c1738-1968.

Papers and drawings rel to the fabric of Woburn Abbey 18th-20th cent, incl work by Flitcroft, Holland and Wyatt; Woburn Abbey catalogues, inventories, etc 17th-20th cent and household accounts and papers 18th-20th cent, with papers rel to the park 19th-20th cent; papers rel to Chenies mainly 19th-20th cent; papers rel to other houses 18th-20th cent, incl Streatham, Endsleigh, Oakley, Bedford House (London) and Belgrave Square (London); misc local papers 16th-20th cent, incl Beds militia orders 1760-86 and Woburn Abbey Hospital 1914-19.

Appointments and commissions mainly 18th-19th cent; Russell family corresp and papers 16th-20th cent, incl misc papers of the 1st-4th Earls, papers of Sir William Russell (later Lord Russell of Thornhaugh) as Lord Deputy in Ireland 1594-7, papers of Lord and Lady Russell 1658-1701, despatches of Admiral Russell (later Earl of Orford) 1692-5, political, diplomatic, Irish, military, business, personal and family corresp and papers of the 4th Duke c1725-71, Irish and other papers of the 6th Duke 1786-1839, political and other corresp and papers of the 7th Duke c1805-61, papers of later Dukes late 19th-mid-20th cent, and diplomatic and other papers of Lord (George) William Russell mainly 1832-46; Howland family accounts and papers c1660-1706; military, estate and personal papers of the 3rd Earl Ludlow (d1842); papers of Gladys Scott Thomson, historian, and Mrs Georgiana Blakiston 20th cent; papers rel to the Pantheon and King's Theatre, Haymarket 1790-1815; misc parliamentary, genealogical and other papers 16th-20th cent.

In private possession. Documents less than one hundred years old are not available for research. Enquiries to the Bedford Estates Archivist, Woburn Abbey, Woburn, Beds MK43 OTP. HMC *Second Report, App*, 1871, pp1-4; *Papers of British Politicians 1782-1900*, 1989, p91. NRA 26179.

[j] Personal vouchers (clothing, etc) 1664-99.

Victoria and Albert Museum, National Art Library. Catalogue of English non-illuminated manuscripts in the National Art Library up to December 1973, nos 15-17. NRA 13466.

Related collections: Percy, Dukes of Northumberland, no 82, including papers relating to the Earl of Bedford's estates (Covent Garden, Thorney, etc) ?17th cent; Townshend, Marquesses Townshend, no 107, including papers of Ralph Peirson, Thorney agent 1665-1702; Cavendish, Dukes of Devonshire, no 17, and Pelham-Clinton, later Pelham-Clinton-Hope, Dukes of Newcastle no 81, including papers of Rachel, Lady Russell.

[91] SACKVILLE, Barons Sackville

The Sackville family was settled in Essex in the twelfth century, but acquired Buckhurst (Sussex) around 1200. Bolebroke (Sussex), inherited in the late fourteenth century, later passed, with a daughter of the third Earl of Dorset, to the Tufton family (see Tufton, Barons Hothfield, no 108). Sir Richard Sackville (1507-66), Chancellor of the Court of Augmentations, acquired extensive properties in Sussex and Kent (including the site of Lewes Priory 1560), and Salisbury House (later Dorset House, later Dorset Gardens, London) in 1564. His son Thomas Sackville (c1530-1608), Lord Treasurer 1599-1608, received further grants of land, including the reversion of Knole (Kent) in 1566. He was created Baron Buckhurst 1567, came into possession of Knole, which thenceforward became the principal seat, in 1603, and was created Earl of Dorset in 1604.

The third Earl of Dorset married in 1609 Anne Clifford, daughter and heir of the third Earl of Cumberland, but the Clifford estates did not descend in the Sackville family (see Cavendish, Dukes of Devonshire, no 17; Tufton, Barons Hothfield, no 108). The fourth Earl (1590-1652) married in 1612 Mary, daughter and heir of Sir George Curzon (d1622), through whom estates in Derbyshire (Croxall, etc) and Staffordshire were inherited, including land formerly in the possession of the Leveson family. The fifth Earl (1622-77) married c1637 Frances Cranfield, sister of the third Earl of Middlesex (d1674), who left estates in Essex (Copt Hall, formerly belonging to the Heneage family), Sussex (Wiston, acquired from the Shirley family) and Warwickshire and Gloucestershire (Milcote, Welford-on-Avon, etc, acquired from the Greville family) to his nephew the sixth Earl of Dorset. The seventh Earl (1688-1765) was created Duke of Dorset in 1720, and was Lord Lieutenant of Ireland 1730-7, 1751-5 and Lord President of the Council 1745-51.

The Kent and Sussex estates were much reduced by sales from 1614 onwards. The Copt Hall estate was sold in 1701, and Croxall in 1783. The third Duke (1745-99), however, repaired the family fortunes, buying back lands in Sussex and Kent, and in 1790 marrying Arabella, daughter and co-heir of Sir Charles Cope, 2nd Bt (d1781), of Bruern (Oxfordshire). (She married secondly Charles Whitworth (1752-1825), Earl Whitworth, who was descended from the Whitworth family of Adbaston and Batchacre (Staffordshire), and who left his property to her at his death.)

On the death of the fourth Duke in 1815 the dukedom passed to a cousin, Charles Sackville-Germain, second Viscount Sackville, of Drayton (Northamptonshire), but the Sussex, Kent, London, Oxfordshire, Gloucestershire and Warwickshire estates were left, after the death of the third Duke's widow in 1825, to her daughters the Countess of Plymouth (dsp1864) and Elizabeth, Countess De La Warr. In 1864 the latter became sole heir, and was created Baroness Buckhurst. On her death in 1870, however, the Sackville estates were divided. Buckhurst, together with the London and Oxfordshire estates, passed thenceforward with the earldom of De La Warr, but the Knole estate, together with property in Sussex (Chiddingly, etc), Gloucestershire and Warwickshire, passed to younger sons, first to the Hon Reginald Sackville-West and then, on his succeeding his brother as seventh Earl De La Warr in 1873, to the Hon Mortimer Sackville-West, who was created Baron Sackville in 1877.

Many early Sackville muniments are thought to have been destroyed by fire with Dorset House in 1666.

Estates in 1883: Sussex 4,080 acres, Gloucs [and Warwicks] 2,391 acres, Kent 1,960 acres, Herts 120 acres, total 8,551 acres worth £11,250 a year.

[a] Deeds 12th-20th cent, incl Kent (Sackville and Whitworth) 15th-20th cent, Sussex and Essex (Sackville and Cranfield) 13th-19th cent, Derbys and Staffs (Sackville and Whitworth) 13th-18th cent, Gloucs and Warwicks 12th-19th cent, Herefs (Sackville) 16th-17th cent and London and Middlesex (Sackville, Cranfield and Whitworth) 16th-19th cent; wills, settlements and related papers 15th-20th cent, incl Sackville 17th-20th cent, Cranfield 17th cent, Greville 15th-early 17th cent, Cope 1741-1821, Whitworth and related families (Wyndham and Strode) 17th-18th cent, and West (Earls De La Warr) late 17th-early 19th cent; legal and case papers 15th-20th cent, incl Greville estates 15th-17th cent and partition of the Sackville estates 19th cent; manorial court records 14th-20th cent, incl Kent 15th-19th cent, Sussex (Wiston, Charlton, etc) 14th-20th cent, Beds (Cranfield) 16th-17th cent, Essex (Sheering) 14th-17th cent, Gloucs and Warwicks (Welford-on-Avon, Stratford-on-Avon, etc) 15th-20th cent and Staffs (Adbaston, etc) 14th-15th cent; Otford (Kent) honour records 1386-1704.

Kent and Sussex (Knole and Buckhurst) estate records 16th-20th cent, incl leases from 16th cent, surveys and valuations from mid-16th cent, maps and plans 18th-19th cent, rentals and accounts 17th-early 20th cent, corresp 19th-20th cent, farm accounts mainly 19th cent, and papers rel to churches and livings, Ashdown forest, etc; papers rel to London and Essex (Sackville) estates 17th-18th cent, incl London (Dorset Gardens) leases and rentals; Derbys and Staffs (Curzon, later Sackville) estate records 16th-18th cent, incl leases, rentals and map of Croxall 1687; Gloucs and Warwicks estate records 16th-early 20th cent, incl leases, surveys, rentals and accounts; misc estate records rel to Surrey (West Horsley: Sackville) early 17th cent, Beds, Essex, Herts and Sussex (Cranfield) 16th-17th cent, Oxon, etc (Cope) late 18th-early 19th cent, Staffs (Batchacre: Whitworth) 1814-24, Somerset (Blackford, etc: Wyndham, later Whitworth) 17th-18th cent, Sussex (Sheffield Park: Abergavenny, later De La Warr) 1736-74, Cambs (De La Warr) 1858-60 and Ireland (Glenogra, Co Limerick: Sackville) 1881-7; Devon (Tawstock, etc: Bourchier Earls of Bath) estate records 1628-55.

Papers rel to Knole 17th-early 20th cent, incl inventories, accounts and vouchers, visitors' books 1805-1928 and papers rel to the garden and park; papers rel to Buckhurst Park and Stoneland Lodge (Sussex) 1624-1873, London houses (Sackville and Cranfield) 17th cent, Copt Hall 1623-1701, Milcote and Sezincote (Warwicks and Gloucs) 1625-44 and Wiston 1629-30; Bath household accounts 1703; papers rel to Kent and Sussex affairs 17th-19th cent, incl lieutenancy and militia, commission of the peace, elections, Kent charities 18th-19th cent and Sackville College (East Grinstead, Sussex) 1630-1797; papers rel to Essex, Gloucs and Warwicks affairs 16th-17th cent, and to the borough and peculiar of Stratford-on-Avon 16th-18th cent.

Patents, commissions, licences, etc 15th-19th cent, Sackville, Cranfield, Whitworth and Greville; Sackville family corresp, accounts, vouchers and papers 16th-20th cent, incl diary of Lady Anne Clifford 1603-19 (copy), corresp and notebooks of the 5th Earl of Dorset *c*1640-77, papers of the 6th Earl as Lord Chamberlain 1689-97, political, Irish and other corresp and papers of the 1st Duke *c*1714-63, and papers of the 3rd Duke as Lord Steward and ambassador to France 1782-96; corresp and papers of the 1st, 2nd and 3rd Earls of Middlesex, incl extensive business and official papers of Lionel Cranfield (1st Earl); papers of the 5th Earl of Bath and his wife (later Lady Middlesex) 1639-54, and of the Earl of Falmouth and his wife (later Lady Dorset) 1660-77; Whitworth family papers 17th-early 19th cent, incl diplomatic corresp and papers of Lord Whitworth early 18th cent, military papers of Sir Francis Whitworth 1777-1805 and diplomatic, Irish and other papers of Earl Whitworth 1778-1819; corresp of the 2nd, 4th and 5th Earls De La Warr 18th-19th cent and of Elizabeth, Countess De La Warr 1834-53; journals or notebooks of Ludovic Greville 1564-86, Lady Rachel Fane 1623-33 and the 6th Earl of Plymouth 1809; misc genealogical and literary papers 17th-19th cent; Feckenham forest (Worcs) swanimote roll 1493.

Centre for Kentish Studies (U 269). Deposited by the 4th Baron Sackville and the Trustees of the Knole Second Trust Fund 1950-96, with additional material deposited in Sevenoaks Library *c*1945 from the collection of HW Knocker and transferred to the Archives Office 1963 (Acc 1008). F Hull, *Guide to the Kent County Archives Office*, 1958, pp150-6; *First supplement 1957-1968*, 1971, p143; *Second supplement 1969-1980*, 1983, pp130-2. HMC *Fourth Report, App*, 1874, pp276-317; *Seventh Report, App*, 1879, pp249-60; *Sackville I, II*, 1940, 1966; *Private Papers of British Diplomats 1782-1900*, 1985, pp58, 72; *Papers of British Politicians 1782-1900*, 1989, p111. NRA 8575.

[b] Copy of grant of the borough of East Grinstead, etc 1606/7; account of Thomas

Medley as receiver for the Sackville estates 1687.

East Sussex Record Office (Portman of Buxted Place papers, AMS 6270/91-2). Acquired 1987. NRA 12274.

[c] Stratford-on-Avon manorial court rolls 1463-1548; Feckenham forest swanimote roll 1552.

Shakespeare Birthplace Trust Records Office (DR 75). Purchased 1949. NRA 4523.

[d] Household accounts of Lady Cranfield kept by Sir Lionel Cranfield (later 1st Earl of Middlesex) 1615, with additions 1619-21.

British Library, Manuscript Collections (Eg MS 1933). Purchased from James McCarthy 1861.

[e] Household books of the Earl and Countess of Middlesex 1622.

Lambeth Palace Library (MSS 1228, 3361). Transferred from Fulham Palace 1828, 1960.

[f] Sussex militia letter book of the 3rd Earl of Dorset 1614-24, with misc papers c1621-7, kept by his secretary Evan Edwards.

Flintshire Record Office (Rhual MSS, D/HE nos 732-41 *passim*). Deposited by Major BHP Heaton 1972 and transferred from the National Library of Wales 1985. NRA 13672.

[g] Corresp and papers of Edward Sackville-West, 5th Baron Sackville c1917-88.

British Library, Manuscript Collections (Add MSS 68904-21). Purchased 1988. Further letters and papers were acquired by the Harry Ransom Humanities Research Centre, University of Texas, Austin, Texas (*Location Register of twentieth-century English literary manuscripts and letters*, 1988, ii, p830).

Related collections: Earls De La Warr (East Sussex Record Office D 397-9, 680, etc, NRA 8607, 14454), including deeds, settlements and manorial records relating to Sackville estates in Sussex 16th-19th cent, Buckhurst terrier 1597-8, rental (all Sackville estates) 1618-19, Sussex maps 1799, London (Dorset Gardens) deeds and leases 17th-19th cent, and a few papers of the 1st Earl of Dorset 1599-1603; diplomatic papers of Lord Whitworth early 18th cent (British Library, Manuscript Collections Add MSS 37348-97, formerly at Buckhurst Park, see HMC *Third Report*, *App*, 1872, pp218-20); Stopford-Sackville MSS (in private possession, HMC *Stopford-Sackville MSS I, II*, 1904, 1910; University of Michigan, William L Clements Library, Ann Arbor, *see* HMC *Guide to the location of collections*, 1982, p59), including Irish and other papers of the 1st Duke of Dorset; Cope of Hanwell and Bramshill (Hampshire Record Office 43 M 48, NRA 540), including Bruern estate records late 17th cent; Whitworth

(Adbaston, etc) deeds and papers (William Salt Library, Stafford WSL 26/22, NRA 8250).

[92] SEYMOUR, Dukes of Somerset

Edward Seymour (d1552), from a Wiltshire family, was created Duke of Somerset in 1547, and received large grants of former monastic lands in Wiltshire (Savernake Forest), Somerset and elsewhere. The Savernake estate passed to Edward Seymour (1537-1621), the Duke's son by his second marriage, created Earl of Hertford in 1559, and eventually to the Earls and Marquesses of Ailesbury (see Brudenell-Bruce, Marquesses of Ailesbury, no 12). However, Sir Edward Seymour (d1593), a son of the Duke by his first marriage, succeeded an elder brother in the Maiden Bradley (Wiltshire) estate in 1552, and the following year was granted his father's manor of Berry Pomeroy (Devon). His son Sir Edward Seymour (1563-1611) was created a baronet in 1611.

Sir Edward Seymour, sixth Bt (1695-1757), married in 1717 Mary, daughter and heir of Daniel Webb of Monkton Farleigh and Melksham (Wiltshire), by Elizabeth Somner of Seend (Wiltshire). In 1750, on the death of the seventh Duke of Somerset, Sir Edward Seymour succeeded to the dukedom, though not to any of the estates that had been held with it (see Percy, Dukes of Northumberland, no 82). In the eighteenth century Maiden Bradley became the principal seat, and the Maiden Bradley estate was later extended with purchases of nearby property in Somerset (Witham Friary) and Dorset (Silton). The tenth Duke (1718-93) married in 1769 Anna Bonnell, who appears to have brought property in the Spalding district of Lincolnshire and the Wisbech district of Cambridgeshire. The eleventh Duke (1775-1855) acquired Bulstrode (Buckinghamshire) from the third Duke of Portland in 1810.

On the death of the twelfth Duke in 1885 his estates were divided. The Berry Pomeroy and Maiden Bradley estates, both reduced, passed to his next brother as thirteenth Duke, but his other properties, including land in Buckinghamshire, Cambridgeshire and Lincolnshire, passed to his daughters.

Estates in 1883: Devon 8,138 acres, Somerset 6,553 acres, Wilts 5,824 acres, Lincs 2,865 acres, Bucks 1,640 acres, Cambs 289 acres, Dorset 46 acres, Norfolk 32 acres, total 25,387 acres worth £37,577 a year.

[a] Deeds 13th-19th cent, mainly Wilts but incl some for Somerset and Dorset and small quantities for Bucks 13th-19th cent, Cambs 17th-18th cent, Lincs 17th-19th cent and other counties; settlements, wills, trust papers and executorship papers 16th-early 20th cent, mainly Seymour, incl letters patent, etc rel to the marriage of Henry VIII and Jane Seymour

1536; legal papers 16th-19th cent, incl Duke of Somerset's estates 1548-52 and Somerset peerage claim 1750; manorial records 14th-19th cent, mainly Wilts and Somerset 18th-19th cent; Wilts, Somerset and Dorset estate records 17th-20th cent, incl leases, surveys and valuations, rentals and accounts, and papers rel to tithes; misc estate records for Bucks 18th-19th cent (incl particular and maps 1840), Cambs 18th cent and Lincs 17th-19th cent (incl maps 1665, *c*1780); valuation of Duke of Somerset's estates 16th cent (copy); survey of Sir Francis Popham's manors 1673; misc Duke of Somerset (Seymour and Percy) legal and estate papers early 18th cent, Sussex, Wilts, Somerset, Middlesex, Cambs, Northumberland and Yorks, incl Strand (Middlesex) rental 1747, Cheveley (Cambs) leases early 18th cent and Cambs, etc rentals 1729-31, 1733; Egremont (Cumberland, Wilts, Somerset) estate accounts 1764, 1779.

Maiden Bradley inventories 18th-19th cent, plans rel to alterations 1887 and household papers early 19th cent; Seend (Wilts) inventory 1769; lists of fixtures at Burton Hall (Leics) 1896; Cheveley plans 18th cent and inventory 1737; misc Seymour (Dukes of Somerset) papers early 18th cent, incl household accounts 1709; militia papers 1660-1800; Seymour patents, grants and commissions 16th-19th cent; misc Seymour family papers mid-17th-early 20th cent, incl naval, military and political papers of Sir Edward Seymour, 4th Bt (1633-1708), letter book of the 11th Duke and diary of ?the 12th Duke 1880; misc genealogical and other papers 17th-18th cent; accounts, etc of the 6th Duke of Somerset as Master of the Horse 1702-16; Maiden Bradley Priory charters, etc 12th-15th cent, incl Rules late 13th cent.

Wiltshire and Swindon Record Office (WRO 1332, WRS 2056). Deposited by the 18th and 19th Dukes of Somerset 1964-84. HMC *Fifteenth Report, App VIII*, 1899, pp52-151. NRA 32135 (partial list).

[b] Devon deeds 13th-18th cent (Berry Pomeroy, Bridgetown, etc); misc legal papers 15th-19th cent, incl grant of wardship and marriage, Pomeroy family 1495; misc Devon manorial court rolls, accounts, etc 14th-18th cent, incl account of Pomeroy manors in Devon and Cornwall 1384, Teignharvey account 1390 and Totnes court roll 1463-5; Devon estate papers mid-16th-early 20th cent, incl leases *c*1557-1835, surveys and maps from 1700, rentals and accounts 18th-19th cent, and misc corresp and papers 17th-20th cent; grant of Bridgetown market 1603; plans and view of Berry Pomeroy House 18th cent; militia papers 1595-1800; commission to survey the Marquess of Winchester's Devon, etc estates 1687; letter book of Sir Edward Seymour 1596-7.

Devon Record Office (D 3799, D 3799 M add, add 2). Transferred from Wiltshire Record Office 1983-4 and deposited 1991. NRA 32135.

[c] Devon manorial records (Berry Pomeroy, Bridgetown, Harberton, Stockleigh Pomeroy, Great Totnes) 15th-16th cent; Berry Pomeroy estate records 1764-1951, incl leases and agreements 1892-1927, surveys and rentals from early 19th cent, accounts from mid-19th cent, letter books 1863-1925, corresp 20th cent, and papers rel to tithes, fishing, Bridgetown Quay, etc 19th-20th cent.

Devon Record Office (867B). Deposited by Michelmore, Loveys & Carter, land agents, Totnes 1960. NRA 8073. A few additional papers 1823-1927, nd, found in the record office in 1992, have been catalogued as 4984B (NRA 4613).

Related collections: Manners, Dukes of Rutland, no 68; Percy, Dukes of Northumberland, no 82; Wyndham, Barons Leconfield and Egremont, no 117; Pennington-Ramsden of Byram and Muncaster (Buckinghamshire Record Office D/RA, NRA 11704; Devon Record Office 1392 M, NRA 12798; in private possession, NRA 24077), including Bulstrode deeds and estate papers 16th-20th cent, miscellaneous Devon deeds and estate papers 13th-20th cent (mainly *temp* the 12th Duke of Somerset), Seymour family papers late 16th-early 19th cent (some calendared in HMC *Fifteenth Report, App VIII*, 1899) and political and personal papers of the 12th Duke.

[93] SHIRLEY, Earls Ferrers

The Shirley family was settled at Ettington (Warwickshire) by 1086 and Shirley (Derbyshire) by *c*1129. Property in Nottinghamshire (Ratcliffe-upon-Soar), Leicestershire (Ratcliffe-on-the-Wreake, Ragdale, etc) and elsewhere was inherited from the last Baron Bassett (d1390) of Drayton. In the fifteenth century Brailsford (Derbyshire) and Staunton Harold (Leicestershire) were acquired through marriages to heiresses while another marriage, that of John Shirley and Jane, daughter and heir of Thomas Lovett, in 1558 brought the Astwell estate (Northamptonshire) and lands in other counties. Sir George Shirley was created a baronet in 1611.

In 1646, on the death of his uncle Robert Devereux, third Earl of Essex, the fourth Bt inherited Chartley (Staffordshire) and a moiety of the barony of Farney (County Monaghan), the remainder of Essex's property passing to his sister Frances, Marchioness of Hertford (see Thynne, Marquesses of Bath, no 104). An estate at Garsdon (Wiltshire) was acquired through the marriage of Robert Shirley (created Earl Ferrers 1711) and Elizabeth, daughter and heir of Sir Laurence Washington, but on the first Earl's death in 1717 his estates were divided between the children of this marriage and those of his second marriage to Selina Finch, daughter of the London merchant George

Finch. Garsdon (sold 1741) passed to a younger son by Elizabeth Washington and the Ettington and County Monaghan estates to the sons of the second marriage (see Shirley of Ettington, no 94), whilst the remaining estates were settled on the second Earl, a son by the first marriage.

The Northamptonshire and some of the Derbyshire property was sold by the fifth Earl (d1778) and further Derbyshire and Leicestershire lands were alienated in the nineteenth century. The Chartley and Staunton Harold estates were disposed of in 1904 and c1949-53 respectively. The eleventh Earl, who succeeded his cousin the tenth Earl in 1912, was descended from a brother of the sixth Earl, Walter Shirley, rector of Loughrea (County Galway), the founder of an ecclesiastical dynasty.

Property at Tamworth (Staffordshire) was acquired through the marriage of Robert Shirley (d1698), son of the first Earl, to Anne, daughter and heir of Sir Humphrey Ferrers. Their son Robert, Viscount Tamworth (d1714) had no issue but their daughter Elizabeth, Baroness Ferrers (d1741) married the fifth Earl of Northampton and had issue Charlotte, wife of the first Marquess Townshend, to whose family the Tamworth estate descended (see Townshend, Marquesses Townshend, no 107). Wiston (West Sussex), brought by the marriage of Beatrice (d1440), daughter and heir of Sir John de Braose, to Sir Hugh Shirley, devolved upon a junior branch of the Shirley family.

Estates in 1883: Staffs 6,862 acres, Leics 1,801 acres, Derbys 2 acres, total 8,665 acres worth £12,707 a year.

[a] Deeds 12th-19th cent, mainly Derbys, Leics and Staffs but incl Lincs, Notts, Warwicks, Yorks, etc 12th-18th cent and Wilts from 14th cent; de Braose family cartulary 15th cent; wills, settlements, and executorship, legal and trust papers 13th-19th cent; sequestration and related papers of Sir Robert Shirley c1648-52; manorial court records, Derbys 15th-19th cent and Leics 14th-19th cent; Duffield (Derbys) wood moot rolls 1497-1505; misc manorial court rolls 14th-19th cent, incl Rippingale (Lincs) 1413-16, Strixton (Northants) 1357-1430 and Chartley 1814-44, with customary of Ingoldmells and Addlethorpe (Lincs) 17th cent.

Leics and Staffs estate records 14th-20th cent, mainly from 18th cent, incl surveys, valuations, maps, plans, particulars, rentals, vouchers and accounts, with Leics colliery and lime works accounts 1762-79 and Shirleywich (Staffs) salt works accounts 1705-42; other estate papers 14th-19th cent, incl Derbys survey and valuation 1768, plans for Derbys and Happisburgh (Norfolk) 18th-19th cent, Bucks estate accounts 1455, and Wilts estate papers 18th cent, with Shirley family estate valuations 1413-14, 1431 and rentals 17th cent, and rental of the 2nd

Earl's estates c1720; Staunton Harold house building accounts 1762-8, 1857-61 and church building accounts c1656-68; Staunton Harold library inventory 1834; misc household records 17th-20th cent (Staunton Harold and Chartley), incl Staunton Harold garden accounts 1827-1904; Kensington (Middlesex) household accounts 1911-18; inventories of household goods of Sir Henry Unton 1596, 1600 and of goods at Astwell 1622.

Family corresp and papers 16th-20th cent, incl misc appointments and commissions from 16th cent, account book of Sir George Shirley of Astwell 1592-6, accounts and papers of the 5th Earl, accounts, corresp and papers of the 8th Earl as manager of Viscount Dudley's Staffs collieries 1782-1820, and solicitors' accounts for the Revd Walter Shirley 1778-1803 and the 9th Earl 1842-59; misc papers from 17th cent, incl Shirley pedigree 1632, Devereux and Ferrers pedigree 1627, Ferrers Bible c1656, and inventory of goods and manuscripts of Sir Isaac Newton 1727.

Leicestershire Record Office (26 D 53, DE 2638). Deposited by the 12th and 13th Earls Ferrers 1953-84. (Staunton Harold estate and church accounts c1656-68 (6 D 61) were received from a private depositor in Ashby-de-la-Zouch 1961.) HE Broughton, *Family and Estate Records in the Leicestershire Record Office*, 1991, pp 28-9. NRA 874.

[b] Misc deeds 1849-59; legal papers 1854-1910, incl some rel to the Stafford and Uttoxeter Railway and to the sale of the Chartley estate; estate records 1833-77, incl Leics and Staffs leases 1833-68, rentals of the Staffs estate 1853-67 and the 9th Earl's estates 1854, Derbys estate valuation 1847, and Derbys, Leics and Staffs accounts 1857-77; misc plans 19th cent, incl drawings for Staunton Harold; vouchers and accounts of Augusta Annabella, Countess Ferrers 1854-68 and accounts of the 11th Earl 1898-1923.

Leicestershire Record Office (25 D 60). Deposited by Crane & Walton, solicitors, Ashby-de-la-Zouch 1960. NRA 874.

[c] Shirley family corresp mainly 18th-19th cent, incl the Revd Walter Shirley (d1858), the Revd Walter Augustus Shirley (1797-1847) and the Revd Walter Waddington Shirley (d1866).

Leicestershire Record Office (22 D 64). Purchased 1964. NRA 874.

[d] Warwicks shrievalty accounts, Sir John Ferrers 1614-15, with misc deeds and a Warwicks rental 1720.

Leicestershire Record Office (23 D 66, 4 D 68). Deposited through Northumberland Record Office 1966, 1968. NRA 874.

[e] Account book of John Johnson, Staunton Harold steward 1724-55.

Leicestershire Record Office (5 D 69). Purchased 1969. NRA 874.

[f] Cartulary of Sir George Shirley Bt of Astwell (d1622).

Leicestershire Record Office (15 D 72). Deposited 1972. NRA 874.

[g] Court rolls for Shirley family manors (Ragdale, Willowes, Ratcliffe-on-the-Wreake, etc) 1375-1560.

Leicestershire Record Office (DE 1452/1). Deposited by Eland Hore Patersons, solicitors, London 1974. HMC *Accessions to Repositories 1974.*

[h] Staffs estate valuation late 18th cent, vouchers 1841-80, accounts 1868-1905 and corresp 1848-87; Astwell rent accounts 1720-1; accounts of the estate of the Revd Walter Shirley, rector of Brailsford 1775-95; misc Shirley family corresp and papers 1693-1859; misc accounts of the first Earl; corresp and papers 1779-1825 and personal and household vouchers 1789-1830 of the 8th Earl, incl accounts as manager of Viscount Dudley's Staffs collieries 1802; corresp and accounts of the Revd Walter Shirley 1780-1823, incl accounts as executor of his mother Henrietta Shirley; Tamworth poll book 1710.

Staffordshire and Stoke on Trent Archive Service, Staffordshire Record Office (D 591, D 3794). Deposited by the City Museum and Art Gallery, Stoke-on-Trent 1959 and by Northumberland Record Office 1982. NRA 7148.

[i] Staffs deeds 1567-1675 and estate papers 19th cent, incl leases 1839-67 and valuations 1851-65; Leics and Staffs estate accounts 1885-89; Staffs tithe papers 1761-1834.

Staffordshire and Stoke on Trent Archive Service, Staffordshire Record Office (D 1702/10-14). Deposited by Crane & Walton, solicitors, Ashby-de-la-Zouch, through Leicester Museum 1943. NRA 3516.

[j] Records of Shirley family manors (Brailsford, Shirley, etc) 18th cent.

Derbyshire Record Office (D 769/12/5/1-2). Deposited by Taylor, Simpson & Mosley, solicitors, Derby 1986. HMC *Accessions to Repositories 1986.*

[k] Deeds, Glen Magna and Ratcliffe-on-the-Wreake (Leics) 1655-1804, with list of legal expenses; inventory of books, pictures and furniture held in trust under the will of the 7th Earl 1828.

Public Record Office (C 108/183, 208).

[l] Breedon Priory (Leics) cartulary 13th cent.

John Rylands University Library of Manchester (Latin MS 222). Formerly in the possession of the Earls Ferrers (Phillipps MS 21710). GRC Davis, *Medieval Cartularies of Great Britain,* 1958, p10.

Related collections: Shirley of Ettington, no 94; Thynne, Marquesses of Bath, no 104; Townshend, Marquesses Townshend, no 107.

[94] SHIRLEY of Ettington

The Shirley family of Ettington (Warwickshire) descended from Robert Shirley, first Earl Ferrers and his second wife Selina, daughter of the London merchant George Finch (see Shirley, Earls Ferrers, no 93). Robert Shirley, the eldest son of this marriage, received the ancestral family estate of Ettington in tail male. This passed on his death without issue in 1738 to his next brother George Shirley (d1787). The County Monaghan estate, however, consisting of a moiety of the barony of Farney, inherited from Robert Devereux, third Earl of Essex (for whom see also Thynne, Marquesses of Bath, no 104), was divided equally between the four sons of the second marriage. These portions were united in the possession of George Shirley following the childless deaths of his younger brothers in 1765 and 1768; some Irish property was sold c1789-90. The Warwickshire and County Monaghan estates descended together to the heirs of George Shirley. Property in Middlesex, including a mansion at Twickenham, was settled on Robert Shirley (d1738) by his father but this seems to have been disposed of by the early nineteenth century. A quantity of papers of the Shirley family was collected by Evelyn Philip Shirley, an antiquarian member of the Ettington branch, from Staunton Harold and transferred to Ettington about 1830.

Estates in 1883: Warwicks 1,769 acres, Worcs 605 acres, Co Monaghan 26,386 acres, total 28,760 acres worth £23,744 a year.

[a] Deeds 13th cent-1886, mainly Warwicks, but incl some for Derbys, Devon (Dowager Countess of Orford's lands 1746-54), Dorset, Hants, Middlesex (Harrow, Hendon and Twickenham 1600-1840), Notts (Stoke estate of Stanhope family), Oxon, Staffs (Chartley estate 1737-43), Yorks and Argyllshire (Malcolm of Poltalloch estate 1833-43); Co Monaghan deeds 1731-1866; wills, settlements, executorship papers and trust papers 16th-20th cent, incl executorship papers for the Stanhope family, Earls of Chesterfield 18th-19th cent; legal papers 17th-19th cent, incl draft division of the 3rd Earl of Essex's estates c1653 and papers rel to the division of the Co Monaghan estate 1851; manorial court records for Ettington 1562-1866 and Ilmington (Warwicks) 1683-1700.

Warwicks estate records mainly 18th-20th cent, incl plans 1738-1862, rentals and valuations 1726-1855, and accounts, farm journals, stock books and papers 1759-1934; Co Monaghan estate plans, rentals, valuations and papers 1657-1882; rental of Shirley family estates 1657-66; Chartley estate accounts 1692-1842; Bretby (Derbys) estate rental 1776 and accounts 1747-1827, Stanhope family, with rental of the 4th Earl of Chesterfield's estates 1773; Ettington Park and parish church plans and building accounts 18th-20th cent; household accounts, Ettington 1793-1882, Alveston (Warwicks) 1794-1803 and Stanhope family 1835-7; Warwicks shrievalty papers of Evelyn Philip Shirley 1867; records of Ettington school 1806-34 and book club 1835-54; papers rel to Edgehill Turnpike Trust 1794-1876; Co Monaghan election expenses of Evelyn John Shirley 1830, with papers rel to Co Monaghan high shrievalty 1835; records of the Irish Society 1837-9 and Beresford Trust 1874-81; commissions and appointments 17th-19th cent; Shirley family corresp and papers 1596-20th cent, incl diaries 1798-1882, naval papers of Admiral Thomas Shirley 1777-91, military papers of General Horatio Shirley 1848-79 and Major-General Arthur Shirley 1851-70, and papers of Evelyn John Shirley 1810-58, Evelyn Philip Shirley 1830-82 and the 8th and 9th Earls Ferrers 1837-49; literary and genealogical papers 16th-19th cent.

Warwickshire County Record Office (CR 229, 464, 2131, 2485, 2747). Deposited by Evelyn Charles Shirley and Major JE Shirley 1952-89. HMC *Papers of British Politicians 1782-1900*, 1989, p95. NRA 17508. The family papers described in HMC *Fifth Report, App*, 1876, pp362-9, were mostly dispersed by sale in 1929 and 1947 (see HMC *Guide to the Location of Collections*, 1982, p56).

[b] Warwicks estate papers 18th-20th cent, incl Lambcote map 1766.

Warwickshire County Record Office (CR 1273). Deposited by Godfrey Payton & Co, Warwick 1970.

[c] Misc Irish deeds 1576-1889; legal papers 1607-1935, incl some rel to the partition of the Co Monaghan estate late 17th cent; Co Monaghan estate records 17th-20th cent, incl leases from 1738, surveys, maps, plans and valuations from 1655, rentals from 1695, accounts from 1708 and journals 1848-1915, corresp 17th-20th cent, tenants' petitions mid-19th cent, Cloughvally and Tyrogarvan limekiln accounts 1851-1906 and Carrickmacross market toll receipts 1876-1904; Irish Land Commission sale papers c1880-1930; Lough Fea (Co Monaghan) household, garden, desmesne and building accounts 1830-20th cent; South Warwicks and Co Monaghan election papers c1826-1901; Carrickmacross Savings Bank ledgers 1832-48; misc appointments and com-

missions 1573-1891; family and misc papers 17th-20th cent, incl diaries of Irish tour by George Hardinge MP 1792-3 and papers of Evelyn John Shirley (d1856).

Public Record Office of Northern Ireland (D 3531). Deposited by Major JE Shirley 1981, 1989. HMC *Papers of British Politicians 1782-1900*, 1989, p95. NRA 25608.

[d] Shirley family wills 1509-1778 (copies) and legal papers 1586-1651; executorship accounts of Thomas Fermor of Somerton (Oxon) 1580; Ettington Park alterations book and visitors' book ?19th cent; household book of the 1st Earl Ferrers 1684-7; Astwell household inventory 1614, Sir George Shirley; Shirley family papers 16th-19th cent, incl corresp of Evelyn John and Evelyn Philip Shirley, letters of Ralph Shirley, rector of Welford (Berks) 1714-54, journal of the Hon Lewis Shirley's voyage to China 1700-2 and commonplace books of Eliza Shirley 1813-41; corresp of the 1st Earl Stanhope and Lord Treasurer Godolphin 1705-8; household receipts and commonplace books of the 2nd Earl of Chesterfield (d1713); journals of Sir Nicholas Lechmere 1613-80 (copy), Sir Fulwar Skipwith, 1st Bt (d1678), Selina, Lady Skipwith 1767-1830 and Alexander Thistlethwayte's Italian tour 1775-6; genealogical papers, Shirley and Lechmere families; literary and misc papers, incl royal letters 1795-1840.

In private possession. Enquiries to the Historical Manuscripts Commission. HMC *Fifth Report, App*, 1876, pp362-9. NRA 7573.

Related collections; Shirley, Earls Ferrers, no 93; Herbert, Earls of Carnarvon, no 49, including further Stanhope papers.

[95] SIDNEY, Barons De L'Isle and Dudley, later Viscounts De L'Isle

By the fifteenth century the Sidney family owned estates in Surrey, at Alfold near Cranleigh, and in Sussex. These were sold in the early sixteenth century by Sir William Sidney (d1554), who received grants of property in the north and east ridings of Yorkshire. In 1539 he exchanged these for the Robertsbridge Abbey (Sussex) estates, which were retained until their sale to Sir Robert Webster in 1726. The Penshurst (Kent) estate was granted to him by Edward VI in 1552. Sir Henry Sidney (d1586), Sir William's son, was co-heir through his grandmother Anne, daughter of Sir William Brandon, to the last Brandon Duke of Suffolk and from him inherited property including the Cromwell family foundation of Tattershall College (Lincolnshire), with former Cromwell family manors in Lincolnshire, Leicestershire, Norfolk, Nottinghamshire and elsewhere. This was largely sold to the Earl of Lincoln in 1574 and descended to the Earls Fortescue (see no 39).

Sir Henry's son Robert Sidney (d1626) was created Baron Sidney 1603, Viscount Lisle 1605 and Earl of Leicester 1618. He inherited Leicester House, Westminster, and property in Warwickshire on the death of his uncle Robert Dudley, Earl of Leicester, in 1588 and was bequeathed by Anne Dudley, Dowager Countess of Warwick (d1604), a claim to the Berkeley family estates in Gloucestershire, which gave rise to litigation but no permanent passage of property to the Sidney family. Through his marriage in 1584 to the daughter and heir of John Gamage, Robert Sidney acquired the Coity (Glamorganshire) estate, while in 1604 he was granted the honour of Otford (Kent).

The fourth Earl of Leicester was succeeded on his death in 1702 by three sons in turn as fifth, sixth and seventh Earls. The fifth Earl (d1705) and another son, the Hon Thomas Sidney (d1728), married the sisters and co-heirs of Sir Robert Reeve, second Bt, of Thwaite (Suffolk), thereby acquiring property in Norfolk (Ranworth, Panxworth, etc) and Suffolk (Thwaite, Monewdon, etc). On the death of the seventh Earl without legitimate issue in 1743, the family peerages were extinguished but the estates descended to Elizabeth, younger daughter of the Hon Thomas Sidney and wife of William Perry (d1759) of Turville Park (Buckinghamshire). The Glamorganshire estate was settled, however, on an illegitimate daughter of the seventh Earl, who married Henry Streatfeild of Chiddingstone (Kent) in 1752; and some division of the Thwaite property occurred in connection with the claims of Elizabeth Perry's sister Mary (d1758, wife of Sir Brownlow Sherrard, fourth Bt). The bulk of the Sidney property, however, and the Perry estates in Buckinghamshire and Oxfordshire (Chalgrove, Pyrton), with property in Gloucestershire, Herefordshire (Eardisley, Knighton) and Radnorshire (Old Radnor), passed to Elizabeth, the daughter of William Perry. She married, as his second wife, Bysshe Shelley of Castle Goring (Sussex). Her estates devolved upon the eldest son of this marriage, Sir John Shelley-Sidney (d1849), who took the surname Sidney in 1793 and was created a baronet in 1818. His son was raised to the peerage as Baron De L'Isle and Dudley in 1835. The sixth Baron was created Viscount De L'Isle in 1956. The Dudley inheritance, except for the Leicester House estate in Westminster, appears to have been disposed of in the seventeenth century and the family property outside Kent (eg Turville, sold 1796) to have been alienated by the early nineteenth century.

In 1850 the second Baron married the daughter and heiress of Sir William Foulis, eighth Bt, of Ingleby Manor (Yorkshire, North Riding). Ingleby had been purchased in 1608 by Sir David Foulis, created a baronet 1620, and the North Riding estate was extended by his son Sir Henry Foulis, through his marriage to the daughter of Sir Thomas Layton of Sexhow.

Estates in 1883: Yorks NR 4,896 acres, Kent 4,356 acres, total 9,252 acres worth £10,232 a year.

[a] Kent and Sussex deeds 12th-18th cent, incl Robertsbridge Abbey charters 1160-1537 (c638 items); deeds for Lincs 13th-17th cent, Middlesex (Leicester House and Fields) 17th-18th cent, Norfolk and Warwicks 16th-18th cent and Glamorgan 15th-18th cent, incl charters for Tattershall College 1406-1566, with misc deeds for Bucks, Gloucs, Hants, Herefs and Radnorshire, etc 13th-18th cent; Irish deeds 1186-1700 (16 items); register of Gamage family deeds c1600; abstracts of title 16th-18th cent, incl one for the estates of Robert Dudley, Earl of Leicester c1581; inquisitions *post mortem*, Seyntclere family of Penshurst c1408-23, Robert Deyncourt 1442, Ralph, Lord Cromwell 1456 and Robert Pakenham 1595; wills, settlements, probate and trust papers 15th-19th cent, mainly Sidney and Perry families, incl wills of Sir William Sidney 1548 and Maud, Lady Cromwell 1417, and will and executorship accounts for Ralph, Lord Cromwell 1454-9; legal and financial papers 16th-19th cent, Sidney, Perry and Reeve families, incl case papers rel to the Berkeley properties 16th-17th cent, the estate of the 7th Earl of Leicester (d1743) and the barony of L'Isle c1780-1835.

Kent manorial records c1300-1800, incl Otford honour and manor 14th-16th cent, Penshurst 14th-18th cent, and Ashurst 1627-42, with Tonbridge perambulations 1258-79 and court roll 1393-5; misc Sussex (Robertsbridge, etc) manorial records c1225-1713; Tattershall College and Cromwell family manorial court rolls, rentals and accounts 1363-1597, mainly Lincs but incl Leics, Northants, Notts, Rutland, etc; surveys and accounts, Glamorganshire manors (Coity, Newlands, etc) c1590-1632; misc manorial records, incl Abberley (Worcs) accounts 14th-16th cent, Michelmarsh (Hants) extent 1323 and rental 1369, and estreat roll, Lincs and Yorks manors of Thomas, Earl of Surrey 1499-1500.

Records of the Sidney family estates from 15th cent, mainly accounts, vouchers and papers for Penshurst (Kent) 15th-early 19th cent and Robertsbridge (Sussex) 15th-early 18th cent, general estate rentals 1519, 1574, accounts 1542-1580 and stewards' corresp c1580-early 18th cent; surveys, valuations and rentals for Lincs, Rutland and Michelmarsh (Hants) 16th cent, etc; iron works accounts, Robertsbridge and Panningridge (Sussex) 1541-73, 1700-2 and Glamorgan 1564-8; Middlesex (Leicester Fields) estate records 17th-18th cent, incl building leases and rentals; misc Warwicks (former Dudley) estate papers 16th-17th cent, incl abstract of the Earl of Leicester's revenues c1585 and Balsall and Long Itchington receipts

1615-18; estate papers, Glamorganshire 16th-18th cent, incl rentals and accounts 1594-1650, and Norfolk and Suffolk (Reeve family estate) 17th-18th cent, incl particulars and valuations c1735-79; Perry family estate papers 17th-18th cent, incl Bucks (Turville), Oxon (Pyrton), Herefs and Radnorshire rentals and accounts 1730-83 and Deeping Fen (Lincs) rentals 1765-6; Tattershall Castle estate accounts c1410-81; estate records, Earl of Romney's Irish estates c1675-1700, Viscount Strangford's Westenhanger (Kent) estate c1629-67 and the Countess of Huntingdon's Loughborough (Leics) estate c1596-1607; extent of Sir Nicholas Louvaine's property c1375; valuation of the Duke of Suffolk's estates c1551; estate records for Cranfield (Beds) 1605, Stoke Poges (Bucks) 1598, Bisley (Gloucs) 1603-6, Leominster (Herefs) c1605, Hampton-in-Arden (Warwicks) c1600-6 and Sir Thomas Cheadle's Welsh estate c1650.

Penshurst household records 16th-19th cent, incl building accounts 18th cent, muniment room register c1582, household inventories 1623, 1627, 1677, ordinances c1620 and accounts from c1539; records for Sir Henry Sidney's Welsh and Irish households and the 1st Earl's Flushing household late 16th-early 17th cent; other household records 16th-19th cent, incl inventories of Baynard's Castle 1622-6, Leicester House 1670-18th cent, Berkeley Square 1748 and Ranworth Hall 1736-58, and accounts for Robertsbridge 16th-17th cent and Baynard's Castle 1600-1; Tattershall Castle household accounts 1434-75; papers rel to local affairs 14th-19th cent, incl the mastership of Leycester's Hospital, Warwick 17th-19th cent, the Thames navigation at Dagenham (Essex) c1715-47 and the lieutenancy of Radnorshire mid-18th cent, with accounts for papal assessments of Lincs deaneries mid-14th cent and a clerical subsidy in the archdeaconry of Stow and the Parts of Lindsey 1535, Kent lay subsidy assessments 1601 and freeholders' book 1781, Exmoor forest particulars 1603-4 and a Cardiganshire association roll 1688.

Patents and appointments 16th-20th cent; family, personal and business accounts, vouchers, corresp and papers 16th-19th cent, mainly Sidney family; Welsh and Irish papers of Sir Henry Sidney (d1586), incl letters of Sir Francis Walsingham; papers of the 1st Earl of Leicester, incl some as governor of Flushing, and of the 2nd Earl, incl journal as ambassador to Denmark 1632 and Irish lieutenancy accounts 1641-3; papers of the Earl of Romney (d1704), of William Perry (d1759), his wife Elizabeth Perry and of the antiquary Arthur Collins (d1760); personal inventory of Robert Dudley, Earl of Leicester 1583; accounts of the 10th Earl of Northumberland 1639-40; genealogical, literary and misc papers 15th-20th cent, Sidney and Perry families, incl roll of swan marks c1536, book of royal annuitants 1570-1, Sidney pedigree 1588 and *liber comptrarotula-*

menti of Sir William Knollys (comptroller of the Queen's household) 1595-6; Robertsbridge Abbey accounts 1416-38, with inventory and legal papers c1256-1500; Tattershall College records c1441-1571, incl statutes c1450-60 and building accounts 1457-82; Sheen Priory (Surrey), Worcs estate accounts 1504-5.

Yorks NR deeds 13th-19th cent, with misc deeds for Bucks, Suffolk, etc 16th-18th cent; wills, settlements, probate, executorship and legal papers 17th-19th cent, Foulis family, incl inventory and executorship accounts for Sir William Foulis 1845-8; misc Yorks NR manorial records (Ingleby Greenhow and Battersby) 16th-18th cent; Yorks NR estate papers 16th-19th cent, incl maps 18th-19th cent, particular and rental 1607 and account book 1757-1802; misc papers rel to Yorks NR affairs 14th-18th cent, incl taxation papers mainly 16th-17th cent (Layton family), shrievalty accounts (Foulis family) 1764-5, 1802-4, Yarm bridge accounts 1565 and Ingleby Greenhow parish Easter offering acounts 1588; Foulis and Layton family and business corresp and papers 16th-19th cent; misc papers 16th-18th cent, incl diet book for the household of Prince Charles 1610.

Centre for Kentish Studies (U 1475, 1500, 1886). Deposited by the 1st Viscount De L'Isle 1969, 1975, 1988. HMC *Third Report, App*, 1872, pp227-33; *De L'Isle and Dudley I-VI*, 1925-66. NRA 17989, 11837.

[b] Penshurst halimote *alias* Otford Weald manorial records 17th-20th cent, with rentals 1830-43.

Centre for Kentish Studies (U 1000/9). Formerly amongst the Sevenoaks Library Collection. Transferred 1963. NRA 18189.

[c] Robertsbridge Abbey charters 12th-14th cent.

British Library, Manuscript Collections (Eg Ch 371-403). Acquired 1874. A medieval Robertsbridge Abbey register acquired in 1870 (Add MS 28550) and further medieval deeds amongst the Campbell, Egerton and Addititonal charters seem also to derive from the Penshurst muniments: see HMC *De L'Isle and Dudley I*, 1925, pp xii-xiii.

[d] Letters to the 2nd Earl and Countess of Leicester from William Hawkins 1636-7.

British Library, Manuscript Collections (Eg MS 807). Purchased at Sotheby's, 9 May 1840.

[e] Sidney family papers c1559-1709, incl corresp of Sir Henry Sidney (d1586) and the 1st Earl of Leicester (d1626).

British Library, Manuscript Collections (Add MS 15914). Purchased at W Upcott's sale of 22 June 1846, lot 166.

[f] Misc Sidney family letters and papers 1572-1726, incl accounts of Henry Sidney as Lord Deputy of Ireland 1577-8.

British Library, Manuscript Collections (Add MS 17520). Purchased 1848.

[g] Poetical MSS of the 1st Earl of Leicester.

British Library, Manuscript Collections (Add MS 58435). Purchased at Sotheby's 1975 (sale of 19 Nov 1974, lot 390).

[h] Corresp of Sir Henry Sidney as Lord Deputy of Ireland 1565-70.

Trinity College Library, Dublin (MS 745). Purchased at Viscount Kingsborough's sale 1842, lot 598. NRA 19217.

[i] Corresp of Sir Philip Sidney (d1586).

Yale University, Beinecke Library (Osborn Collection). Purchased at Sotheby's sale of Phillipps MSS 26 June 1967, lot 741 (formerly Phillipps MS 11762). Letters from Sidney to Canon Robert Dorset in the same sale (lot 742) were acquired for Christ Church, Oxford, but the whereabouts of further Sidney family papers 16th-17th cent (lot 743) has not been traced (P Beal, *Index of English Literary Manuscripts, Vol 1, part 2*, 1980, pp465-88).

[j] Penshurst household inventory 1632; inventory of pictures and statues delivered for His Majesty's use from Viscount L'Isle's house at Sheen 1660.

National Library of Wales (Mansel Franklen collection, NLW MS 6596). Amongst the antiquarian collections of JM Traherne presented by Lady Mansel Franklen 1928-9. NRA 34361.

Related collections: Streatfeild of Chiddingstone (Centre for Kentish Studies U 908, NRA 39835), including Sidney wills, settlements, legal papers and family papers 17th-18th cent; Shelley of Avington (Hampshire Record Office 18 M 51, NRA 8990), including deeds and legal papers for the Sidney and Perry estates 17th-early 19th cent; Pelham, Earls of Chichester, no 80; Heathcote-Drummond-Willoughby, Earls of Ancaster, no 48; Thynne, Marquesses of Bath, no 104.

[96] SOMERSET, Dukes of Beaufort

Charles Somerset (c1460-1526), natural son of Henry Beaufort, second Duke of Somerset (executed 1464), married in 1492 Elizabeth, daughter and heir of William Herbert (c1455-91), second Earl of Pembroke and Earl of Huntingdon. William Herbert (d1469), created Earl of Pembroke in 1468, had inherited Raglan Castle (Monmouthshire), and had acquired estates in Monmouthshire (Chepstow, etc, with Tidenham in Gloucestershire), Breconshire (Crickhowell and Tretower), Glamorganshire (Gower and Kilvey), Pembrokeshire (surrendered in 1479) and Somerset (Dunster: later restored to the Luttrell family, see no 66). Charles Somerset was created Baron Herbert in 1503 and Earl of Worcester in 1514. The second Earl of Worcester (d1549) acquired Tintern Abbey lands (mainly Monmouthshire, but including Woolaston in Gloucestershire) in 1537, and the reversion of Chalton (Hampshire) in 1542. The Troy (Monmouthshire) estate was purchased in 1584 but settled on a younger son.

The fourth Earl (c1550-1628) purchased Badminton (Gloucestershire) in 1612, and settled this property on his younger son Thomas (d1649), later Viscount Somerset of Cashel. The fifth Earl (d1646) married in 1600 Anne Russell, daughter and heir of Lord Russell, son of the second Earl of Bedford, through whom properties including Acton (Middlesex: settled on a younger son), Chulmleigh and Denbury (Devon) and Chaldon Herring (Dorset) came to the Somerset family. The fifth Earl also acquired Poston (Herefordshire: again later settled on a younger son) and the manor of Monmouth. He was created Marquess of Worcester in 1643, but suffered the destruction of Raglan Castle and its library and the sequestration of his estates.

The third Marquess of Worcester (1629-1700) restored the family fortunes, inheriting Badminton from his cousin Elizabeth Somerset, daughter of Viscount Somerset of Cashel, in 1655, and purchasing Troy from the estate of his uncle Charles Somerset (d1655) in 1663. He made Badminton the principal seat, and was created Duke of Beaufort in 1682. The second Duke (1684-1714) married in 1706 Rachel, daughter and co-heir of the second Earl of Gainsborough (see Cavendish-Bentinck, Dukes of Portland, no 18; Noel, Earls of Gainsborough, no 74): the Beaufort moiety was sold in 1742. The third Duke (1707-45) married Frances Scudamore, but her Holme Lacy (Herefordshire) estate later descended through her daughter by her second husband (see Fitzalan-Howard, Dukes of Norfolk, no 37).

The fourth Duke (1709-56) married in 1740 Elizabeth, sister and heir of Norborne Berkeley, Baron Botetourt (d1770), through whom estates in Gloucestershire (Stoke Gifford, Stapleton, etc), Wiltshire (Hilmarton), Norfolk (Brancaster) and Suffolk were eventually inherited. During the time of the fifth Duke (1765-1803) the outlying estates of Chalton, Chaldon Herring, Chulmleigh and Denbury, together with Beaufort Buildings (Strand, Middlesex: the site of Worcester (previously Russell) House) and the former Berkeley estates in Norfolk and Suffolk, were sold, but the Gloucestershire and Monmouthshire estates were extended (notably by the purchase of the Usk and Trelleck (Monmouthshire) estate from Lord Clive in 1770).

The Stapleton estate was sold in 1859-65, and Tidenham and Woolaston in 1872. During the time of the ninth Duke (succeeded 1899, d1924) further and more extensive sales took place, leaving a reduced Badminton estate and some Glamorganshire property.

The fifth Duke was executor of Lady Anne Somerset (d1763), daughter of the first Duke and wife of the second Earl of Coventry, through which connection some Coventry papers came to Badminton House.

Estates in 1883: Gloucs 16,610 acres, Wilts 1,939 acres, Monmouthshire 27,299 acres, Breconshire 4,019 acres, Glamorganshire 1,218 acres, total 51,085 acres worth £56,226 a year.

[a] Gloucs and Wilts deeds 13th-19th cent (Somerset and Berkeley); deeds for Dorset 16th-18th cent, Hants 17th-18th cent, Herefs 17th cent, London and Middlesex 15th-19th cent, and Norfolk and Suffolk (Norborne, later Berkeley) 14th-18th cent; trust accounts and papers, 2nd Duke decd 1714-32 and 4th Duke decd c1756-74; legal and case papers 17th-19th cent, incl sequestration papers 1645-60; manorial court records 14th-20th cent, mainly Gloucs (Great Badminton, Tidenham, Woolaston, etc) but incl Wilts (Hilmarton, etc) 14th-18th cent, Norfolk (Brancaster, etc) 17th-18th cent and other counties 14th-17th cent.

General estate surveys, rentals, accounts, etc 16th-19th cent; Badminton (Gloucs and Wilts) estate records late 16th-early 20th cent, incl leases, surveys, valuations, maps from early 17th cent, rentals, accounts, corresp, and papers rel to timber, enclosure, tithes, roads and charities; Tidenham and Woolaston estate records 16th-19th cent (some with Welsh and general accounts, etc), incl leases, maps, rentals, accounts, and papers rel to enclosure, Severn and Wye fisheries, Severn royalty and Wye navigation; records for outlying Somerset family estates 16th-18th cent, incl Chulmleigh and Denbury, Chaldon Herring, Chalton, Poston and Netheravon (Wilts); Beaufort Buildings (Strand, Middlesex) rentals and accounts 18th cent; Stoke Gifford and Stapleton (Gloucs) estate records 16th-early 20th cent, incl leases, surveys, maps, rentals, accounts, papers rel to liberty of Kingswood and Kingswood collieries 17th-19th cent, and papers rel to the Warmley Brass and Copper Co 1761-83; records for outlying Berkeley and Norborne estates (Norfolk, Suffolk and Wilts) mainly 18th cent; misc records rel to South Wales (Somerset) estates (with general estate accounts, etc) 16th-early 19th cent; papers of Edmund Estcourt (auditor of Welsh estates) c1770-1806; Berkeley of Stoke Gifford general estate accounts 1377-1482; account of former Evesham Abbey (Worcs) lands c1550 (Hoby, later Russell); Sir Thomas Somerset, Irish rental 1620-2; corresp rel to sale of an estate in the Bahamas (Somerset, formerly Granville) to the Crown 1733-85; Coventry family (Worcs, etc) estate rentals, accounts and related papers mainly 1691-1748.

Badminton House and Grosvenor Square building accounts and related papers 18th cent; Badminton park and farm accounts 18th-19th cent; Stoke Gifford building accounts 1760-3; Berkeley of Stoke Gifford household accounts 1424-42; Croome Court (Worcs: Coventry family) building accounts 1640-9; lease of Heythrop House (Oxon) and related schedule 1819-26; Beaufort Hunt papers 1860-85; misc papers, incl fragments of medieval MSS; Glastonbury Abbey almoner's account 1531-2.

Gloucestershire Record Office (D 2700, 3022). Deposited by the 10th and 11th Dukes of Beaufort 1972-96. *Handlist of the contents of Gloucestershire Record Office*, 3rd edn, 1995, pp164-7. NRA 6282.

[b] Settlements and related deeds 1824-99.

Gloucestershire Record Office (D 2492). Given by Williams & James, solicitors, London 1969. NRA 6282.

[c] Tidenham and Woolaston legal and estate papers 1658-1920, incl manorial court papers 1794-1837, leases, and rental 1842.

Gloucestershire Record Office (D 1430). Deposited by Evans & Ellis, solicitors, Chepstow 1957. *Handlist*, 3rd edn, 1995, p200. NRA 5922.

[d] Gloucs (Cross Hands petty-sessional division) magistracy papers, mainly of the 5th Duke of Beaufort, 1713-84.

Gloucestershire Record Office (D 1401 (PS/CR)). Deposited by the 10th Duke 1956. NRA 9255.

[e] Wills, settlements and related trust, executorship and case papers 1600-early 20th cent, mainly Somerset family, incl the 1st Marquess of Worcester decd 1631-57, 1st Duke of Beaufort decd c1700-14, 6th Duke decd 1835-51 and 8th Duke decd 1899-1902, but also incl the 3rd Duke of Somerset decd (Duchess of Beaufort executor) 1671-6, the 6th Earl of Thomond decd c1700-7, Lady Coventry decd 1763-71, Lord Botetourt decd 1770-89 (with Berkeley and Norborne wills and settlements from late 16th cent), and the 5th Duke of Rutland (5th Duke of Beaufort a trustee) 1787-1800; legal and case papers 15th-19th cent, incl papers rel to the 3rd Duke's divorce 1739-44, the barony of Botetourt 1474-1803 and the Coventry family early 18th cent; papers rel to the attainder of the Duke of Ormonde (Lady Coventry's brother-in-law) 1715-16.

Papers rel to Badminton House 17th-20th cent, incl building account summaries, inventories, muniment catalogues and related papers, accounts and vouchers, and papers rel to garden plants and trees; inventories and accounts rel to Stoke Gifford 18th-early 20th cent, and to

London houses 17th-19th cent; Raglan Castle inventory of plate 1639, with papers late 17th cent rel to the Castle before the Civil War; inventories or accounts rel to Troy House 1687-90, c1700, and Netheravon House 1758; Croome Court and Snitterfield (Warwicks) catalogues and accounts 1698-1745; London and Richmond (Duke of Ormonde) establishment books 1712-15; Governor's palace, Williamsburg (Lord Botetourt as Governor of Virginia), inventory 1770; Uley (Gloucs) inventory and valuation c1464.

Papers rel to the lieutenancy of Gloucs and Monmouthshire 17th-18th cent, Gloucs militia 1750-66, Monmouthshire militia 1770-1831, Gloucs, Monmouthshire, etc politics 18th-19th cent and the Forest of Dean 1565-1831; papers of the 1st Duke as President of the Council of Wales 1672-85 and governor of Chepstow Castle; Duchy of Lancaster receivership accounts and papers (Monmouthshire, etc) 1779-1822; Gloucs shrievalty account 1564-5 (Sir Richard Berkeley); papers rel to Stoke Gifford spinning school late 18th cent and to Mary Webb's charity, Stapleton 1730-1893; Beaufort Hunt papers 19th-early 20th cent.

Patents, commissions, etc, Somerset 17th-20th cent, Berkeley 18th cent and 2nd Earl of Coventry 1686-1700; Somerset family papers 17th-20th cent, incl political, official and other corresp and papers of the 1st and 2nd Marquesses of Worcester and the 1st, 2nd, 4th, 5th and 6th Dukes of Beaufort; corresp of Mary, Duchess of Beaufort (d1715), with some Capell and Seymour letters and papers 17th cent; corresp and papers of Emily, Duchess of Beaufort (d1889), with Indian letter books of Charles Smith 1758-81, papers of his son Culling Charles Smith (the Duchess's father) 1802-51 and misc Wellesley family corresp; Berkeley of Stoke Gifford family papers 15th-18th cent, incl Sir Richard Berkeley's 'Discourse upon the felicity of man' 1598, papers rel to Gloucs affairs 17th cent and Virginia governorship papers of Lord Botetourt 1768-70; papers of Lady Coventry (d1763), with political and other corresp and papers of the 2nd Earl of Coventry; genealogical papers 17th-19th cent; Garter statutes c1400; household accounts of Archbishop Sheldon 1674-5; inventory of goods, Earl of Grantham c1708.

In private possession, property of the Somerset Trust. Enquiries to the Archivist, Badminton House, Badminton, Avon GL9 1DB. HMC *Twelfth Report, App IX*, 1891, pp1-115; *Papers of British Politicians 1782-1900*, 1989, p97. NRA 6282.

[f] Maps of Littleton Drew (Wilts) 1840 (2 items).

Wiltshire and Swindon Record Office (WRO 374/315). Deposited by Mullings & Ellett, solicitors, Trowbridge. NRA 1556.

[g] Norfolk and Suffolk deeds (Brancaster, Great and Little Waldingfield, Burgate (Suffolk), etc) 16th-18th cent; legal and manorial papers rel to Brancaster 16th-18th cent; misc Norfolk and Suffolk estate papers 17th-18th cent, incl rental 1738 and accounts 1736-60 (Norfolk only from 1744).

Norfolk Record Office (Q 187 A-B). Deposited by Loynes, Son & Baron, solicitors, Wells-next-the-Sea 1970, having been transferred from Badminton to the then owner of the Brancaster estate in 1922.

[h] Deeds for Breconshire, Glamorganshire and Monmouthshire c1200-20th cent (c400 medieval); settlements and related papers 17th-18th cent, Somerset family; legal and case papers 16th-20th cent, Somerset and Powell families, incl papers rel to forfeited Somerset family estates 1650-60; manorial court records 13th-20th cent, Breconshire (Crickhowell, Tretower, etc), Glamorganshire (seignory and manor of Gower, Kilvey, Swansea, etc), Monmouthshire (Portgaseg, Raglan, Usk, etc), and Gloucs (Tidenham and Woolaston 15th-19th cent).

Welsh estate records (Breconshire, Glamorganshire and Monmouthshire) 15th-20th cent, incl leases 16th-20th cent (numerous), lease registers and abstract books from 17th cent, surveys from 16th cent, maps 17th-19th cent, rentals from early 17th cent, receiver-generals' accounts 1538-54, audit rolls 1477-1641, other financial records 17th-20th cent, and papers rel to tithes, enclosure, fisheries, schools, chapels, etc; papers rel to canals 18th-19th cent, incl the Trewyddfa Canal c1794-1853, and to railways 19th cent; papers rel to coal mining and industrial undertakings 16th-20th cent, incl Gower coal mining, copper and tin-plate works, Llanelly and Llangattock (Breconshire) coal and ironworks 18th-19th cent, Monmouth forge, and Tintern (Monmouthshire) iron and wire works 16th-19th cent; papers rel to urban development in Swansea and elsewhere mainly 19th cent; papers rel to Chepstow, Raglan and Swansea castles, incl plan of Raglan Castle 1652-3; misc Tidenham and Woolaston rentals, accounts etc 15th-18th cent (with Monmouthshire estate records); Wilts, Devon and Dorset rental 1712-18 and misc accounts 1700-63; Earls of Pembroke, Welsh (Pembrokeshire, etc) accounts 1412-76, Dunster accounts 1461-79 and Monmouthshire arrears 1706.

Monmouthshire shrievalty account 1666-71; papers rel to Breconshire, Cardiff and Monmouth elections mid-18th cent; papers rel to the borough of Swansea 17th-19th cent (incl lease register 1706-87), borough and parish of Monmouth 17th-19th cent (incl church rebuilding 1736-8), Chepstow market and tolls 18th-19th cent, Usk town hall and market 1775-1859 and Newport (Monmouthshire) market 19th cent; Wentwood Forest (Monmouthshire) papers 16th-17th cent, incl map 1678; papers rel to Lady Scudamore's charity 1727-1862; Duchy of Lancaster appointments and receivership papers 17th-early 19th cent; accounts of Sir William Powell of Lanpill (d1611); Lord Grey of Ruthin estate accounts 1393-4; Earl of Pembroke's estate accounts 1707-8; account of stock, etc in Ireland (Sir John Perrott Lord Deputy) 1585-6.

National Library of Wales. Deposited by the 10th Duke of Beaufort 1941-89. Purchased 1993. NRA 12100, 12101.

[i] Misc papers rel to the Monmouthshire estates mainly 19th cent, incl Chepstow manorial records, draft leases, rental 1803, papers rel to Chepstow market and Wye fishery, and sale papers 1899.

Gwent Record Office (D 25). Deposited by Evans & Evill, solicitors, Chepstow 1950. NRA 6968.

[j] Monmouthshire legal and estate papers c1733-1838, incl draft leases, tenancy papers, and maps and surveys early 19th cent.

West Glamorgan Archive Service (D/D Beau). Deposited from the Beaufort Estate Office, Swansea 1978, 1990. Hilary M Thomas, *A catalogue of Glamorgan estate maps*, 1992, pp70-2.

[k] Papers rel to the jointure of the Countess of Dundonald (Dowager Duchess of Beaufort) 1620-1717, incl marriage settlement 1712 and Chalton rental 1678.

Public Record Office (C 107/22). Some early 17th-century Monmouthshire court rolls in C 116/191-193 (Beaufort *v* Dundonald) were noted as missing in 1996.

[l] Somerset family corresp 1631-1709, 1746-9, mainly on public affairs, incl letters from Robert Price 1688-99.

Bodleian Library, Oxford (MS Carte 130). Presented with the Ormonde papers by John Carte 1753. *Summary Catalogue of Western Manuscripts*, vol iii, 1895, p135 (MS 10575).

[m] Letters to Charlotte, Duchess of Beaufort from her mother the Marchioness of Stafford 1774-1805.

Birmingham University Information Services, Special Collections Department. Purchased from J Browning 1984 (having perhaps descended to the family of Lord Granville Somerset, the Duchess's younger son). NRA 29832.

Related collections: Capell, Earls of Essex, no 16, including papers of Arthur, Lord Capell (d1649); Cavendish-Bentinck, Dukes of Portland, no 18, including Titchfield estate papers; Osborne, Dukes of Leeds, no 78, including papers of and relating to the 2nd Duke of Beaufort and his wife c1702-12;

Russell, Dukes of Bedford, no 90, including Chulmleigh and Denbury court rolls, etc 15th-16th cent; Stuart, later Crichton-Stuart, Earls and later Marquesses of Bute, no 100, including Glamorganshire (Beaufort) colliery papers 1823-35; Coventry, Earls of Coventry (in private possession); Sloane MSS (British Library, Manuscript Collections), including lists of plants at Badminton 1696-1713 (Sloane MSS 4070-2).

[97] SPENCER, Earls Spencer

The Spencer family originated as graziers and sheepbreeders in Warwickshire and Northamptonshire in the late fifteenth century. Sir John Spencer of Snitterfield (Warwickshire) purchased Wormleighton (Warwickshire) in 1506 and Althorp (Northamptonshire) in 1508. Sir John Spencer (d1599) married Mary, daughter of Sir Robert Catlin (d1574) and heiress of property in Bedfordshire, Leicestershire, Northamptonshire and Dorset, much of which, however, was sold between 1575 and 1617. Their son Robert Spencer was created Baron Spencer of Wormleighton in 1603, and the third Baron was created Earl of Sunderland in 1643.

The third Earl of Sunderland (c1674-1722) married in 1700 Anne, second daughter and co-heir of the first Duke of Marlborough (see Spencer-Churchill, Dukes of Marlborough, no 98). In 1733, on the death of his maternal aunt Henrietta, Countess of Godolphin and *suo jure* Duchess of Marlborough, the fifth Earl of Sunderland (1706-58) succeeded to the dukedom and the Blenheim estates. He resigned the Althorp estates to his younger brother John Spencer (1708-46), who on the death of Sarah, Duchess of Marlborough in 1744 also succeeded to her paternal estates in Hertfordshire (Sandridge, etc) and to her purchased properties in Surrey (Wimbledon, etc), Berkshire (Shillingford, etc), Norfolk (North Creake), Northamptonshire (Steane), Staffordshire and elsewhere. (Her trustees continued to make purchases after her death.) John Spencer's son purchased the Battersea (Surrey) estate in 1763, and was created Earl Spencer in 1765.

The third Earl Spencer (1782-1845) married in 1814 Esther, daughter and heir of Richard Acklom of Wiseton (Nottinghamshire). The fourth Earl (1798-1857) married in 1830 Elizabeth, daughter and co-heir of William Poyntz of Midgham (Berkshire)(d1840) by Elizabeth, sister of George Browne, eighth Viscount Montagu (d1793), and co-heir to the Cowdray (Sussex) estates. Records for these estates survive among the Spencer papers, but the Midgham and Cowdray estates themselves were sold in 1843 and were never held with the Althorp estates.

The Althorp estates in Northamptonshire and Warwickshire, with outliers in Buckinghamshire and Leicestershire, were consolidated in the nineteenth century. But there were sales of other outlying properties, including land in Wimbledon (though not the manorial lordship) in 1846, the Wiseton estate in 1848 and remaining properties in Bedfordshire by 1883.

Estates in 1883: Northants 16,800 acres, Warwicks 3,392 acres, Herts 3,017 acres, Norfolk 2,533 acres, Bucks 771 acres, Leics 670 acres, Surrey 2 acres, total 27,185 acres worth £46,764 a year.

[a] Deeds for Spencer properties 12th-late 19th cent (c1,000 medieval), mainly Northants and Warwicks but incl Beds, Berks, Bucks, Herts, Kent, Leics, Lincs, Norfolk, Notts, Surrey and other counties; deeds for alienated Catlin properties 12th-16th cent, mainly Beds and Leics, incl Waltham Abbey and Haliwell Priory charters; Browne and Poyntz deeds 12th-early 19th cent, mainly Surrey and Sussex, incl Waverley Abbey charters; wills, settlements and related executorship and trust papers 16th-late 19th cent, mainly Spencer but incl Churchill early 18th cent, Poyntz 16th-19th cent and Agar family (Viscounts Clifden) late 18th-late 19th cent; legal papers 14th-early 20th cent, incl formulary 14th-15th cent, bonds 15th-16th cent, solicitors' papers (mainly Wimbledon) 19th cent and Poyntz and Browne papers (Berks, Surrey and Sussex estates) 16th-18th cent; manorial court records 13th-20th cent, incl Beds (Millow, etc) from 13th cent, Herts 16th-19th cent, Norfolk (North Creake) late 16th-early 20th cent, Northants (Brington, Muscott, Nobottle, etc) 14th-18th cent, Surrey (Wimbledon, Battersea, etc) 1460-early 20th cent, Sussex, etc (Montagu manors) 15th-18th cent and Warwicks (Priors Marston and Hardwick, Wormleighton, etc) from 14th cent.

Misc early estate records 14th-early 17th cent, mainly Northants and Warwicks but a few for Beds, etc, incl leases, rentals and tithe papers; Althorp estate papers c1775-early 20th cent, Northants, Warwicks, Bucks and Leics, incl rentals, accounts, vouchers, stewards' corresp and papers rel to building and repairs, woods, etc; Surrey (Wimbledon, etc) estate records 17th-early 20th cent, incl survey 1617, rentals from 1786 and papers rel to proposed enclosure of common 1864-70; records for other Spencer estates 16th-early 20th cent, incl Beds mainly late 18th-19th cent, Berks (Shillingford) late 18th-19th cent, Dorset (Mappowder) 18th cent, Herts 17th-19th cent, Kent (Agney, a Jennings property) c1690-1746, Middlesex (St James's Place) c1790-1866, Norfolk (North Creake) 19th-early 20th cent, Notts (Wiseton estate) c1650-1848 and Staffs (former Fauconberg, previously Fowler, property) c1738-79; misc Berks (Midgham) and Sussex (Cowdray) estate papers 17th cent-1843; papers rel to Althorp house (incl library), gardens and park late 18th-19th cent, with household accounts from c1775; Althorp weather records 1815-71; papers rel to

Spencer House (London) late 18th-early 20th cent, Holywell House and gardens (Herts) 1724-1816, Wimbledon Park late 18th-early 19th cent and Wiseton Hall 1743-1847.

Papers rel to Northants affairs 16th-19th cent, incl shrievalty account 1511-12 and election papers 18th-19th cent; St Albans charity papers 18th-20th cent, incl papers rel to estates at Crowhurst (Surrey) and Marston Jabbett (Warwicks); papers rel to London and Middlesex charities late 18th cent; grant of arms, Sir John Spencer 1504; inventory, Sir Robert Spencer 1628; Spencer family papers 18th-20th cent, incl papers of the 1st, 2nd, 5th and 6th Earls; misc Poyntz and Browne patents, pedigree rolls, etc 16th-18th cent, with some papers of the Revd Charles Poyntz late 18th cent; misc Drake and Martyn family papers 18th cent; Exchequer quietus rolls 1709-25; legal papers of the 13th Baron Bergavenny early 18th cent; naval account of Philip Papillon 1694.

Northamptonshire Record Office (S(A)). Purchased 1986-7. NRA 10410 (partial list).

[b] Rentals (all estates) 1872-4 (3 vols).

Northamptonshire Record Office (ZB 764/1-3; Acc 1988/106). Given through Kent Archives Office 1988. NRA 10410.

[c] Althorp and Pytchley hunt journals, hound books and related papers 1767-1922; Althorp weather records 1830-45.

Northamptonshire Record Office (Acc 1985/259). Purchased 1985. NRA 28669.

[d] Spencer family trust, executorship and related papers early 16th-early 19th cent, incl the 1st Baron Spencer, John Spencer decd 1747-58, guardianship accounts for the 1st Earl Spencer 1746-54 and Lady Spencer decd 1814-22; Duchess of Marlborough executorship and trusteeship papers mainly 1744-69; trust papers for Poyntz and related families c1681-1866, incl Viscounts Montagu late 18th-early 19th cent and the Revd Charles Poyntz as executor for members of the Monteage, Martyn and Butterworth families; Acklom trust papers 1814-19; legal and case papers rel mainly to Northants and Warwicks estates 16th-17th cent; misc manorial court records, Whitchurch Canonicorum (Dorset) 1571-83 and Mattersey (Notts: Acklom) 1605-33.

Misc Northants and Warwicks estate and farm records late 15th-20th cent, incl maps 18th-20th cent, misc rentals and accounts 16th-17th cent, enclosure papers early 16th cent, wood sale accounts 16th-17th cent, shepherds' and farm accounts 1498-1640 and Althorp and Wiseton farm and livestock accounts (3rd Earl) 1808-45; agency corresp of George Appleyard 1836-54; maps and misc papers for Norfolk (North Creake) and Middlesex (St James's) estates 18th-20th cent; Beds (Burgoyne family) estate papers 16th cent; maps for other counties 17th-20th cent, incl Berks, Herts, Kent, Leics, Staffs and Surrey (Coombe); papers rel to Althorp 17th-19th cent, incl building papers 1787-1802, 1844-81, inventories from early 17th cent and household accounts; papers rel to Spencer House (London) 1791-1942; Harlestone House (Northants) inventory 1866; inventories and other papers rel to Marlborough House (London), Holywell House and Blenheim Palace mainly 1690s-1749, with bills for a house in Dover Street (London) 1738-40; Nevill (Barons Bergavenny) household bills 1710-37; papers rel to Northants and Warwicks taxation and county affairs 1524-1680.

Spencer family papers 1485-early 20th cent (extensive), incl Sir John Spencer (d1522), the 1st Baron as envoy to Wurttemberg 1603, John Spencer 1726-46, Georgiana, Countess Spencer 1755-1814, and official, political, personal and family corresp of the 2nd, 3rd, 4th and 5th Earls; misc papers of the Catlin family 1583-1657 and of the Revd Thomas Burgoyne of Sandy (Beds) 1519-46; misc corresp and papers of the 1st Duke and Duchess of Marlborough c1682-1744, incl household books for James, Duke of York 1682-5, letters from Queen Anne and narratives of the Duchess's conduct; papers of the Poyntz and connected families 17th-early 19th cent, incl diplomatic and official papers of Stephen Poyntz mainly 1722-51, personal and parochial papers of the Revd Charles Poyntz of North Creake 1757-1808, and misc papers of the Browne family 17th-18th cent, the Drake family of Buckland (Devon) 18th cent and Thomas Martyn MP (d1750); corresp and papers of the 1st-5th Earls of Cumberland *temp* Henry VIII-1636, the 1st and 3rd Earls of Burlington 1627-1741, the 1st and 2nd Marquesses of Halifax 1661-1721 and Sir William Coventry 1665-7 (all formerly among the papers of the Dukes of Devonshire); Seymour and Biddulph papers 19th cent; corresp of the 13th Baron Bergavenny and his wife 1712-43; misc papers mainly 16th-18th cent, incl naval treatise by John Mountgomerie 1574, diplomatic letter book of Edmund Poley 1684 and volume 2 of George Lockhart's account of Scottish affairs 1702-8.

British Library, Manuscript Collections. Purchased 1985. HMC *Papers of British Cabinet Ministers 1782-1900*, 1982, p 59; *Papers of British Politicians 1782-1900*, 1989, p98.

[e] Architectural drawings 18th-20th cent, incl Althorp 1789-91 and Wimbledon Park 1801 (Henry Holland), Spencer House 1760s-1926 and Harlestone House 1809-11.

British Library, Manuscript Collections. Purchased 1986, 1989.

[f] Misc Spencer papers 1522-1656, incl household accounts 1599-1605, 1622, 1634, 1643-47, personal vouchers 1602-36 and Northants muster papers 16th-early 17th cent.

British Library, Manuscript Collections (Add MSS 25079-83). Purchased 1863.

[g] Accounts for personal expenses of Margaret Spencer 1610-13, audited by her father the 1st Baron Spencer.

British Library, Manuscript Collections (Add MS 62092). Purchased 1981 (Sotheby's, 17 Dec, lot 16).

[h] Travel diaries, commonplace books, etc 1815-75, Spencer, Seymour and Poyntz families.

British Library, Manuscript Collections (Add MSS 62911-23). Purchased from Winifred A Myers (Autographs) Ltd 1983.

[i] Corresp and papers of Sir JG Shaw-Lefevre (d1879) as auditor of the Spencer estates 1814-45, incl lease book 1827-35, misc surveys (Wimbledon, etc) 1814-32, Surrey and Middlesex (St James's Place) rentals 1826-33, audit book 1818-28, corresp mainly 1828-43, letter books 1827-35, memorandum books 1826-30, papers rel to Wimbledon church and Park House 1840-1, papers rel to sale of property in Wimbledon 1845, and Herts and Norfolk vouchers 1840-5.

House of Lords Record Office (Shaw-Lefevre papers). Thought to have been left in the Parliament Office on his retirement as Clerk of the Parliaments 1875. NRA 7118, 28247.

[j] Wimbledon court rolls 1669-1729 and steward's accounts 1788-98.

Surrey History Centre. Transferred from Croydon Central Library 1975.

[k] Custumal early 19th cent and formulary c1830-51 for Surrey manors.

Surrey History Centre (Acc 117). Deposited by Frere, Cholmeley & Co, solicitors, London, through the British Records Association 1950. NRA 3518.

[l] Map of the manor of Wimbledon by J Corris 1787.

Wandsworth Local History Collection, Battersea Library. Purchased at an auction sale in Wellington, New Zealand 1980.

[m] Surrey, etc rental 1811-14.

Lambeth Archives Department. Guide, p10.

[n] Staffs (Sow, etc) rental 1779.

William Salt Library, Stafford (unnumbered collections no 554). NRA 7279.

[o] Sandridge rental and account book 1732-6.

In private possession 1967.

[p] Library catalogues 18th-19th cent.

John Rylands University Library of Manchester
(Spencer 575, 22427, 22479-82, 22738, 22887,
23124). Acquired with the library from Althorp
by Mrs Rylands 1892. *Hand-list of the collection
of English manuscripts in the John Rylands Library
1928*, pp16-18.

Related collections: Spencer-Churchill, Dukes of
Marlborough, no 98, including Jennings deeds
and further papers relating to the 1st Duke of
Marlborough, Sarah, Duchess of Marlborough
and the 3rd Earl of Sunderland; Cavendish,
Dukes of Devonshire, no 17, including further
Clifford, Boyle and Savile (Halifax) papers, and
further papers of Georgiana, Countess Spencer;
Cecil, Marquesses of Exeter, no 19, including
further papers relating to the sale of the
Cowdray estate; Fox-Strangways, Earls of
Ilchester, no 40, including papers relating to the
Wilton (Yorkshire, North Riding) estate of the
2nd Earl of Sunderland.

[98] SPENCER-CHURCHILL, Dukes of Marlborough

John Churchill (1650-1722), general and statesman, was created Duke of Marlborough in
1702, and was granted the manor of Woodstock
and hundred of Wootton (Oxfordshire). He
began the construction of Blenheim Palace near
Woodstock in 1705. In 1678 he had married
Sarah, daughter and co-heir of Richard Jennings
of Sandridge (Hertfordshire). The properties
inherited by her, however, together with the
estates purchased by her in Surrey and other
counties, passed at her death in 1744 to her
grandson John Spencer, younger brother of the
fifth Earl of Sunderland (see Spencer, Earls
Spencer, no 97).

Estates in Wiltshire (Overton, Lockeridge, West
Lavington, etc) were acquired from 1709
onwards, and estates in Buckinghamshire
(Waddesdon, etc) in 1725. In 1722 the Duke of
Marlborough was succeeded in the dukedom
and the Blenheim estates by his eldest daughter
Henrietta, wife of the second Earl of
Godolphin. On her death in 1733 they passed
to her nephew Charles Spencer, fifth Earl of
Sunderland as third Duke of Marlborough (see
Spencer, Earls Spencer, no 97, and, for the
descent of the Godolphin estates, Osborne,
Dukes of Leeds, no 78).

In 1751 the third Duke purchased the
Cornbury (Oxfordshire) estate, but this, with
West Lavington, was settled on a younger son of
the fourth Duke, created Baron Churchill in
1815. The Blenheim estates in Oxfordshire were
consolidated between the late eighteenth and
mid-nineteenth centuries, but the remaining
Wiltshire estates were reduced by sales c1866-

77, and the Buckinghamshire estate was sold to
Baron Ferdinand de Rothschild in 1875.
Property in Sussex was acquired by Lord
Robert Spencer, third son of the third Duke, in
the late eighteenth century, but passed out of
the family on his death in 1831.

Estates in 1883: Oxon 21,944 acres, Wilts 1,534
acres, Berks 33 acres, total 23,511 acres worth
£36,557 a year.

[a] Deeds for Churchill estates 12th-20th cent,
principally Oxon 13th-20th cent (mainly from
16th cent) but incl Bucks 12th-19th cent, Lincs
17th-18th cent, Middlesex 17th-18th cent,
Sussex 18th-19th cent and Wilts 16th-19th
cent; deeds for Jennings properties in Herts,
Kent, Middlesex, etc 14th-18th cent; wills, settlements and related trust accounts and papers
1694-early 20th cent, mainly Churchill family,
incl the 1st Duke of Marlborough decd 1725-
44, the Duchess of Marlborough 1715-27 and
the 3rd Baron Trevor (d1764, uncle of
Elizabeth, wife of the 3rd Duke); legal papers
mainly 18th-20th cent, incl draft conveyances,
abstracts of title, schedules, mortgage register
1687-1758 and papers rel to the Surrey estate
1875; Oxon manorial court records 16th-20th
cent, incl North Leigh, Witney and Witney borough, and Woodstock and members; Wootton
(Oxon) hundred court books and papers 1684-
1804; misc Bucks and Wilts manorial records
18th-19th cent.

Blenheim estate records 18th-20th cent, incl
leases and agreements, surveys and particulars,
maps and plans, rentals and accounts, corresp,
and papers rel to buildings and improvements,
timber, enclosure, tithes and schools on the
estate; papers rel to the building of Woodstock
town hall and Hensington House 1767-70;
Bucks estate records 18th-19th cent, incl leases,
surveys and rentals; Wilts estate records 18th-
19th cent, incl surveys, maps, rentals and
accounts; misc estate papers, Beds and Lincs
mid-18th cent, Sussex 18th-19th cent and
Middlesex (London properties) 18th-20th cent;
papers rel to Blenheim Palace 18th-20th cent,
incl drawings and plans of the palace, garden
and park, building papers, inventories 19th-20th
cent, papers rel to the Sunderland library and
its sale 18th-19th cent, and visitors' books;
papers rel to Lockeridge House (Wilts) 18th
cent; survey and map of Langley Park (Bucks)
1721, with papers rel to its rebuilding c1756;
Marlborough House (London) building
accounts 1709-10 and inventory 1740; inventories, Sunderland House (London) 1722,
house at Bath 1783 and Upper Winchendon
(Bucks) 1789; Overton (Hants) turnpike papers
1734-6; Oxford city election papers 1796;
Bladon (Oxon) parish meeting book 1886-1938.

Churchill family appointments and commissions
17th-19th cent; Churchill family papers mainly
18th-19th cent, incl misc diplomatic, military
and financial papers of the 1st Duke of

Marlborough 1701-22, accounts, commonplace books and other papers of Sarah, Duchess of Marlborough 1687-1744, and papers of the 7th Duke as Lord President of the Council and Lord Lieutenant of Ireland 1867-80; misc treaty and other papers of the 2nd Earl of Sunderland 1665-82; political, official and misc papers of the 3rd Earl of Sunderland *c*1698-1722; Trevor family corresp *c*1714-44; literary and misc papers 16th-19th cent, incl account of Sir Henry Lee for repairs at Woodstock 1593-5, an account of Scottish affairs 1702-8 by George Lockhart (vol 1), and log of the *Wyvern* 1846.

In private possession. Not normally available for research. Enquiries to His Grace the Duke of Marlborough, Blenheim Palace, Woodstock, Oxon OX20 1PX. NRA 8130, 8510.

[b] Misc charters, grants and commissions 16th-18th cent; executorship papers, 3rd Earl of Sunderland (d1722); military, official and personal corresp and papers of the 1st Duke of Marlborough, incl papers rel to Blenheim Palace and Marlborough House (London); political, business, personal and family corresp of Sarah, Duchess of Marlborough; papers of later Dukes of Marlborough 18th-19th cent, incl the 3rd and 4th Dukes; diplomatic and other papers of the 2nd Earl of Sunderland late 17th cent; extensive official and political papers of the 3rd Earl of Sunderland, with papers rel to the Sunderland Library 1699-19th cent; other personal papers 17th-19th cent, incl the 1st Earl of Cardigan 1606-54, the 2nd Earl of Bristol 1646-67, the Trevor family of Bromham (Beds) 17th-early 18th cent, Sir John Wildman (d1693) and Sir Richard Steele (1672-1729, father-in-law of the 3rd Baron Trevor); misc catalogues, tracts, etc.

British Library, Manuscript Collections (Add Ch 76069-76142, Add MSS 61101-61710). Accepted for the nation in lieu of tax and allocated to the Library 1978.

[c] Corresp, case papers and other papers of Henry Joynes, comptroller of the works, rel to the building of Blenheim Palace 1705-27.

British Library, Manuscript Collections (Add MSS 19591-19618). Acquired 1853.

[d] Corresp and papers of the 1st Duke of Marlborough and his secretary Adam Cardonnel 1697-1714.

British Library, Manuscript Collections (Add MSS 70938-46). Purchased 1992.

[e] Misc Churchill papers 1698-1784, chiefly of Sarah, Duchess of Marlborough, incl Privy Purse accounts 1706-7.

British Library, Manuscript Collections (Eg MS 2678). Acquired 1887.

[f] Letters to James Craggs senior, financial secretary to Sarah, Duchess of Marlborough, from the Duke and Duchess 1711-18.

British Library, Manuscript Collections (Stowe MS 751). Acquired 1883.

[g] Astronomical corresp and papers of the 4th Duke 1781-97.

British Library, Manuscript Collections (Add MSS 72847). Acquired 1996 (AR Heath of Clifton, Bristol, sale catalogue July 1996, item 71).

[h] Misc Oxon deeds 1803-20 (7 items); wills, settlements and related legal and estate papers 1790-1866.

Bodleian Library, Oxford (MSS Dep. Deeds Hautenville Cope c. 1-4). Presented by Mr EDR Eagar to Berkshire Record Office 1949 and transferred 1950. NRA 3966.

[i] Survey of Charlbury and Walcot (Oxon) 1761.

Bodleian Library, Oxford (Dep. c. 379). Deposited from the Blenheim Palace Estate Office 1969-70. *Curators' Report 1969-70*, p23.

[j] Journal of the 3rd Earl of Sunderland 1705.

Bodleian Library, Oxford (MS Rawl. d. 601).

[k] Misc Wilts estate records 1758-19th cent, incl survey 1784 and valuation (West Lavington) 1812.

Wiltshire and Swindon Record Office (WRO 79, 113). Deposited by Messrs Elwell & Co, solicitors, Highworth 1948. NRA 881.

[l] Papers of William Townesend, mason, rel to work at Blenheim Palace 1722-32, incl letters from Sarah, Duchess of Marlborough; papers of Joseph Brooks of Woodstock as agent for the 4th Duke of Marlborough mainly 1798-1809, incl election papers 1802.

Berkshire Record Office (D/ESv(B) F 29-30, D/ESv(M) B 6-18 *passim*). Deposited by Mrs B Stevens 1963 and by Mrs Ward of Bradfield 1965. NRA 10469.

[m] Blenheim garden accounts 1705-10 (4 items).

Untraced. Winifred A Myers (Autographs) Ltd, catalogue no 13, 1986.

[n] Corresp and papers of the 1st Duke of Marlborough 1697-1714, incl corresp with Sir Charles Hedges and battle plans 1703-10.

Churchill Archives Centre, Churchill College, Cambridge (MARL). Deposited from Chartwell 1977. NRA 29995.

[o] Letters from Sarah, Duchess of Marlborough to her lawyer (Mr Waller) 1737-41 (96 items).

Yale University, Beinecke Library (Osborn MSS fc 25). NRA 18661.

[p] Misc accounts and papers of the 1st Duke and Sarah, Duchess of Marlborough 1704-24, incl household accounts 1717-24, accounts for work in Windsor Great Park 1717-22, Ordnance account 1713-14 and accounts of the Duchess as Keeper of the Privy Purse, etc 1707-10.

Hove Central Library (Wolseley/RUSI MSS). Deposited with papers of Viscount Wolseley (author of a *Life of Marlborough*) in the Royal United Services Institution, and transferred to Hove Corporation 1968. NRA 10471.

[q] American letters and papers of the 3rd Earl of Sunderland 1704-10.

Huntington Library, San Marino, California. Purchased at Sotheby's, 1-2 July 1920, lots 156-251 *passim*. Other papers were purchased by the Maryland Historical Society. A number of items from this sale, however, including charters for St Alban's (Herts) 1248-1540 (9 items) (lots 133-141) and misc MSS of Sir Richard Steele (lot 37), are untraced. (See HMC *Eighth Report, App, part I*, 1881, pp1-60.)

[r] Astronomical papers of the 4th Duke, with those of Thomas Hornsby.

Museum of the History of Science, Oxford (MSS Radcliffe 15-16, 35-40, 75). NRA 9532.

[s] Political corresp and papers of the 7th Duke of Marlborough 1840-80, incl papers as Lord Lieutenant of Ireland 1876-80.

Cambridge University Library (MS Add 9271). NRA 38803. Acquired from Mr Peregrine Churchill 1994.

[t] Autograph letters 1706-1926 (3 vols, 2 albums).

Library of Congress, Washington DC (Acc 3569). Presented by the 9th Duke of Marlborough 1929.

Related collections: Spencer, Earls Spencer, no 97; Brudenell, Earls of Cardigan, no 11, including further papers of the 1st Earl of Cardigan.

[99] STANLEY, Earls of Derby

Sir John Stanley, second son of Sir William Stanley of Storeton (Cheshire) acquired estates in Lancashire, including Lathom and Knowsley, through his marriage in 1390 to Isabel, heiress of Sir Thomas Lathom. He also acquired estates in Cheshire, where the family were hereditary Stewards and Master Foresters of Macclesfield,

and was granted the Lordship of Man in 1405. His grandson, Sir Thomas, created Lord Stanley in 1456, acquired Hawarden and Mold (Flintshire) in 1443 and Bosley (Cheshire) in 1446. Thomas, second Lord Stanley, was created Earl of Derby in 1485. His son George married Joan, heiress of Lord Strange of Knockin, and inherited the Strange title and estates in Shropshire, including Ellesmere, and the Welsh marches. The first Earl of Derby and his son Lord Strange were granted the manor of Holborn (Middlesex) in 1474, and estates in Lancashire, Cheshire, Flintshire (Hope), Westmorland (Witherslack), Northamptonshire (King's Sutton and Brackley), Cumberland (Bassenthwaite), London and elsewhere. Estates in Yorkshire (Burton-in-Lonsdale and Mewith in the West Riding, and Thirsk and Kirkby Malzeard in the North Riding) were also acquired at this time. The third Earl bought Burscough Priory, Dieulacres Abbey and Manchester College estates, and in 1545 exchanged estates in Lincolnshire, Derbyshire and Nottinghamshire for Eynsham Abbey's estates in Oxfordshire.

On the death of the fifth Earl in 1594, the earldom and entailed estates in Lancashire, Cheshire and North Wales went to his brother, William, who also secured the Isle of Man, but the Brackley and Ellesmere estates passed to the heirs general (see Egerton, Earls of Ellesmere, no 33). Substantial outlying estates, including Eynsham, were sold in the late sixteenth and early seventeenth centuries, and further property, including Mold, was lost on the execution of the seventh Earl and forfeiture of his estates in 1651. On the death of the ninth Earl in 1702 he was succeeded by his brother, as tenth Earl, in most of the family estates, but Lathom, Childwall and other Lancashire manors passed to the ninth Earl's daughter, the Countess of Ashburnham (see Ashburnham, Earls of Ashburnham, no 3). In 1705 the tenth Earl married Mary, daughter and heir of Sir William Morley of Halnaker (Sussex), but part of her estate was sold to pay her family's debts. The tenth Earl also sold his Yorkshire manors, but in 1724 he bought Sir Cleave Moore of Bankhall's properties in Bootle, Kirkdale and Liverpool. In 1736, on his death without issue, the Isle of Man and the barony of Strange passed to his heir general, the second Duke of Atholl (see Murray, later Stewart-Murray, Dukes of Atholl, no 71), but the entailed estates descended with the earldom to Sir Edward Stanley, fifth Bt, of Bickerstaffe (Lancashire).

Sir Henry Stanley, son of Sir James Stanley of Cross Hall, the younger brother of the second Earl, acquired Bickerstaffe through marriage in 1563. His son Edward was created a baronet in 1627. In 1697 Sir Thomas, fourth Bt, inherited the manor of Thornley and Patten House in Preston (Lancashire) through his marriage to Elizabeth, daughter and heir of Thomas Patten. Their son Edward married Elizabeth, daughter of Robert Hesketh of Rufford, and succeeded to the earldom in 1736. His son James (dvp1771) inherited estates in Ireland and Hamerton (Huntingdonshire) through his marriage to Lucy, daughter and co-heir of Hugh Smith of South Weald (Essex). The twelfth Earl acquired The Oaks (Surrey) from his aunt's husband, General John Burgoyne (d1792), but it was sold in 1833. The thirteenth Earl sold the site of Patten House and, in 1847, part of the Moore estate in Liverpool. Irish estates were also sold in the mid-nineteenth century. Estates in Kent and Surrey were late nineteenth-century purchases.

Estates in 1883: Earl of Derby: Lancs 57,000 acres, Cheshire 9,500 acres, Surrey 1,400 acres, Kent 950 acres, Flintshire 92 acres, total 68,942 acres worth upwards of £163,273 a year, excluding 900 acres leased for buildings and returned in the tenants' names; Hon F Stanley (in 1873): Westmorland 1,431 acres worth £737 a year.

[a] Deeds early 13th-20th cent, mainly Lancs but incl Cheshire 15th-18th cent, Flintshire (Hope, Mold and Hawarden) 1570-19th cent, Oxon (Eynsham, etc) 1383-1635, Salop (Knockin, etc) 1249-1447, Sussex (East Lavant and Halnaker) 18th cent, Westmorland (Beetham and Witherslack, etc) 1448, 1540-18th cent, Yorks NR and WR 15th-18th cent and Ireland 18th cent; registers and calendars of deeds 20th cent; abstracts of title, settlements, wills and inquisitions *post mortem* 15th-18th cent; papers rel to sequestration of the 7th Earl's estates 1650-2; legal and case papers 16th-19th cent, incl Flints estates late 17th cent and Bishop of Sodor and Man *v* Earl of Derby 1738-58; manorial court records 1566-20th cent, mainly Lancs but incl Devon (Bradworthy) 1555, Salop 1588-92, Sussex 1565, Westmorland (Beetham and Witherslack) 1690-1717 and Yorks NR (Thirsk) 1424-77.

Estate papers, mainly Lancs, incl leases from mid-16th cent, lease registers and related papers late 17th-20th cent, maps and plans 17th-20th cent, surveys, valuations and particulars from 16th cent, rentals late 14th cent-20th cent, accounts 1512-20th cent, estate corresp 18th-20th cent and papers rel to canals, drainage, mining, railways, patronage, etc 18th-20th cent; estate papers for Cheshire (Macclesfield, etc) 17th-20th cent, Flints (mainly Hope) 17th-19th cent, Oxon, incl Eynsham leases nd and Milton bailiff's account 1384-6, Warwicks 17th-18th cent, Westmorland (Beetham and Witherslack) 1628-19th cent, and Yorks NR and WR 17th-early 18th cent; Middlesex (Colham and Hillingdon) bailiffs' accounts 1372-1418; survey and valuation of 12th Earl's lands in London, Middlesex and Essex 1776; Ellesmere bailiffs' accounts 1378-80; Salop rental 1629; Northumberland (Fleetham) survey 1658; Cumberland (Whicham and Corney) rental c1660; Sussex (Halnaker) rental 1710-11;

Glassmore (Isle of Ely) rental 1774-7; Newmarket (Suffolk) maps and plans late 19th-20th cent; accounts and papers rel to Smith estates in Ireland, Middlesex, Yorks, Essex and Hunts 1747-59; Irish estate papers 1747-1873.

Household records 16th-19th cent, incl ordinances and accounts 1562, list of servants at Knowsley and Lathom 1702, housekeeper's account 1728-9 and London household journal and vouchers 1812-34; catalogue of pictures at Knowsley 1875; Duchy of Lancaster papers 1568-19th cent; Lancs lieutenancy and militia papers 1692-1814, with corresp rel to riots 1842; Lancs election papers late 17th-19th cent; Preston election corresp 1706-1820 and accounts 1780-97; papers rel to Preston 18th-19th cent, incl plan of cockpit 1790 and race course papers early 19th cent; papers rel to Ormskirk (Lancs) 16th-19th cent, incl book of orders for regulating the town 1613-1725 and papers rel to the church and town hall; misc papers rel to Lancs local affairs; accounts of the Keeper of the Great Seal of Chester Exchequer 1682-97 and bailiff itinerant in Cheshire 1693; papers rel to the Countess of Derby's almshouses in Boxgrove, East Lavant and Tangmere (Sussex) 1717, and to Hulme's charity for graduates of Brasenose College, Oxford 18th cent.

Appointments, commissions and patents 1439-19th cent; misc family papers from 15th cent, incl dispensation for marriage of Thomas Stanley and Elizabeth Welles 1498, Earl and Countess of Derby's letter of confraternity from Ely Priory 1507, Eton accounts of Edward and James Stanley 1768-70 and genealogical papers 1632-1844; ministers' and receivers' accounts of Lord Lovell 1446, the Duchess of Exeter 1472, the Duchess of Norfolk 1477, 1495, the Countess of Richmond 1504 and Sir Robert Broughton 1505; Burscough Priory account 1537; papers rel to the Hesketh family of Rufford 1650-95, incl many Rufford leases.

Lancashire Record Office (DDK). Deposited by the 17th Earl of Derby and others from 1946. *Guide to the Lancashire Record Office*, 1985, pp262-70; *Supplement 1977-89*, 1992, p118. SA Moore, *Calendar of the Muniments of the Earl of Derby*, privately printed 1894. NRA 53 (partial list).

[b] Lancashire leases from early 19th cent and plans c1790-20th cent; Bury and Pilkington rentals 1907-23; estate corresp 19th-20th cent.

Lancashire Record Office (DDKb). Deposited by the Bury Estate Company 1956. *Guide to the Lancashire Record Office*, 1985, pp270-1.

[c] Preston borough election account 1826, Hon E G Stanley.

Lancashire Record Office (DDX 123). Transferred from the Harris Museum, Preston

1981. *Guide to the Lancashire Record Office, Supplement 1977-89*, 1992, p118.

[d] Letters to EH Stanley (later 15th Earl of Derby) from his grandfather the 13th Earl 1850.

Lancashire Record Office (DP 446). Purchased 1980. *Guide to the Lancashire Record Office, Supplement 1977-89*, 1992, p118.

[e] Misc Lancs deeds mainly late 16th cent; wills of the 3rd Earl 1572 and Henry Stanley of Bickerstaffe 1598 (with funeral account); legal and estate papers late 16th-late 17th cent, incl leases, surveys, rentals and corresp; household accounts and papers c1561-90; corresp 16th-17th cent, incl 3rd Earl's letter book 1532-9.

Lancashire Record Office (Farington of Worden papers, DDF nos 985-1015, 2420-31, etc). *Guide to the Lancashire Record Office*, 1985, pp261-2. HMC *6th Report, App*, 1877, pp426-48. NRA 334.

[f] Trust and settlement papers 1841-57; papers rel to the will and estate of the 15th Earl 1893; papers rel to the 14th Earl's claim to the dukedom of Hamilton 1838-9; estate corresp and papers 19th-20th cent, incl list of Tipperary tenants c1830 and statements of Knowsley accounts 1896-1914; corresp and papers rel to advowsons 19th-20th cent; misc household accounts and vouchers mainly 19th cent; corresp with London and Knowsley architects late 19th cent; corresp and papers rel to Coworth Park, Derby House and Knowsley 20th cent; corresp and papers rel to paintings, porcelain, etc 20th cent; local and election papers 19th-20th cent; corresp and papers of the 13th Earl, incl papers rel to his natural history collections c1810-51; extensive personal and political corresp and papers of the 14th, 15th, 16th and 17th Earls c1816-1948, incl journals of the 15th Earl 1848-93; papers rel to Lord Randolph Churchill's biography of the 17th Earl.

Liverpool Record Office, Local Studies and Family History Service (920 DER). Deposited by the 18th Earl of Derby 1968-84. HMC *Papers of British Cabinet Ministers 1782-1900*, 1982, pp60-1; *Private Papers of British Diplomats 1782-1900*, 1985, p63; *Private Papers of British Colonial Governors 1782-1900*, 1986, pp54-55; *Papers of British Politicians 1782-1900*, 1989, p97. NRA 20084, 20761 (partial lists). A recipe book of Elizabeth, Countess of Derby (1714-76) was acquired in 1961 (920 MD 417; NRA 18456).

[g] Corresp and papers mainly 20th cent.

In private possession. Not normally available for research.

[h] Isle of Man deeds 1379, early 17th-early 19th cent; abstracts of deeds (1607-1736) c1740; papers rel to the 10th Earl's will and settlement 1736-8; legal and case papers 1598-

c1810, incl Derby *v* Regina (succession to Isle of Man) 1598, Crown *v* Derby (Rushen Priory rent) 1673-82, Bishop of Sodor and Man *v* Derby 17th-19th cent, and Atholl *v* Derby 1736-51; Isle of Man manorial court roll 1576; Manx estate records 16th-18th cent, incl leases 1598-1723, surveys and valuations 1506-1703, rental 1607, book of fines due from Manx tenants 1704, and receivers' and bailiffs' accounts 1521-1735; misc accounts c1700-35, incl voyages of the *Henrietta* to and from Liverpool 1704-18, cattle bought in the island for the 10th Earl's use 1704-14, and sale of puffins, rabbits and cattle grazing on the Calf of Man 1735; corresp and papers rel to the government of Man 17th-18th cent, incl book of customary laws 1667, copies of charters and statutes, appointments, establishment orders c1607-1736, customs papers c1661-1735 and inventories of arms 1661-1702; Stanley family pedigrees 1753.

Manx National Heritage Library (MD 401). Presented by the 18th Earl of Derby 1967. *Guide to the Lancashire Record Office*, 1985, pp262-70. NRA 53, 39139 (partial lists).

[i] Records of the manor and forest of Macclesfield 1700, c1790-1936; misc estate papers 19th-20th cent, incl inventories and other papers rel to Crag Hall, Wildboarclough (Cheshire) 1842-67.

Cheshire Record Office (D 5075). Purchased 1994. NRA 39460.

[j] Survey of Manchester College 1654, with copy of conveyance to George and Edward Chetham 1654.

Chetham's Library, Manchester (E.2.8.S1; Mun. A.5. Leases (a)6). Presented to the Trustees of Chetham's Hospital by the 15th Earl of Derby 1885.

[k] Receiver of Molesdale's account of Lord Stanley's properties in Molesdale and Hawarden (Flintshire) 1476-7.

Flintshire Record Office (D/DM/426). Purchased at Sotheby's 1975. NRA 24328.

[l] Bolton-cum-Adgarley (Lancs) manorial records 1836-1949.

Cumbria Record Office, Barrow (BD/HJ/204-5). Deposited by Hart, Jackson & Sons, solicitors, Ulverston 1977-8. NRA 32581.

[m] Kirkby Malzeard (Yorks WR) manorial court rolls 1512, 1620-8.

West Yorkshire Archive Service, Leeds (Bostock MSS 34-38; Acc 1653). Acquired from the 18th Earl of Derby by Godfrey Bostock, Esq and transferred from Lancashire Record Office 1971. NRA 39454.

[n] Misc papers of the 4th Earl of Derby *c*1583-9, incl estate accounts.

British Library, Manuscript Collections (Add MS 63742). Purchased from Pickering and Chatto 1986.

[o] Natural history papers 18th-19th cent (13th Earl's collection).

British Library, Manuscript Collections (Add MSS 28534-48). Presented by the 15th Earl of Derby 1870.

[p] Letter books and corresp of the 13th Earl of Derby 1799-1850.

National Museums and Galleries on Merseyside, Maritime Archives and Library (MM/8K). Given by the executors of the 13th Earl 1851-2. NRA 37366.

[q] Knowsley game book 1807-18, incl personal notes of the 13th Earl of Derby.

Merseyside Naturalists' Association. GDR Bridson, *Natural History Manuscript Resources in the British Isles*, 1980, p131.

[r] Corresp and papers of Mary, Countess of Derby (1824-1900).

In private possession. Access restricted. Enquiries to the Librarian and Archivist, Hatfield House, Hertfordshire.

[s] Stanley family papers 1841-1921, incl corresp of Frederick Stanley, later 16th Earl of Derby, and his wife Constance (née Villiers) during his Governor-generalship of Canada 1883-93.

Corpus Christi College, Cambridge. Deposited by RF Hobbs 1969. HMC *Private Papers of British Colonial Governors 1782-1900*, 1986, pp54-5. NRA 11916.

[t] Two volumes of working papers 1869-79 collected by Frederick Stanley, later 16th Earl of Derby, while Secretary of State for War.

National Army Museum (ARC 8806/31). Purchased 1988. NRA 33449.

[u] Autograph letter collection of Lady Emma Talbot (d1928), daughter of the 14th Earl of Derby, mainly 19th cent but incl some papers 17th-20th cent.

In private possession. Enquiries to West Sussex Record Office. NRA 23389.

[v] Family papers of Sir Patrick Chetwynd-Talbot (1817-98) and Lady Emma Talbot (née Stanley), incl Stanley family corresp and papers 19th cent; collected papers rel to the Talbot family, Earls of Shrewsbury 15th-20th cent.

In private possession. Not normally available for research.

Related collections: Egerton, Earls of Ellesmere, no 33; Murray, later Stewart-Murray, Dukes of Atholl, no 71; Stanley of Cross Hall (Lancashire Record Office DDCr, NRA 6251); Barons Kenyon (Lancashire Record Office DDKe, NRA 19460, and in private possession).

[100] STUART, later CRICHTON-STUART, Earls and later Marquesses of Bute

John Stuart, a son of Robert II of Scotland, was created hereditary sheriff of Buteshire (the islands of Bute, Arran and Cumbrae) *c*1385. The first Earl of Bute, so created in 1703, married in 1680 Agnes, daughter of Sir George Mackenzie of Rosehaugh (Ross and Cromarty), but following the death of the second Earl in 1723 the Mackenzie estates passed to a younger son, James Stuart, later Stuart-Mackenzie (d1800). The third Earl of Bute (1713-92, Prime Minister 1762-3) married in 1736 Mary Wortley-Montagu (d1794), heiress of estates in Yorkshire and Cornwall. These estates, however, passed to their second son James Archibald Stuart-Wortley (1747-1818), who also inherited the Mackenzie estates from his uncle and took the additional name of Mackenzie in 1803. The third Earl acquired the Luton Hoo (Bedfordshire) estate in 1763, but it was sold in 1844.

In 1766 John Stuart, later fourth Earl and (1796) first Marquess of Bute, married Charlotte, daughter and heir of the second Viscount Windsor (d1758), through whom descended estates and coalfields in South Wales formerly belonging to the Earls of Pembroke (see Herbert, Earls of Pembroke, no 50), and the Axwell (County Durham) estate of her mother's family of Clavering.

Lord Mount Stuart (d1794), son of the first Marquess, married in 1792 Elizabeth McDouall-Crichton, daughter of the sixth Earl of Dumfries (d1803), bringing estates in Ayrshire and Wigtownshire to the Stuart family. Originally seated at Sanquhar (Dumfriesshire)(later sold), the Crichton family had been established in Ayrshire since the seventeenth century. William Crichton was created Viscount of Air in 1622 and Earl of Dumfries in 1633. The third Earl (d1694) was succeeded by his sister Penelope, who married in 1698 William Dalrymple, second son of the first Earl of Stair. On her death in 1742 the Dumfries estates passed to her son as fifth Earl of Dumfries: he also succeeded in 1760 to the earldom of Stair, as fourth Earl, but not to the Stair estates. On the death of the fifth Earl of Dumfries in 1768 the title and estates passed to his nephew Patrick McDouall of Freuch (Wigtownshire).

The second Marquess of Bute (1793-1848) married secondly, in 1845, Sophia Rawdon-Hastings (d1859), second daughter of the first

Marquess of Hastings and Flora Campbell, *suo jure* Countess of Loudon (d1840) (see Rawdon-Hastings, later Abney-Hastings, Marquesses of Hastings and Earls of Loudon, no 88), through whom a large quantity of Campbell and Hastings papers passed to the Marquesses of Bute. Sanquhar and Drumlanrig accounts and papers formerly at Drumlanrig (see Montagu-Douglas-Scott, Dukes of Buccleuch and Queensberry, no 70) were acquired from a dealer in 1897: the Drumlanrig papers were returned to the ninth Duke of Buccleuch in 1981. In the twentieth century the fourth Marquess of Bute added extensively to the manuscript collections at Mount Stuart House and elsewhere.

Estates in 1883: Ayshire 43,734 acres, Buteshire 29,279 acres, Wigtownshire 20,157 acres, Glamorganshire 21,402 acres, Breconshire 59 acres, Monmouthshire 12 acres, Co Durham 1,953 acres, Beds 72 acres, total 116,668 acres worth £151,135 a year, exclusive of Ayrshire minerals worth £2,506.

[a] Bute and Arran charters c1400-1800; Ayrshire and Wigtownshire charters and writs (Crichton, McDouall, etc) 15th-19th cent, with some for Dumfriesshire, Edinburgh, etc 14th-17th cent; wills, settlements and related papers 16th-20th cent, Stuart, Crichton, etc, incl Bute sederunt book 1766-1827 and papers rel to Lady Bute's trust c1867-1910; legal and case papers, Crichton 16th-19th cent and Stuart mainly 18th-19th cent, incl sasines, papers rel to teinds and feu duties, and Mackenzie case papers 18th cent; Ardwell (Wigtownshire) barony court minutes 1658.

Bute estate records late 17th-mid-20th cent, incl tacks, surveys and maps from mid-18th cent, rentals and accounts from c1700, crop books 1747-63, letter books from late 18th cent, corresp from late 18th cent, and papers rel to buildings, drainage and plantations; Mount Stuart home farm accounts and herd books early 20th cent; Ayrshire (Dumfries House, etc) estate records 17th-20th cent, incl tacks, maps, rentals, accounts and vouchers, memoranda, letter books, corresp, and papers rel to minerals; Wigtownshire estate records mainly 18th-19th cent, incl tacks, rentals, accounts and corresp; papers rel to Clackmannanshire (Crichton) estate 17th-mid-18th cent, Dumfriesshire estate 19th cent and Irish (McDouall) estates c1690-1780; Welsh legal and estate papers mainly 19th-20th cent, incl copies of trust deeds, agreements, accounts, reports, and papers rel to railways and canals, Cardiff docks and harbour, sales, etc.

Papers rel to the fabric of Mount Stuart House 18th-20th cent, incl drawings mid-18th cent, papers rel to alterations late 18th cent, and papers rel to the rebuilding by Sir Robert Rowand Anderson 1880-1912; papers rel to the contents of Mount Stuart House 18th-20th

cent, incl inventories and catalogues, with household and garden accounts and papers from early 18th cent; papers rel to Liefnorris, later Dumfries, House 17th-20th cent, incl Adam drawings and papers 1750s, papers rel to contents from late 18th cent, and household accounts and papers 19th-20th cent; papers rel to Edinburgh houses 18th-20th cent, Mochrum Castle 19th cent, Cardiff Castle 18th-20th cent (incl drawings and reports by William Burges), Castell Coch and Caerphilly Castle 19th-20th cent, and London houses 19th-early 20th cent; Luton Hoo library book lists 1827-41 (2 vols); papers rel to Falkland Palace and Pluscarden Priory 19th-20th cent; Buteshire lieutenancy papers late 18th-mid-20th cent, incl minutes 1795-1808, 1824-62; papers rel to Rothesay (Bute) 18th cent, and to Cumbrae (Arran) parish 1805-7.

Stuart, later Crichton-Stuart, patents and commissions 18th-19th cent; Stuart and Crichton-Stuart family papers 16th-20th cent, incl the 1st and 2nd Earls of Bute 1683-1763, prime ministerial, scientific, estate and other corresp of the 3rd Earl, and extensive corresp and papers of the 1st, 2nd, 3rd and 4th Marquesses; diplomatic and other papers of James Stuart Mackenzie (d1800); military and American papers of General Sir Charles Stuart (1753-1801); Crichton family papers mainly 18th-early 19th cent, incl corresp of the 5th and 6th Earls of Dumfries; McDouall of Freuch family papers 17th-18th cent; corresp and papers of Sir John Dalrymple and Colonel William Dalrymple late 17th-early 18th cent, and of the 2nd and 3rd Earls of Stair 18th cent; Windsor family pedigree rolls, etc 17th-18th cent; misc and collected papers 14th-20th cent, incl Boyd of Penkill (Ayrshire) papers 1518-1716, journals of Bulstrode Whitelocke 1605-75 (2 vols), papers of John Hough, Leghorn merchant 17th cent, Kirkcudbright testaments 1642-1750 and town council minutes 1629-83, Stuart and Jacobite papers 18th cent, Gibraltar garrison accounts 1733-52 (1 vol), letters of Lady Mary Wortley-Montagu to Lady Mar and Mme Michielli 1740-62 (2 vols), diplomatic and family corresp of Lord Stuart de Rothesay (1779-1845), weather records (Mount Stuart, etc) 18th cent, tracts and pamphlets, and photographs 19th-20th cent.

Ayrshire (Loudon and Rowallan) charters and legal papers late 12th-early 19th cent; estate records, Ayrshire 16th-mid-19th cent, Ireland (Rawdon estates) 17th-18th cent, and Leics and Derbys (Hastings estates) 18th-19th cent; Ayrshire and Leics mining records 18th-early 19th cent; household papers 18th-19th cent, Loudon Castle, Donington Park (Leics), Moira House (Dublin), etc; Campbell and Hastings family papers 16th-19th cent, incl papers of the 3rd, 4th and 5th Earls of Loudon 18th cent, military, political, Indian and other corresp and papers of the 1st Marquess of Hastings, and corresp and papers of his wife (*suo jure*

Countess of Loudon) and family; Mure of Rowallan (Ayrshire) family papers 17th cent; misc papers 17th-19th cent, incl register of returns of stock, etc mid-17th cent and scroll account book of James Hamilton, Provost of Glasgow 1615-20.

In private possession. Access restricted. Enquiries to the National Register of Archives (Scotland) (NRA(S) 631). HMC *Third Report, App*, 1872, pp202-9, 402-3; *Fifth Report, App*, 1876, pp617-20; *Papers of British Politicians 1782-1900*, 1989, p25; *Guide to the Location of Collections*, 1982, p9. NRA 15459 (partial list).

[b] Buteshire, Dumfriesshire and Wigtownshire rentals and states of account 1859-60.

National Archives of Scotland (CS 96/2375).

[c] Glamorganshire and Monmouthshire deeds 16th-19th cent, with some for Beds 16th-19th cent; wills and inventories, settlements and related trust deeds and papers, Herbert, Windsor and Crichton-Stuart 16th-early 20th cent, incl 7th Earl of Pembroke decd late 17th cent; legal and case papers 16th-early 20th cent; Glamorganshire and Monmouthshire manorial records 14th-20th cent, incl boroughs of Llantrisant and Cardiff 16th-19th cent; misc English manorial records 16th-18th cent.

Monmouthshire lease registers 1617-1706; Glamorganshire and Monmouthshire estate records 16th-20th cent, incl leases, surveys and valuations from 16th cent, maps and plans 18th-20th cent, rentals and accounts 16th-19th cent, corresp from late 16th cent, letter books 1757-1848 and enclosure papers 16th-19th cent; leases, etc rel to the Herberts of Swansea 16th cent-1716; agent's corresp rel to the Herberts of Cogan Pill late 16th-early 17th cent; papers rel to minerals and ironworks 16th-early 20th cent, incl mineral leases 19th-20th cent, accounts of coal shipped from Neath, etc 1626-82, and quarry and lime kiln accounts 19th cent; railway, dock and harbour papers and plans 19th-20th cent, incl Bute Dock cash book 1830-41; Worcs estate accounts (Windsor family) 1724-7; papers rel to Cardiff Castle 16th-19th cent, incl inventories 1581, 1585, estimate of repairs 1590 and plans of grounds; Glamorganshire yeomanry and militia papers 1815-37 and election papers 1837; corresp of Alice, Lady Windsor 1757-76 and of the 2nd Marquess of Bute, 1804-55 (incl letters rel to Beds, Cambs (Kirtling: Lady Bute's property) and Co Durham estates); misc records, incl Montgomeryshire Crown accounts 1528-31, muster roll for hundreds of Wentlooge and Caldicot (Monmouthshire) 1601 and description of Glamorgan by Rice Lewis 1596-1600.

National Library of Wales. Deposited by the 5th Marquess of Bute 1950 and later. *National Library of Wales Journal*, vol VII no 3, summer 1952. NRA 581.

[d] Misc deeds, incl exchanges 19th-20th cent; Glamorganshire manorial records 1877-1957; Glamorganshire estate records 18th-20th cent, incl survey 1824, vouchers and corresp; papers rel to minerals and easements 1889-1956, Bute Docks and railways 19th-20th cent, Aberdare Canal 1793-1961, Penydarren and Tredegar Iron companies 1831-7 and Llantrisant Town Trust 1880-93, 1949-50.

Glamorgan Record Office (D/D/A-B). Deposited from the Rothesay estate office c1965-70. NRA 10781.

[e] Deeds for Beds, Herts, Middlesex and Worcs 17th-19th cent.

Glamorgan Record Office (1989/409). Transferred from South Glamorgan County Library, among the collection of deeds of the former Cardiff Central Library. In course of cataloguing 1998.

[f] Misc deeds, legal papers and estate accounts and papers rel to Windsor estates in Glamorganshire, Worcs, Bucks and elsewhere 17th-18th cent, incl surveys of Broadlands (Hants) c1720, 1724; misc manorial records 1738-1815; misc Glamorganshire and Monmouthshire estate records 1707-1893, incl Glamorganshire estate accounts 1840-84 and letter books 1824-40; report on Glamorganshire and Luton estates c1827; South Wales canal, railway and dock papers 18th-20th cent; papers rel to minerals and ironworks 18th-early 20th cent; catalogue of pictures at Cardiff Castle 1886-7; Crichton-Stuart family papers 1764-1918, incl papers of the 2nd Marquess as lord lieutenant of Glamorgan 1815-48 and papers rel to politics in Beds; Stuart Mackenzie papers 1748-98, incl Perthshire and Forfarshire estate accounts, and drawings and accounts rel to Belmont Castle (Perthshire); Adderbury (Oxon), etc rental 1757 (Argyll, later Buccleuch); Glamorganshire (Beaufort estate) colliery papers c1823-35.

South Glamorgan Library Service, Cardiff Central Library (CL/Bute, Cardiff MSS 4.709-5.85 *passim*). Acquired c1940. NRA 10781.

[g] Drawings of proposed alterations to Cardiff Castle by William Burges late 19th cent.

Cardiff Castle. Transferred from Cardiff City Library c1974.

[h] Luton Hoo estate and household corresp and papers 1789-1859, incl some local political corresp of the 1st Marquess of Bute.

Bedfordshire and Luton Archives and Record Service (G/DDA). Presented to Glamorgan Record Office by Arthur Andrews, who had purchased them at auction, and transferred to Bedfordshire Record Office 1965, 1967. NRA 10481.

[i] Luton court rolls 1470-1558, with accounts of the guild of the Holy Trinity of Luton 1527-47 (1 vol).

Bedfordshire and Luton Archives and Record Service (Z 486). Purchased from the 6th Marquess of Bute 1983.

[j] Co Durham deeds 17th-early 20th cent; trust deeds and related trust and executorship papers 18th cent-1906, mainly Crichton-Stuart; legal papers 18th-20th cent, incl abstracts, schedules, case papers and corresp, mainly Co Durham but some for Welsh and Scottish estates 19th cent; Chopwell (Co Durham) court book 1681-1740; misc Co Durham estate records 18th-20th cent, incl rentals, accounts, plans and sale papers; Co Durham mining papers 18th-20th cent, incl leases, wayleaves, accounts and corresp; misc rentals for south Wales estates 1824-56; papers rel to Kirk Newton (Northumberland) advowson 1877; Winlaton (Co Durham) manor and partnership estate records 16th-19th cent.

Durham County Record Office (D/CG 6, 19, 20). Deposited by Sir WW Gibson and Wilkinson, Marshall, Clayton & Gibson, solicitors, Newcastle-upon-Tyne 1963-76. NRA 26390.

[k] Additional Co Durham deeds, trust papers and legal papers 16th-20th cent; additional mining papers and plans 18th-20th cent; letter book 1778-1819.

Durham University Library, Archives and Special Collections (PD/CG/Bute). Deposited by Sir WW Gibson c1960. NRA 26390.

[l] Co Durham surveys, plans and related papers c1811-56 (papers of Thomas Bell as surveyor).

Durham County Record Office (Bowes Museum collection D/BO/G43, 98). Transferred 1963, 1970. NRA 23425.

[m] Co Durham mineral rent account book 1901-33.

Durham County Record Office (D/X 1173). Deposited 1997.

[n] Falkland (Fife) estate papers 1820-1973, incl rentals, accounts and corresp; Falkland Palace visitors' books 1879-1933; Co Durham estate papers 1820-56, incl rent account 1846.

In private possession. Enquiries to the National Register of Archives (Scotland) (NRA(S) 3663). NRA 40343. (The Falkland estate was purchased in 1887, and on the death of the third Marquess in 1900 passed to his second son Lord Ninian Crichton-Stuart.)

[o] Adam drawings for Bute (later Lansdowne) House (London) and Luton Hoo 1750s-60s.

Victoria and Albert Museum, National Art Library. Purchased 1995.

[p] Letter book of the 3rd Earl of Bute 1761-3.

In private possession (c1956). Untraced 1997. NRA 5699.

[q] Account book of the 3rd Earl 1764-6.

Cambridge University Library (Add 9399). Purchased 1996 (Sotheby's, 25 Oct, lot 913).

[r] Scottish travel journal of the 1st Marquess of Bute 1788.

National Library of Scotland (MS 9587). Purchased 1965 (Sotheby's, 2 Mar, lot 445). (A quantity of the 1st Marquess's papers passed to his daughter Frances, whose grandson the 5th Earl of Harrowby sold many of them in 1903. For papers now in the British Library Manuscript Collections, the John Rylands University Library of Manchester and remaining with the Harrowby papers see HMC *Private Papers of British Diplomats 1782-1900*, 1985, pp65-6.)

Related collections: Herbert, Earls of Pembroke and Montgomery, no 50; Rawdon-Hastings, later Abney-Hastings, Marquesses of Hastings and Earls of Loudon, no 88; Montagu-Douglas-Scott, Dukes of Buccleuch, no 70; Barons Wharncliffe (Sheffield Archives WhM, NRA 1077; Dundee City Archives and Record Centre GD/Wh, NRA 32926; and see HMC *Guide to the location of collections*, 1982, p65); Earls of Harrowby (in private possession, NRA 1561), including correspondence of the 1st Marquess of Bute; Watson of Rockingham Castle (Northamptonshire Record Office, NRA 25867), including Glamorganshire and Luton manorial court papers 1817-24 (WR 1280, 1283/5-7).

[101] SUTHERLAND-LEVESON-GOWER, Dukes of Sutherland

The wool merchant James Leveson (d1549) acquired the monastic estates of Trentham Priory (Staffordshire) and Lilleshall Abbey (Shropshire) between 1537 and 1543 as well as other property in Staffordshire (such as Wolverhampton, from the Duke of Norfolk, in 1531, and Penn and Rowley Somery c1540) and Shropshire (including Leegomery, from the Audley family, c1528, and Sheriff Hales, from the Earl of Oxford, in 1546). Walter Leveson bought a moiety of Newport (Shropshire) in 1579. On the death of Sir Richard Leveson of Trentham in 1605, these estates came to Sir Richard Leveson of Halling (Kent) (d1661), a descendant of James Leveson's brother Nicholas Leveson (d1539), who had purchased Halling and acquired an Essex estate (Black Notley) by marriage. Sir Richard Leveson alienated the Kent and Essex estates between 1627 and 1650, and on his death in 1661 his Trentham and Lilleshall estates were inherited by Sir William Leveson-Gower (d1691), youngest son of his niece Frances Leveson by Sir Thomas Gower, second Bt, of Stittenham (Yorkshire, North Riding). In 1689, on the death of his nephew the third Bt, Leveson-Gower succeeded to the baronetcy and to Stittenham, which had been owned by the Gower family since the twelfth century. His son was created Baron Gower in 1703 and his grandson Earl Gower in 1746.

Through the marriage of the fourth Bt to Lady Jane Granville, aunt and co-heir in her issue of the third Granville Earl of Bath (d1711), the first Earl Gower inherited a portion of the Granville estates in Devon and Cornwall and a reversionary interest in the estates (including Grindon, Staffordshire) of Elizabeth, second Duchess of Albemarle, who died in 1734 (see Montagu-Douglas-Scott, Dukes of Buccleuch, no 70). This inheritance seems, however, to have been largely disposed of by 1760.

George Granville Leveson-Gower (1758-1833) succeeded his father as second Marquess of Stafford (so created 1786) in 1803 and was raised to the dukedom of Sutherland in 1833. He married in 1785 Elizabeth Gordon, *suo jure* Countess of Sutherland, daughter of the eighteenth Earl of Sutherland by Mary, daughter and co-heir of William Maxwell of Preston (Kirkcudbrightshire). The Earls of Sutherland were established in Sutherland in the thirteenth century and by the sixteenth century owned extensive property in the east of the county, centred on Dunrobin, including Golspie, Dornoch, Brora and Helmsdale. Aboyne (Aberdeenshire) came through the marriage of Elizabeth, sister of the ninth Earl (d1514), to Adam Gordon but was exchanged with the Earl of Huntly for Strathnaver (Sutherland). The Sutherland estate was extended by the purchase of Skelbo in 1787, the property of the Gordon family of Carrol (Gordonbush, etc) in 1812, Armadale and Strathy in 1813, and the West Sutherland lands of the Barons Reay (Tongue, etc) in 1829.

On the death of his uncle the third Duke of Bridgewater in 1803, the first Duke of Sutherland inherited the Bridgewater estates in Northamptonshire and Lancashire, together with the canal property and Bridgewater House (London), with remainder to his second son Francis Leveson-Gower, who was created Earl of Ellesmere in 1846 (see Egerton, Earls of Ellesmere, no 33).

In 1849 an estate in Ross-shire entered the family on the marriage of the third Duke with Anne, *suo jure* Countess of Cromartie, the daughter of John Hay-Mackenzie of New Hall and Cromartie. At her death in 1888, however, this property and her title passed by special remainder to her second surviving son Francis, second Earl of Cromartie.

The Staffordshire and Shropshire estates were consolidated by piecemeal purchase between the sixteenth and the nineteenth century. Borough electoral influence in Staffordshire came with acquisitions at Newcastle-under-Lyme (in the late seventeenth and early eighteenth century) and Lichfield (in the mid-eighteenth century), but these interests were disposed of before 1832, the latter to Lord Anson. Between 1912 and 1917 the Yorkshire and Shropshire estates and Stafford House (London, bought 1827) were sold and Trentham House demolished, though estates in Staffordshire and Scotland were retained and Sutton Place (Surrey) was acquired c1919 as a residence. On the death of the fifth Duke in 1963 the family estates passed to his niece Elizabeth, *suo jure* Countess of Sutherland, but his cousin the fifth Earl of Ellesmere succeeded as sixth Duke.

Bill Hill (Berkshire) was purchased in 1734 by Mary, Countess of Harold, who married the first Earl Gower as his third wife in 1736. On her death in 1785 it was inherited by her son the Hon John Leveson-Gower, to whose heirs it passed.

Estates in 1883: Salop 17,495 acres, Staffs 12,744 acres, Yorks NR 1,853 acres Sutherland 1,176,454 acres, Ross-shire 149,999 acres, total 1,358,545 acres worth £141,667 a year.

[a] Deeds 12th-20th cent (many medieval), mainly Salop and Staffs, with some for Cheshire, Derbys, Essex, Kent, Leics, Warwicks, Yorks, etc, incl deeds for properties of monastic houses at Croxden and Trentham (Staffs) and Lilleshall and Wombridge (Salop) 12th-16th cent; grants of confraternity and indulgence 15th cent; abstracts of title 16th-19th cent; copies of Sutherland writs 1499-1851 (3 vols); inquisition *post mortem*, Sir Thomas Giffard 1560; wills, settlements and executorship, trust and legal papers 15th-19th cent, incl papers rel to Lady Margaret Leveson's lunacy c1611-40, the prize ship *St Valentine* of Lisbon c1603-25, the 16th Baron Cobham decd c1597-1610, William and Francis Coppinger of All Hallows (Kent) decd c1580-96 and Sir Edward Barrett of Belhus (Essex) decd early 17th cent; legal and financial papers rel to the Devon and Cornwall estates of the 3rd Earl of Bath 18th cent; manorial records, Staffs (Trentham, Great Wyrley, etc) 14th-20th cent and Salop (Ketley, Leegomery, Sheriff Hales, etc) 15th-19th cent; misc manorial records, Freasley (Warwicks) 14th cent and Braunston (Northants) 15th-16th cent.

Agents' records for the English and Scottish estates generally c1799-20th cent, incl corresp and reports, with misc private papers of James and George Loch (agents 1812-77); survey and valuation of Sir Walter Leveson's estates 1599; Staffs and Salop estate records 14th-20th cent (particularly full from 18th cent), incl leases 14th-20th cent, surveys, maps, plans, valuations and rentals 16th-20th cent, accounts and vouchers 14th-20th cent and corresp and papers mainly 18th-20th cent, with records of the Lichfield and Newcastle-under-Lyme estates mainly mid-18th-19th cent; records of Trentham and Lilleshall home farms 1776-1915 and savings banks 1817-93; Blurton (Staffs) tilery accounts 1848-55; Wappenshall (Salop) wharf dues 1835-49; papers rel to Staffs and Salop cottages, improvements, drainage and estate buildings 18th-20th cent; records of Trentham Gardens Ltd 1933-68; papers rel to coal mining in north Staffs (Meirheath and Florence collieries, etc) and in south Staffs and Salop (Wolverhampton, Lilleshall, etc) mainly 18th-20th cent, incl leases, plans and royalty and other accounts, with north Staffs limeworking papers 1815-25; solicitors' papers for Staffs and Salop estates 17th-19th cent (transferred to Trentham by Messrs Fenton of Newcastle-under-Lyme c1851).

Yorks NR estate records 17th-20th cent, incl surveys and maps 18th-20th cent, rentals, accounts and vouchers c1661-20th cent, drainage accounts 1801-72 and corresp c1814-1924; Middlewich (Cheshire) salt working papers mainly 17th-18th cent, incl survey and valuation 1712-15; Kent estate terrier c1540 and misc Kent and Essex rentals, accounts and vouchers c1600-34; papers rel to proposed lease of Wimbledon Park (Surrey, Spencer estate) 1827 and to Leveson-Gower properties at Woolmers (Herts) 1801-15, Willows (Windsor, Berks) c1834-96 and Sutton Place (Surrey) 1916-18; estate papers for Davington (Kent, Coppinger family) late 16th cent, Lord Cobham's Kent estate c1603-10 and Barrett family properties in Essex (Belhus), Berks (Stanford Dingley) and Hants (Foxcott and Wolverton) c1600-8; Grindon (Staffs, former Albemarle estate) rentals and papers c1700-51; misc estate papers 15th-20th cent, incl Walsall (Staffs) survey late 16th cent, Dudley (Worcs) barony accounts 1489-1522 and rentals of Worcs lands of Sir Hugh Conway 1495 and the Newport (Salop) estate of William Yong c1539-40; Sutherland estate rentals, accounts and papers c1815-1910, incl factory minutes from 1888; papers rel to the 2nd Earl of Cromartie's estates c1853-94.

Trentham household and park records from 17th cent (mainly 19th-20th cent), incl architectural plans and drawings c1727-20th cent, building records c1632-9, 1834-47, inventories 1605, 1696, accounts c1632-95, accounts and vouchers 19th-20th cent, and cellar books mid-18th cent-1879; records of Stafford House c1820-1912, incl building papers c1820-44, inventory 1833 and accounts and vouchers c1822-1912; Bridgewater House vouchers 1833-4; inventory of the 3rd Duke of Bridgewater's plate 1804; records of other family residences 17th-20th cent, incl plans and drawings for Lilleshall Abbey c1841-1914, inventories and accounts for Halling c1602-12 and Sheriff Hales c1670-82, and accounts for Stittenham c1668-

73, London 17th cent-early 18th cent, Cliveden (Bucks) mid-19th cent and Willows (Windsor, Berks) c1889-1902; inventory of the Queen's Palace at Canterbury (Kent) 1598; Cobham Hall (Kent) household accounts 1603-4.

Staffs election papers 18th-early 19th cent, incl poll books and accounts for Lichfield and Newcastle-under-Lyme c1740-1818; papers rel to Staffs affairs 17th-19th cent, incl lieutenancy papers 18th cent and list of recusants indicted at quarter sessions 1640-1; misc papers rel to Staffs and Salop parochial matters 16th-20th cent, incl accounts of Trentham parish Easter dues c1550-2, Kinnersley (Salop) terrier 1748, Lilleshall parish school minutes 1818 and Tittensor (Staffs) National school accounts 1888-1901; Trentham gardens bowling club minutes 1913-17; extensive Kent lieutenancy papers c1550-1614, incl inventory of Dover Castle artillery 1576, Rochester market book 1586-7 and records of subsidies, musters and purveyance; New Malton (Yorks NR) burgage rentals c1670; Ross-shire, Cromarty, Sutherland and Caithness-shire volunteers and militia papers mid-19th cent; Golspie farmers club minutes 1847.

Appointments and commissions 16th-19th cent; family accounts and papers 17th-20th cent, incl papers of Sir John Leveson of Halling (d1615), Sir Richard Leveson (d1661), the 1st Earl Gower and the 2nd Duke of Sutherland, accounts with Drummond's Bank 1792-1913, and vouchers rel to the yacht *Ondine* 1847-51; diaries and papers of the 3rd Duke and his first wife, incl royal corresp, with records of Stafford House and Mansion House committees for the relief of Turkish soldiers, South African aid, etc, mainly 1877-9; corresp and papers of the Dukes' private secretaries 1835-1918; corresp of Princess Lieven and the 2nd Earl Grey 1823-41; literary and misc papers 16th-20th cent, incl printed pamphlets and tracts.

Monastic records 13th-16th cent, mainly Lilleshall Abbey, incl Lilleshall cartulary 13th cent, case papers 13th-16th cent, court roll (various manors) 14th-15th cent, account rolls, 14th cent, c1516 and chief rent receipts 1515-25, with case papers for Wombridge and Trentham priories, etc; accounts of Lichfield Dean and Chapter 1297 and former estates of Wombridge Priory 1565-6; rental 15th cent and accounts 1422 of St John's hospital, Bridgnorth (Salop); Wolverhampton hospital ordinances c1395.

Staffordshire and Stoke on Trent Archive Service, Staffordshire Record Office (D 593). Deposited by the Trustees of the will of the 4th Duke of Sutherland and Elizabeth, Countess of Sutherland 1955-82. The collection includes papers deposited at the William Salt Library 1944 (WSL D1709) and 1959 (WSL D1822) and transferred 1963. HMC *Papers of British Cabinet Ministers 1782-1900*, 1982, p38; *Private*

Papers of British Diplomats 1782-1900, 1985, p39; *Papers of British Politicians 1782-1900*, 1989, pp33, 61, 102. NRA 10699. Printed books, with some MSS, were sold at Sotheby's 19-24 Nov 1906 and further MSS at Christie's 2 July 1975, lots 242-54. Certain MS items from the earlier sale were aquired by the British Library (lot 1123, Egerton MS 2862), Durham Cathedral Library (Uhtred de Boldon, lot 1667, MS.A.IV.33, see NR Ker, *Medieval Manuscripts in British Libraries*, II, 1977, p486), and by several repositories in the United States (*Census of Medieval and Renaissance Manuscripts in the United States and Canada*, i, p1040 (lot 545), ii, p2027 (lot 175) and *Supplement*, p56 (lot 439))).

[b] Leveson and Leveson-Gower family and political corresp 16th-19th cent (12 vols).

Staffordshire and Stoke on Trent Archive Service, Staffordshire Record Office (D 868). Transferred from Dunrobin 1966. HMC *Fifth Report, App*, 1876, pp135-214. NRA 10699.

[c] Misc deeds and conveyances 1893-1974; family settlement 1596; executors' accounts for the 4th Duke 1913-56; extensive Salop and Staffs leases and agreements *c*1517-1800, with misc leases 1876-1947; misc Staffs estate papers 19th-20th cent, incl Trentham rentals 1930-5 and wage books 1856-79, 1933-47; records of Trentham Gardens Ltd 1933-56 and the Florence Coal and Iron Co 1896-1939; Staffordshire Coal and Iron Co corresp 1930-5; Lilleshall royalty accounts 1941-55; misc papers 19th-20th cent, incl Trentham house plans *c*1840-7.

Staffordshire and Stoke on Trent Archive Service, Staffordshire Record Office (D 4092). Deposited from Trentham by Trentham Gardens Ltd 1984. NRA 10699.

[d] Misc papers 19th-20th cent, incl Lilleshall plans 1914-17 and catalogue of Stafford House pictures 1908.

Staffordshire and Stoke on Trent Archive Service, Staffordshire Record Office (D 4401). Retrieved from Trentham and deposited 1986. NRA 10699.

[e] Staffs deeds and agreements 1840-1976 (mainly copies or drafts); misc papers 1901-78, incl plans 1919.

Staffordshire and Stoke on Trent Archive Service, Staffordshire Record Office (D 5569). Deposited by G Short 1997. NRA 10699.

[f] Abstracts of title 1883-1919; estate and mining leases 1697-1882, mainly Staffs.

Staffordshire and Stoke on Trent Archive Service, Staffordshire Record Office (D 3272/1/20/1-5). Deposited by Rigby, Rowley & Cooper, solicitors, Newcastle-under-Lyme 1978. NRA 25766.

[g] Great Wyrley (Staffs) manorial records 18th-20th cent.

Staffordshire and Stoke on Trent Archive Service, Staffordshire Record Office (D(W)/05,06; D(W) 1452-4). Deposited at the William Salt Library by the 5th Duke of Sutherland and through Fowler, Langley & Wright, solicitors, Wolverhampton 1927-35, and transferred 1966. NRA 7816.

[h] Meirheath (Staffs) colliery accounts 1757-90; particulars of Sir Richard Leveson's estates *c*1650 (copy).

Staffordshire and Stoke on Trent Archive Service, Staffordshire Record Office (D 4193). Deposited by P Bell 1984. NRA 10699.

[i] Trentham architectural drawings 1834-1914 (*c*800 items), incl many by Sir Charles Barry *c*1834-51.

Stoke-on-Trent City Museum and Art Gallery. Purchased 1996. *Friends of the National Libraries Annual Report*, 1996, pp27-8. Other Barry drawings for Trentham are in the custody of the J Paul Getty Museum, Malibu, California and the British Architectural Library.

[j] Lichfield burgage rental 1824-7.

Staffordshire and Stoke on Trent Archive Service, Lichfield Record Office (D 4363/N). Deposited at Staffordshire Record Office by Hinkley, Birch & Exham, solicitors, Lichfield 1985 and transferred 1993. NRA 8864.

[k] Stowheath (Staffs) map, survey and extent 1838.

Wolverhampton Archives and Local Studies (DX/17, Acc 40). Provenance unrecorded. NRA 21915.

[l] Salop deeds 12th-16th cent, incl some for Lilleshall Abbey; misc deeds, legal papers and manorial papers 15th-19th cent, incl will of James, 5th Baron Audley 1431 and Cleveland Court (Middlesex) agreements 1805-7; Salop leases, surveys, maps and plans 15th-20th cent, incl Wem survey 1631 (Earl of Arundel's estate), Lilleshall survey 1744 and map 1679, maps of Sheriff Hales 1600 and the Wealdmoors 16th-17th cent, and estate maps by Thomas Burton *c*1717-23; Salop rentals and accounts *c*1797-1918, letterbooks and corresp *c*1815-1906, reports 1822-1908, cottage rentals 1821-1914 and cropping and drainage books 1820-1909, with papers rel to sales *c*1894-1922 and game and timber 1796-1915; accounts of Lilleshall colliery royalties 1852-88 and Donnington Wood tilery 1884-1912; records of Lilleshall savings bank 1818-93 and water works 1908-25 and of Wappenshall and Lubstree wharves 1835-50; Hilton and Honnington turnpike minutes and toll books 1823-67; Lilleshall and Sheriff Hales clothing club accounts 1895-

1903; Lilleshall picture catalogue 1909 and misc household and garden accounts 1818-1918.

Shropshire Records and Research Centre (SRO 38/1-346, 72/1-3, 673, 972). Deposited by the Trustees of the will of the 4th Duke of Sutherland 1947-59. *Guide to the Shropshire Records*, 1952, p102. NRA 33433 (partial list), 11563 (Accessions Mar-May 1955, Dec 1958-May 1959).

[m] Newport (Salop) manorial court records 1337, 1542-1652, with related deeds and legal and misc papers 17th-19th cent.

Shropshire Records and Research Centre (SRO 6000/19296-460). Acquired by CWS Dixon, who purchased the lordship of Newport from the 5th Duke 1920, and deposited by Miss Dorothy Dixon 1961.

[n] Lilleshall Abbey charters 12th-16th cent, with appointments and pardons of abbots 14th-16th cent, patent 1539, court rolls 1404, 1423 and related medieval papers.

Shropshire Records and Research Centre (SRO 6000/16193-331 passim). Collected by CWS Dixon and passed to the Revd PH Bradley of Newport, from whom they were purchased for Shropshire Local Studies Library 1959.

[o] Leveson family deeds 1555-1639; Lilleshall court rolls 1631-55, particular 1650 and rental (with Sheriff Hales) 1661; Newport market and fair toll book 1633-4; misc papers rel to Lilleshall Abbey and Newport 13th-19th cent, incl Lilleshall Abbey bailiff's account 1524-5.

Shropshire Records and Research Centre (SRO 1910). Collected by CWS Dixon and deposited with Newport parish records by the Revd JC Hill 1967. NRA 11563.

[p] Lilleshall estate letter books 1906-7.

Shropshire Records and Research Centre (SRO 3670/1/22). Deposited by Liddle & Heane, solicitors, Newport 1977. NRA 11563.

[q] Shipley (Salop) estate map by Thomas Burton 1725.

Shropshire Records and Research Centre (SRO 1008/1). Presented by Reading University Department of Geography 1959. NRA 11563.

[r] Lilleshall estate sale plans 1912.

Shropshire Records and Research Centre (SRO 1450/1). Presented by the County Records Officer, Gloucestershire 1964. NRA 11563.

[s] Writs and charters 13th-19th cent, mainly Sutherland, with some for Aberdeenshire, Morayshire and Ross-shire; misc Caithness-shire writs 15th-17th cent; inventories of writs 16th-19th cent; marriage contracts and executry, legal and related papers 15th-19th cent, incl

tutory and curatory papers for the 13th Earl of Sutherland 1615-39 and 1st Duchess c1766-85, papers rel to the minority of Mary Maxwell (afterwards 18th Countess) c1721-61, and legal papers rel to the Skelbo and Assynt estates 18th cent; Sutherland regality court papers 1711-48 and barony court roll 1756.

Sutherland estate records 16th-20th cent, incl tacks 17th-19th cent, maps and plans 18th-20th cent, rentals and accounts 16th-20th cent, vouchers 1743-20th cent, cropping books 1829-69, tenantry amelioration book 1828-53, factors' and solicitors' corresp 18th-20th cent, and estate architect and surveyor's letter books, William Fowler 1859-81; Sutherland fisheries papers 17th-20th cent; Sutherland estate papers 18th-20th cent, incl papers rel to removals and emigration mid-19th cent and to Brora colliery, Golspie sawmill, woods, roads, railways, bridges and harbours (Helmsdale, etc) mainly 19th-20th cent; Sutherland savings bank records 1834-52; Preston (Kircudbrightshire) estate papers c1721-70, incl accounts and vouchers from c1741; Rosebank (Inveresk, Midlothian) estate rental 1753 and vouchers 1729-58 (Lady Strathnaver's estate); Ross-shire estate papers 1811-45; Sutherland estate papers of the Barons Reay 1764-1829; Stittenham (Yorks NR) rentals and accounts 1807-34.

Records of building at Dunrobin 1841-60, incl plans 1848 and letters of the architect William Leslie 1846-51; misc Dunrobin household accounts and papers 17th-19th cent, incl inventories 1721-1822 and accounts 1688-94, 1745; Tongue House inventories 1825-9 (7th Baron Reay); estimate for alterations at Dean's House (Dornoch) 1775; papers rel to building at Dornoch Cathedral c1834-1922; papers rel to Sutherland affairs 17th-19th cent, incl cess and quartering rental 1649, minutes of commissioners of supply 1720, electoral roll 1740 and militia and volunteer papers 1796-1813; Scottish Home Industries, Sutherland Association records c1894-1914; papers rel to Sutherland Drove Road Association 1818-27 and Wick (Caithness-shire) harbour and burgh mid-19th cent, incl election papers 1830-2; misc Orkney and Shetland vice-admiralty papers 1717-28.

Personal inventories and family accounts 17th-19th cent, incl inventories for the 16th and 17th Earls of Sutherland 1722, 1766 and accounts of Jean, Countess of Angus 1650-4, Katherine, Lady Strathnaver (d1765) and George Urquhart of Cromarty, merchant 1718-38; political and family papers 16th-19th cent, incl military papers of the 13th Earl 1648-68, and letters of the 1st Duke of Gordon c1684-7, the 3rd Baron Reay (d1748) and General James St Clair (d1762); corresp and papers of the 15th and 17th Earls, with records of their regiments 1702-7, 1759-63; papers rel to the Jacobite risings of 1715 and 1745; papers of the 1st and 2nd Dukes and Duchesses, incl letters from Sir

Walter Scott and CK Sharpe 1808-45 and papers of the 2nd Duke rel to Scottish affairs (church building, highland depopulation, etc); personal, family and genealogical papers of Sir Robert Gordon, 1st Bt, of Gordonstoun (Aberdeenshire) (1580-1656); misc papers 13th-19th cent, incl Dornoch cathedral charter c1223-45, Fearn Abbey (Ross-shire) kalendar 15th-17th cent, corresp of General Robert Monro rel to continental warfare c1632-6 and antiquarian letters of Cosmo Innes (d1874).

Papers of the Gordon family of Carrol 16th-19th cent, incl legal papers 1616-1819, misc accounts 1612-93, accounts of Gordonbush house building 1803-8, accounts of John Gordon's company of Sutherland Fencibles 1762 and genealogical papers 18th-19th cent.

National Library of Scotland (Dep 313-14; Accs 10225, 10853). Deposited by Elizabeth, Countess of Sutherland 1980-93. HMC *Second Report, App,* 1874, pp177-80; *Private Papers of British Diplomats 1782-1900,* 1985, p39; *Papers of British Politicians 1782-1900,* 1989, pp61, 102. NRA 11006.

[t] Sutherland factory papers 18th cent, mainly of Dugald Gilchrist (d1797), incl Skelbo and Pulrossie rentals 1743-83, corresp 1750-60, papers rel to Dunrobin 1752-89 and papers rel to the Earl of Sutherland's regiment 1746-60 and the Sutherland Fencibles 1781-97.

National Archives of Scotland (GD 153). Deposited with papers of the Gilchrist family of Ospisdale by Miss Lyon in 1959 and 1981. For summary details of the later deposit see *Keeper's Report 1985,* pp21-2.

[u] Lilleshall Abbey cartulary 13th cent.

British Library, Manuscript Collections (Add MS 50121). Deposited from Trentham c1950 (Loan MS 39) and purchased 1959.

[v] Berlin diary of Harriet, Dowager Duchess of Sutherland 1864; diary of Lord Ronald Charles Sutherland-Gower 1903-5.

British Library, Manuscript Collections (Add MSS 45109-10). Bequeathed by Frank Hird 1938. HMC *Papers of British Politicians 1782-1900,* 1989, p102.

[w] South African journals and papers of Colonel Robert Jacob Gordon 1751-92.

Brenthurst Library, Johannesburg, South Africa. Acquired by the 1st Marquess of Stafford from Gordon's widow c1795, deposited at Staffordshire Record Office from Trentham and sold at Christie's 4 Apr 1979, lot 73, by the Trustees of the Countess of Sutherland's settlement. NRA 10699.

Related collections: Egerton, Earls of Ellesmere, no 33; Leveson-Gower, Earls Granville (Public Record Office PRO 30/29, NRA 8654), includ-ing personal, family and official correspondence and papers of the 1st Earl Gower and 1st Marquess of Stafford; Montagu-Douglas-Scott, Dukes of Buccleuch and Queensberry, no 70, including Albemarle papers; Mackenzie, Earls of Cromartie (National Archives of Scotland GD 305, NRA 9756); Leveson-Gower of Bill Hill (Berkshire Record Office D/EMP, NRA 41171).

[102] TALBOT of Margam

Sir Hugh Mansel of Scurlage Castle in Gower (Glamorganshire) acquired Penrice and Oxwich (also in Gower) c1400 through marriage to the daughter and heir of Sir John Penrice. Beaupre in eastern Glamorganshire came with the marriage of Sir Rice Mansel (1487-1559) to the daughter and heir of James Bassett but returned to the Bassett family on the marriage of Mansel's daughter to William Bassett (d1593). Margam Abbey (Glamorganshire) was bought in 1540 by Sir Rice Mansel, who also purchased other Margam Abbey lands. Sir Edward Mansel, third Bt (1637-1706), extended the Glamorganshire estate after 1660, purchasing the former Herbert family manors of Landimore, Reynoldston and Weobley in 1666 and the manor and borough of Kenfig in 1668. The manor of Llandough and St Mary Church passed to him c1685 on the death of his mother-in-law Martha Bassett, daughter and heir of Edward Carne of Ewenny (Glamorganshire).

The fourth Bt, created Baron Mansell of Margam in 1712, was succeeded by his grandson Thomas Mansel (d1744), who was in turn succeeded by his uncle Christopher Mansel (also d1744) of Newick Place (Sussex), a property acquired through the first Baron's marriage to the daughter and heir of Francis Millington of London and Newick. The third Baron had sold Glamorganshire property (Henllys, etc) to his nephew the second Baron in 1732 and purchased further Newick property in 1734.

On the death in 1750 of Bussy, fourth and last Baron Mansell, the Margam and Penrice estates passed to the Revd Thomas Talbot (d1758) of Collingbourne (Wiltshire), whose father, John Ivory Talbot of Lacock (Wiltshire), had married Mary, daughter of the first Lord Mansell. The Sussex estate passed to the fourth Baron's daughter, Louisa Barbara (d1786), wife of George Venables-Vernon, second Baron Vernon of Kinderton. Briton Ferry (Glamorganshire), which had been inherited from a distant relative, Thomas Mansel (d1706), also descended to Lady Vernon, before passing to her mother's relatives the Villiers family, Earls of Jersey.

Thomas Talbot was succeeded by his son Thomas Mansel Talbot (d1813), who married Mary Lucy Fox-Strangways, daughter of the second Earl of Ilchester (see Fox-Strangways, Earls of Ilchester, no 40). Their son Christopher Rice Mansel Talbot (d1890) was active from *c*1834 in the development of Port Talbot (Glamorganshire). Following the death in 1918 of his daughter Emily Charlotte Talbot, Margam was inherited by her nephew Andrew Mansel Talbot Fletcher of Saltoun (East Lothian), while Penrice passed to her niece Evelyn, wife of the fourth Baron Blythswood. The bulk of the Margam estate was sold in 1941.

Estates in 1883: Glamorganshire 33,920 acres, worth £44,057 a year, inclusive of the profits of lessees of mines on the estate.

[a] Glamorganshire deeds 12th-19th cent (over 500 medieval), incl Margam Abbey charters 12th-16th cent and Penrice deeds 13th-19th cent; misc deeds for Breconshire 17th cent and Carmarthenshire 13th cent; Lincs deeds (Cumberworth, etc) 12th-16th cent (*c*80 medieval) and misc deeds for Somerset 13th-17th cent, Dorset 17th cent, Wilts 17th-18th cent and Devon and Sussex 18th cent; abstracts and schedules of deeds 13th-19th cent, incl Margam Abbey charter rolls 13th-14th cent; inquisitions *post mortem* for Sir Rice Mansel 1559 and John Carne 1644; wills, settlements and trust and executorship papers, Mansel 16th-18th cent and Talbot 18th-19th cent; legal papers 13th-19th cent, incl papers rel to proposed marriages with the Morgan family of Tredegar (Monmouthshire) *c*1682-8 and disputes between the 3rd Bt and Sir Humphrey Mackworth *c*1704-6; Glamorganshire manorial records 16th-19th cent, incl North Cornelly court rolls and Kenfig manor and borough surveys 16th-19th cent, and Laleston court rolls 17th-19th cent.

Margam, Penrice and east Glamorganshire estate records 16th-19th cent, incl leases 16th-19th cent, surveys 17th-19th cent, maps and plans 18th-19th cent, particulars, valuations, rentals and accounts 16th-19th cent and corresp 17th-19th cent; papers rel to wrecks 16th-19th cent, game, timber and tithes 17th-19th cent and railways 19th cent; papers rel to mines, quarries and industrial undertakings 17th-19th cent, incl coal leases 17th-19th cent, Margam estate colliery records 1727-36, papers rel to the English Copper Company *c*1811-80, shipbuilding accounts 1736-8 and Oxwich cliffage accounts 1708, 1732; records of church building and repairs 17th-19th cent, incl some for Margam church 1802, and of the development of Port Talbot 19th cent; surveys, accounts and papers for the Glamorganshire estate of the 3rd Baron *c*1723-32; accounts of Martha Bassett's Glamorganshire property 1675; survey of the estate of Thomas Morgan of Tredegar 1687.

Penrice Castle building accounts 1777; papers rel to repairs at Margam 18th-19th cent and Llandough Castle 1799-1800; household inventories 17th-18th cent, incl catalogues of books at Margam 1747 and Newick 1751 and inventories of Llandough Castle 1685, 1757 and

Margam 1765; misc Margam and Penrice household accounts 17th-19th cent; shrievalty papers for Glamorganshire 16th-18th cent and Monmouthshire 16th cent, Mansel and Carne families; papers rel to Glamorganshire politics and affairs 16th-19th cent, incl papers rel to assessments 17th-19th cent, poll book 1734 and canvass papers 1820, militia papers 17th-18th cent and quarter and petty sessions papers 18th cent, with papers rel to Cardiff bridge repairs 16th-18th cent; Newcastle (Glamorganshire) hundred freeholders' papers 17th-18th cent and churchwardens' accounts 1677-1702; accounts for Margam school 1702-6 and Christmas charity 1768-94; papers rel to Swansea racecourse 1804-6; Swansea Association for the Prosecution of Felons subscription book 1799.

Appointments and commissions 16th-18th cent; Mansel and Talbot family corresp and papers 16th-19th cent, incl papers of Sir Edward Mansel, 3rd Bt, as Vice-Admiral of South Wales *c*1662-82 and steward of the royal manor of Penkelly (Breconshire), papers of the 1st Baron as Comptroller of the Household *c*1704-5, accounts of the 4th Baron with the Navy commissioners 1747-8, papers rel to Thomas Mansel Talbot's foreign travel and acquisition of paintings and statuary 1769-75, and financial papers of Christopher Rice Mansel Talbot *c*1824-77; literary, genealogical and historical MSS 17th-19th cent, incl some of Philip and Llewelin Williams of Plas Dyffryn Clydach (Glamorganshire) 17th-18th cent; valuation of Robert Southwell's Suffolk, Essex, Surrey and Kent property *c*1599, with will of Thomas Southwell 1567-8 (copy); Gower Anglicana surveys 16th-17th cent; survey and valuation of the Earl of Warwick's estates in Gower 1700.

National Library of Wales (Penrice and Margam). Deposited 1941 by Lady Blythswood, Mrs Olive Douglas Methuen-Campbell and the trustees of the late Emily Charlotte Talbot. NRA 30000.

[b] Margam estate and household wages book 1851-6.

National Library of Wales (MS 12594). Presented by Miss Hilda M Davies 1967. *Handlist of MSS*, iv, p253.

[c] Corresp and papers rel to Glamorganshire mineral extraction and industrial concerns 18th-19th cent, incl corresp of Thomas Mansel Talbot 1795-1805; Margam timber sales account 1799; Margam building estimate 1760 and plan 19th cent.

National Library of Wales (MSS 6561, 6582). Amongst the MS collections of the antiquary John Montgomery Traherne. Presented by Lady Mansel Franklen 1928-9. *Handlist of MSS*, ii, pp192, 194. NRA 34361.

[d] Marriage settlement of Louisa Barbara Mansel and George Venables-Vernon 1757; misc Glamorganshire manorial records 17th-

20th cent, incl rentals (Margam, Kenfig, Penrice, etc) 1682-1706 and North Cornelly court book 1766-1928; Glamorganshire estate records 17th-20th cent, incl Margam and Penrice lease book 1758, surveys, maps and plans 19th cent, extensive rentals and accounts 18th-20th cent, stewards' accounts 1715-16, 1771-1840, vouchers c1700-1900 and corresp 19th-20th cent; tithe papers 19th cent; Port Talbot brick and tile works account book 1845-59; particulars of the 3rd Baron's Glamorganshire estate 1729; inventory of linen 1862-1932 and household accounts 1874-90 (?Margam); Ogmore hundred (Glamorganshire) poll book 1820; misc Talbot family papers 19th-20th cent, incl financial papers of Emily Charlotte Talbot 1890-1908; misc papers of Sir Christopher Cole (d1836), incl ships' log books 1806-8, 1813-14; draper's ledger 1784-1808.

West Glamorgan Archive Service (D/D Ma). Acquired by Glamorgan Record Office from various sources, and mostly transferred to West Glamorgan Archive Service 1983. Additional material was deposited 1993 and further papers were transferred from Glamorgan Record Office 1994. A Margam Abbey Charter 1358, acquired by Glamorgan Record Office 1984, has also been transferred (A/Ma 1). *Annual Report*, 1993-4, p45 and 1994-5, p44; *Guide*, 1998, pp 93, 100. NRA 7621. Photocopies of miscellaneous papers in private possession are available through West Glamorgan Archive Service.

[e] Gower deeds c1725-1920; trust account of William Morgan of Tredegar (d1680) 1681-5; misc legal case papers 19th cent; misc Gower manorial records 18th-20th cent; Penrice estate leases, surveys, maps, plans, particulars and valuations, rentals and accounts 18th-20th cent and corresp 1746-8, 1755, c1845-1900, with papers rel to timber 18th cent, railways 19th cent, minerals and tithes 19th-20th cent, etc; account book of the smack *Gulliver* of Port Talbot 1844-61; Oxwich cliffage account book 1869-99; building papers 18th cent, incl Penrice building accounts 1778-80 and architectural drawings for Margam orangery c1785; catalogue of books at Margam c1750; Penrice household accounts and vouchers 18th cent and wine cellar book 1912-15; misc papers rel to Glamorganshire affairs 18th-20th cent, incl militia lists 1705-6, 1798, Newcastle hundred land tax and window tax assessments c1700-10, election papers 18th cent and Oxwich, Penrice and Porteynon school board accounts c1882-1906; solicitors' accounts for Christopher Rice Mansel Talbot 1832-5.

West Glamorgan Archive Service (D/D P). Deposited in Glamorgan Record Office 1952, transferred to West Glamorgan 1983 and, with further papers deposited from Penrice in 1994, purchased for West Glamorgan Archive Service 1994. *Annual Report*, 1994-5, p45; *Guide*, 1998, p102. NRA 39992. Further family papers are understood to remain in private possession: see

Joanna Martin (ed), *The Penrice Letters 1768-1795*, Swansea, 1993.

[f] Margam Abbey charters 12th-16th cent (c170 medieval).

British Library, Manuscript Collections (Harleian Ch 75 A-D).

Related collections: Fox-Strangways, Earls of Ilchester, no 40, including correspondence relating to Talbot estates in Glamorganshire 1803-60; Earls of Jersey (National Library of Wales, NRA 30009), including papers relating to the Mansel estate at Briton Ferry; Barons Tredegar (National Library of Wales, NRA 28351); Talbot of Lacock (in private possession, NRA 26045).

[103] THROCKMORTON of Coughton

The Throckmorton family, originally from Worcestershire, acquired estates in Warwickshire and Buckinghamshire in the fifteenth century through two marriages. Sir John Throckmorton (d1445) married Eleanor Spiney of Coughton (Warwickshire). Their son Thomas married Margaret, daughter and heir of Sir Robert Olney of Weston Underwood (Buckinghamshire). Robert Throckmorton (d1650) was created a baronet in 1642.

Sir Robert Throckmorton, second Bt (1662-1721), married Mary Yate of Buckland (Berkshire), who brought the Buckland estate and property in Worcestershire (Chaddesley Corbett) into the Throckmorton family. George Throckmorton (dvp1767) married Anna Paston of Horton (Gloucestershire), who through her mother, daughter and heir of John Courtenay of Molland (Devon), inherited property in Devon and Somerset. The Sampford Brett (Somerset) estate, however, was sold in the mid-nineteenth century.

Estates in 1883: Warwicks 7,618 acres, Devon 6,589 acres, Worcs 3,618 acres, Berks 3,008 acres, Bucks 1,552 acres, total 22,385 acres worth £27,092 a year.

[a] Deeds for Warwicks, Worcs, Bucks and Berks 12th-19th cent: deeds for other counties 12th-19th cent, incl Beds 12th-14th cent, Oxon 13th-18th cent, Devon 16th-18th cent and Northumberland, etc (Collingwood of Eslington) 1613-1710; wills, settlements and related papers 14th-19th cent, incl Arundell trusteeship 18th-19th cent; legal and case papers 14th-19th cent, mainly 16th-18th cent; bonds and financial papers 16th-18th cent; Weston Underwood manorial accounts 1295-6; misc Warwicks manorial papers 16th-18th cent.

Warwicks and Worcs estate records 14th-early 20th cent, incl leases from 14th cent, surveys and valuations mainly 18th-20th cent, maps and plans 17th-20th cent, rentals and accounts from late 16th cent, and papers rel to tithes and advowsons 16th-19th cent, enclosure 18th-19th cent, timber 17th-20th cent, and Coughton church and school; Bucks estate records mainly 16th-18th cent, incl maps, rentals, accounts, and papers rel to boring for coal at Weston Underwood 1674-5; Berks estate papers 16th-early 20th cent, incl rentals, accounts and papers rel to timber; papers rel to Coughton Court 16th-19th cent, incl papers rel to repairs 1663-5, 1782-95, inventories from 17th cent and household accounts from 1585-6; inventories, Throckmorton (Worcs) 1590, Buckland 17th-19th cent, Weston Underwood 1749, and Chillington (Staffs: Giffard family) 1746, 1750; Llanblethian (Glamorganshire) household accounts 1815-19.

Commissions, liveries, pardons, grants of stewardship, etc 15th-19th cent, mainly Throckmorton family; papers rel to recusancy and Catholic disabilities late 16th-early 19th cent, incl licences, pardons, sequestration papers, papers rel to Titus Oates 1681-3 (1 vol), corresp of priests at Buckland 18th cent and papers rel to the emancipation movement late 18th-early 19th cent; Throckmorton family corresp and papers 15th-19th cent, incl papers rel to the trial (c1554) and French embassy (1563-4) of Sir Nicholas Throckmorton, corresp of Sir John Throckmorton, 5th Bt (1753-1819), and Sir Robert Throckmorton, 8th Bt (1800-62), and corresp of Miss Mary Throckmorton (1832-1919) rel to the Austrian court; freemasonry papers 18th-19th cent; Yate family corresp 17th-early 18th cent; pedigrees, genealogical papers and biographical papers 15th-19th cent; religious and historical MSS; household account of the Duke of York 1671; letters and poems of William Cowper (2 vols, 17 items).

Warwickshire County Record Office (CR 1998). Deposited by Sir Robert Throckmorton, 11th Bt 1980-3. Accepted for the nation in lieu of tax and allocated to the record office 1997. HMC *Third Report, App*, 1872, pp256-8. NRA 741.

[b] Throckmorton manorial court roll 1776, 1779; Warwicks and Worcs estate records 18th-19th cent, incl surveys and valuations 1744-1820 and rate books 1863; valuation of land in Buscot (Berks) and Bampton (Oxon) 1744; draft tithe award for Buckland 1839.

Warwickshire County Record Office (CR 2323). Purchased from R Ford, antiquarian bookseller, London 1984. NRA 741.

[c] Deeds 14th-19th cent, mainly Warwicks, Worcs, Devon and Somerset; legal papers 15th-19th cent, incl case papers (Earl of Warwick decd c1450, etc) and abstracts of title; manorial court records 13th-19th cent, incl Buckland 13th-18th cent (with rentals 1544-1712), Weston Underwood 13th-18th cent (with rentals

1444-1721), Warwicks 14th-early 19th cent (Coughton, Oversley, Sambourn, etc), Worcs 14th-early 19th cent (Chaddesley Corbett, Throckmorton, etc) and Anglesey 14th cent; Warwicks and Worcs estate papers 16th-19th cent, mainly leases but incl memoranda of wood sales 1675-6 and Sambourn enclosure papers 17th-18th cent; Devon and Somerset estate papers 16th-19th cent, incl leases, lease register 18th-19th cent, surveys early 19th cent (Devon) and rental 1818-26; misc papers 14th-19th cent, incl Carnarvonshire charter roll (Paris family) 1374-80, survey of Brewood White Ladies (Staffs and Salop) 1587, particular of Worlaby (Lincs) 1633, memorandum rel to Howman charity, Solihull (Warwicks) 17th cent, and Coughton Court inventory and related papers 1819.

Shakespeare Birthplace Trust Records Office (DR5). Deposited by Sir Robert Throckmorton, 11th Bt, and others 1936-84. Accepted for the nation in lieu of tax and allocated to the record office 1997. NRA 28045.

[d] Throckmorton court rolls 1600-32.

Shakespeare Birthplace Trust Records Office (DR 282). Purchased from Bernard Quaritch Ltd 1973. NRA 4523.

[e] Sampford Brett leases 1659-1822, with related deeds and papers 1815-62.

Somerset Archive and Record Service (DD/TK). Deposited by Lilian, Lady Throckmorton c1950. NRA 4331.

[f] Berks deeds 17th-19th cent; Buckland manorial court records 16th-18th cent; Berks legal and estate papers 17th-early 20th cent, incl survey 1748, accounts, and papers rel to Buckland rectory and tithes; Weston Underwood estate accounts 1698-1748; Giffard of Chillington estate and executorship accounts 1718-58.

Berkshire Record Office (D/EWe). Deposited by R Wellesley 1964-76, the deeds and legal papers having originated from the offices of the Throckmorton family's London solicitors. NRA 11515.

[g] Manorial court records, Martinhoe and Molland (Devon) 1487-1570, Sampford Brett 1584-6 and Birdingbury (Warwicks) 1396-7.

Devon Record Office (248M). Deposited by R Wellesley of Buckland 1955. NRA 4613.

[h] Buckland missal 15th cent.

Bodleian Library, Oxford (MS Don. b. 5). Presented by Sir John Noble, Bt, 1933, having been sold by the Throckmorton family in 1909 and re-sold in 1932. HMC *Tenth Report, App, part IV*, 1885, p169. Other devotional MSS mentioned in the *Report* remain at Coughton Court, having been purchased by the National Trust in 1991, except for the *Mirror of the*

Church (p171), purchased by Lambeth Palace Library in the same year.

[104] THYNNE, Marquesses of Bath

The Thynne or Botevile family was well established at Stretton (Shropshire) by 1500. Sir John Thynne (d1580), steward to Lord Protector Somerset, acquired estates in Somerset and Wiltshire (including former Glastonbury Abbey lands), Shropshire (Minsterley, a former Stafford property) and Gloucestershire (Kempsford). Longleat House (Wiltshire) as it now stands was largely built under his close direction during the years 1567-80.

Kempsford passed to a junior branch of the family, which also acquired Caus Castle and other property in Shropshire in the early seventeenth century. Sir Thomas Thynne, second Bt (1640-1714), of that branch, succeeded his cousin Thomas Thynne in the Longleat estates in 1682. He had married c1673 Frances, daughter of the third Earl of Winchilsea and granddaughter of Frances, Duchess of Somerset, sister and co-heir of Robert Devereux, third Earl of Essex (d1646). Through his wife Sir Thomas Thynne (created Viscount Weymouth in 1682) acquired former Devereux properties in Herefordshire (Ross-on-Wye, Weobley, etc) and Ireland (County Monaghan) (see also Shirley of Ettington, no 94). He also purchased the Drayton Bassett (Staffordshire) estate from the Duchess of Somerset's executors. As an executor himself he further acquired records relating to other Devereux properties in Herefordshire, Wales and elsewhere, to Ferrers properties in Staffordshire, Derbyshire, Warwickshire and other counties, and to the Bourchier Earls of Essex, together with records relating to the Seymour Dukes of Somerset and to Robert Dudley, Earl of Leicester, second husband of Lettice Knollys, Countess of Essex.

The second Viscount Weymouth (1710-51) married in 1733 Louisa Carteret, daughter of the second Earl Granville. On the death of the third Earl Granville in 1776 Granville and Carteret estates in Cornwall, Devon and Bedfordshire (Haynes or Hawnes Park) passed to a younger son of the second Viscount Weymouth, Henry Frederick Thynne, who was created Baron Carteret in 1784. The third Viscount Weymouth (1734-96) married in 1759 Elizabeth Bentinck, daughter of the second Duke of Portland, through whom some Harley and other papers came to Longleat, and was created Marquess of Bath in 1789.

Estates in Staffordshire, Warwickshire, Dorset and Gloucestershire were sold between c1790 and 1805. The widow of the second Marquess acquired Muntham Court (Findon, Sussex) in 1850. The Norton Hall (Northamptonshire) estate, with land in Northamptonshire and Shropshire, passed under the will of Beriah

Botfield (d1863) to his widow and then to Lord Alexander Thynne, second surviving son of the fourth Marquess. On Lord Alexander's death in 1918 the estate passed to his sister Lady Beatrice Thynne, and then, on her death in 1941, to the future sixth Marquess of Bath.

Estates in 1883: Marquess of Bath: Wilts 19,984 acres, Somerset 8,212 acres, Salop 3,508 acres, Herefs 699 acres, Sussex 409 acres, Co Monaghan 22,762 acres, total 55,574 acres worth £68,015 a year; Mrs Alfred Seymour (formerly Botfield) (in 1873): Northants 2,211 acres, Salop 2,697 acres, total 4,908 acres worth £7,323 a year.

[a] Deeds for Thynne properties c10th-19th cent, many medieval, incl Somerset and Wilts c10th-19th cent, Herefs and Salop 13th-19th cent, and Dorset, Gloucs, Middlesex (London) and Staffs 13th-18th cent; Beds and Hants (Carteret) deeds 18th-19th cent; deeds for misc Devereux, Ferrers (of Chartley, Staffs), Bourchier, Dudley and Seymour properties in Berks, Derbys, Devon, Essex, Hunts, Kent, Leics, Norfolk, Northants, Notts, Warwicks, Carmarthenshire, Pembrokeshire, etc 10th-17th cent; wills, settlements, trust papers and executorship papers 16th-20th cent, Thynne, Devereux, Dudley and Seymour, incl Sir John Thynne decd c1604-7, Sir HF Thynne decd 1680-3, guardianship for the 4th Marquess of Bath 1837-52, the 1st Earl of Essex decd 1576-86, the Earl of Leicester decd 1588-1608 and the Duchess of Somerset decd 1674-1703; Thynne family legal, financial and case papers 15th-20th cent; Carteret (later Thynne of Hawnes) legal papers 16th-20th cent, incl papers rel to the Rotherhithe (Surrey) estate 1795-1852; Devereux, Dudley and Seymour legal papers 16th-17th cent.

Manorial court records 13th-20th cent, mainly Somerset (Cheddar, Frome, etc) and Wilts (Longbridge Deverill, Monkton Deverill, Warminster, etc) from 13th cent but incl Beds (Hawnes, Wilshampstead) 18th-19th cent, Devon (Berry Pomeroy, etc) 14th-16th cent, Essex (Asheldham, Halstead, Stansted, etc) 13th-16th cent, Gloucs (Kempsford, etc) 14th-early 19th cent, Herefs (Ledbury, Ross-on-Wye, etc) 14th-19th cent, Salop (Caus, Minsterley, etc) 14th-20th cent, Staffs (Devereux manors) 14th-early 19th cent, Suffolk (Bildeston) 14th-16th cent, Warwicks 13th-early 19th cent and Wales (Devereux and Dudley manors in Pembrokeshire, etc) 14th-16th cent; records for Bath and Wells bishopric manors 1407-1529, Marquess of Dorset's manors in Devon, Dorset, etc 1533-44 and Lord Stourton's manors in Dorset, Wilts and Somerset 1549-55; Cheddar and Winterstoke (Somerset) hundred rolls 15th-17th cent.

Somerset and Wilts (Thynne) estate records mainly 16th-20th cent, incl leases and agreements, lease registers, surveys, maps and plans from 17th cent, rentals, accounts, corresp, and papers rel to enclosure, tithes, timber, allotments, sales and purchases, railways, etc; Longleat, etc farming accounts c1571-1679 and farm wages books c1862-1902; papers rel to Longbridge Deverill almshouses 1668-1936 and to Frome Woodlands church and school 1709-1920; papers rel to Gloucs, Herefs and Salop estates 14th-20th cent, incl leases, maps, surveys, rentals and accounts; Staffs and Warwicks estate rentals, accounts and papers 14th-early 19th cent; Dorset and Oxon leases, rentals, etc mainly 18th cent; Wye fisheries accounts 1566-8; Irish (Co Monaghan) estate records 16th-20th cent, incl leases and agreements 17th-18th cent, surveys and valuations late 16th-early 19th cent, rentals and accounts from late 16th cent, agency corresp and papers, and papers rel to Carrickmacross school 1711-1894; Beds and Cornwall (Carteret) estate papers 18th-20th cent, with papers for the Channels Islands 16th cent and North Carolina c1728-80; misc Bohun, Bourchier, Devereux, Dudley and Ferrers estate records 13th-17th cent, Essex (Bourchier accounts, etc 14th-16th cent), Hunts (Keyston, etc), Northants (Bugbrooke, etc), Norfolk (Dudley properties late 16th cent), Warwicks (Kenilworth), Wales, etc; misc records rel to the estates of the Stafford family, Dukes of Buckingham 14th-16th cent, the Stourton estates 1548-60 and the Seymour estates c1535-early 18th cent.

Papers rel to the fabric and contents of Longleat House 16th-20th cent, incl building accounts from the 1540s, drawings and accounts for alterations and interior decoration 19th cent, and inventories and catalogues 16th-20th cent; Longleat, etc household accounts and papers 16th-20th cent, incl kitchen, etc accounts from 1577, servants' wages 19th-20th cent and cellar books 1777-1946; papers rel to Longleat stables, gardens and park 16th-20th cent; inventories and papers rel to Kempsford, Caus Castle, Cannon Row and other Thynne houses 16th-18th cent, with papers rel to London houses and to Norton Hall 19th-20th cent; Seymour, Devereux and Dudley household accounts and inventories 16th-17th cent; Sir William Coventry, butler's book 1667-85; papers rel to Wilts and Somerset affairs 16th-early 20th cent, incl magistracy, shrievalty, militia and yeomanry; papers rel to Warminster (Wilts), incl petty sessions roll 1625 and papers rel to the grammar school c1705-90; Gloucs assessment roll 1516-17 and militia papers early 17th cent; Herefs assize roll 1442; Salop forest and other papers 14th-17th cent; Staffs election and other papers 1680-1702; Windsor (Berks) sessions roll 1463, with Windsor Castle constable's roll 1484-5 and Forest fines roll 1582.

Patents, commissions, etc 15th-20th cent, Thynne, Devereux, Dudley, Seymour, etc; Thynne family corresp and papers 1542-20th cent, incl letters and papers of Sir John Thynne (d1580), political, diplomatic and personal corresp and papers of the 1st Viscount Weymouth, papers of Henry Frederick Thynne (d1705) as Royal Librarian and Treasurer to the Queen Dowager c1675-1700, corresp and papers of the 1st Marquess of Bath as Secretary of State 1768-79, naval papers of the 3rd Marquess 1810-28, and political and other corresp of the 4th Marquess c1850-96; Carteret papers 17th-18th cent, incl papers of Sir George Carteret as governor of Jersey 1643-51 and misc papers of Earl Granville as Secretary of State, etc c1719-52; Seymour papers 1532-1674, incl papers of the Duke of Somerset 1532-50 and the 1st Earl of Hertford c1559-1612; account book of Lady Arabella Stuart 1609-14; Bourchier corresp and papers 15th cent; Devereux papers 1571-1641, incl corresp and papers of the 1st, 2nd and 3rd Earls of Essex; Dudley papers, incl corresp and papers of Robert Dudley, Earl of Leicester 1559-88; Harley papers 16th-18th cent, incl royal and political corresp of the 1st Earl of Oxford 1694-1714 and letters to the 2nd Earl from Alexander Pope 1721-39; corresp, diplomatic papers and literary papers of Matthew Prior c1685-1721; corresp and papers of Margaret, Duchess of Portland c1712-81; Coventry papers c1596-1687, incl extensive papers of Henry Coventry as Secretary of State 1672-80 and naval and other papers of Sir William Coventry; Whitelocke papers 1562-1684, incl papers of Bulstrode Whitelocke, Keeper of the Great Seal; papers of William Burton (1609-57, antiquary); Dr George Harbin (librarian to the 1st Viscount Weymouth) and Canon JE Jackson (*temp* the 4th Marquess).

Misc and collected MSS 14th-19th cent, incl household accounts of the Countess of Oxford 1389 and the 13th Earl of Oxford 1507-8, accounts of the 3rd Earl of Stafford 1391-2 and the Duke of Buckingham 1506-18, household book 1420-1 and estate accounts 1421-2 of the Earl of Warwick, Royal Household accounts and papers 15th-17th cent, naval and diplomatic papers 16th-17th cent, Talbot (Earls of Shrewsbury) corresp and papers 1569-1608, Privy Council proceedings 1658-9, newsletters 1666-1711, excise papers 1754-80, merchant's ledger 1762-3 and report on the Earl of Devon's Irish estates 1847.

Glastonbury Abbey muniments mainly late 12th-early 16th cent, incl general cartulary c1338-40, registers, inquisition of manors late 12th cent, charters and grants from ?681 (?10th cent), court rolls, leases and accounts; other monastic and ecclesiastical records 12th-17th cent, incl Cirencester (Gloucs) cartulary fragment late 12th cent, Thame Abbey (Oxon) cartulary 13th-15th cent, Maiden Bradley Priory (Wilts) register, rentals, etc 14th-16th cent, Bisham Priory (Berks) compotus 1337-8, Dorchester Abbey (Oxon) account roll 1487-8, Wells deanery account 1509, Red Book of Bath Priory, Robertsbridge Abbey (Sussex) formulary, Shaftesbury Abbey (Dorset) accounts and papers early 16th cent, Strata Florida (Cardiganshire) rental and custumal 16th cent, St Peter's Abbey (Gloucester) accounts 1524-5, and Kingswood Abbey (Gloucs) valor 1547 and compotus 1568-9.

In private possession. Enquiries to the Librarian and Archivist to the Marquess of Bath, The Estate Office, Longleat, Warminster, Wilts BA12 7NW. HMC *Third Report, App,* 1872, pp180-202; *Fourth Report, App,* 1874, pp227-51; *Bath I-V.* GRC Davis, *Medieval cartularies of Great Britain,* 1958; Kate Harris and William Smith, *Glastonbury Abbey records at Longleat House: a summary list,* Somerset Record Society, 1991. The following sections of the Longleat MSS have been microfilmed by Microform (Wakefield) Ltd, Main Street, East Ardsley, Wakefield, West Yorkshire WF3 2AT: Thynne papers (first series) (96703), Seymour Papers 1517-1703 (96702), Devereux Papers 1372-1664 (96701), Dudley Papers 1556-1608 (first five volumes only, 96700), Portland Papers 1516-1784 (96766), Prior Papers 1685-1721 (96698), Coventry Papers *c*1596-1687 (96699), Whitelocke Papers 1562-1684 (96737), Talbot Papers 1569-1608 (96839), Carteret/Granville correspondence *c*1615-1727 (96840), Miscellaneous MSS (96777-96780), catalogue of Library MSS (96804). (Films of individual medieval manuscripts are available only from Longleat and not from the publisher.) Glastonbury Abbey accounts and court papers have been microfilmed by Cedric Chivers Ltd, 9a/9b Aldermoor Way, Longwell Green, Bristol BS15 7DA. The London University Institute of Historical Research holds the most nearly complete set of these films, but the British Library, Cambridge University Library and the Bodleian Library, Oxford also have holdings.

[b] Manorial court rolls for various Thynne manors in Somerset, Wilts, Gloucs, etc 1568-9.

John Rylands University Library of Manchester. Formerly in the possession of Canon JE Jackson. *Handlist of charters, deeds and similar documents in the possession of the John Rylands Library,* part II, 1935, p6.

[c] Somerset, Wilts and Gloucs estate papers mainly 1727-8 (John Ord, steward, decd), with surveys, abstracts of rentals, etc from *c*1663.

Public Record Office (C 108/182).

[d] Thynne estate accounts (Wilts and Somerset) 1602-6.

Somerset Archive and Record Service (DD/X/HY/ 2-3). Given by Mrs DL Hayward 1937. *Bulletin of the Institute of Historical Research,* xvi, 1938-9, p205. NRA 4320.

[e] Gloucs estate account book 1730-56.

Bodleian Library, Oxford (MS Top. Glouc. b. 4). Purchased 1971-2. *Annual Report 1971-2,* p15.

[f] Legal papers rel to the sale of the Drayton Bassett estate 1790 (1 vol), incl settlements of 1711 and 1759 (copies), and abstract of title.

Staffordshire and Stoke on Trent Archive Service, Staffordshire Record Office (D 1158). NRA 17112.

[g] Northants (Botfield) deeds 17th-19th cent, with settlements and legal papers 19th-20th cent.

Northamptonshire Record Office. Deposited by Farrer & Co, solicitors, London 1961. NRA 35394.

[h] Salop (Botfield) deeds and related legal papers 17th-early 20th cent; Thynne family trust deeds 1759-1829.

Shropshire Records and Research Centre (SRO 1150). Deposited by Farrer & Co, solicitors, London through Northamptonshire Record Office and Shrewsbury Borough Library 1961. NRA 33337.

[i] Salop (Botfield) legal and estate papers *c*1850-60.

Shropshire Records and Research Centre. Deposited by Salt & Sons, solicitors, Shrewsbury 1959. *Accessions October-December 1959.* NRA 11563.

[j] Co Monaghan estate papers *c*1870-85.

National Library of Ireland. HMC *Accessions to repositories 1971,* p68.

[k] Papers of WS Trench as Co Monaghan agent mainly 1865-75.

Public Record Office of Northern Ireland (Loughton Papers, D 4141). NRA 40374.

[l] Misc Seymour financial papers.

Devizes Museum (shelf 242). Acquired 1895. Formerly in the possession of Canon JE Jackson. HMC *Bath IV,* 1968, pviii. A further 30 fragments are in the Royal Library, Windsor Castle.

[m] Misc Thynne, Dudley, Seymour, Coventry and other letters and papers *c*1559-1688.

British Library, Manuscript Collections (Add MSS 32091-6). Collected by Dr George Harbin and later in the possession of the Malet family of Wilbury (Wilts). Acquired 1882. HMC *Fifth Report, App,* 1876, pp308-20; *Seventh Report, App,* 1879, pp428-33.

[n] Carteret family papers 1649-1783, incl a grant by Charles II 1649.

Société Jersiaise. Deposited by Farrer & Co, solicitors, London, through the British Records Association 1986. (Other Carteret family papers from the offices of Farrer & Co, distributed to

Wiltshire Record Office in 1955 and to Rhodes House Library, Oxford in 1986, were subsequently transferred to Longleat.)

Related collections: Brudenell-Bruce, Marquesses of Ailesbury, no 12, including papers of the Dukes of Somerset and their Savernake estate 16th-17th cent; Cavendish-Bentinck, Dukes of Portland, no 18, including Harley papers; Seymour, Dukes of Somerset, no 92; Shirley, Earls Ferrers, no 93; Shirley of Ettington, no 94, including Co Monaghan estate records; Sidney, Barons De L'Isle and Dudley, later Viscounts De L'Isle, no 95; Thynne of Hawnes (Beds) and Stratton (Cornwall) (Bedfordshire and Luton Archives and Record Service DDSA, X520, NRA 33545; University of British Columbia Library, NRA 34810; Devon Record Office 178B/M/E 20-25, NRA 9922; North Devon Record Office 2239/B add 2, add 7, NRA 18680; Cornwall Record Office DDX 117, NRA 4185); correspondence and papers of the 1st Earl Granville (British Library, Manuscript Collections Add MSS 22511-45, presented by Lord John Thynne 1858).

[105] TOLLEMACHE, Barons Tollemache

The Tollemache family was established in Suffolk from the twelfth century and acquired Helmingham by marriage in the fifteenth century. The Harrington (Northamptonshire) estate came from the Stanhope family by marriage in the early seventeenth century. Sir Lionel Tollemache was created a baronet in 1611. Sir Lionel Tollemache, third Bt, married in 1647 Elizabeth Murray (d1697), Countess of Dysart, and added her property in Surrey (Ham, Ham House and Petersham) to the Tollemache family estates. (She later married the Duke of Lauderdale.) Their eldest son succeeded his mother as third Earl of Dysart and in 1680 married Grace, daughter and co-heir of Sir Thomas Wilbraham, third Bt, of Woodhey (Cheshire), through whom extensive estates in north and south Cheshire passed to the Tollemache family.

On the death of the sixth Earl without issue in 1821 the family property was divided. The Cheshire, Northamptonshire and Suffolk estates, with part of the Surrey estate (Kingston Canbury), descended to his nephew, Admiral John Halliday (afterwards Tollemache), whose own family had some property in the West Indies. Other Surrey property (Ham and Petersham) devolved upon the sixth Earl's eldest sister Louisa, *suo jure* Countess of Dysart. In 1765 she had married John Manners of Grantham Grange (Lincolnshire), the illegitimate son of Lord William Manners (d1772, second son of the second Duke of Rutland), and heir to his property in Leicestershire (Buckminster, Sewstern) and Lincolnshire (Hanby Hall). These estates passed to her descendants, the Tollemache Earls of Dysart.

The Cheshire estates were consolidated by exchange and purchase in the late eighteenth and early nineteenth centuries. About 1825 property at Alpraham, Alvanley and Tarporley was acquired from the second Baron Alvanley. About 1840 John Tollemache (1805-90, succeeded his father Admiral Tollemache 1837, created Baron Tollemache 1876) purchased from the first Baron Mostyn the Beeston (Cheshire) estate, where he built Peckforton Castle between 1844 and 1850. In 1843 he sold his Surrey property to the eighth Earl of Dysart. Harrington (Northamptonshire) was sold in the 1860s, and there were sales of Suffolk property in the late nineteenth century.

Estates in 1883: Cheshire 28,651 acres, Suffolk 7,010 acres, Denbighshire 35 acres, Flintshire 30 acres, total 35,726 acres worth £43,345 a year.

[a] Deeds late 13th-20th cent, mainly Suffolk, incl some for Dodnash Priory; St Kitts and Antigua deeds 1690-19th cent; Tollemache cartulary 15th cent; wills, settlements and trust papers 14th-20th cent; legal papers 14th-20th cent, incl some rel to the Stanhope family 16th-17th cent and the De Burgh family 19th cent (Marrianne, daughter of Admiral Tollemache, married Hubert De Burgh of West Drayton (Middlesex) 1827); bonds, receipts and other financial papers 16th-17th cent; manorial records, Suffolk 14th-20th cent (incl Framsden court rolls 1464-1748 and rentals 1525-1835 and Helmingham court rolls 1343-1738) and Cheshire (Tiverton) 1712-69; Suffolk estate records 13th-20th cent, incl leases 18th-19th cent, maps and plans from 17th cent, surveys and valuations 16th-19th cent, rentals from 13th cent, accounts from 17th cent, vouchers 19th-20th cent and Helmingham cash books 20th cent, with papers rel to woods and timber 17th-20th cent; Surrey (Ham and Petersham) estate records 17th-18th cent, incl accounts of rents 1685-99 and accounts for the Duchess of Lauderdale 1684-96; estate papers for Harrington and Middlesex (De Burgh family) 19th cent; plantation accounts and papers for Antigua c1764-1838.

Papers rel to Helmingham Hall 16th-20th cent, incl plans and drawings 18th-20th cent, building accounts 18th cent, inventories from 1598 and household accounts 18th-19th cent; Peckforton Castle building papers 19th cent; Norfolk and Suffolk shrievalty papers 16th cent; papers rel to Suffolk affairs 14th-19th cent, incl lieutenancy, vice-admiralty and militia papers 17th-18th cent and Helmingham school papers 19th cent; family corresp and papers 16th-20th cent, incl naval log books of Admiral Halliday (afterwards Tollemache) late 18th cent, corresp of Mary, Lady Tollemache (1889-1932, wife of the 2nd Baron) and colonial, diplomatic, and other papers of Sir JW Ridgeway (d1930, grandfather of the 4th Baron); genealogical, heraldic and misc papers 15th-20th cent, incl pedigrees and papers for EDH Tollemache's *The Tollemaches of Helmingham and Ham.*

In private possession. Enquiries to the Rt Hon Lord Tollemache, Helmingham Hall, Stowmarket, Suffolk IP14 4EF. Records deposited in Suffolk Record Office by Peake & Co, solicitors, London in 1977 (HA 405) were transferred to Helmingham in 1978. MSS from the library at Helmingham, including those described in HMC *First Report, App,* 1870, pp60-1, were mostly sold between 1953 and 1971 (see HMC *Guide to the Location of Collections,* 1982, p61). See also HMC *Private Papers of British Diplomats 1782-1900,* 1985, p56. NRA 6277, 6957 (Ridgeway papers).

[b] Suffolk deeds 19th-20th cent; settlement, Magdalen Lewis (second wife of 5th Earl of Dysart) 1791; manorial records late 19th-20th cent (incl Framsden 1898-1933); Suffolk estate records 20th cent, mainly for Helmingham; valuation of books and MSS in the library at Helmingham Hall 1928.

Suffolk Record Office, Ipswich branch (HB 133: 6706). Deposited by Lee & Pemberton, solicitors, London, through Cheshire Record Office 1983. NRA 6277.

[c] Dodnash Priory and Bentley (Suffolk) deeds 13th-early 14th cent.

Suffolk Record Office, Ipswich branch (HD 1047). Formerly in the collection of William Stevenson Fitch (MSS 447, 448), acquired by Sir Thomas Phillipps 1859 (MS 16734) and purchased by Suffolk Record Office 1982. NRA 26046.

[d] Dodnash Priory deeds and cartulary c1200-1506; Helmingham deeds 1309-1704; marriage settlement, Bridget Tollemache 1650; Helmingham household account book 1587-8.

Suffolk Record Office, Ipswich branch (HD 1538). Formerly in the collection of Sir Thomas Phillipps (MSS 15391, 15795, 16732), acquired by the Earl of Iveagh 1914 and purchased by Suffolk Record Office 1987. NRA 39544.

[e] Deeds 17th-20th cent, mainly Cheshire, incl royal grant of manors of Longdendale and Mottram 1690-1, with a few for London, Antigua, etc, 18th-19th cent; abstracts of title 18th-19th cent; wills and settlements 17th-20th cent, Wilbraham and Tollemache families; executorship and trust papers 19th-20th cent, incl papers of John Tollemache as a trustee for the Cholmondeley estates late 19th cent; legal and financial papers 17th-19th cent, incl Chancery papers rel to Castle Northwich (Cheshire) 18th cent; manorial records 17th-19th cent, mainly Cheshire (Mottram in Longdendale, Alpraham, etc).

Cheshire estate records 17th-20th cent, incl leases 17th cent, maps and plans 18th-19th cent, surveys, valuations, rentals and accounts from

17th cent, farm accounts 1810-20, 1873-1908 and letter books 20th cent; household inventories 20th cent, incl some for Peckforton and Helmingham; papers rel to London houses 18th-20th cent; records of Sir Roger Wilbraham's almshouse, Nantwich 17th cent.

Cheshire Record Office (DTW). Deposited at various dates since 1955 by Lord Tollemache and the Tollemache Estate Trustees, Messrs Strutt & Parker (Peckforton Estate Office), Messrs Peake & Co, solicitors, London, and others. NRA 30085.

[f] Wettenhall (Cheshire) book of reference 1794.

Cheshire Record Office (D 4173/1). Transferred from Chester City Record Office. NRA 5236.

[g] Abstracts of deeds and draft deeds, Surrey (Ham, Petersham and Kingston Canbury) 19th cent.

Surrey History Centre (4016). Deposited by the 5th Baron Tollemache 1992. NRA 3518.

[h] Letter and order book of Admiral Halliday (afterwards Tollemache) 1809-15.

National Maritime Museum (LBK/53). Purchased from Gordon A Storey 1959. NRA 30121.

Related collection: Earls of Dysart (Surrey History Centre 58, 4468, NRA 3518, 17204, and in private possession, NRA 23003), including Suffolk legal and estate papers 15th-17th cent; Roundell of Dorfold (John Rylands University Library of Manchester, NRA 1288), including Cheshire (Wilbraham and Tollemache) deeds and papers 13th-19th cent.

[106] TOWNELEY of Towneley, later TOWNELEY-O'HAGAN, Barons O'Hagan

The De La Legh, later Towneley, family of Hapton and Cliviger (Lancashire) inherited Towneley (Lancashire) in the fourteenth century. Gateford (Nottinghamshire) came with the marriage of Sir John Towneley (d c1540) to Isabel, daughter and heir of Sir Charles Pilkington, but was subsequently sold. The marriage of Sir Richard Towneley (d1554) to Frances, daughter of Sir Christopher Wymbish, brought the Nocton (Lincolnshire) estate, sold to meet debts c1660. Standish (Lancashire) entered the family through the marriage of William Towneley (1714-41) to Cecilia, daughter and heir of Ralph Standish (d1755), but this estate passed to William Towneley's youngest son Edward Towneley-Standish, who however also succeeded his eldest brother Charles Townley in the Towneley estates on the latter's death without issue in 1805.

On the death of Edward Towneley-Standish in 1807 Standish passed to his nephew Thomas Strickland of Sizergh (Westmorland), but the Towneley estates were inherited by his uncle John Towneley (1731-1813). John Towneley had already inherited the Lancashire estate of Leighton, formerly owned by the Middleton family, on the death of his uncle George Towneley in 1786, and the Stella (County Durham) estates of the Widdrington family, Barons Widdrington, to whom he was related through his mother, on the death of Thomas Eyre of Hassop (Derbyshire) in 1792.

In 1835 John Towneley's son Peregrine Edward Towneley (d1846) bought the manor of Slaidburn and the Bowland Forest estate of about twenty thousand acres in the West Riding of Yorkshire from the Duke of Buccleuch. Properties in Leicestershire (Bittesby), Herefordshire (Pembridge, Welsh Newton, etc) and elsewhere, however, acquired by John Towneley from the Talbot family in the mid-eighteenth century, were sold c1837, and the Leighton estate was disposed of before 1875.

Following the deaths of Charles Towneley in 1876 and his brother John Towneley in 1878, both without male issue, the estates were divided among their daughters. The Towneley Hall estates, mainly in Lancashire but extending into the West Riding east of Burnley, were divided equally between the three daughters of Charles Towneley, Caroline, wife of Lord Norreys, later seventh Earl of Abingdon, Emily, wife of Lord Alexander Gordon-Lennox, and Alice, wife of Thomas O'Hagan, first Baron O'Hagan. Lady O'Hagan received Towneley Hall, which was sold to Burnley Corporation in 1901, the library manuscripts having been sold by auction in 1883. In 1921 the Gordon-Lennox portion of the Lancashire estates (Worsthorne, etc) was inherited by Lady Alice Reyntiens, daughter of the seventh Earl of Abingdon and grandmother of Sir Simon Towneley of Dyneley (Lancashire). The Bowland Forest and County Durham estates were left to the daughters of John Towneley, the longest survivor of whom died in 1928.

Estates in 1873: Charles Towneley: Yorks WR 23,153 acres, Lancs 14,086 acres, Co Durham 2,826 acres, total 40,065 acres worth £26,979 a year. In 1883 the daughters of Charles Towneley each held 4,695 acres in Lancs and 604 acres in Yorks WR, and the daughters of John Towneley jointly held 21,341 acres in Yorks WR and 2,826 acres in Co Durham.

[a] Deeds 12th-19th cent (over 1,700 medieval), mainly Lancs from 12th cent (incl Whalley Abbey deeds) but incl Yorks WR 13th-19th cent, Westmorland 13th-17th cent, Notts 13th-early 18th cent, Lincs 12th-18th cent, Co Durham 13th-19th cent, other counties 13th-18th cent and Calais 14th-15th cent; wills, settlements and related trust and executorship

papers 14th-20th cent, mainly Towneley family from 14th cent but incl Wymbish family ?14th-16th cent, Widdrington 17th-18th cent, Standish 18th cent, Middleton 16th-mid-18th cent, Talbot Earls of Shrewsbury 1663-1726, the Countess of Strafford 1783-96, Sir William Stanley 1786-92 and the Petrogalli family 1790-1808; legal papers 16th-19th cent, Towneley, Wymbish, Widdrington, Middleton, etc; recusancy papers, Towneley and Middleton 16th-17th cent; misc Lancs manorial court rolls 14th-early 18th cent (Ightenhill, Leighton, Warton, Yealand, etc); Blackburn (Lancs) wapentake records late 14th-early 18th cent; honour of Clitheroe survey 17th cent and accounts 1488-9, 1558, 1827-34, 1852-3.

Towneley Hall (Lancs and Yorks WR) and N Lancs estate records 16th-19th cent, incl leases from 16th cent, valuations 18th-19th cent, maps and plans, rentals 16th-19th cent, accounts 17th-19th cent, corresp 18th cent, and papers rel to collieries late 16th-19th cent, Warton tithes 1624-49, mills 1718-50 and the Rochdale Canal 18th-19th cent; misc Bowland (Yorks WR) estate papers late 16th-19th cent, incl maps, accounts and papers rel to Grindleton mill 1591-1723; Lincs (Nocton, etc) estate papers 16th-18th cent, incl Nocton survey 1651, rentals early 16th cent and misc papers 17th cent; Co Durham estate papers 17th-mid-19th cent, incl leases, maps, and papers rel to mining and smelting; Blankney (Lincs) survey ?17th cent; valuation of Gloucs and Herefs estate 1837; Wetheral and Warwick (Cumberland) estate papers 17th-early 19th cent; Chesterfield (Derbys: Knight family) rental 1411; papers rel to Towneley Hall 18th cent, with schedules of furniture at Towneley and Stella 18th cent; Towneley household accounts c1680-early 19th cent; household accounts (?Middleton) 1652-4.

Papers rel to Lancs affairs 14th-17th cent, incl shrievalty papers late 14th cent, Lancs subsidy book late 16th cent, Blackburn wapentake rate book 1628 and papers rel to bailiwick of Blackburnshire 16th-17th cent; Hyning in Yealand charity papers 1783-1803; papers rel to the borough and port of Great Yarmouth (Norfolk: Middleton family) 15th-17th cent; Towneley appointments and commissions 14th-19th cent; Towneley family papers 17th-19th cent, incl misc antiquarian and scientific papers of Christopher and Richard Towneley 17th cent, personal and estate corresp of Charles, John and PE Towneley late 18th-early 19th cent, accounts 17th-19th cent, and Catholic Committee papers late 18th-early 19th cent; household book of Anne Middleton 1675; commission of the 1st Baron Widdrington as deputy lieutenant for Northumberland 1662, with Berwick-upon-Tweed garrison accounts 1660; misc and collected papers from 14th cent, incl Eddisford (Lancs) leper hospital cartulary 1317, Whalley Abbey accounts early 16th cent and evidence book of Sir Edward Plumpton 1614.

Lancashire Record Office (DDTo). Deposited by the 3rd and 4th Barons O'Hagan 1953, 1971, 1974 and subsequently purchased by the Record Office. NRA 1302.

[b] Misc deeds c1200-1894, Lancs, Lincs, etc; Towneley settlements and trust papers 17th-19th cent; misc bonds, legal papers, etc 14th-18th cent, incl Lancs and Lincs evidence book 1612-20.

Lancashire Record Office (DDTo, Accs 2396, 2580, 2705). Deposited by Lawrence, Graham & Co, solicitors, London, through the British Records Association 1968-70. NRA 1302.

[c] Towneley trust deeds 1847-78 (5 items).

Lancashire Record Office (DDTo, Acc 2474). Deposited by Thomas Cooper & Co, solicitors, London, through the British Records Association 1969. NRA 1302.

[d] Survey of Charles Towneley's estate 1735.

Lancashire Record Office (DP/322). *Guide*, 1985, p339.

[e] Letters and papers rel to Hapton coal mines 1797-1804.

Lancashire Record Office (DX/911-929). NRA 6038.

[f] Records of the manor of Winlaton (Co Durham) 17th-20th cent, incl maps of Towneley properties 19th cent.

Durham County Record Office D/CG). Deposited by Sir WW Gibson and Messrs Wilkinson, Marshall, Clayton & Gibson, solicitors, Newcastle-upon-Tyne 1963-76. NRA 26390. (In the nineteenth century the Towneley family owned 36/96ths of the lordship of Winlaton, the Bowes family 7/96ths (see Bowes-Lyon, Earls of Strathmore, no 8) and the Crichton-Stuart family 1/96th (see Stuart, later Crichton-Stuart, Earls and later Marquesses of Bute, no 100).)

[g] Co Durham (Widdrington) estate rental 1765-73.

Durham County Record Office (D/X 978). Deposited 1992. Probably HMC *Fourth Report, App*, 1874, p412 (original MS XXVII); Sotheby's, 27-28 June 1883, lot 228. NRA 18297.

[h] Corresp of PE Towneley 1807-37, mainly rel to Co Durham coal mining; papers rel to the Towneley library and collections late 18th-early 19th cent.

Bodleian Library, Oxford (MSS Add. D. 70-73c). Sotheby's, 19-20 April 1877, lot 670. *Summary catalogue*, vol 5, 1905, pp561-2.

[i] Scientific papers of Richard Towneley (1628-1707) and his family 17th cent.

Bodleian Library, Oxford. Acquired 1985 (Sotheby's, 22-23 July, lot 546).

[j] Antiquarian papers of Christopher Towneley (1604-74), mainly transcripts of deeds, etc; collected MSS 14th-18th cent, incl cartularies of the Pedwardine family late 14th cent and St James's Hospital Thanington (Kent) 1474.

British Library, Manuscript Collections (Add MSS 32097-32116). Acquired 1883. HMC *Fourth Report, App*, 1874, pp408-16 (original MSS I, X, transcripts I-XXXIX *passim*); Sotheby's, 27-28 June 1883 (Towneley Hall sale), lots 75-232 *passim*. For further antiquarian and collected MSS deriving from the 1883 sale see also below, [k]-[n], [p].

[k] Further transcripts of Lancs and other evidences by Christopher Towneley; misc original Towneley MSS 16th-18th cent, incl commonplace book and astronomical MSS of Christopher Towneley, and catalogues of books, Christopher Towneley 1647 and Charles Towneley 1771; commonplace book of Roger Dodsworth 17th cent; accounts of executors of Robert Nowell 1569.

Chetham's Library, Manchester (MUN. D.3. 1-11; MUN. A.2. 93, 97, 121; MUN. A.3. 110; MUN. A.6. 25, 50; etc). HMC *Fourth Report, App*, 1874, pp408-16 *passim* (original MSS XXII, XXV ?, transcripts XVII-XXXVII *passim*); Sotheby's, 27-28 June 1883, lots 29-162 *passim*; sale of JE Bailey's library 1889. NRA 17002.

[l] Further antiquarian papers of Christopher Towneley, mainly transcripts of Lancs muniments copied c1621-74; Whalley Abbey (Lancs) accounts c1485-1538.

Manchester Central Library, Local Studies Unit (Farrer collection L1/47). HMC *Fourth Report, App*, 1874, pp408-16 *passim* (original MS II, transcripts III-XXXIV *passim*); Sotheby's, 27-28 June 1883, lots 70-227 *passim*. NRA 17338.

[m] Transcripts of Plumpton family evidences; Wilstrop family cartulary 15th cent.

West Yorkshire Archive Service, Leeds (Chambers MSS 1-9). Purchased 1972. HMC *Fourth Report, App*, 1874, pp408-10 (original MS III, transcripts I-LVI *passim*); Sotheby's, 27-28 June 1883, lots 189-192, 229, 241. NRA 19413.

[n] Further transcripts by Christopher Towneley (4 vols); Eastbridge (Canterbury) hospital register 16th cent.

Bodleian Library, Oxford (MSS Top. Lancs. c. 6, Top. Yorks. c. 12, Top. Kent c. 2, Top. Derbyshire b. 1; MS Lyell Empt. 33). Acquired at the Towneley sale 1883 (lots 76, 89, previously HMC *Fourth Report, App*, 1874, pp409-10, original MS VI and transcripts XLI), from the Countess of Abingdon 1933 (lots 209, 224), and from the executors of James PR Lyell (d1940) (lot 203, previously HMC *Fourth Report, App*, 1874, p408, transcript XII). Further transcripts by Christopher Towneley (8 vols, purchased 1938 from Bernard Halliday of Leicester), are now in Wigan Record Office (D/DZ A4; see *Journ Soc Archivists*, vol 3, no 10, Oct 1969, pp577-8). Untraced items from the Towneley sale 1883 include Lancs legal papers early 17th cent (lot 114, purchased by Lord Norreys) and papers relating to the Herefordshire, etc (former Talbot) estates c1687-1793 (lots 144, 167, 200, 214).

[o] Misc financial and estate papers mid-18th-early 19th cent, incl income and expenditure account 1780-7; inventories of Towneley Hall pictures, etc 1805-68; papers rel to London houses (Park St, Westminster, etc) mainly 1770s; personal, family and antiquarian corresp and papers of Charles Townley c1755-1807, incl estate and family corresp c1768-1803, general and antiquarian corresp 1765-1804, and papers rel to the Townley Marbles and their acquisition by the British Museum; misc Towneley family corresp and papers 17th-early 20th cent, incl papers of John Towneley 1746-1812 and Peregrine Towneley 1776-1845.

British Museum Central Archives (TY). Purchased 1992 (Sotheby's, 21-22 July 1992, lot 334). *The Townley Archive in the British Museum*, British Museum Occasional Paper no 138, forthcoming. Other papers once in Charles Townley's possession were sold at Sotheby's 23 July 1985, lots 550-559.

[p] Account book of Charles Townley 1787-98.

Wigan Archives Service (D/DZ A 13/20). Sotheby's, 27-28 June 1883, lot 141. Acquired 1939.

[q] Political, legal, personal and family corresp and papers of the 1st Baron O'Hagan c1825-85.

Public Record Office of Northern Ireland (D 2777). Deposited by the 4th Baron O'Hagan 1971. HMC *Papers of British Politicians 1782-1900*, 1989, p78. NRA 18813.

[r] Further Irish corresp of the 1st Baron O'Hagan 1850-85.

National Library of Ireland (MSS 17864-74). Acquired with the papers of his great-nephew Sir William Teeling. HMC *Papers of British Politicians 1782-1900*, 1989, p78.

[s] Misc deeds and papers 14th-19th cent, incl maps of the Towneley Hall estate 1661, corresp of Cecilia Towneley 1742-55 and MS catalogue of the Townley Marbles 1804.

In private possession. Not normally available for research.

Related collections: Eyre of Hassop (Sheffield Archives, Bagshawe collection, NRA 7871),

including Widdrington (Co Durham and Northumberland) deeds and leases 14th-18th cent; Standish of Standish (Wigan Archives Service D/DSt, NRA 26876), including Towneley family correspondence mid-18th cent-1807; Earls of Abingdon (Bodleian Library, Oxford MSS D.D. Bertie c. 2/38-41, c. 3/15, MS Top. gen. c. 89, MS Eng. misc. d. 240, NRA 4474; John Rylands University Library of Manchester Eng MS 735-7), including Hapton estate wages book 1911-19, Towneley library catalogues early 18th cent, papers of Christopher Towneley 1639 and miscellaneous correspondence and antiquarian papers of Charles Towneley c1782-1802; Witham, Weld & Co (Lancashire Record Office DDX 754, NRA 3510; Wigan Archives Service D/DX Wel, NRA 15633), including Towneley (later Earls of Abingdon) deeds and leases 1859-1912, settlements 1762-1922 and coal mining papers 19th-20th cent; Slaidburn manorial records 14th-20th cent (Lancashire Record Office DDHCL, NRA 40716); Worsthorne estate records (in private possession), mainly 1887 onwards but including deeds from 14th cent and Towneley estate maps and rentals 19th cent.

[107] TOWNSHEND, Marqesses Townshend

The Townshend family was settled at East Raynham (Norfolk) by the late fourteenth century, and greatly extended its estates around Raynham in the sixteenth century. Out-county properties were also acquired, including Wivenhoe (Essex), purchased from the Earl of Oxford in 1584 but sold during the seventeenth century. Sir John Townshend (1568-1603) married Anne, daughter and co-heir of Sir Nathaniel Bacon of Stiffkey (Norfolk) (c1546-1622). Their son Sir Roger Townshend (d1637) married Mary, daughter and co-heir of Lord Vere of Tilbury (a grandson of the fifteenth Earl of Oxford), and built Raynham Hall. Their son Horatio married Mary, daughter and heir of Sir Edward Lewkenor, through whom the Denham (Suffolk) estate (sold in 1803) was inherited, and was created Baron Townshend 1661 and Viscount Townshend 1682.

The second Viscount (d1738), statesman and agriculturist, married firstly (in 1698) Elizabeth Pelham, whose mother was a co-heir of the Jones family of Ramsbury (Wiltshire), and secondly (in 1713), Dorothy (1686-1726), sister of Sir Robert Walpole, of Houghton Hall, Norfolk, first Earl of Orford. The third Viscount (1700-64) married Audrey, daughter and heir of Edward Harrison, through whom the Townshends obtained the Balls Park (Hertfordshire) estate (sold 1901) and the Soham and Fordham (Cambridgeshire) estate (sold c1806).

The first Marquess Townshend (1724-1807), so created 1787, Field Marshal and Lord

Lieutenant of Ireland, married in 1751 Charlotte Compton, *suo jure* Baroness Ferrers (d1770), only daughter of James Compton, fifth Earl of Northampton, and through her mother heiress of the Ferrers family of Tamworth Castle (Warwickshire), with estates in Derbyshire, Staffordshire and Warwickshire (see Compton, Marquesses of Northampton, no 24; Shirley, Earls Ferrers, no 93). These estates, which included Walton-upon-Trent (Derbyshire), a secondary seat of the Ferrers family, and further Derbyshire properties inherited through the Bradbourne family in the late sixteenth century, were mostly sold in the early nineteenth century, although Tamworth Castle itself was bought back and remained in the family until 1897.

There were extensive sales from Raynham Hall in the early twentieth century, and manuscripts were widely dispersed at auction in 1911 and 1924. A quantity of papers appears to have left Tamworth Castle in the early nineteenth century, passing into the collection of Sir Thomas Phillipps.

Estates in 1883: Norfolk 18,343 acres, Herts 1,565 acres, Warwicks 2 acres, total 19,910 acres worth £22,560 a year, exclusive of tithes and shooting rents worth *c* £1,000.

[a] Deeds 12th-19th cent, incl Norfolk from 12th cent, Derbys, Staffs and Warwicks from 13th cent, Cambs and Herts from 13th cent, and Essex, Suffolk, Bucks, etc (Earls of Oxford, Townshend, etc) 13th-18th cent; Townshend wills and settlements 14th-19th cent, with executorship and trust papers from 16th cent; trust papers, Earls of Oxford 14th-16th cent, Jones (of Ramsbury, Wilts) 1680s and Harrison (of London and Balls Park, Herts) 17th-18th cent; Ferrers, Bradbourne and Shirley settlements and related papers 16th-18th cent, incl Lady Catherine Shirley decd 1736-7; Compton settlements and related papers 17th-18th cent, incl the Earl of Wilmington decd 1743-4; legal and case papers 15th-20th cent, mainly Townshend but incl Ferrers and other families; manorial court records, Norfolk 13th-18th cent (Helhoughton, Langham, Raynham, Stiffkey, etc, incl many medieval extents, rentals and accounts), Derbys 14th-16th cent (Walton-upon-Trent, etc), Essex 14th-16th cent, Gloucs 14th-17th cent (Kempsford, etc), Cambs 17th cent (Soham and Fordham), Suffolk 13th-17th cent (Akenham, Desning, etc), and Clerkenwell (Middlesex: Compton family) 1650-1733.

Norfolk estate records 14th-20th cent, incl leases, surveys and valuations from 15th cent, field books, rentals and accounts, papers rel to sheep farming on the Raynham estate late 15th-early 17th cent, papers rel to the Stiffkey estate 16th-early 17th cent, vouchers and corresp; Essex and Suffolk estate records 15th-18th cent (Wivenhoe, Denham, etc), incl leases, rentals and accounts; Earl of Oxford, estate accounts 1434-7; Herts estate records 18th-early 19th

cent, incl leases, agreements and rentals; Derbys, Staffs and Warwicks estate records 15th-19th cent (Tamworth, Walton-upon-Trent, etc), incl leases, valuations, rentals and accounts; Middlesex (Compton) estate records 1598-1749 (Canonbury, Clerkenwell), incl leases and rental 1749; Northants (Compton) valuation 1715; Elkington (Northants) estate papers 1734-41, with maps 1680, 18th cent.

Raynham Hall building accounts 1618-24, drawings (Hall and park) 18th-20th cent, and inventories and catalogues from late 16th cent; Raynham household accounts and vouchers 16th-19th cent; accounts for Raynham gardens 1731-1821, kennels 18th cent and home farm 1783-1806; Stiffkey Hall drawing 1570s, household accounts late 16th-early 17th cent and garden accounts 1626-36; Balls Park household accounts 18th-early 19th cent and inventory 1732; inventories, Aldersgate (Ferrers) 1572 and Tamworth Castle 1730; Brook St (London) house building account 1728-30 (Earl of Northampton).

Papers rel to Norfolk affairs (lieutenancy, shrievalty, commission of the peace, etc) 16th-late 18th cent, Townshend and Bacon, incl lieutenancy papers of the 1st Viscount 1660s and assessment and subsidy papers 16th-17th cent; Tamworth election papers late 18th cent; Derbys shrievalty papers 1573-4 (Sir Humphrey Bradbourne); appointments and commissions 17th-19th cent, mainly Townshend; Townshend family papers 16th-19th cent, incl financial papers of Sir Roger Townshend late 16th cent, corresp and papers of the 2nd Viscount as Secretary of State 1714-16, 1721-30, and corresp and papers of the 1st Marquess rel to Quebec 1758-9, Ireland 1767-72 (accounts, etc), Norfolk politics and family affairs; local and personal papers of Sir Nathaniel Bacon late 16th-early 17th cent; Harrison papers 17th-18th cent, incl register of Edward Harrison as surveyor-general for the Bedford Level 1729-32; personal and business papers of Nathaniel Browne of Ely mainly 1670s-80s; Bedford agency and other papers of Ralph Peirson 1665-1702; misc Ferrers family papers 16th-17th cent; misc Compton family papers 17th-mid-18th cent, incl papers of the Earl of Wilmington as Paymaster-General, etc 1722-30 and misc papers of the 5th Earl of Northampton (d1754) and his wife Lady Ferrers; genealogical and misc papers 16th-19th cent; Coxford Priory (Norfolk) records 12th-early 16th cent, incl cartulary 13th-14th cent, register 1318-20, rentals and accounts; Binham Priory (Norfolk) survey 14th-15th cent.

In private possession. Enquiries to Norfolk Record Office. HMC *Eleventh Report, App IV* (HMC 19), 1887. HW Saunders, *The Official Papers of Sir Nathaniel Bacon of Stiffkey as a Justice of the Peace 1580-1620*, Camden Society, 3rd Series, vol XXVI, 1915. NRA 1224.

[b] Misc Norfolk and Essex (Wivenhoe, etc) deeds mainly 15th-17th cent; Townshend settlement 1627; misc legal papers 17th-19th cent, incl case papers rel to the Earl of Wilmington 1729-31 and corresp rel to the marital affairs of Lord Charles Townshend 1809-11; misc Norfolk manorial records 1286-1678; misc Bacon and Townshend estate, financial and other papers 16th cent-1904.

Norfolk Record Office (BRA 926). Deposited in Norwich Public Libraries by Foyer, White & Prescott, solicitors, London, through the British Records Association 1955. NRA 15371.

[c] Misc Norfolk and Suffolk manorial court records 15th-16th cent, incl Langham with Morston court book *c*1554-5; Raynham shepherd's accounts 1569-72; misc Stiffkey, etc estate accounts and papers 16th-17th cent; Great Yarmouth election corresp 1747.

Norfolk Record Office (MC 1868). Deposited by Emmett & Tacon, solicitors, Norwich 1975. NRA 7825.

[d] Raynham and Tamworth estate papers 1806-11 (1st Marquess decd), incl leases, surveys, rentals, accounts and corresp; inventories of Raynham Hall, Tamworth Castle, etc 1811.

Public Record Office (C 107/38-9, Blake *v* Townshend).

[e] Norfolk deeds 12th-17th cent; wills, settlements, trust and executorship papers and legal papers 15th-18th cent, mainly Townshend but incl papers rel to the purchase of Stiffkey by Sir Nicholas Bacon 1569-75; manorial court records 13th-17th cent, mainly Norfolk (Helhoughton, Raynham, etc); misc Norfolk estate papers late 14th-19th cent, incl maps 17th-19th cent, Raynham sheep accounts 1489-90 and estate accounts 1501-18, and Stiffkey estate accounts 1577-89; misc Soham estate papers 18th cent; map of Balls Park estate 1736; Raynham inventories 1630s, 1764 and household accounts 17th cent; Stiffkey household accounts 1592-6; Townshend family papers 16th-early 19th cent, incl memorandum book (farm accounts, etc) of Roger Townshend 16th cent, diplomatic and political corresp of the 2nd Viscount 1709-28 (2 vols) and local defence corresp of the 1st Marquess 1794-1803; misc papers of Sir Nathaniel Bacon late 16th-early 17th cent, incl Poor Law papers; Coxford Priory register 14th cent.

Norfolk Record Office (Bradfer-Lawrence collection). Given by the executors of HL Bradfer-Lawrence to the Norfolk and Norwich Archaeological Society 1967. NRA 27666. See also A Hassell Smith, GM Baker and RW Kenny, *The papers of Nathaniel Bacon of Stiffkey, vol 1, 1556-77*, Norfolk Record Society, 1979, pp xx-xxxvii, for an account of the dispersal of Bacon MSS from Raynham Hall. For further substantial groups of Townshend and Bacon papers formerly at Raynham Hall, and deriving mainly from the sales of 1911 and 1924, see [f]-[z] below.

[f] Weasenham bailiffs accounts 1496-1508; Stiffkey manorial accounts 1573-4; misc Townshend and Bacon estate accounts 16th-early 17th cent; papers of Sir Nathaniel Bacon as a magistrate, commissioner for musters, etc *c*1580-1619, incl notebook 1584-91; misc Townshend papers 15th-early 18th cent.

Norfolk Record Office (MC 1872). Deposited by Martyns & Gane, solicitors, London 1970. FW Brooks, 'Supplementary Stiffkey papers', *Royal Historical Society, Camden 3rd S*, LII, 1936; Hassell Smith, *op cit*, p xxiii. NRA 41876.

[g] Misc legal and trust papers 14th-18th cent, incl executorship accounts for Sir Nicholas Bacon 1573-94; Norfolk manorial records 14th-18th cent (Helhoughton, W Raynham, E Rudham, Weasenham, etc); Tamworth court roll and accounts 1353-68, 1663; misc Norfolk estate papers 15th-19th cent, incl Stiffkey rental 1487, Raynham valuations and accounts 16th-17th cent, sheep accounts 1480-2, 1491, 1565-72, and Threxton enclosure papers 1809-10; Middlesex (Canonbury and Clerkenwell) rental 1753; Raynham Hall building account 1620 and household accounts 1740-52; papers rel to local affairs 16th-18th cent, incl Norfolk militia *c*1661-1800 and Great Yarmouth elections 1701, 1709; misc Townshend family papers 16th-18th cent; papers of Sir Nathaniel Bacon *c*1580-1620; Compton family pedigree; Coxford Priory charter 1230.

Norfolk Record Office (NNAS Safe II; Q 189A; S 154 D; T 188 A; MSS 1420-1631, 2641-74, 20096, 20384-20462, 20513-27, 20581-2, 20645, 21508; etc). Acquired by Norfolk and Norwich Archaelogical Society, Norwich Public Libraries and Norfolk Record Office at auction and by gift or purchase 1911-84. The Record Office also has microfilm copies of MSS located elsewhere.

[h] Misc Bacon and Townshend papers *c*1554-1711, incl map of Stiffkey early 17th cent.

Norfolk Record Office (HMN 7/218-28). Collected and deposited by Anthony Hamond (d1991). NRA 40234.

[i] Misc Townshend family corresp and related papers *c*1657-1806 (*c*108 pieces).

Norfolk Record Office (MC 1601, Acc 1997/16). Purchased 1997 (Bloomsbury Book Auctions, catalogue of MSS, etc largely from the stock of Frank Marcham, no 246). NRA 41765.

[j] Coxford Priory cartulary 13th-15th cent.

Norfolk Record Office (Norwich diocesan records, DN/SUN/8). (Microfilm copy: MF/RO 342/4, 344/7.) GRC Davis, *Medieval Cartularies of*

Great Britain, 1958, no 280. NRA 9364. An early fifteenth-century cartulary, discovered in a London junk shop by TS Blakeney, is British Library Add MS 44784 (Davis, *op cit*, no 281).

[k] Norfolk estate accounts 1698-1705, 1738-66 (8 vols).

Untraced. Sotheby's (Pulborough), 9 Mar 1984, lot 1,922.

[l] Norfolk lieutenancy book of the 1st Viscount 1660-76.

British Library, Manuscript Collections (Add MS 11601). Acquired 1839. See RM Dunn, ed, *Norfolk lieutenancy journal 1660-1676*, Norfolk Record Society xlv, 1977. For other Townshend MSS acquired by the British Museum before 1900 see Stowe MS 150 (Ferrers and Bacon family correspondence 1526-1623), King's MS 265 (military and naval papers early 17th cent, Vere and Townshend) and Eg MSS 892-4 (diplomatic papers of the 2nd Viscount 1709-10).

[m] Townshend wardship and executorship accounts 1637-47, with legal papers early 17th cent; Norfolk manorial court book 1537-41 (E and W Rudham, etc); misc estate papers 16th-early 17th cent, mainly Norfolk but incl Akenham survey 1576; Raynham Hall accounts and inventories 1609-1755; papers rel to Norfolk lieutenancy, musters and subsidies 1582-1711; Tamworth election account 1741 and poll book 1765; Townshend family papers 15th-19th cent, incl memorandum books of Lady Townshend 1487-99 and Roger Townshend 1500-1, corresp of the 2nd Viscount as ambassador to Holland and Secretary of State (despatches from Paris, etc), and papers of the 1st Marquess, mainly rel to military affairs and to Ireland; misc corresp and papers of Sir Nathaniel Bacon 1573-1624; religious papers of Sir Edward Lewkenor of Denham late 16th-early 17th cent; letters to the 4th Earl of Northampton, with account book of the 5th Earl 1744-54.

British Library, Manuscript Collections (Add Ch 66712-13, 75479-91; Add MSS 37634-8, 34892-38508, 41139-52, 41178K, L, 41305-8, 41654-6, 45902, 46856, 48981-2, 50006-12; Eg MS 3124). Acquired 1908-59, mainly at or following the sales of 1908, 1911 and 1924.

[n] Deeds c1200-17th cent, mainly Norfolk but a few for Essex, Cambs, etc; misc Townshend, Bacon and Compton family corresp and papers 16th-19th cent, incl letters to the 2nd and 3rd Viscounts, military patronage corresp of the 1st Marquess 1767-72, and corresp of the 5th Earl of Northampton.

British Library, Manuscript Collections (Add Ch 76153-76383, Add MSS 63079-63111 *passim*). Bequeathed by TS Blakeney 1976.

[o] Townshend executorship papers mainly 1590-5; misc papers of Ralph Peirson as JP for the Isle of Ely 1693-1701.

Lincolnshire Archives (CRAGG 9). Deposited by Major WJR Cragg 1953. *Archivists' Report 5*, 1953-4, p33.

[p] Canonbury court rolls 1468-1500, 1559-97, 1650-1719.

Islington Archives. Acquired from F Marcham 1949. Sotheby's, 14 July 1924, lot 27. *Trans London and Middlesex Arch Soc*, NS XI, part 1, 1954, p96.

[q] Horsham St Faith rental 1724-61; Raynham labourers' accounts 1666-7; misc militia papers 18th cent; corresp and papers of the 1st Marquess, mainly as Lord Lieutenant of Ireland 1767-72.

John Rylands University Library of Manchester (Eng MSS 938-41). Purchased 1939. *Handlist of additions to the collection of English manuscripts …1937-1951*, p202.

[r] Legal, estate, local and misc corresp and papers 16th-17th cent, Bacon and Townshend.

Folger Shakespeare Library, Washington DC. (L.d.1-1036). Purchased 1924. NRA 20984. Additional groups were purchased from Bernard Halliday following the 1924 sale (Norfolk shrievalty roll 1585-6, inventories of Lady Berkeley's apparel 1605-18, etc (Xd.256-8, 522, etc)) and from Hofman and Freeman in 1970 (papers of Sir Nathaniel Bacon 1574-1622, 51 items (Xd.502)).

[s] Misc accounts and papers of Sir Nathaniel Bacon 1576-1626, incl Stiffkey Hall building accounts.

University of Chicago Library, Department of Special Collections (Percy Millican collection). Sotheby's, 7 Apr 1970, part of lots 518-520. (Other papers from this sale are mainly untraced. Copies in Norfolk Record Office, Q 189 A.) Further Bacon papers late 16th-early 17th cent have been acquired by the Pierrepont Morgan Library, New York (including letters from Sir Thomas Gresham) and the Francis Bacon Library, Claremont, California (including a justice's recognisance book). (See Hassell Smith, *op cit*.)

[t] Farm, etc accounts of Sir Nathaniel Bacon 1576-1626 (mainly 1577-89).

Reading University Library (Historical Farm Records, NORF 20). Deposited by Rothamstead Experimental Station 1966. (Formerly Bernard Halliday, of Leicester, catalogue 126, 1930. The remainder of the 1577-89 volume is in the Bradfer-Lawrence collection, [e] above.) Reading University Library, *Historical Farm Records*, 1973, p219. NRA 41577.

[u] Raynham household account book 1626-37; misc Bacon building and other papers 1575-87, incl Gorhambury (Herts) building accounts.

Huntington Library, San Marino, California (HM 26559, 41753-6). Purchased 1962 and 1973 (Sotheby's, 18 July, lot 175). *Guide*, 1982, p283.

[v] Diplomatic and other corresp and papers of the 2nd Viscount 1709-29; letters to the 1st Marquess from his brother Charles Townshend 1754-66.

Bodleian Library, Oxford (MSS Top. Oxon. c. 164, e. 125; Eng. Hist. c. 194, d. 117-18, 147-9, 211). Acquired *c*1912-43.

[w] Townshend family papers *c*1709-1811 (12 boxes), incl misc letters to the 2nd Viscount, and papers of the 1st Marquess rel to Ireland 1767-72 and to the Westminster election 1789.

Yale University, Beinecke Library (Osborn collection). NRA 20037. The Library has also acquired some eighteenth-century diplomatic papers (see *Sixth Biennial Report*, 1980) and a Stiffkey mill account book 1576-80.

[x] Corresp and letter book of the 2nd Viscount as ambassador to Holland 1709-12.

Hertfordshire Archives and Local Studies (D/EX 736). Presented by J Crozier 1986. NRA 3507. Further papers of the 2nd Viscount have been acquired by Trinity College Library, Dublin (letters from William King 1717-24: MSS 1995-2008, NRA 20078) and the National Library of Australia (MS 1458: see *Archives*, vol XXI, no 92, Oct 1994, p206).

[y] Corresp and letter books of the 1st Marquess 1767-1807, mainly as Lord Lieutenant of Ireland.

University of Michigan, William L Clements Library, Ann Arbor. Acquired 1924-8 (see Sotheby's, 14-16 July 1924, lot 109). *Guide*, 3rd edn, 1978, pp140-1. Other Irish, military and miscellaneous correspondence and papers of the 1st Marquess have been acquired by the National Archives of Ireland (M 648-735); the National Library of Ireland; the Representative Church Body Library, Dublin (MS 20, NRA 28346); the National Army Museum (6806-41, 8604-81, 9107-9146, NRA 18641, 20834, partial lists); the National Library of Wales (MSS 1489D, 2115C: *Handlist of MSS, I*, 1943); the Queen's Dragoon Guards Museum, Cardiff (NRA 20951); the National Archives of Canada (MG 18 L7: *General inventory of manuscripts*, vol 3, 1974, p100); Flinders University of South Australia Library, Special Collections; Duke University, William R Perkins Library, Durham, North Carolina (*Guide*, 1980, p578); Boston Public Library, Massachusetts (MS Eng. 180, NRA 22724); Yale University, Lewis Walpole

Library, Farmington, Connecticut (NRA 22338).

[z] Papers of the Earl of Wilmington 1731-44.

Library of Congress, Washington DC. PM Hamer, ed, *A guide to archives and manuscripts in the United States*, 1961, pp85, 120. For other papers of the Earl of Wilmington see [a] above and British Library Add Ch 71290-7, Add MS 45733.

[aa] Executorship, legal and case papers 14th-18th cent, Ferrers and Bradbourne, incl executorship papers for Dorothy Cockayne of Ashbourne (Derbys) late 16th cent and case papers rel to Princes Risborough (Bucks); manorial court records 1438-1670, incl Walton-upon-Trent and Tettenhall (Staffs); estate records 16th-early 19th cent, Derbys, Warwicks, etc, incl surveys, rentals and accounts; household accounts (?Tamworth and Walton); papers rel to local administration *c*1550-1667, incl Needwood Forest, honour of Tutbury and Derbys and Warwicks musters and subsidies; Ferrers family corresp and papers 16th-18th cent, incl letters to Sir Humphrey Ferrers (d1608); estate, legal and other papers of the Ellerkers of Risby (Yorks ER) (family of the 2nd Marquess's wife) 18th cent.

Folger Shakespeare Library, Washington DC (MS ADD 744). Purchased 1977 (Sotheby's, 12 Dec, lot 14). Formerly Phillipps MSS 11013-35124 *passim*, and probably all or mostly from the Tamworth Castle muniments. NW Alcock, 'The Ferrers of Tamworth collection: sorting and listing', *Archives* vol XIX, no 86, Oct 1991, pp358-63. Additional items *c*1558-1773 were acquired in 1985 (Add 882: Phillips's, 10 Apr, lot 595; NRA 24945). Related groups of papers, all former Phillipps MSS, have been acquired by Derbyshire Record Office (Sotheby's, 13 Apr 1981, lot 30, including deeds for Walton-upon-Trent), Leicestershire Record Office (Ferrers deeds 13th-early 17th cent: Sotheby's, 13 Apr 1981, lot 53) and Shropshire Records and Research Centre (Ferrers legal and manorial records 1352-1609, including manorial accounts for Claverley (Salop), Tamworth, Walton-upon-Trent, etc 1450-1509, 1606-7: Acc 4229; Sotheby's, 13 Apr 1981, lot 170; NRA 11563).

[bb] Legal and sale papers rel to the Tamworth estate 1814-34, with misc Ferrers and Townshend deeds and papers 14th-18th cent.

Staffordshire and Stoke on Trent Archive Service, Staffordshire Record Office (D 5368). Probably acquired with other papers from a Tamworth solicitor's office by JF Woody. Deposited by his descendant Mrs Hollins 1995. NRA 40705.

Related collections: Compton, Marquesses of Northampton, no 24; Shirley, Earls Ferrers, no 93; Ferrers of Baddesley Clinton (Shakespeare Birthplace Trust Records Office, NRA 16993), including misc Townshend and Ferrers of Groby and Tamworth deeds, etc 1385/6-1847.

[108] TUFTON, Barons Hothfield

The Tufton family was settled in the Rainham district of Kent from the twelfth century. Hothfield (Kent) was purchased *c*1542, and the family also acquired estates in Sussex (mainly near the Kent border) and other counties.. Sir Nicholas Tufton, second Bt (1578-1631), was created Earl of Thanet in 1628. The second Earl married in 1629 Margaret Sackville, daughter of the third Earl of Dorset by Anne, *suo jure* Baroness Clifford. Through her (who married secondly the fourth Earl of Pembroke) the Tufton family inherited former Clifford estates in the West Riding of Yorkshire (Skipton Castle, etc) and Westmorland (Appleby Castle, Brough, Brougham, etc, with the hereditary shrievalty of Westmorland), and the Sackville property of Bolebrooke (Sussex) (sold in 1770: see also Sackville, Barons Sackville, no 91).

Robert de Clifford, Baron Clifford 1299, and his nephew the third Baron inherited the extensive estates of the Vipont or Veteripont family in Westmorland and elsewhere. The first Baron was also granted Skipton, Skelton (Cumberland) and other estates by Edward I. The ninth Baron (d1461) married Margaret, daughter and heir of Henry de Bromflete, Lord Vessy, through whom estates in the East and North Ridings of Yorkshire (Bromflete, Londesborough, Malton, etc) were inherited. The eleventh Baron Clifford (1493-1542) was created Earl of Cumberland in 1525, and considerably extended the West Riding estates, notably by the acquisition of the Percy Fee in Craven and the Bolton Abbey lands. In the second half of the sixteenth century, however, there were extensive sales both of estates in Craven and of outlying properties. On the death of the fifth Earl of Cumberland in 1643 the Bolton Abbey and Londesborough estates passed to his daughter, who married Richard Boyle, Viscount Dungarvan and later Earl of Cork and Earl of Burlington (see Cavendish, Dukes of Devonshire, no 17), but the Skipton Castle and Westmorland estates passed to his cousin Lady Pembroke (see above).

On the death of the sixth Earl of Thanet in 1729 the barony of Clifford fell into abeyance among his daughters (for the Dungeness lighthouse dues, that passed to his third daughter, the Countess of Leicester and *suo jure* Baroness Clifford, see Coke, Earls of Leicester, no 23), but the bulk of the family estates passed to his nephew as seventh Earl. He married in 1722 Mary Savile, daughter and co-heir of the second Marquess of Halifax (d1700), through whom, on the partition of the unentailed Halifax estates in 1742, some Derbyshire property was inherited. (See also Lumley-Savile of Rufford, no 65, and, for Savile properties inherited by the Boyle family, see Cavendish, Dukes of Devonshire, no 17.)

The eleventh Earl of Thanet was succeeded in 1849 by his natural son Sir Richard Tufton, Bt, whose son was created Baron Hothfield in 1881.

Estates in 1883: Westmorland 17,093 acres, Yorks WR 11,953 acres, Kent 10,144 acres, Cumberland 86 acres, total 39,276 acres worth £45,937 a year.

[a] Deeds late 12th-20th cent, mainly Kent *c*1200-20th cent but incl Sussex 13th-17th cent, Cheshire, Leics, London, Middlesex and Northants 14th-19th cent, and Westmorland and Yorks WR 19th-20th cent; wills, settlements and related papers 16th-20th cent, mainly Tufton, incl trust papers 19th-20th cent; legal and case papers 16th-20th cent, incl papers rel to the sequestration of the Tufton estates 1642-59; manorial court records, Kent (Hothfield, etc) 13th-18th cent, Northants (Newbottle, etc) 16th-18th cent and Sussex (Framfield, Peasmarsh, etc) 15th-18th cent.

Kent estate records (Hothfield and Rainham) 16th-20th cent, incl leases, surveys, maps, rentals, accounts and papers rel to woods; misc estate records, Sussex 17th-18th cent, Cheshire (Hurlston, etc) 1673-80, Northants 16th-18th cent and Derbys 17th-19th cent; misc records for northern estates 17th-19th cent, incl map of Appleby 1754 and Westmorland accounts 1684-94; Virginia estate papers 1613-*c*1667; household inventories 17th-19th cent (Hothfield, etc) and accounts 1706-12; Hothfield farm and garden accounts 19th cent; Kent sewers papers 17th-18th cent; Hothfield parochial and charity papers 17th-19th cent; appointments, pardons, pedigrees, etc 17th-19th cent; Privy Purse account book 1721-5.

Centre for Kentish Studies (U 455, 991, 1095). Deposited by the Hon PJS and Mrs Tufton 1954, Mrs M Tufton 1967, and Cumberland and Westmorland Joint Archives Committee and Dawson & Co, solicitors, London 1963. *Guide to the Kent County Archives Office*, 1958, pp156-8; *first supplement*, 1971, pp124, 153. NRA 4391.

[b] Kent deeds 17th-19th cent and legal papers 19th cent; Kent manorial court records (Hothfield, etc) 16th-20th cent; Kent and Sussex estate records 17th-19th cent, incl surveys, rentals, accounts and tithe papers; Hothfield charity papers 16th-19th cent.

Centre for Kentish Studies (U 55, U 1000/7/M29, 30). Presented by HW Knocker and his executors 1940-5, and through Sevenoaks Public Library (HW Knocker collection) 1963. NRA 5406, 18189.

[c] Misc Kent manorial court records (Fowsley in Hothfield, Ripple) 17th-19th cent; misc

Hothfield legal and estate papers c1650-1899, incl draft survey c1840, sketch maps, and accounts 1819, 1821, 1842.

Centre for Kentish Studies (U 442/B1, E9, M50-52, 87). Presented by Dr Gordon Ward to the Kent Archaeological Society and transferred to Kent Archives Office 1954. NRA 5301. (These documents derive, like some in [b] above, from the legal firm of Norwood of Charing.)

[d] Kent estate maps c1630-1888.

Centre for Kentish Studies (U 1095). Purchased 1964. NRA 4391.

[e] Rental of Kent estates 1923-50.

Centre for Kentish Studies (U 2538). Deposited by Mr Oliver of Hothfield 1982. NRA 4391.

[f] Rent account 1830-1944.

Centre for Kentish Studies (U 3056). Deposited by Miss C Blocksidge 1991. NRA 4391.

[g] Accounts of John Billington as Hothfield steward 1759-67.

Centre for Kentish Studies (U 1045/E1). Deposited by Hallett & Co, solicitors, Ashford 1963. NRA 11066.

[h] Deeds 13th-20th cent, mainly Westmorland but incl some for Cumberland and Yorks WR and a few for Derbys (Savile property 18th cent); wills, settlements and related trust and executorship papers 16th-20th cent, Tufton, Clifford and Savile, incl inquisitions *post mortem* (mainly copies); legal and case papers 16th-20th cent, incl Lady Anne Clifford's claims 17th cent; documents rel to Westmorland knights' fees and cornage rents 14th-17th cent.

Westmorland estate records (Appleby, Brough, etc) 16th-20th cent, incl leases, tenancy papers, surveys and valuations, rentals, accounts, and papers rel to enclosure, advowsons and tithes, Mallerstang and Stainmore chapels, Kirkby Stephen market, lead mining and railways; misc Yorks and Derbys estate and mining papers 18th-19th cent; London and Southwark, etc estate accounts 1743-55; papers rel to the hereditary shrievalty of Westmorland 16th-19th cent, incl writs and accounts 18th cent, and to the borough of Appleby 16th-19th cent, incl lists of burgages from 1528 and election papers 18th cent; other papers rel to Westmorland affairs 14th-19th cent, incl Brough market charter 1330; patents, licences, etc 17th cent; family corresp and papers 16th-18th cent, Clifford and Tufton, incl alchemical and medical books of the 10th Baron Clifford, letters to the 3rd Earl of Cumberland and narratives of his privateering voyages 1586-98, letters to Lady Anne Clifford, and her Great Books of Record 1649-75; genealogical and misc papers.

Cumbria Record Office, Kendal (WD/Hoth). Deposited 1962-86, material originally deposited at Carlisle being afterwards transferred to Kendal. Includes records formerly held at Appleby Castle, by the Tufton family, and in the offices of Messrs Dawson & Co, solicitors, London and Hoares Bank, London. HMC *Eleventh Report, App, Part VII*, 1888, pp81-90; *Accessions to Repositories* 1962, 1964, 1986. NRA 12905 (partial list). A further copy of the Great Books of Record was recorded in George C Williamson, *Lady Anne Clifford*, 1922, as being *penes* the Hodgson, formerly Leveson-Gower, family of Bill Hill (Berkshire), by descent from the sixth Earl of Thanet. In 1983 further Appleby Castle estate papers c1856-1962 were deposited by J Dixon (Secretary, Corlands Minerals Ltd) from the office of E & EA Heelis, Appleby (Archivist's Report September-December 1983).

[i] Westmorland manorial court records 16th-20th cent (Appleby, Dufton, Kirkby Stephen, etc), incl boundary rolls and enfranchisement papers; misc Westmorland legal and estate records 17th-20th cent, incl rentals 1841, 1844 and enclosure papers 18th-20th cent; records rel to the borough of Appleby 14th-20th cent, incl deeds, leases 1612-1865, burgage rental 1528 and election returns 1641-1852.

Cumbria Record Office, Kendal (WD/HH (Accs 930, 1048, 1049, 1380, 2057, A 415)). Deposited by E & EA Heelis, solicitors, Appleby c1971-83. NRA 41063 (partial list).

[j] Legal corresp rel to the Tufton estates 1749/50-1856.

Cumbria Record Office, Kendal (WDX 71 (Acc 4)). Purchased from Mr E Hall 1963. Archivist's Report March 1963.

[k] Yorks WR deeds 13th-19th cent; marriage settlements 16th cent; inquisitions *post mortem*; legal and case papers 15th-20th cent, incl book of grants (Craven properties) 1558-1650 and schedule of evidences 1739; Yorks WR manorial court records 14th-19th cent, incl manor, borough and honour of Skipton; manorial rentals and accounts (Yorks WR and ER: Bromflete and de Aton families) 15th cent; Yorks WR (Craven) estate records 15th-19th cent, incl leases, surveys, maps, rentals, accounts, and papers rel to tithes 16th cent, coal mining 17th cent, enclosure 18th cent, and canals and railways 18th-19th cent; Skipton Castle and Londesborough household accounts 1628-9; Skipton Castle visitors' book 1902-26; alchemical MSS *temp* the 10th Baron Clifford (2 items).

West Yorkshire Archive Service, Yorkshire Archaeological Society, Leeds (D 121, 121 add, 174, 214). Deposited by Veteripont Ltd from the Skipton Estate Office 1955-86. *Guide to the* archive collections, 1985, pp20-1. NRA 12905 (partial list).

[l] Yorks WR manorial court records 17th-19th cent (Silsden, manor and honour of Skipton, etc).

West Yorkshire Archive Service, Yorkshire Archaeological Society, Leeds (Bradfer-Lawrence collection, MD 335/boxes 1, 5). NRA 546.

[m] Beamsley Hospital (Skipton) records 16th-20th cent.

West Yorkshire Archive Service, Yorkshire Archaeological Society, Leeds (DD 240). Deposited 1993.

[n] Abstracts of legal evidences, Clifford family 17th cent.

British Library, Manuscript Collections (Add MS 49972). Acquired 1958. (For transcripts of evidences at Londesborough and Skipton Castle c1646 see Bodleian Library, Oxford MSS Dodsw. 70, 74, 83, 92.)

[o] Register of estate papers c1684-1729, rel mainly to the Westmorland and Yorks estates.

Bodleian Library, Oxford (MS Don. c. 85). Acquired 1961 from Messrs Quaritch, through the Friends of the Bodleian Library. *Summary catalogue of post-medieval western manuscripts*, vol 1, 1991, p136.

[p] Clifford family corresp 16th cent, incl letters to the 1st Earl of Cumberland.

British Library, Manuscript Collections (Add MS 48965). Purchased 1955 (Hodgson's, 2 June, lot 243).

[q] Clifford family accounts 1551-1659, mainly of the 4th and 5th Earls of Cumberland.

Hull University, Brynmor Jones Library (DDCV/204/38-59). Deposited by Crust, Todd & Mills, solicitors, Beverley. NRA 6482.

[r] Account book of Lady Anne Clifford 1600-2.

Yale University, Beinecke Library (Osborn Mss b 27). NRA 18661.

Related collections: Cavendish, Dukes of Devonshire, no 17; Coke, Earls of Leicester, no 23; Lowther, Earls of Lonsdale, no 63, including Westmorland accounts and rentals 1690-1724 (Cumbria Record Office, Carlisle D/Lons/L12/3/7/9); Sackville, Barons Sackville, no 91; Spencer, Earls Spencer, no 97, including further Clifford and Savile papers.

[109] VANE, Barons Barnard

The Vane or Fane family, a younger branch of the Fane Earls of Westmorland (see no 34), was settled at Hadlow (Kent) in the fifteenth century. Sir Henry Vane senior (1589-1654) sold Hadlow but purchased the Fairlawn (Kent) estate and extensive properties in County Durham, including Raby Castle, in the early seventeenth century. An estate at Long Newton (County Durham) was settled on a younger son, Sir George Vane (see Vane-Tempest-Stewart, Marquesses of Londonderry, no 110), but the other Kent and County Durham estates descended to Sir Henry Vane junior (1613-62), the republican politician, and eventually to his son Christopher Vane (d1723), who married in 1676 Elizabeth, sister and co-heir of John Holles, Duke of Newcastle (see Pelham-Clinton, later Pelham-Clinton-Hope, Dukes of Newcastle, no 81) and was created Baron Barnard in 1698.

In the next generation Raby Castle passed to the second Baron (1678-1753), who married Mary Randyll of Chilworth (Surrey), but Fairlawn passed to a younger brother, William (c1680-1734), who also inherited some property in County Durham and a reversionary interest in the Newcastle estates. William Vane married in 1703 Lucy, daughter and co-heir of William Jolliffe of Caverswall (Staffordshire), and was created Viscount Vane in 1720. The second Viscount sold Caverswall (retaining, however, a life interest) and disposed of his reversionary interest in the Newcastle estates (to the second Duke of Newcastle). After his death in 1798 Fairlawn was also sold, but some County Durham property reverted to the senior line.

The third Baron Barnard (c1705-1758) married in 1725 Grace, daughter of Charles Fitzroy, Duke of Cleveland by his second wife Anne Pulteney, aunt of William Pulteney, Earl of Bath, and was created Earl of Darlington in 1754. The second Earl (1726-92) married in 1757 Margaret, sister and eventually co-heir of James Lowther, Earl of Lonsdale (see Lowther, Earls of Lonsdale, no 63), through whom property in Barbados was inherited, and was residuary legatee of the second Duke of Cleveland (d1774).

The third Earl of Darlington (1766-1842) inherited in 1805 extensive estates in Shropshire (High Ercall, Wroxeter, etc), Staffordshire (Wolverhampton), Northamptonshire (Brigstock and Sudborough), Cheshire (Minshull Vernon) and Montgomeryshire (Deythur or Deuddwr). These estates had all or mostly been acquired by the Earl of Bath from the Newport family, Earls of Bradford (see Bridgeman, Earls of Bradford, no 10), and had descended to Frances Pulteney and her husband Sir William Johnstone, afterwards Pulteney, fifth Bt (d1805) (see Hope-Johnstone of Raehills, no 54). Following the deaths of their daughter Henrietta Laura (created Countess of Bath 1803) in 1808 and her husband Sir James Murray-Pulteney, Bt, in 1811 Lord Darlington also inherited property in Somerset (Bathwick and Wrington). The Cheshire and Montgomeryshire estates and some Shropshire properties were sold between 1805 and 1824, and the Somerset properties reduced by sale in the late nineteenth century, but the bulk of the Shropshire, Staffordshire and Northamptonshire estates were retained into the twentieth century.

Lord Darlington was created Duke of Cleveland in 1833. In 1787 he had married Katherine, daughter and co-heir of the sixth Duke of Bolton (see Orde-Powlett, Barons Bolton, no 77). Her interest in the Bolton estates in Cornwall, Devon, Dorset and Wiltshire passed to her younger son Lord William Vane, who in January 1864 succeeded as third Duke of Cleveland. As divided under a private Act of 1863 the Vane family received estates in Cornwall (Ludgvan, etc), Devon (Brixham, etc) and Wiltshire (Imber, etc).

Lord Harry Vane (1803-91), younger brother of the second and third Dukes, inherited some land in County Durham from his father. He also acquired the Battle Abbey estates in Sussex (from Sir Augustus Webster, seventh Bt, in 1858) and other properties in Sussex and Kent. In September 1864 he succeeded as fourth Duke of Cleveland, inheriting the Vane and former Pulteney estates in County Durham, Shropshire and other counties, and former Bolton estates in Cornwall, Devon and Wiltshire (except those that passed to the third Duke's widow). On the fourth Duke's death without issue in 1891 the dukedom of Cleveland was extinguished, but the barony of Barnard, together with the bulk of the Vane and Pulteney estates, passed to a distant cousin, Henry de Vere Vane (1854-1918), son of Sir Henry Morgan Vane (1808-86) by Lousia, daughter and co-heir of the Revd Richard Farrer of Ashley (Northamptonshire). The former Bolton estates, however, together with the Sussex and Kent properties, passed to the widow of the fourth Duke. (The Battle Abbey estate was repurchased by the Webster family following her death in 1901.) The Ashton Keynes (Wiltshire) estate, purchased in the 1840s, was left in 1891 to the fourth Duke's great-nephew AWH Hay (later Hay-Drummond).

Estates in 1883: Duke of Cleveland: Co Durham 55,837 acres, Salop 25,604 acres, Sussex 6,025 acres, Somerset 4,784 acres, Northants 3,482 acres, Kent 2,449 acres, Staffs unstated (rental £3,970), Cornwall 1,997 acres, Wilts 1,511 acres, Devon 1,085 acres, Gloucs 11 acres, total 102,785 acres worth £95,755 a year; Dowager Duchess (in 1873): Wilts 886 acres, Cornwall 523 acres, total 1,409 acres worth £1,643 a year, with 2,456 acres in Devon, worth £3,087 a year, held jointly with the Earl of Sandwich; HM Vane (in 1873): Northants 329 acres, Leics 15 acres, total 344 acres worth £817 a year.

[a] Deeds 14th-19th cent, incl Co Durham from early 17th cent, Salop from 14th cent and

Northants and Leics (Farrer properties) 16th-19th cent; wills, settlements, trust papers and legal papers 17th-19th cent, incl Vane and Pulteney families, the Duke of Cleveland 1730s, and Farrer and Parkyns (of Bunny and Great Leake, Notts) families 17th-19th cent; misc manorial court records 17th-19th cent, incl Barnard Castle court book 1637-1733, Bower in Molash (Kent) presentments 1732-89 and Medbourne (Leics) court book 1736-1822.

Co Durham (Raby Castle and general) estate records early 17th-mid-20th cent, incl leases and agreements 19th-20th cent, lease books c1680-1707, surveys and maps from 18th cent, rentals and accounts from 1614, corresp 18th-20th cent, letter books 1865-1949, and accounts and papers rel to farms and cropping, buildings, enclosure, tithes, timber, drainage, collieries and game; home farm accounts late 18th-late 19th cent; papers rel to the Co Durham estate of Lord Harry Vane (later 4th Duke) 1842-65; Co Durham (highland or Upper Teesdale) estate records 18th-20th cent (mainly from early 19th cent), incl agreements, letting book 1808-34, surveys, valuations, reference books, rentals, accounts, corresp from c1816, letter books 1850-1949, and papers rel to timber, tithes, drainage and brick and tile works; Teesdale mining accounts and papers 18th-20th cent, incl lead account 1737-46; Teesdale fishing permits 1896-1948; Barnard Castle (Co Durham) estate records 19th-20th cent (mainly from 1867) incl reports 1839-94 and market toll accounts 1856-1917; Darlington (Co Durham) estate records c1867-1928, incl maps, accounts and letter books.

Records rel to the former Pulteney estates in Salop, Staffs and Northants 17th-20th cent (mainly 1805 onwards), incl leases 17th-19th cent, surveys and valuations, rentals and accounts, Salop and Staffs mining papers, Salop wood accounts, Northants brickyard papers, papers rel to Wolverhampton (Staffs) deanery and tithes, papers rel to urban property in Wolverhampton, and papers rel to churches and schools; papers rel to Minshull Vernon (Cheshire) 1806-17 and to Deythur (Montgomeryshire) mainly 1805-25; papers rel to the Bathwick and Wrington (Somerset) estates 19th cent (from c1808), incl Bathwick waterworks papers 1814-24, and to properties at Muswell Hill (Middlesex) and Keyingham (Yorks ER) 1808-11; Kent (Fairlawn) estate papers c1727-98, incl rentals and accounts, with Caversfield (Staffs) rental 1767 and Duke of Newcastle estate rental (Notts, Lincs, etc) c1746; Bolton estates rental (Cornwall, Devon, Dorset, Wilts) 1853; Loders (Dorset) estate papers 1903-6; Farrer (Northants and Leics) estate papers 18th-19th cent, incl map of Market Harborough (Leics) ? late 18th cent, with Cornish mining papers 1848-55.

Papers rel to Raby Castle 18th-20th cent, incl plans and drawings for alterations 18th-19th cent, workmen's accounts 1806-1923, inventories 1711-1891, household accounts and vouchers 1811-1927, and cellar books 1805-1905; drawings and papers rel to the park and plantations 18th-19th cent, incl list of trees planted 1743-50; Staindrop Hall (Co Durham) valuation 1795-6; inventory of London house (Viscount Vane) 1736; plan of Cleveland House (London) 1892; London household accounts 1788-90; Ashley (Northants) household accounts 1812-52; papers rel to Co Durham affairs 18th-20th cent, incl militia and volunteers late 18th cent and elections 18th-19th cent; papers rel to Market Harborough volunteers 1803-14.

Patents and commissions 17th-20th cent, mainly Vane family; Vane family papers 18th-20th cent, incl papers of the 1st and 2nd Earls of Darlington, the 1st Duke of Cleveland, Sir HM Vane, the 10th Baron Barnard and the 1st and 2nd Viscounts Vane; Seal Office and other papers of the 3rd (Fitzroy) Duke of Cleveland *c*1731-74; interest account of General Pulteney 1765; misc Farrer family papers 18th-mid-19th cent, with papers of the Groves family of Market Harborough early 18th cent; misc papers, incl drawings for gate and screens at Brocket Hall (Herts) *c*1830, a German merchant's accounts 1803 (2 vols), Staindrop Farmers' Club minutes 1846-74 and documents acquired by Sir HM Vane.

In private possession. Not normally available for research.

[b] Manorial records for Co Durham 17th-19th cent (Barnard Castle, Middleton-in-Teesdale, Raby with Staindrop, etc); Co Durham surveys and valuations 1745, 1763, 1772.

Durham County Record Office (D/Bo/A). Deposited by the 10th Baron Barnard in the Bowes Museum and transferred to the Record Office 1963. NRA 23425.

[c] Transcripts of Barnard Castle manorial court rolls 1621-1788, with presentments 1817.

Durham County Record Office (D/HH/11/142, 203). Deposited on behalf of the late ER Hanby Holmes 1981. NRA 18998.

[d] Case papers Vane *v* Barnard 18th cent; manorial court records, Barnard Castle, Middleton-in-Teesdale and Raby 16th-late 19th cent; misc Co Durham estate records 19th-early 20th cent, incl maps early 19th cent, Raby estate conveyances and leases 1896-1923 and Darlington conveyances and plans *c*1890-1920.

Durham County Record Office (D/Wat). Deposited by Col WI Watson, solicitor, Barnard Castle 1984. NRA 40371.

[e] Misc Teesdale estate records 1803-64 (5 vols), incl rentals and accounts.

Durham University Library, Archives and Special Collections (SR.19.E (Vane MSS)). Purchased from AB Walker, bookseller, Whitby 1970.

[f] Salop manorial court records 16th-19th cent, incl Hinstock, Loppington and Wem court books 1578-1878; misc Salop and Montgomeryshire estate records *c*1561-1847, incl Wem survey 1561, Salop and Montgomeryshire surveys 1746-8 and Deythur valuation 1813.

Shropshire Records and Research Centre (SRO 167, 168/1-4, 248). Deposited by Sprott, Stokes & Turnbull, estate agents, Shrewsbury 1948-9. NRA 11563, 35526. (Other Wem and Loppington manorial records 1711-82 are among the Whitfield papers, SRO 3607/III/A/2-10; NRA 21443.)

[g] Salop manorial papers (presentments, etc) 1787-1804.

Shropshire Records and Research Centre. (SRO 1011). Deposited by Salt & Son, solicitors, Shrewsbury 1959. NRA 11563.

[h] Wolverhampton manorial court records 1653-1928; rental, Earl of Bradford 1716-27, with misc Wolverhampton estate papers 19th cent; lease register, Bolton estates (Cornwall, Devon, Dorset, Wilts) 1752-4.

Staffordshire and Stoke on Trent Archive Service, Staffordshire Record Office (D 1804). Deposited by the 10th Baron Barnard and Messrs Sprott, Stokes & Turnbull 1957. NRA 5946.

[i] Papers of SP Cockerell (1753-1827) as surveyor to the Pulteney estates 1793-1806, incl copies of deeds and accounts.

British Architectural Library (COC Add 5/51-72). NRA 34210.

[j] Ashton Keynes estate papers *c*1825-1917, incl maps, particular 1912 and rentals 1871-1910; Cove House (Ashton Keynes) inventories and gardener's book early 20th cent.

Wiltshire and Swindon Record Office (WRO 374 *passim*). Deposited by Mullings, Ellett, solicitors, Cirencester 1956. NRA 1556.

[k] Barbados plantation accounts 1756, 1825-35; misc Vane family papers 1737-1892, incl corresp of Viscount Barnard (later 2nd Duke of Cleveland) rel to his candidature for Totnes 1822-5 and corresp of the 4th Duke.

British Library, Manuscript Collections (Add Ch 70791; Add MSS 43507, 69420-1). Presented by HC Price 1933 and M Llewellyn 1989.

[l] Corresp of the 4th Duke and his wife *c*1843-93, with misc papers of the Duchess.

Centre for Kentish Studies (U 1590/C 502-12). Deposited among the Stanhope papers by the

Chevening Trustees 1971. (Catherine, sister of the 5th Earl Stanhope, married firstly Lord Dalmeny, son of the 4th Earl of Rosebery, and secondly, in 1854, Lord Harry Vane, later 4th Duke of Cleveland.) NRA 25095.

[m] Journals and other papers of the 4th Duke 1840-91.

National Library of Scotland (MSS 10206-16). Presented with the Rosebery papers by Lord Primrose 1966. NRA 22490.

Related collections: Bridgeman, Earls of Bradford, no 10; Lowther, Earls of Lonsdale, no 63; Orde-Powlett, Barons Bolton, no 77; Pelham-Clinton, later Pelham-Clinton-Hope, Dukes of Newcastle, no 81; Vane-Tempest-Stewart, Marquesses of Londonderry, no 110; Earls of Sandwich (Dorset Record Office D 45, NRA 5472), including records of the Bolton estates 1700-1879; correspondence of Sir William Pulteney (formerly Johnstone), 5th Bt (Huntington Library, San Marino, California); Webster of Battle Abbey (East Sussex Record Office BAT, Acc 4693), including Battle Abbey estate records 1858-1902 and Somerset (Bathwick and Wrington) estate accounts and vouchers 1870-81; Fisher and Sanders collection (Northamptonshire Record Office FS, NRA 22321), including Farrer of Ashley estate papers 18th-20th cent (FS 10).

[110] VANE-TEMPEST-STEWART, Marquesses of Londonderry

The Stewart family settled in the early seventeenth century in County Donegal, where Ballylawn became its seat. Alexander Stewart (1699-1781) married his cousin Mary, sister and heir of Sir Robert Cowan (d1738), through whom he inherited property in County Londonderry, and he also bought lands in County Down, acquiring the manors of Newtown and Comber in 1744. The County Down estates were extended by his son Robert (1739-1821), who built Mount Stewart, and who was created Baron Londonderry 1789, Viscount Castlereagh 1795, Earl of Londonderry 1796 and Marquess of Londonderry 1816.

The second Marquess (1769-1822), known for most of his political career as Lord Castlereagh, married in 1794 Amelia (or Emily), daughter and co-heir of the second Earl of Buckinghamshire (for the descent of her properties see Kerr, Marquesses of Lothian, no 58, and below, Addenda (Family Names A-K)). He was succeeded by his brother Charles (1778-1854), who in 1819 had married Frances Anne, daughter of Sir Henry Vane-Tempest, second Bt (1771-1813). She was heir through her father to the Vane and Tempest estates in County Durham (see below), and though her mother, *suo jure* Countess of Antrim, to Carnlough and

other properties in County Antrim. The County Durham estates descended to her son Lord Vane (see below), but the County Antrim properties, following the death of her grandson Lord Herbert Vane-Tempest in 1921, to the family of her daughter Frances, Duchess of Marlborough.

The Tempest family was of medieval origin in County Durham, and enlarged its estates by marriages with the Heath and Wharton families in 1642 and 1706 respectively. John Tempest (1710-76) purchased Wynyard and other estates, but his son John died without surviving issue in 1794, leaving his estates to his nephew Sir Henry Vane, later Vane-Tempest, second Bt, son of Sir Henry Vane, first Bt, of Long Newton, County Durham by his (Tempest's) sister Frances. Long Newton had been purchased in 1635 by Sir Henry Vane of Raby (see Vane, Barons Barnard, no 109), and settled on his second son George in 1640.

The third Marquess of Londonderry, having succeeded to the County Durham estates in right of his wife, added to them by purchase, the most notable acquisition being Seaham in 1821-2. Also in 1822 he bought Holdernesse (later Londonderry) House in London. On his death in 1854 the Irish estates passed to his son by his first marriage, as fourth Marquess, but the County Durham estates, after his second wife's death in 1865, to his son by her, George Vane (later Vane-Tempest) (1821-84). He succeeded his father as Earl Vane, by special remainder, and also succeeded as fifth Marquess to the Irish estates on the death of his half-brother in 1872. In 1846 he had married Mary, daughter and heir of Sir John Edwards, first Bt, of Garth and Plas Machynlleth (Montgomeryshire).

Following the death of the seventh Marquess in 1949 the County Durham estates passed to his son as eighth Marquess, and the Irish estates to his youngest daughter, Lady Mairi Bury. Londonderry House and the Welsh estates were sold (Plas Machynlleth being given to the town of Machynlleth).

Estates in 1883: Co Durham 12,823 acres, Montgomeryshire 7,399 acres, Merionethshire 2,685 acres, Co Down 23,554 acres, Co Londonderry 2,189 acres, Co Donegal 1,673 acres, total 50,323 acres worth £100,118 a year.

[a] Deeds for Cos Down and Donegal 17th-20th cent and Co Antrim 18th cent; wills; settlements and related trust accounts and papers 18th-20th cent, mainly Stewart family; legal papers 18th-20th cent, incl schedules, abstracts of title and Irish Land Commission papers; Irish estate records (Cos Down, Donegal and Londonderry) 17th-20th cent (mainly early 18th cent onwards), incl leases 17th-19th cent (mainly Co Down), tenancy papers, maps and plans, rentals and accounts, corresp and letter books 19th-20th cent, and papers rel to prop-

erty in Newtownards and Comber (Co Down); papers rel to roads and sea banks early 19th cent, proposed reclamation of Strangford Lough early 19th cent, lead mining 1780-1867, Craiganu (Co Down) slate quarry 1807-18 and Mount Stewart home farm 19th-20th cent; moss books 1796-1893; papers rel to Mount Stewart 18th-19th cent, incl drawings for stables by James Wyatt *c*1780-3, building accounts and vouchers 1805, inventories and catalogues, household accounts and vouchers, and garden papers 20th cent; drawings for ?a new house at Wynyard by James Gibbs *c*1740-6.

Co Down lieutenancy papers 19th cent, incl live and dead stock returns 1803; Co Down election papers 18th-19th cent; papers rel to the borough of Newtownards 19th cent, with report on markets 1861; Stewart family commissions and appointments 18th-19th cent; Stewart family corresp and papers 18th-20th cent, incl business papers of Alexander Stewart (1699-1781), and papers of the 2nd, 3rd, 6th and 7th Marquesses, Frances Anne, Marchioness of Londonderry, Theresa, Marchioness of Londonderry (1856-1919) and Edith, Marchioness of Londonderry (1879-1959); Indian corresp and papers of Sir Robert Cowan mainly 1720-35; political and other papers of the 1st Viscount Chaplin (father-in-law of the 7th Marquess) late 19th-early 20th cent; Newtownards Agricultural Society subscription book 1860-2; Newtownards cotton yarn spinner's book 1807-11.

Public Record Office of Northern Ireland (D 654, 2846, 3030, 3099). Deposited by Edith, Marchioness of Londonderry and Lady Mairi Bury 1954-76. HMC *Papers of British Cabinet Ministers 1782-1900*, 1982, pp12, 61-2; *Private Papers of British Diplomats 1782-1900*, 1985, pp64, 68; *Papers of British Politicians 1782-1900*, 1989, pp105-6. NRA 12865, 19803, 25609, 28860.

[b] Deeds, trust papers and legal papers 1812-*c*1880 (*c*11 bundles), incl 2nd Marquess of Londonderry decd.

Public Record Office of Northern Ireland (D 665). Deposited by Galway, McIlwaine & Seeds, solicitors, Belfast. *Deputy Keeper's Report 1954-59*, pp46-7.

[c] Legal and case papers rel to the Co Down and Co Londonderry estates 1678-1918.

Public Record Office of Northern Ireland (D 2364). Transferred from the Public Record Office of Ireland. *Deputy Keeper's Report 1966-72*, p200.

[d] Corresp and papers of the Revd John Cleland as trustee for the Londonderry estates (particularly Comber) late 18th-early 19th cent, with papers rel to the United Irishmen 1797-1801.

Public Record Office of Northern Ireland (D 714, 3232). Deposited by RC Lytton-White and Mrs J Rea. *Deputy Keeper's Report 1954-59*, p65, *1976-9*, pp152-3.

[e] Corresp and papers of the Revd Mark Cassidy as agent for the Londonderry estates in Co Down *c*1810-39, incl corresp on election matters.

Public Record Office of Northern Ireland (D 1088). Deposited by Captain FP Cassidi. *Deputy Keeper's Report 1954-59*, p31.

[f] Co Down and Co Donegal maps and surveys 1824-48; misc papers 1810-*c*1860, incl receipts for secret service payments to Lord Castlereagh 1810.

In private possession. Copies in Public Record Office of Northern Ireland (T 1536). *Deputy Keeper's Report 1954-59*, p64.

[g] Deeds late 12th-20th cent, mainly Co Durham; wills, settlements and related trusteeship and executorship papers 16th-20th cent, mainly Vane, Tempest, Heath, Vane-Tempest-Stewart and related families, incl 2nd Earl of Buckinghamshire (d1793) and Caroline, Countess of Buckinghamshire (d1817); legal and case papers 18th-20th cent; Seaham and Dawdon (Co Durham) manorial records 1712-1809; Co Durham (Wynyard, Long Newton and Seaham) estate records 17th-20th cent (mainly 19th-20th cent), incl leases and agreements, surveys and maps, rentals and accounts, reports, agents' corresp, and papers rel to enclosure, tithes, churches and livings, schools 1858-1929, purchases and sales, Wynyard home farm 1834-1950, Wynyard and Long Newton tileries mid-19th cent, Vane and Seaham iron works mid-19th cent, and shipping 1857-1903; Co Durham colliery papers 17th-20th cent (mainly 1800 onwards), incl leases, wayleave agreements, valuations, plans, reports, accounts, and records of Londonderry Collieries Ltd 1864-1953; papers rel to Seaham foreshore, harbour and urban development mainly 1822-20th cent; misc Mount Stewart estate accounts and papers 19th cent; Carnlough estate papers mid-19th cent; Plas Machynlleth estate rentals and accounts 1906-51, with corresp rel to sales 1945-51; papers rel to Fulham (Middlesex) leasehold estate 1829-50 and to Springfield and Ranksborough (Rutland) estate 1919-38.

Papers rel to Wynyard Park *c*1819-1950, incl building papers, inventories, household accounts, and garden and stable accounts; papers rel to Seaham Hall 19th cent, incl accounts and cellar books, and to Holdernesse (later Londonderry) House 1822-1950, incl papers rel to alterations 1823-32, inventories 1857-1950 and accounts; papers rel to Garron Tower (Co Antrim) mid-19th cent; inventories of Rogerley (Co Durham: Maddison family) 1647 and Blickling (Norfolk: Earl of

Buckinghamshire) 1793; papers rel to Wynyard Park stud c1875-1951 and shooting 1821-1937; papers rel to Kepier grammar school, Houghton-le-Spring (Co Durham) 19th cent.

Appointments and commissions 18th-20th cent; Vane family papers 17th-early 19th cent, incl accounts of the Revd Sir Henry Vane (d1794) as Treasurer of Durham Cathedral 1763-5; diplomatic and other papers of the 2nd Marquess of Londonderry; diplomatic, political and business corresp and papers of the 3rd Marquess; misc Vane-Tempest-Stewart family papers 19th-20th cent, incl papers of the 5th, 6th and 7th Marquesses, Frances Anne, Marchioness of Londonderry, Theresa, Marchioness of Londonderry and Edith, Marchioness of Londonderry; papers of Sir John Duck, mayor of Durham, and Ralph Clerke, of Sunderland, coal fitter late 17th cent; papers of the 1st Viscount Chaplin as executor of the 3rd Duke of Sutherland (d1892); papers of John Buddle (1773-1843), agent and colliery viewer 1818-43; Seaham Colliery Explosion Fund records 1880-1930.

Durham County Record Office (D/LO). Deposited by the 8th and 9th Marquesses of Londonderry and others 1963-87. HMC *Papers of British Cabinet Ministers 1782-1900*, 1982, pp12, 61-2; *Private Papers of British Diplomats 1782-1900*, 1985, pp64, 68; *Papers of British Politicians 1782-1900*, 1989, pp105-6. NRA 11528.

[h] Co Durham deeds, trust papers and legal papers 1699-1873.

Durham County Record Office (D/X915). Given by Denton Hall Burgin & Warren, solicitors, London, through the British Records Association 1990. NRA 18297.

[i] Legal papers rel to Londonderry Collieries Ltd 1916-39.

Durham County Record Office (D/X784). Deposited by Warrens, solicitors, London, through the British Records Association 1985. NRA 18927.

[j] Gilligate (or Gilesgate) (Durham) manorial records 1634-1964.

Durham County Record Office (D/X790). Deposited by Longden, Mann & Wright, solicitors, Seaham 1985. NRA 28524.

[k] Montgomeryshire and Merionethshire deeds 16th-19th cent; wills and settlements 18th-19th cent, Edwards, Owen and Herbert; Montgomeryshire and Merionethshire estate records 18th-20th cent, incl leases, maps and plans, rentals and accounts 1848-1921, and papers rel to tithes, timber, lime-burning and sheepwalks; papers rel to slate quarrying 19th cent and to lead mining 19th-early 20th cent; patent and grant of arms, Sir John Edwards 1838; legal precedent book 17th cent.

National Library of Wales. Deposited by the 7th and 8th Marquesses of Londonderry 1940-1, 1952. *Annual Report 1940-1*, p21. NRA 28748.

[l] Plas Machynlleth account book 1879-97.

National Library of Wales (Henry Evans (Machynlleth) records, no 348). Deposited by Henry Evans, solicitor, Machynlleth 1981-2. NRA 38540.

[m] Misc family papers 1805-1957, incl corresp and papers of the 3rd Marquess and papers of H Montgomery Hyde as private secretary to the 7th Marquess.

Public Record Office of Northern Ireland (D 3084/C). Deposited 1991, 1995 following the deaths of H Montgomery Hyde and his widow. NRA 40370.

Related collections: Kerr, Marquesses of Lothian, no 58, including Bellaghy (Co Londonderry) estate papers 1811-42 and family correspondence of Amelia, Marchioness of Londonderry; Marquesses Camden (Centre for Kentish Studies U 840, NRA 8410), including family correspondence of Frances, Marchioness of Londonderry; Earls of Antrim (Public Record Office of Northern Ireland D 2977, NRA 28832), including Carnlough estate records 1835-1920; further papers of John Buddle (Durham County Record Office NCB 1/JB, NRA 19490); Seaham Harbour Dock Co Records 1898-1979 (Durham County Record Office D/SHD, NRA 29256).

[111] VERNEY, Barons Willoughby de Broke

The Verney family was established at Bramshall (Staffordshire) in the thirteenth century but settled at Compton Verney (Warwickshire) in the fifteenth century. Sir Richard Verney (d1630) married Margaret, sister and co-heir of Sir Fulke Greville, first Baron Brooke and *de jure* fifth Baron Willoughby de Broke. Through this marriage were inherited properties in Cambridgeshire (Steeple Morden, Long Stanton), Gloucestershire (Tytherington), Hertfordshire (Cottered), Leicestershire (Kimcote and Walton), Lincolnshire (Frampton, Gayton-le-Marsh, Helpringham, Tothill), Somerset (Poyntington, later transferred to Dorset) and Staffordshire (Penkridge, Rodbaston). These estates formed part of the inheritance of Elizabeth, Baroness Willoughby de Broke, who married Sir Fulke Greville, grandfather of the first Baron Brooke, in 1526, and derived from the families of Willoughby, Cheyney, Latimer and Champernowne. (For other Willoughby estates, including moieties of the Lincolnshire, Gloucestershire and Staffordshire properties, see Greville, Earls Brooke and Earls of Warwick, no 45, and, for the west country estates, Orde-Powlett, Barons Bolton, no 77.)

William Verney of Compton Verney died unmarried in 1683, being succeeded by his great-uncle Sir Richard Verney (1621-1711) of Allexton (Leicestershire) and Belton (Rutland), who secured the revival of the peerage as eleventh Baron Willoughby de Broke. The twelfth Baron married in 1683 Margaret, daughter of Sir Robert Heath (1575-1649), Chief Justice. The sixteenth Baron married in 1829 a daughter of Sir John Williams, first Bt, of Boddelwyddan (Anglesey).

Margaret Peyto of Chesterton (Warwickshire) (d1746) left estates in Warwickshire and a property in Northamptonshire (Sulby and Buckby) to the Verney family. The Warwickshire estates were also consolidated in the early nineteenth century, when the Cambridgeshire, Gloucestershire and Hertfordshire estates were sold and the Lincolnshire and Somerset holdings reduced. The remaining outlying estates were sold in 1906-9, and Compton Verney itself in 1921.

Estates in 1883: Warwicks 12,621 acres, Lincs 2,930 acres, Northants 929 acres, Somerset 588 acres, Staffs 555 acres, Leics 126 acres, Anglesey 396 acres, total 18,145 acres worth £23,915 a year.

[a] Deeds 12th-19th cent, mainly Warwicks but incl a few for Cambs 15th-early 18th cent, Northants, Staffs and other counties; Verney and Peyto wills, settlements and trust deeds and papers mainly 16th-20th cent; inquisitions *post mortem* 1425-1656; Willoughby family deeds 1296-1542; Heath settlements 17th cent; legal and case papers 14th-20th cent, mainly Warwicks; Warwicks manorial court records 13th-20th cent (Compton Verney, Kingston in Chesterton, Sowe in Coventry, etc); Warwicks estate records 14th-19th cent, incl leases, surveys, maps and plans, rentals, accounts, Chesterton glebe and tithe papers 1556-1664, Lighthorne enclosure papers 1720s and turnpike accounts 1770-91; misc rentals, accounts, etc for Leics, Lincs, Northants and Staffs estates 16th-19th cent; papers rel to sale of land in Cambs, Herts and Somerset early 19th cent, house in Richmond (Surrey) 1829-30 and land in Lincs 1855-6; papers rel to Otford (Kent) rectory and tithes 1747-1840.

Chesterton House (Peyto family) building papers 1657-62, with Compton Verney and Chesterton inventories, drawings, catalogues, etc 17th-19th cent; Warwicks shrievalty papers 16th-19th cent and taxation papers early 17th cent; Verney and Peyto appointments, commissions, etc mainly 16th-18th cent; Verney family corresp and papers 16th-19th cent, incl papers rel to John Verney's resignation as Master of the Rolls 1741; Peyto papers 16th-18th cent, incl artillery accounts of Sir E Peyto 1642-3; Heath family appointments, accounts and papers 1599-1685.

Shakespeare Birthplace Trust Records Office (DR 98). Deposited by the 19th and 20th Barons Willoughby de Broke 1914-71. NRA 2638.

[b] Warwicks deeds late 16th-20th cent, mainly 18th-19th cent, with related legal and misc estate papers; deeds and related papers for Gloucs, Kent, Leics, Lincs, Northants, Staffs and Surrey estates 18th-20th cent; trust deeds and papers 18th-20th cent, incl settlement 1793 and will 1859.

Shakespeare Birthplace Trust Records Office. (DR 622, 636, 951). Deposited by Boodle, Hatfield & Co, solicitors, London, through the British Records Association 1987, 1988, 1997. NRA 2638.

[c] Estate accounts (incl out-county properties) 1868, 1894 (2 vols).

Shakespeare Birthplace Trust Records Office (DR 956). Presented by HJR Wing 1997.

[d] Misc deeds and legal papers 14th-19th cent, mainly Warwicks; misc manorial and estate papers rel to Sowe in Coventry and its sale 1655-1853.

Warwickshire County Record Office (CR 556). Deposited by Campbell, Brown & Ledbrook, solicitors, Warwick 1958. NRA 11903.

[e] Cottered deeds and legal papers 14th-early 19th cent; Cottered manorial records 1307-1727.

Hertfordshire Archives and Local Studies (Acc 223). Deposited by the 20th Baron Willoughby de Broke through Boodle, Hatfield & Co. NRA 9299.

[f] Manorial court records, Stone Hall in Frampton and Helpringham with Bicker 1729-1925, with related papers 18th-19th cent.

Lincolnshire Archives (Acc 88/55). Deposited by Boodle, Hatfield & Co, solicitors, London, through the British Records Association 1988. NRA 33269.

[g] Deeds 13th-19th cent, some for Warwicks (Chesterton) but mainly for outlying properties, incl Cambs 13th-17th cent, Gloucs 13th-early 19th cent, Herts 13th cent-c1600, Kent (Brasted, etc) 14th-18th cent, Leics (Kimcote, Allexton, etc) 13th-17th cent, Lincs 13th-18th cent, Northants 14th-early 19th cent, Somerset 14th-18th cent and Staffs (Bramshall, Penkridge, etc) 13th-18th cent; manorial court records 13th-18th cent, incl Steeple Morden (Cambs) 1280-1437, Tytherington (Gloucs) 1343-1622, Kimcote (Leics) 14th-18th cent, Lincs (Frampton Stone Hall, Helpringham with Bicker, etc) 14th-18th cent, Stepney and Hackney (Middlesex) 15th-16th cent, Poyntington 1560-1636 and Warwicks 14th-15th cent; estate papers 16th-early 19th cent, Gloucs, Leics, Lincs and Somerset, incl surveys

and rentals; misc estate papers for Cambs and Staffs 15th-17th cent, and for Kent, Middlesex and Rutland (Heath estates) 17th cent.

Inventories, Rolls House (London) 1741 and Heath family mainly 17th cent; commissions, etc 1549-1723, Verney, Greville and Heath families, incl appointment of Fulke Greville as Treasurer of the Navy 1598; account book of the 14th Baron as churchwarden of St George's Hanover Square (Middlesex) 1769-70; Heath family papers 17th cent, incl papers of Sir Robert Heath as Chief Justice, sequestration papers 1643-52, papers of Sir Edward Heath rel to Rutland affairs and papers of Sir John Heath as Treasurer of the Inner Temple and JP, etc, for Kent; account roll, Countess of Norfolk *c*1377; roll of Common Pleas in Rutland 1386-7.

British Library, Manuscript Collections (Eg Ch 645-2116, Eg MSS 2978-3008, 3779). Purchased from the 19th and 20th Barons Willoughby de Broke 1917, 1966.

[h] Case papers rel to the Cambs properties 1590-1616; rentals and accounts 1721-30, incl Cambs, Herts, Leics, Lincs and Northants.

Warwickshire County Record Office (CR 1987). Deposited by the Society of Genealogists 1980. NRA 3519. (Apparently left in the hands of the Revd J Harvey Bloom following the selection of MSS by the British Museum in 1917, and given by him to the Society of Genealogists. See also [i]-[n] below.)

[i] Willoughby de Broke legal and trust deeds and papers 17th-18th cent, with Kimcote and Walton legal papers 16th-18th cent; legal and estate papers, Allexton and Brasted (John Verney) 17th-18th cent, and Cottesmore (Rutland) and Horninghold (Leics) (Heath family) 17th cent.

Leicestershire Record Office (DG 8/69-146). Deposited with Leicestershire County Council by the Society of Genealogists 1940. NRA 6099.

[j] Lincs deeds 15th-18th cent (Helpringham, etc); case papers 1723-31; surveys 1680 (Frampton), 1855 (all Lincs estates); Heath family corresp and papers rel to their North Ingelby (Lincs) estate 17th cent.

Lincolnshire Archives. Deposited in the Lindsey Muniment Room by the Society of Genealogists 1940. *Archivists' Report 8*, 1956-7, pp16-18.

[k] Deeds and related papers 16th-19th cent, mainly Northants; survey of Long Buckby 1596 and of Coton 17th cent; rentals, Long Buckby 1742, Long Stanton 1726, Cottered 1731, 1736, Kimcote 1729 and Scredington (Lincs) 1727.

Northamptonshire Record Office (Acc 1940/33). Acquired by Northamptonshire Record Society 1940, probably from the Society of Genealogists. NRA 4039.

[l] Misc Northants (Verney) deeds and papers 16th-early 19th cent, incl Coton and Ravensthorpe manorial court roll 1721 and estate accounts (with other properties in Cambs, Herts, Leics and Lincs) 1744, 1750; Heath family legal papers, estate papers and corresp 17th cent, mainly rel to the Colleyweston (Northants) estate.

Northamptonshire Record Office (Acc 1962/51; NPL 1337-1465). Deposited by Northampton Public Library 1962. NRA 25682.

[m] Misc Staffs deeds 16th-18th cent and manorial records (Bramshall, etc) 1538-1611; misc Staffs estate records 15th-early 19th cent, incl rentals 1668, 1729, 1796-7 and accounts 1487-8, 1574; misc legal and family papers 16th-17th cent, incl honour of Tutbury receivers' accounts 1648, 1684-5.

Staffordshire and Stoke on Trent Archive Service, Staffordshire Record Office (D 1553). Deposited by the Society of Genealogists 1940. NRA 3516.

[n] Northbourne (Kent) stewards' accounts (Heath family) 1667-72; Otford tithe accounts 1821-38.

Centre for Kentish Studies (U 1542/E 2-3). Deposited by the Society of Genealogists 1972. NRA 3509.

[o] Legal, estate and family corresp and papers 17th-early 18th cent, Heath family, incl papers rel to Otford rectory and the Brasted estate.

Centre for Kentish Studies (U 55/E100-104). HW Knocker collection. NRA 5406.

[p] Heath family papers 17th cent, incl papers of Sir Robert Heath.

University of Illinois Library, Urbana. PM Hamer, ed, *A guide to archives and manuscripts in the United States*, 1961, p170. Hodgson's, 2 June 1950, lot 429.

[q] Political corresp of the 19th Baron Willoughby de Broke mainly 1907-20.

House of Lords Record Office (Historical Collection 142). Deposited by the 20th Baron 1973. NRA 21684.

Related collection: Greville, Earls Brooke and Earls of Warwick, no 45.

[112] VYNER of Gautby and Newby

The Vyner family was settled in Gloucestershire in the early sixteenth century. Sir Robert Vyner

(1631-88), third son of William Vyner of Eathorpe (Warwickshire) and an eminent London goldsmith, was created a baronet in 1666 and was Lord Mayor in 1675. He bought estates in Lincolnshire, Cheshire, Leicestershire and London, which descended to his nephew Thomas. The Leicestershire and London estates were later sold, but the Gautby (Lincolnshire) and Bidston (Cheshire) estates were retained until the twentieth century.

Henry Vyner (1805-61), younger brother of Robert Vyner of Gautby (1789-1872), married in 1832 Mary, daughter of Thomas Robinson, third Baron Grantham and second Earl De Grey (see Robinson, Marquesses of Ripon, no 89). On the death of Lord De Grey in 1859 Lady Mary Vyner inherited the Robinson property of Askrigg (Yorkshire, North Riding), together with a half-interest in the Clifton estate near York (North Riding). She also inherited Yorkshire properties that had come to the Robinsons from the Weddell family of Newby Hall, principally the Newby (West Riding) estate but including Huntington (North Riding), Leppington and Barthorpe (East Riding), and a small part of the Craven (Wigglesworth, etc) estate in the West Riding. (For the major portion of the Craven estate and the other half-share in the Clifton estate see Cowper, Earls Cowper, no 25.)

In 1872 Henry Frederick Clare Vyner (1836-83), son of Henry and Lady Mary Vyner, inherited the Vyner estates from his uncle Robert. Gautby was demolished, and Newby Hall became the principal Vyner seat. HFC Vyner was succeeded by his brother Robert Charles de Grey Vyner (1842-1915), and he in turn by his daughter Mary Evelyn, who in 1886 had married Lord Alwyne Compton, third son of the fourth Marquess of Northampton (see Compton, Marquesses of Northampton, no 24). The Lincolnshire and Clifton estates were sold in 1918-20.

Lord Alwyne Compton, later Compton-Vyner, had inherited the Torloisk (Mull, Argyllshire) and Kirkness (Kinross-shire) estates from his father in 1897. In the twentieth century they appear to have passed to his eldest grandson Alwyne Compton, who in 1945 took the name of Farquharson on succeeding to his mother's Invercauld (Aberdeenshire) estate, whilst his younger brother Robert Compton succeeded to Newby.

Estates in 1883: HFC Vyner: Lincs 14,443 acres, Yorks WR and NR 9,039 acres, Cheshire 3,223 acres, total 26,705 acres worth £37,693 a year; Cowper and Vyner: Yorks NR 496 acres (the Clifton estate) worth £2,198 a year; Marquess of Northampton: Argyllshire 8,000 acres, Kinross-shire 864 acres, total 8,864 acres worth £2,465 a year.

[a] Yorks WR and NR deeds 12th-20th cent, Weddell and Robinson; deeds for other counties 14th-19th cent, mainly Vyner, incl Lincs 14th-19th cent, Gloucs 14th-18th cent, Cheshire 17th-19th cent and London and Middlesex 16th-18th cent; wills, settlements and related papers 16th-19th cent, mainly Vyner and Robinson, incl Sir Robert Vyner decd c1665-1712, Colonel William Robinson decd 1739-42 and the Hon George Pelham (of Barnoldby-le-Beck, Lincs) decd 1835; legal and case papers 16th-20th cent, Vyner, Robinson and Weddell, incl the Earl of Derby's claim on the Bidston estate 1650-1805; manorial court records 15th-18th cent, incl Swanland (Yorks ER) 15th-16th cent and Bidston 1706-80.

Yorks WR and NR (Newby Hall, etc: Weddell, later Robinson) estate records 16th-20th cent, incl surveys from 16th cent, maps and plans, rentals and accounts, corresp, enclosure papers, Huntington tithe accounts 1860-91 and other tithe papers 19th-20th cent; Yorks NR and WR (Newby Park, Clifton, Askrigg, etc: Robinson) estate records 16th-20th cent, incl leases 18th cent, surveys from 1600, maps and plans, rentals and accounts, and papers rel to Newby and Dishforth woods 18th cent, Clifton enclosure 1762 and Worton (NR) fee-farm rents 17th-18th cent; papers for the Elcock (later Weddell) family's estates near York c1695-1715; Lincs and Cheshire estate records 17th-20th cent, incl surveys and valuations, maps, rentals, accounts, vouchers, and papers rel to Birkenhead docks (Cheshire); papers rel to Newby Hall and Givendale (WR) farms and Fairfield, Newby and Thornton-le-Street (NR) studs 19th-20th cent; papers rel to Newby Hall 18th-20th cent, incl papers rel to repairs and alterations, inventories, household accounts, and garden papers 19th-20th cent; papers rel to Newby Park and ? York town house (Robinson) mainly 18th cent; schedule of furniture, Swakeleys (Middlesex: Vyner) 1741; Strensall (Yorks NR: Robinson) plans 1695; accounts and papers for Fairfield, Coombe Hurst (Surrey), London house and Cannes late 19th-early 20th cent.

Yorks NR militia papers 17th cent; papers rel to York 17th-18th cent, mainly Robinson family, incl elections, Navigation and Assembly Room; papers rel to Topcliffe (NR) church and advowson 16th-18th cent, Dishforth chapel 17th-18th cent and Skelton (WR) parish 19th-20th cent; City of London port books 1717-19 (3 vols); commissions and appointments 17th-19th cent, Vyner and Robinson; Vyner family papers 17th-early 20th cent, incl business papers of Sir Robert Vyner (d1688) and game books 1875-1948; Robinson family corresp and papers 17th-19th cent, incl naval papers of Sir Tancred Robinson early 18th cent, continental journal 1683 and family corresp 1736-67; Weddell family accounts and corresp late 17th-18th cent; papers of John Aislabie as Treasurer of the Navy 1714-26; genealogical (Vyner and Robinson), literary and misc MSS, incl Whitby Abbey voucher book *c*1470.

West Yorkshire Archive Service, Leeds (Newby Hall collection). Deposited 1957-88. West Yorkshire Archive Service, *Report 1988-9*, p91. NRA 5836.

[b] Misc legal and estate papers *c*1697-1853, incl 2nd Earl of Hardwicke executorship account 1790-7, Duke of Kent estate terriers and rentals 1697-1716, De Grey (Yorks NR and WR) estate accounts 1829-44 and Baldersby (Yorks NR: Duke of Devonshire, later De Grey) estate papers 1789-1844.

West Yorkshire Archive Service, Leeds (Acc 2718). From the offices of Nicholl, Manisty & Co, solicitors, London. Purchased 1984 (Phillips's, 16 Feb, lot 445). NRA 5836.

[c] Yorks NR (Worton, etc) deeds 17th-18th cent; Worton, etc legal and case papers mainly 17th-18th cent; Wensleydale (Worton, etc) estate papers early 17th cent-1770, incl leases, rentals and accounts; misc accounts and vouchers for other Robinson (Yorks NR) properties *c*1754-70.

West Yorkshire Archive Service, Leeds (Acc 3646). Deposited by Birch Cullimore & Co in Cheshire Record Office 1969 (DBC Acc 1621) and transferred 1992. NRA 41227.

[d] Yorks NR deeds 16th-18th cent (Huntington, etc); Yorks NR and WR manorial papers (Huntington, Swinefleet, etc) 1616-1850.

North Yorkshire County Record Office. Transferred from Cheshire Record Office *c*1965-6. NRA 38114.

[e] Clifton and York deeds 16th-18th cent; legal and case papers 16th-18th cent, Robinson family; Yorks NR (Robinson) estate papers 1592-1773, mainly Clifton but some for the Newby (near Topcliffe) estate, incl leases 1610-1732, lease register 1611-40, rentals (Newby, Rawcliffe, etc) and papers rel to tithes, manorial incidents and fee-farm rents.

York City Archives Department (YC/AE). Presented by Lady Alwyne Compton-Vyner and Lady Lucas *c*1919. NRA 11988.

[f] Architectural drawings for Newby Hall, gardens and estate buildings 18th-19th cent, incl designs by William Belwood and Robert Adam; drawings rel to Gautby (Lincs) 18th-early 19th cent, Bidston early 19th cent and Wrest Park (Beds) before 1833; misc designs by Thomas Robinson and others 18th cent.

In private possession. Enquiries to the District Archivist, West Yorkshire Archive Service, Leeds.

[g] Deeds and legal and case papers, mainly Cheshire 17th-20th cent but incl Yorks ER, NR and WR 18th-20th cent and London, Middlesex and Surrey late 19th-early 20th cent; Vyner settlements and trust papers 19th-20th cent; misc Bidston and Upton (Cheshire) manorial records 18th-19th cent; Cheshire estate papers mainly 19th-20th cent, incl leases and agreements, maps and plans, and papers rel to enclosure, tithes, Wirral railways, Birkenhead docks, Wallasey embankment, Bidston Hill residential development and sales; Yorks estate survey ?19th cent; Lincs estate papers early 19th cent-1920, incl maps, accounts and sale papers; papers rel to contents of Newby Hall 1915-23.

Cheshire Record Office (DBC, Accs 1063, 3298, 4710, 4855, 5434). Deposited by Birch Cullimore & Co, solicitors, Chester 1963-97. NRA 38114.

[h] Particulars of Cheshire estates *c*1885-1926, with maps and plans late 19th-early 20th cent.

Cheshire Record Office (D 1719, 2797). Deposited by Denton Clark & Co, surveyors and land agents, Chester 1971, 1980. NRA 40342. A survey of Bidston 1665 (formerly Studley Royal MS 5539) remains in the custody of the firm (copy in Cheshire Record Office, Acc 4938).

[i] Lincs (Vyner) deeds, wills and settlements 17th-19th cent; Lincs estate records 1685-1921 (mainly early 19th-early 20th cent), incl surveys and plans 19th cent, rent ledger and accounts early 20th cent, Sotby enclosure award 1804 and Strubby tithe account book 1805-16; Yorks (Vyner) estate papers late 19th cent, with Leppington, etc (Yorks ER) survey 1846.

Lincolnshire Archives (Acc 88/112, 92/60). Deposited by Birch Cullimore & Co in Cheshire Record Office and transferred 1988, 1992.

[j] Torloisk legal and estate papers 17th cent-1889, with Carslogie (Fife: Clephane family) deeds and papers 15th cent-1889 and trust papers (Clephane and Compton) 19th cent.

In private possession. Enquiries to the National Register of Archives (Scotland) (NRA(S) 3283). NRA 34746.

[k] Torloisk estate papers 1871-90.

National Archives of Scotland (GD 314). Deposited by Strathern & Blair, WS, Edinburgh 1975. *Annual Report 1976*, p18. NRA 12629.

[l] Kirkness legal papers 1667-1826.

National Archives of Scotland (GD 1/49).

[m] Papers of Sir Robert Vyner as Goldsmith to the King 1677-90 (3 items).

Victoria and Albert Museum, National Art Library (nos 20, 25-6). NRA 13466.

Related collections: De Grey, Barons Lucas, no 28; Robinson, Marquesses of Ripon, no 89; Compton, Marquesses of Northampton, no 24; Ramsden (later Pennington-Ramsden) of Byram (West Yorkshire Archive Service, Leeds, NRA 7344), including family correspondence of William Weddell *c*1771-92.

[113] WENTWORTH-FITZWILLIAM, Earls Fitzwilliam

The Wentworth family owned Wentworth Woodhouse and Hooton Roberts (Yorkshire, West Riding) by the fourteenth century, and extended its West Riding property by purchase (Barbot Hall 1525, Brampton Bierlow 1606, Newhall 1610, etc) and by marriage, notably that of Thomas Wentworth (d1579) to Margaret, daughter of Sir William Gascoigne, which brought estates at Gawthorpe, Cusworth and elsewhere. Sir William Wentworth was created a baronet 1611 and his son Thomas (executed 1641) was made successively Baron Wentworth 1628, Viscount Wentworth 1629 and Earl of Strafford 1640. Strafford owned extensive Irish estates, mainly in County Wicklow (Shillelagh), County Kildare (Naas), and County Wexford.

At the second Earl's death in 1695 the Wentworth estates passed to his nephew Thomas Watson (afterwards Watson-Wentworth), a younger son of the second Baron Rockingham. He bought estates at Malton (Yorkshire, North Riding) in 1713 and Great Harrowden and Higham Ferrers (Northamptonshire) in 1695, which were extended by his son, created Earl of Malton 1736 and Marquess of Rockingham 1746. Property at Barmby Moor (Yorkshire, East Riding) was added to the Malton estate and further acquisitions, including Barnbrough 1736 and the former Rokeby family possessions at Hoyland (bought *c*1704) and Skyers (bought 1756), were made in the West Riding. The estates of the Bright family near Sheffield (Yorkshire, West Riding) came through the marriage of the second Marquess to Mary Bright in 1752. They had been accumulated in the seventeenth century by Stephen Bright of Carbrook (d1642), whose acquisitions included Ecclesall and Westwell, and his son Sir John Bright (d1688), who bought Badsworth (in 1652) and other West Riding properties.

On the second Marquess of Rockingham's death without issue in 1782 the marquessate lapsed and his estates were inherited by his nephew the fourth Earl Fitzwilliam. However, when the fifth Earl Fitzwilliam died in 1857 his estates were divided, the former Watson-Wentworth properties passing to his elder son the sixth Earl and the former Fitzwilliam properties to his younger son George Wentworth Fitzwilliam of Milton (see Wentworth-Fitzwilliam of Milton no 114). Badsworth (Yorkshire, West Riding) was sold by the sixth Earl *c*1858-9 but the seventh Earl

bought the former Childers family property at Cantley (Yorkshire, West Riding) in 1903-5 and an estate at Wansford (Northamptonshire) from the Duke of Bedford in 1904.

Estates in 1883: Yorks E, N and WR 22,192 acres, Northants 881 acres, Cambs 522 acres, Derbys 308 acres, Hunts 75 acres, Lincs 17 acres, Co Wicklow 89,891 acres, Co Kildare 1,532 acres, Co Wexford 325 acres, total 115,743 acres worth £138,801 a year.

[a] Deeds 12th-20th cent, mainly Yorks WR, with some for Derbys, Essex, Middlesex, Notts, etc; Irish (Strafford) deeds 17th cent; Debden family cartulary (Yorks and Essex estates) 14th cent; inquisitions *post mortem* 14th-17th cent, incl Sir John Fitzwilliam 1418; wills, settlements, executorship and trust papers and legal and financial papers 13th-20th cent, mainly Wentworth, Watson-Wentworth, Bright and Fitzwilliam families, incl Hawkesworth family wills and settlements 16th-17th cent, and executorship papers for the 1st and 2nd Marquesses of Rockingham, the 8th Earl of Shrewsbury *c*1599-1629, Thomas Wentworth of North Elmsall 1677 and Sir Richard Hawkesworth (d1657); legal papers for the families of Gill of Carrhouse and Rokeby of Skellow (both Yorks WR) 17th-18th cent and for the Childers family 17th-19th cent; Yorks WR (Tinsley, Wath-upon-Dearne, Wentworth, etc) manorial records 13th-19th cent; Tickhill (Yorks WR) honour fine roll 1404; Bury, Offham and Wepham (Sussex) manorial court records 1654.

Yorks WR (Wentworth Woodhouse) estate records 15th-20th cent, mainly from mid-18th cent, incl maps (many by William Fairbank senior, d1754, and junior, d1801), rentals, accounts, vouchers, wood accounts 1747-64, and papers rel to enclosure, tithes and canals; records of WR collieries (Elsecar, Lowood, etc) and industrial undertakings 18th-20th cent; farm records 1743-20th cent, incl cropping books from *c*1844; Wentworth Woodhouse stud papers *c*1751-80 and Doncaster and York stables vouchers 1783-1821; Bright of Badsworth estate papers 16th-18th cent, incl Badsworth plan and rental 1632, Handsworth colliery accounts *c*1649-83, lead trade papers mid-17th cent, and Badsworth rectory tithe book 1699-1728; Cantley (Yorks WR and Notts) estate papers mainly 19th-20th cent, incl building leases and mineral extraction papers.

Malton (Yorks NR) leases and estate papers 18th-19th cent; Higham Ferrers (Northants) estate papers *c*1750-1824, 1894-1906 and Milton (Northants) estate corresp 1831-8; Irish estate accounts and papers 18th-19th cent, with survey *c*1655; Sheffield (Yorks WR) estate papers (Bright family as agents) *c*1619-52, incl accounts of the Countess of Kent's property 1652; corresp of John Staniforth, Sheffield agent of the Howard family 1652; Ravenfield (Yorks WR) estate accounts 1829-45; misc estate papers 16th-19th cent, incl Eckington, Edale and Mosborough (Derbys) leases 17th-18th cent, Eaton (Notts) timber valuations 1745-6, and Yorks WR estate papers of the Hawkesworth, Ingram and Wentworth of North Elmsall families 17th cent.

Wentworth Woodhouse household records 17th-20th cent, incl house and mausoleum building accounts 1744-91, house and garden plans 18th-19th cent, household accounts 1617-23, inventories and accounts from c1726 and cellar and stables accounts 1754-1858; other household papers 18th-20th cent, incl Coolattin (Co Wicklow) plans c1800, Malton (Yorks NR) inventory c1750 and records of Grosvenor Square, Parsons Green (Middlesex) and Wimbledon (Surrey) houses c1752-1805; misc Bright family house building and household papers 17th-18th cent, incl Ravensworth Castle (Co Durham) plans early 18th cent and Badsworth garden accounts 1756-61; Sheffield church building vouchers 1658; inventories, Sheffield manor house 1638, North Elmsall Hall 1650 and Carrhouse 1728.

Election records 17th-19th cent, mainly Yorks c1783-19th cent, Malton c1794-1808, York City c1753-1820 and Hull c1802-19, with some for Pontefract 1621, Peterborough 1767-8 and Northants and Cos Wicklow and Wexford 18th-19th cent; Yorks lieutenancy and militia papers 17th-19th cent, incl shrievalty accounts (William Wentworth) 1570-1 and records of WR militia, yeomanry and volunteers 1794-1861; papers rel to Yorks WR affairs 17th-19th cent, incl Ecclesall Bierlow poor book 1703-44, Sheffield rate books and civil parish papers 18th-19th cent, Bradfield, etc rate book 1777, Bradfield chapelry papers mid-17th cent, and papers for Carleton in Craven hospital c1712-22 and Bolsterstone and Hoober schools; Malton and Derwent navigation records 1750-1924; River Don navigation papers c1720-5; Rotherham and Wentworth Woodhouse turnpike records 1767-73, 1788-1829; York racecourse grandstand subscription book 1755; Grove and Rufford Hunt (Notts) accounts 1922-7; Shillelagh (Co Wicklow) workhouse returns 1848-55; Wicklow lighthouse papers 1817.

Pardons, patents and appointments 15th-18th cent; Wentworth, Watson-Wentworth, Bright and Fitzwilliam family corresp and papers 16th-20th cent, incl legal accounts 18th-19th cent, accounts of charitable donations 1804-56, and letters of Selina, Viscountess Milton and GS Foljambe mid-19th cent; political and other papers of 1st Earl of Strafford, incl French travel journal 1612; accounts and papers of the 1st and 2nd Marquesses of Rockingham, the 4th, 5th and 6th Earls Fitzwilliam, Viscount Milton (d1877), Stephen Bright (d1642) and Sir John Bright (d1688) (incl his papers as commissioner for disbanding the army 1660-1); papers of Sir Richard Hawkesworth (d1657), incl some as WR treasurer for lame soldiers

1637-8; political and family corresp and papers of Edmund Burke (d1797), with papers rel to an edition of his letters by Walker King (d1827); corresp of Sir John Wentworth (d1820), Governor of Nova Scotia, Sir Charles Wentworth (d1842), the 3rd Earl of Albemarle 1746-8, and Henry Joseph Wilson, MP 1895-1911; letter books of William Vassell of Boston (Massachusetts) 1769-98; genealogical, literary and misc papers 13th-20th cent, incl royal household ordinance book 1553, MS of Sir Edwin Sandys's *Europae Speculum* 1599, book of offices of the royal household and courts of record 1614, parliamentary journals 1610, 1625-7, and establishment lists 1719, 1734; treatises, handbills and pamphlets 17th-19th cent.

Sheffield Archives (WWM). Deposited by the 9th Earl Fitzwilliam 1949, the 10th Earl Fitzwilliam 1953, 1965, 1970, 1972 and 1974, and the trustees of the Wentworth Woodhouse estates 1986. NRA 1083, 2619, 7622. For the 2nd Marquess of Rockingham, Edmund Burke, Viscount Milton and the 4th, 5th and 6th Earls Fitzwilliam see also HMC *Papers of British Cabinet Ministers 1782-1900*, 1982, pp66, 68-9; *Papers of British Politicians 1782-1900*, 1989, pp16,110. The collection includes letters of the 4th and 5th Earls to Charles Sturgeon 1818-40 presented by Bath Library and Art Gallery 1963. Miscellaneous MSS (mainly untraced), numerous tracts and pamphlets 16th-18th cent and many books from Wentworth Woodhouse library were sold in 1948 (Sotheby's, 1 Mar, 26 Apr). Of these, the Russian letter book of Admiral Sir Charles Knowles (lot 614) was bought by the National Maritime Museum (LBK/80) in 1984 (Sotheby's, 10 May, lot 245), and a late 15th century MS of Cicero (lot 474) was acquired in 1948 for Yale University Library (WH Bond and CU Faye, *Supplement to the Census of Medieval and Renaissance Manuscripts in the United States and Canada*, 1962, p65). The remaining library contents were acquired by CW Traylen (see [b] below). The present location of five Wentworth Woodhouse letter books 1772-1805, sold at Sotheby's, 20 July 1989, lot 270, is not known.

[b] Customs establishment records 1765-6 (3 vols).

Sheffield Archives (MD 2060-2). Purchased 1949 from the book dealer CW Traylen (catalogue no 14, 1949, lot 632), who had acquired over 1,900 printed books and 5 MSS from the Wentworth Woodhouse library in 1948. These were dispersed by auction in 1949 and 1951 (catalogue no 21).

[c] Deeds 17th-19th cent, mainly Yorks WR; testamentary, probate, executorship, trust and legal papers 18th-20th cent, incl papers rel to the Milton and Irish estates 1802-97; manorial court records (Yorks WR) 13th-20th cent, incl Barnbrough 1577-1816, Swinton 1622-1923,

Tinsley 1291, 1462-1812 and Wentworth 1705-99; misc Yorks WR estate papers 16th-19th cent, incl maps and plans 19th cent, field books and surveys 1736, 1750, 1861, chief rentals 1748-54, Tinsley rental 1546, Tinsley Park colliery valuation and inventory 1845, and papers rel to coal and shale working, enclosure, tithes, the Sheffield and Tinsley canal, etc 18th-19th cent; Irish estate rentals (Co Wicklow, etc) 1806-71; rental, King's Co estate of the Hon Frederick Ponsonby 1844-5.

Sheffield Archives (NBC). Deposited by Newman & Bond, solicitors, Barnsley 1968-76. NRA 4701.

[d] Tinsley manorial rentals (2nd Earl of Strafford) 1667.

Sheffield Archives (MD 509). Purchased from the English Book Company 1935. NRA 23246.

[e] Survey of Lord Rockingham's Hoyland (Yorks WR) estate by William Fairbank 1771.

Hull University, Brynmor Jones Library (DX/103). Presented by NI Secker 1975. NRA 10731.

[f] MS of Seneca's *Epistles* 12th cent.

British Library, Manuscript Collections (Add MS 70929). Accepted in lieu of tax on the estate of the 10th Earl Fitzwilliam 1984. Formerly at Wentworth Woodhouse.

[g] English translation for Duke Humfrey of Gloucester of Palladius's *Opus agriculturae* 15th cent.

Bodleian Library, Oxford (MS Duke Humfrey d. 2). Accepted in lieu of tax on the estate of the 10th Earl Fitzwilliam 1984. Recorded at Wentworth Woodhouse 1862.

[h] Deeds 16th-20th cent, mainly Yorks NR; legal papers 19th cent, incl solicitor's accounts 1819-35; manorial court records, Old and New Malton and Hutton Bushel (Yorks NR) 18th-20th cent; Yorks E and NR estate maps and plans 18th-19th cent, terriers, particulars, valuations, surveys and rentals 16th-19th cent, accounts and vouchers from 1751 and corresp and papers 18th-20th cent; papers rel to Barmby Moor enclosure c1814-49 and to Yorks E and NR drainage, embankment, navigation and canals (rivers Derwent, Hertford, Humber and Rye) 18th-19th cent, incl Derwent Navigation accounts 1805-55; Malton cattle market papers 19th-20th cent; Old Malton and Pickering turnpike surveyor's accounts and papers 1786-1814; Malton election papers 17th-19th cent (mainly late 18th-early 19th cent); Yorks NR deputy sheriff's vouchers 1782-6; misc papers, incl private stud and other business papers of William Allen of Malton mid-19th cent.

North Yorkshire County Record Office (ZPB). Deposited from the Malton Estate Office 1967-87. NRA 33762.

[i] Irish estate records early 18th-mid-20th cent, mainly rentals and accounts but incl tenancy records 1727-19th cent, emigration records 1847-56, maps, surveys and valuations 18th-19th cent, memoranda books c1796-1885 and corresp c1784-1843, with some papers rel to Coolattin household; Rathdrum Flannel Hall (Co Wicklow) building accounts 1791-5; Coolattin poor shop register 1830-8; poor rate books 1845; Co Wicklow church and county cess book 1784-91; tax assessments, Shillelagh union 1864-70; papers rel to Co Wicklow schools (Carnew, Coolroe, Mountabower and Shillelagh) 1826-52; Shillelagh Horticultural Society minute book 1856-65; misc papers 18th-20th cent, incl tithe book of the Revd Henry Moore 1832.

National Library of Ireland. Deposited from the Coolattin Estate Office by the Countess Fitzwilliam 1951 and her executors 1978. *Annual Report 1951-2*, p4, *1978*, p11. NRA 31205.

[j] Misc papers of the Bridges family as attorneys for the Marquess of Rockingham's Irish estates 18th cent.

West Yorkshire Archive Service, Bradford (16D86). Deposited, with other family papers, at Leeds District Archives by representatives of the Bardsley-Powell family 1979 and transferred 1986. NRA 30578.

Related collections: Wentworth-Fitzwilliam of Milton, no 114; Ramsden of Byram (West Yorkshire Archive Service, Leeds, NRA 7344), including correspondence and papers of the second Marquess and Marchioness of Rockingham; rental and account book of Sir John Wentworth of North Elmsall 1699-1712 (London University Library MS 277).

[114] WENTWORTH-FITZWILLIAM of Milton

Sir William Fitzwilliam (d1534), household treasurer to Cardinal Wolsey, bought Gaynes Park (Essex) in 1501 and the estates of Milton and Marholm (1502) and Etton (1514) in the Soke of Peterborough (Northamptonshire). The Essex property was sold in 1636 but the Milton estate was extended and included Woodhall and Helpston (bought 1572-6), Northborough and Lolham (bought 1681-2), Maxey (bought 1699) and Upton (bought 1750). William Fitzwilliam (d1644) was ennobled as Baron Fitzwilliam of Lifford (Irish) in 1620, and the third Baron (d1719) was created Earl Fitzwilliam (Irish) in 1716. The first Earl's marriage in 1669 to Anne, heiress of Edmund Cremer, brought an estate in Norfolk (North Runcton, Setchey,

West Winch, etc) while that of the second Earl in 1718 to Anne, heiress of John Stringer, brought one in Nottinghamshire (Clarborough, Eaton, Sutton cum Lound, etc). In the early eighteenth century further property was acquired in Lincolnshire (Algarkirk and Fosdyke in Holland, Billinghay and North Kyme in Kesteven) and Yorkshire (Humbleton and Meaux in the East Riding, Smeaton and Stubbs in the West Riding). These outlying estates were mainly sold c1784-8, the Milton estate being further extended through subsequent purchases in Huntingtonshire (Stanground and Farcet 1796, Great Gidding 1827, Morborne c1854, etc).

In 1782 the fourth Earl inherited the estates of his uncle the second Marquess of Rockingham but in 1857, on the death of the fifth Earl, the former Rockingham estates passed to his elder son (who succeeded as sixth Earl) and the Fitzwilliam (Milton) estates to his younger son George Wentworth Fitzwilliam (see also Wentworth-Fitzwilliam, Earls Fitzwilliam, no 113). Following the death in 1886 of Lady Milton (widow of the sixth Earl's eldest son) the former Rockingham property in Northamptonshire and neighbouring counties (including Higham Ferrers and Great Harrowden) appears to have devolved on GW Fitzwilliam's son George Charles Wentworth-Fitzwilliam (1866-1935), who sold much of it around 1895 (Great Harrowden) and later. In 1952 WTG Wentworth-Fitzwilliam of Milton succeeded a cousin as tenth Earl Fitzwilliam.

The presence of papers of the Godolphin family is explained by the marriage of Anne (1722-1805), daughter of the second Earl Fitzwilliam, to the second Baron Godolphin of Helston (d1785).

Estates in 1883: Northants 18,116 acres, Hunts 5,202 acres, total 23,318 acres worth £39,547 a year.

[a] Deeds and evidences of title, Northants 12th-19th cent, Norfolk 12th-17th cent, Essex 13th-17th cent, Notts 13th-18th cent, Hunts and Lincs 13th-19th cent and London and Westminster 17th-19th cent, with misc deeds for other counties from 13th cent; inquisitions *post mortem*, Robert Wyttelbury 1506 and John Cremer 1611; wills, settlements and trust, legal and financial papers 13th-19th cent, mainly Fitzwilliam and Cremer families, incl wills of John Wyttelbury 1445, Sir William Fitzwilliam 1533 and Sir William Fitzwilliam 1598, Stringer family probate papers 1636-1726, papers rel to legal disputes with Peterborough Abbey and Dean and Chapter 16th cent and papers rel to the will of Sir William Fitzwilliam (d1599); bonds of the Williamson family of Kenwick (Norfolk) 16th-17th cent; manorial records for Hunts (Great Gidding, etc) and Northants (Etton, Marholm, Maxey, etc) 13th cent-1932, incl records of Peterborough Abbey manors

13th-16th cent and Higham Ferrers manor and borough court records 1614-1730; Norfolk (Kenwick, North Runcton and Setchey, etc) manorial records 14th-18th cent; Hemnalls and Gaynes Park Hall (Essex) manor rental 1408 and court roll 1566-79; Emley (Yorks WR) court roll 1424; Nassaburgh (Northants) hundred court records 1452-3.

Milton (Northants and Hunts) estate records 15th-20th cent, incl leases, maps, plans, particulars and surveys, rentals and accounts 16th-20th cent, vouchers 18th-19th cent, letter books 1855-1932, cattle stock book 1582-94, records of wood sales 1571-1904 and papers rel to enclosures, roads and River Nene drainage 18th-19th cent; Norfolk estate records 14th-19th cent, incl leases 17th-18th cent and accounts c1670-1773, with valuation of the property of Nicholas Brooke 1594; accounts and corresp of Francis Guybon as steward of the Milton and Norfolk estates c1678-1709; Lincs, Notts and Yorks ER and WR estate papers 15th-18th cent, incl Lincs and Yorks leases 17th-18th cent, Lincs maps c1660 and c1780, Eaton (Notts) terrier 15th cent, Yorks ER survey 1713 and Lincs, Notts and Yorks accounts 1729-88; Higham Ferrers and Harrowden (Northants) estate records 16th-20th cent, incl leases, surveys and valuations 18th-19th cent, rentals and accounts 1778-1907 and vouchers 1850-6; misc Gaynes Park (Essex) estate papers 16th-17th cent, incl plan of Elizabeth Barrett's estate c1586 and Theydon Garnon terrier 1655; accounts of Lord Fitzwilliam's property at Boxted and Little Coggeshall (Essex) c1709-22; Malton estate rental 1714; Yorks WR (former Rockingham) estate accounts 1781-95; valuation of Sir William Fitzwilliam's Essex, Lincs, London and Northants estates 1575; rental, bishopric of Peterborough estates 1571; misc estate papers 15th-18th cent, incl honour of Tickhill (Yorks WR) rentals and accounts 1684-97 and particulars of estates of the 4th Earl Rivers c1712.

Milton architectural plans, drawings and building papers late 17th-19th cent and household accounts and papers 16th-19th cent, incl inventories 1622-55 and accounts 1583-1617; household papers for Dogsthorpe (Northants) 16th-17th cent, incl building accounts 1579-1601 and inventories 1601-65, and for Setchey 17th cent; inventories, Gaynes Park 1598, Belhus (Essex) 1653, and Great Harrowden 1782; London household vouchers and papers 18th-19th cent; misc Wentworth Woodhouse architectural papers 18th-19th cent, with London building accounts 1812-13; papers rel to Northants affairs 16th-19th cent, incl shrievalty notebook (William Fitzwilliam) 1607, Nassaburgh hundred and Northants (Eastern Division) subsidy papers late 16th-early 17th cent, accounts of Francis Downes (treasurer, Eastern Division) 1630-1 and accounts of musters and royal purveyance in the Eastern Division 1635-7; Peterborough town lands accounts 1560-86 and quarter sessions rolls 1699-1710; poor rate assessments, Peterborough 1848 and Castor 1889-90; Peterborough and Northants election records 1666-19th cent, incl poll books and case papers; Higham Ferrers election accounts 1812-31 and vicarage, college, school and parish papers 16th-19th cent; minutes, North Northants Reform Association (Peterborough District) 1835-6 and Milton Horticultural Society 1908-11; acquittance rolls, Cambs and Hunts escheator 1532-3 and Norfolk sheriff (John Cremer) 1658; Hull election accounts (Earl of Burford) 1790; papers rel to Little Urswick (Lancs) school 17th-18th cent.

Family corresp and papers 16th-20th cent, mainly Fitzwilliam and Cremer families, incl patents, appointments, personal inventories, personal accounts of Thomas Stringer 1677-1705, accounts of charitable payments in the Peterborough neighbourhood 1739-1836, papers of Sir William Fitzwilliam (d1599) mainly rel to Irish affairs, corresp and papers of the 4th and 5th Earls Fitzwilliam, and political corresp and papers of Edmund Burke (d1797); political papers of Sir Walter Mildmay (d1589); accounts rel to William Fitzwilliam's farm of the aulnage of the new draperies *c*1579-1610; genealogical papers 16th-19th cent, Fitzwilliam and Cremer families; literary and misc papers 16th-20th cent, incl MS copy of George Cavendish's *Life of Wolsey* 16th cent, a treatise on trade between England and Friesland 1564 and parliamentary journals 1640-1; papers rel to swans and swan marks 15th-16th cent; Peterborough Abbey records 13th-16th cent, incl Lincs estate accounts 1280, bailiff's accounts 1300-10, Sacristan's court records 1426-7 and rental 1504, with a (forged) charter of 670.

Papers of the Godolphin family, Barons Godolphin of Helston 16th-19th cent, incl testamentary, trust, legal and financial papers 18th cent, Cornish estate valuation 1773 and accounts 1786-7, plans 1766 and papers 18th cent for Westminster (St James's Place) property, Baylies (Bucks) estate accounts and papers 18th cent, inventories of households at Gog Magog Hills (Cambs) 1785 and Baylies 1795, household and personal bills *c*1788-1802 and accounts 1743-1803 of the 2nd Baron and Lady Godolphin, funeral accounts for Henry Godolphin 1731-2, and Godolphin family corresp *c*1675-1802.

Northamptonshire Record Office (Fitzwilliam (Milton) MSS: Accessions 1937/45, 1942/11, 1946/97, 1948/5, 19, 70, 1949/27, 1955/12-13, 1956/23, 1963/66, 77, 1964/154, 1969/109, 1971/89). Deposited by WTG Wentworth-Fitzwilliam (10th Earl Fitzwilliam from 1952) 1937-71. NRA 4120 (Burke papers), 5870. For Sir William Fitzwilliam see *Analecta Hibernica*, no 4, October 1932, pp287-326; for the 4th Earl Fitzwilliam see HMC *Papers of British Cabinet Ministers 1782-1900*, 1982, pp68-9; and for the 5th Earl and Edmund Burke see HMC

Papers of British Politicians 1782-1900, 1989, pp16, 110. See also DR Hainsworth and C Walker, *The Correspondence of Lord Fitzwilliam of Milton and Francis Guybon his Steward 1697-1709*, Northamptonshire Record Society, 1990.

[b] Northants (Higham Ferrers and Harrowden) deeds, abstracts, settlements, mortgages and legal and trust papers 17th-19th cent; probates of the 2nd Baron Godolphin of Helston 1785 and Lady Godolphin 1805; abstract of conveyances of Higham Ferrers burgage properties 1684-1744; Higham Ferrers and Harrowden estate records 18th-20th cent, incl tenancy agreements 1860-1925, maps and plans from 1750, Higham Ferrers survey 1770, and rentals, accounts and vouchers from *c*1735; Wansford and Bedford Purlieus estate records 1904-29 (Lord Fitzwilliam's estate); misc papers, incl rental of the estate of Roger Parker *c*1790.

Northamptonshire Record Office (F/WW/1-502; Accessions 1951/93, 146, 1952/17, 1953/20). Deposited from Wentworth Woodhouse and Sheffield Central Library 1951-3. NRA 5870.

[c] Peterborough Abbey cartulary *c*1322-9.

British Library, Manuscript Collections (Add MS 39758). Purchased from GC Wentworth-Fitzwilliam at Sotheby's, 30 Apr 1918, lot 255. Another medieval Peterborough cartulary, owned by Lord Fitzwilliam in 1636, is Egerton MS 2733. Two further medieval cartularies were privately purchased at the Milton sale of 1918 and subsequently presented to Peterborough Dean and Chapter (MSS 7, 39). See GRC Davis, *Medieval Cartularies of Great Britain*, 1958, pp86-8; JD Martin, *The Cartularies and Registers of Peterborough Abbey*, Northamptonshire Record Society, 1978.

Related collections: Wentworth-Fitzwilliam, Earls Fitzwilliam, no 113; Osborne, Dukes of Leeds, no 78; Barons Harlech (National Library of Wales, NRA 11471), including Godolphin family correspondence; Thomas Carte's collections (Bodleian Library, Oxford MSS Carte 55-8, 131), including further Irish papers of Sir William Fitzwilliam (d1599).

[115] **WILLIAMS WYNN of Wynnstay**

Sir William Williams (1634-1700), son and heir of Hugh Williams of Nantanog, Llantrisant (Anglesey), was Speaker of the House of Commons and Solicitor-General, and was created a baronet in 1688. He added to his Anglesey inheritance by purchasing Llanforda (Shropshire) from Edward Lloyd and Glantanat (Denbighshire) from Edward Thelwall, and by acquiring Glascoed (Denbighshire) through marriage to Margaret, daughter and co-heir of Watkin Kyffin (d1670). The Shropshire and Denbighshire estates descended to his son the second Bt (d1740), who had acquired Plas-y-Ward (Denbighshire) through marriage to Jane, daughter and heir of Edward Thelwall. The property in Angelsey and at Bodelwyddan (Flintshire) was settled on a second son, John Williams of Chester, from whom descended the Williams baronets of Bodelwyddan.

Sir Watkin Williams, third Bt (1692-1749), succeeded by will to the estates of Sir John Wynn, fifth Bt (d1719), whose father was a younger son of Sir John Wynn, first Bt, of Gwydir (d1627). Wynn (on whose death the baronetcy expired) had succeeded his cousin the fourth Bt, but the main Gwydir estates had passed to the fourth Bt's daughter and her husband the first Duke of Ancaster (see Heathcote-Drummond-Willoughby, Earls of Ancaster, no 48). Wynn did, however, inherit some property from his father Henry Wynn and other members of the Wynn family, incl Maenan (Carnarvonshire), Glasinfryn (Anglesey and Carnarvonshire) and Eglwysfach (Denbighshire). Other acquisitions by Wynn included the manors of Valle Crucis and Wrexham Abbot (Denbighshire), while Rhiwgoch (Merionethshire), his mother's inheritance, was settled on him at his marriage. He also purchased property in Shropshire, including the manors of Stanwardine and Much Wenlock, and came into possession of Watstay (Denbighshire) through marriage to Jane, daughter and heir of Eyton Evans. When Sir Watkin Williams inherited Sir John Wynn's estates he renamed this seat Wynnstay and assumed the additional name of Wynn.

The marriage of the third Bt to Anne (d1748), daughter and heir of Edward Vaughan, brought the Vaughan estates of Llwydiarth (Montgomeryshire), Llangedwyn (Denbighshire) and Glan-y-llyn (Merionethshire), and the former Purcell manor of Talerddig (Montgomeryshire). Further property, including the lordship of Cyfeiliog (Montgomeryshire), was purchased during the minority of the fourth Bt. In 1857 Maenan (Carnarvonshire) was sold, and extensive purchases of Crown lands in Denbighshire were made.

Estates in 1883: Montgomeryshire 70,559 acres, Merionethshire 42,044 acres, Denbighshire 28,721 acres, Cardiganshire 361 acres, Flintshire 224 acres, Salop 3,856 acres, Cheshire 5 acres, total 145,770 acres worth £54,575 a year.

[a] Deeds 12th-19th cent, mainly Denbighshire, Merionethshire, Montgomeryshire and Salop, incl medieval charters of Strata Marcella Abbey (Montgomeryshire); inquisitions *post mortem* for Thomas Myddleton 1543 and Owen Vaughan 1620; wills, settlements and executorship, trust, legal and financial papers 16th-20th cent, Williams, Williams Wynn, Kyffin, Purcell, Thelwall, Vaughan and related families, incl trust papers of the Price family of Eglwysegle (Denbighshire) and case papers of the Vaughan

family of Llwydiarth 17th-18th cent; Wynn of Gwydir family settlements and probate, legal and financial papers 16th-18th cent, incl Sir John Wynn, 5th Bt decd; Llwydiarth (Montgomeryshire) sequestration papers 1640-54, Vaughan and Devereux families; manorial records 14th-19th cent, Denbighshire (Valle Crucis, Bromfield and Yale lordship, Chirk and Chirkland, Ruthin, etc), Montgomeryshire (Cyfeiliog, Machynlleth, Talerddig, etc) and Salop (Much Wenlock, etc); ministers' accounts, lordship of Caus (Montgomeryshire and Salop) 1455-6, 1523-4, Anglesey 1555-6, Carnarvonshire 1540-1, and Flintshire 1458-9, 1554-5.

Records of the Williams Wynn estates in Denbighshire, Merionethshire, Montgomeryshire and Salop 17th-20th cent and Carnarvonshire 17th-19th cent (extensive), incl misc surveys and maps, rental and account books 17th-20th cent, vouchers and day books 19th-20th cent, corresp from 17th cent, papers rel to timber, enclosures, tithes, roads and railways 18th-19th cent, and papers rel to game and sporting rights 19th-20th cent; mining and quarrying papers, Denbighshire, Merionethshire, Montgomeryshire and Salop (Cefn, Overley Hall, Plas Isa and Trefarclawdd collieries, etc) 18th-20th cent, incl leases, accounts and royalty returns; misc records for the Williams Wynn estates in Flintshire 17th-20th cent and Cardiganshire and Cheshire 19th-20th cent; Anglesey (Chwaen Isaf) estate rentals 17th cent, Williams family; rentals and estate papers for properties of the Purcell family in Montgomeryshire (Overgorther, Talerddig, etc) 16th-17th cent, the Thelwall family in Denbighshire (Ruthin, etc) 15th-17th cent and the Vaughan family in Denbighshire, Merionethshire and Montgomeryshire 16th-18th cent; Gwydir estate papers (Anglesey, Carnarvonshire, Denbighshire and Merionethshire) 1618-80, incl rentals 1671, 1680 and corresp 1618-19; misc papers for estates of Sir Richard Wynn, 2nd Bt, at Isleworth (Middlesex) and Crowland (Lincs) c1634-53; Wimbledon (Surrey) particulars and quit rent accounts c1638-40.

Papers rel to proposed building at Wynnstay 1770, incl plans, drawings and elevations by James Byres; household inventories, accounts and vouchers 17th-19th cent, Wynnstay and 20 St James's Square (London), incl St James's Square building vouchers and accounts (Robert and James Adam) 1771-6 and Wynnstay inventories 1683-6, 1749 and 1840, with papers rel to the Wynnstay playhouse 18th cent; papers rel to the monument by Rysbrack in Ruabon church (Denbighshire) to Sir Watkin Williams Wynn, 3rd Bt 1750-1; Wimbledon House accounts 1641-9; shrievalty papers, Carnarvonshire, Denbighshire, Merionethshire and Montgomeryshire 16th-18th cent, Kyffin, Purcell, Thelwall, Vaughan, Williams and Wynn families; election papers 1621-1861, incl

Denbighshire 1671, Flintshire Boroughs 1734, 1741 and Montgomeryshire 1678-9, 1714, with parliamentary returns 17th-18th cent; Montgomeryshire and Machynlleth hundred quarter sessions records 16th-18th cent, incl Montgomeryshire sessions files 1614-60; Machynlleth fair toll books 1749-50; militia lists, Bromfield hundred (Denbighshire) c1820; papers rel to local affairs 16th-19th cent, incl Holt (Denbighshire) borough papers 18th-19th cent and Ruthin hundred subsidy roll 1620-1.

Appointments and commissions 16th-18th cent; family corresp and papers 16th-19th cent, Williams, Wynn, Williams Wynn, Kyffin, Lloyd, Purcell, Thelwall and Vaughan families, incl accounts of Simon Thelwall at the Exchequer of North Wales 1553-8, accounts and vouchers of Griffith and Watkin Kyffin 17th cent, accounts of Sir Richard Wynn, 2nd Bt, as treasurer and receiver-general to Queen Henrietta Maria 1629-42, legal, political and family papers of Sir William Williams, 1st Bt (d1700), accounts of Sir Watkin Williams Wynn, 4th Bt, as treasurer for the Ancient Concerts and Handel Commemoration Concerts 1784-7, and fee book of Henry Wynn 1637-43; literary, historical and legal MSS 15th-18th cent, incl collections rel to Welsh laws by William Maurice (d1680); genealogical and misc papers 14th-19th cent, incl accounts of the chamberlain of Chester (William de Melton) 1301, rental of the Rhos, Rhufoniog and Ceinmeirch (Denbighshire) lordship of Richard, Duke of York 1437, receiver-general of North Wales's accounts 1591-2, and surveys and papers rel to Crown revenues in Wales 17th cent.

National Library of Wales (Wynnstay MSS and Documents; Wynnstay Archives). Deposited by the 7th and 10th Bts and the trustees of the Wynnstay estates 1933-52, 1978. *Annual Report 1933-4*, pp46-7, *1940-1*, p29, *1944-5*, pp32-3, *1951-2*, pp35-7, *1978-9*, p86. HMC *Papers of British Politicians 1782-1900*, 1989, p 112. NRA 30545.

[b] Denbighshire, Merionethshire, Montgomeryshire and Salop deeds 19th-20th cent; abstracts of title and schedules of deeds 18th-19th cent; legal, trust and Denbighshire, Merionethshire, Montgomeryshire and Shropshire estate papers 19th-20th cent, incl misc leases, particulars and rentals, estate accounts 1844-5 and estate sales books 1853-6; papers rel to the 6th Bt's Derbyshire election costs 1868.

National Library of Wales. Deposited by Longueville & Co, solicitors, Oswestry 1954-88. NRA 34473 (partial list).

[c] Carnarvonshire, Denbighshire, Merionethshire and Montgomeryshire rental 1719; account of chief rents in Trefeglwys and Llangurig (Montgomeryshire) 1825-69.

National Library of Wales. Deposited by the Powysland Club 1965. *Annual Report 1965-6*, pp57-8. NRA 39382.

[d] Carnarvonshire, Denbighshire, Merionethshire and Montgomeryshire rental and accounts 1725-6.

National Library of Wales (MS 10256). Acquired from the collection of Robert Ellis 1935. *Handlist of MSS*, iii, p205.

[e] Merionethshire rental and accounts 1785-1811

National Library of Wales (MSS 19664-5, 19674). Deposited by Dr Llywelyn ap Ifan Davies 1944-5, 1963. NRA 40909.

[f] Montgomeryshire manorial records and steward's papers 19th cent, incl Cyfeiliog and the town, borough and liberty of Machynlleth; abstracts and copies of Strata Marcella grants and manorial records 19th cent; misc Montgomeryshire estate and agency records 19th-20th cent.

National Library of Wales. Given by Mr and Mrs Percival Bevan 1964. *Annual Report 1963-4*, p23.

[g] Notebooks, travel journals and corresp of Frances (Fanny) Williams Wynn 18th-19th cent; catalogue of the Wynnstay library 1840.

National Library of Wales (MSS 2775-88). Purchased 1917 (formerly in the collection of Canon Trevor Owen). *Handlist of MSS*, i, pp241-2.

[h] Misc receipts and accounts of the 5th Bt c1808-12.

National Library of Wales (RHG Smallwood Deeds and Papers, nos 1008-19, 1024-35, 1037). Amongst the antiquarian collections of RHG Smallwood purchased 1994-5. NRA 33982.

[i] Deeds c1138-20th cent (c114 medieval), mainly Carnarvonshire, Denbighshire, Merionethshire, Montgomeryshire and Salop; inquisitions *post mortem* for John Owen Vaughan 1600, Owen Vaughan 1620 and Sir Robert Vaughan 1631; wills, settlements and related papers 15th-20th cent, Wynn, Williams, Williams Wynn, Evans, Eyton, Kyffin, Thelwall and Vaughan families; Radcliffe trust papers 1740-8, incl building accounts of the Radcliffe Library, Oxford; abstracts and schedules of deeds 17th-20th cent, incl abstracts of deeds rel to the former possessions of Valle Crucis Abbey c1540-1663 and abstract of title to the Watstay estate 1571-1625; legal and case papers 16th-20th cent, incl papers rel to Thelwall, Vaughan and Williams estates c1650-1720 and to settlements of the Wynn estates in Wales 1654-98; misc manorial records 16th-19th cent, Denbighshire, Merionethshire,

Montgomeryshire and Salop, incl papers rel to lordships of Bromfield and Yale (Denbighshire) 16th-19th cent and Dyffryn Clwyd (Denbighshire) 16th-17th cent, with account roll of ringild for the manor of Cyfeiliog 1447-8; ministers' accounts, Flintshire 1506-7 and Montgomeryshire 1557.

Williams Wynn estate records, mainly Denbighshire, Merionethshire, Montgomeryshire and Salop 17th-20th cent, incl leases, surveys, maps and plans, particulars, valuations, rentals, accounts, vouchers and corresp; papers rel to timber and tithes 17th-20th cent and to enclosure, roads, canals, railways and game and sporting rights 18th-20th cent; Carnarvonshire, Denbighshire, Merionethshire, Montgomeryshire and Salop mining and quarrying papers 17th-20th cent; Denbighshire, Merionethshire and Montgomeryshire estate papers of the Vaughan family of Llwydiarth 17th-18th cent, incl particulars and rentals 17th cent; misc estate records 16th-19th cent, incl survey of former Valle Crucis Abbey possessions 1606.

Building papers 18th-19th cent, incl accounts for work by Robert and James Adam and others at 20 St James's Square 1771-6 and by Benjamin Ferrey at Wynnstay 1859-61, with bills and accounts for work at 18 St James's Square 1846-7; inventories 18th-20th cent, incl catalogue of books at Wynnstay 1840; household accounts and vouchers 18th-20th cent, mainly Wynnstay and St James's Square; papers rel to politics and elections in Denbighshire, Flintshire, Merionethshire and Montgomeryshire 17th-20th cent; lieutenancy and militia papers 19th-20th cent, incl Montgomeryshire Imperial Yeomanry papers 1900-4; deeds and papers rel to Welsh charities 17th-20th cent, incl the Llanfyllin and Llanfihangel (Montgomeryshire) charity schools 18th-20th cent; apprenticeship indentures, Merionethshire 1720-5; papers rel to the prosecution of Methodists in Denbighshire 1747; Taunton (Somerset) poll book and related papers 1774.

Family papers 16th-20th cent, Wynn, Williams, Williams Wynn, Kyffin, Thelwall and Vaughan families, incl appointments and commissions 16th-19th cent, corresp 17th-20th cent, parliamentary papers of Sir William Williams, 1st Bt 1671-89, military papers of the 5th Bt 1799-1828 and letters and papers of Watkin Kyffin of Glascoed c1638-70; genealogical and misc papers 16th-17th cent, incl Salesbury pedigree book c1640, account roll of the Shropshire estates of Edward, Duke of Buckingham 1519-20, particular of the late Earl of Leicester's possessions in Montgomeryshire 1620-1 and rent roll of Myddleton lands in Cheshire, Denbighshire, Flintshire, Montgomeryshire and Salop 1650.

Denbighshire Record Office (DD/WY). Deposited by the 10th and 11th Bts 1979-88. NRA 27821.

[j] Wynnstay estate day book 1908-10.

Denbighshire Record Office (DD/DM/1001). Purchased 1991. *Annual Report* 1991, p20.

Related Collections: Heathcote-Drummond-Willoughby, Earls of Ancaster, no 48, incl Wynn of Gwydir papers 1515-1690; Williams Wynn of Coedymaen (National Library of Wales, NRA 22799), including papers of Sir William Williams, 1st Bt; papers of Canon Richard Trevor Owen (National Library of Wales, NRA 26605), including papers of Sir William Williams, 1st Bt; Williams of Bodelwyddan (Plas Bowman papers) and Williams Wynn of Plas yn Cefn (National Library of Wales, NRA 37189, 38558); Denbighshire manorial papers c1848-1937 collected by Edward Hughes (Denbighshire Record Office DD/G); Wynne-Eaton of Leeswood and The Tower (Flintshire Record Office D/LE, NRA 37280), including Wynn of Wynnstay executorship papers mid-18th cent.

[116] WILLOUGHBY, Barons Middleton

The Willoughby family, descendants of Ralph Bugge, a Nottingham merchant, took its name from Willoughby-on-the-Wolds (Nottinghamshire), where he had bought land in the early thirteenth century. It held lands in Derbyshire and Leicestershire by the early fourteenth century. Sir Richard Willoughby (d1362) acquired the manors of Wollaton and Cossall (Nottinghamshire), Risley and Mapperley (Derbyshire) and Dunsby (Lincolnshire) through his marriage to the daughter of Sir Roger Morteyn, and purchased further lands in these and other counties. Risley descended to the illegitimate offspring of his son Hugh, a priest, and other estates, including Mapperley and Sheringham (Norfolk), passed out of the family. Most of the estate, however, was inherited by Sir Richard's son by his second marriage, Sir Edmund. Further lands in Nottinghamshire (Gunthorpe, Loudham, etc), Warwickshire (Middleton, etc), Staffordshire and Herefordshire were acquired through the marriage of Sir Edmund's grandson, Sir Hugh (d1448), to Margaret, sister and co-heir of Sir Baldwin de Freville of Tamworth (Staffordshire).

Their grandson Sir Henry Willoughby (d1528) bought land in Holborn (Middlesex) formerly belonging to Malmesbury Abbey. His son Sir Edward (d1540) gained the Woodlands (Dorset) estate, with lands in Hampshire, Hertfordshire (Standon) and Essex (Steeple Hall), through his marriage to Anne, daughter and co-heir of Sir William Filoll. Their grandson Sir Francis built Wollaton Hall but sold land, including Cossington and Wymeswold (Leicestershire), and left the estate in considerable disarray on his death in 1596. The Holborn property passed (c1570) to his illegitimate brother, George Fox alias Willoughby, and the Woodlands estate to his second daughter's husband, Henry Hastings, younger son of the fourth Earl of Huntingdon.

The Wollaton and Middleton estates, however, passed to his eldest daughter's husband, Sir Percival Willoughby of Bore Place (Kent) (d1643), a descendant of the Willoughby family of Eresby (see Heathcote-Drummond-Willoughby, Earls of Ancaster, no 48), who in order to retain the other family property found it necessary to sell his own estate in Kent, lands in Essex and Smallwood (Cheshire), and Willoughby itself.

Sir Percival Willoughby's grandson Francis Willoughby, the eminent naturalist, was bequeathed further Nottinghamshire lands (South Muskham and South Carlton) by Sir William Willoughby of Selston in 1671. His second son, Thomas Willoughby, succeeded his brother, Sir Francis, first Bt (so created 1677), in 1688, and was created Baron Middleton in 1712. He had already acquired, through his marriage to Elizabeth, daughter and co-heir of Sir Richard Rothwell, further lands in Nottinghamshire (Newark, North Wheatley, etc) and Lincolnshire (Stapleford, etc). His second son, Thomas (d1742), married Elizabeth, daughter and heir of Sir Thomas Sotheby of Birdsall (Yorkshire, East Riding): their son Henry succeeded his cousin as fifth Baron in 1789. The sixth Baron bought an estate in Wharram Percy (Yorkshire, East Riding) in 1833. Lands, mainly in Gloucestershire (Westerleigh, etc), which had been held jointly with the Colston family of Bristol (to whom the Willoughbys were related by marriage), were sold in 1858 by the trustees of the seventh Baron, but the eighth Baron bought the Applecross estate (Ross-shire) in 1862. In 1921 estates in East Nottinghamshire (Saundby and North Wheatley) were sold and, following the deaths of the ninth and tenth barons in 1922 and 1924, most of the estates outside Yorkshire, including Wollaton, Middleton, Stapleford and Applecross, were also alienated.

Estates in 1883: Notts 15,015 acres, Yorks N and ER 14,045 acres, Lincs 3,809 acres, Warwicks 3,641 acres, Staffs 50 acres, Derbys 16 acres, Ross-shire 63,000 acres, total 99,576 acres worth £54,014 a year.

[a] Deeds 12th-20th cent (c5,000 medieval), incl Notts and Yorks 12th-20th cent, Lincs and Warwicks 12th-19th cent, Hants and Worcs 12th-18th cent, Dorset and Leics 12th-17th cent, Norfolk (Freville family) 12th-14th cent, Middlesex (Holborn, etc) 13th-19th cent, Derbys and Staffs 13th-18th cent, Kent 13th-17th cent, Essex, Herts, Salop and Surrey 13th-16th cent, and Cheshire (Smallwood) 14th-16th cent; cartularies, Willoughby estates in Notts, Derbys, Leics, Lincs and Warwicks 13th-17th cent, Cossington (Leics) 15th cent, Standon (Herts) 15th cent, and the chantry chapel of St Leonard Wilcheswood (Dorset) 16th cent; settlements, wills and trust and executorship papers 14th-20th cent, incl wills of Lord Grey of Codnor 1308, the Filoll family 15th cent and

the Willoughby family of Bore Place 16th cent, inventory of goods of Sir Baldwin de Freville 1355, papers rel to the minority of the grandchildren of Sir Edward Willoughby (d1540) 16th cent, and Colston family settlements 17th-18th cent; inquisitions *post mortem* 14th-16th cent, Willoughby, Freville, Filoll, etc; legal and case papers 15th-19th cent, incl extensive legal and financial papers rel to the co-heirs of Sir Francis Willoughby late 16th-early 17th cent and Rothwell family case papers late 17th cent.

Extensive manorial records, Notts and Warwicks 13th-18th cent, incl Thurgarton (Notts) hundred roll ?13th cent and honour of Peverel records 15th-18th cent, and Kent 13th-16th cent, incl Chiddingstone custumal 1373 and hundred rolls for Hoo 1289-90 and Wrotham 16th cent; manorial records, Derbys 13th-16th cent, Dorset, incl Knowlton and Upwimborne hundreds 14th-16th cent, Cheshire (Smallwood) and Staffs 14th-16th cent, Herefs 14th cent, Lincs and Yorks N and ER 15th-18th cent, and Leics 15th-16th cent.

Notts, Warwicks, Lincs, Derbys, Leics, etc estate papers 13th-20th cent, incl leases 14th-19th cent, maps and plans 17th-20th cent, surveys and valuations late 13th-19th cent, rentals, accounts and financial papers 14th-19th cent, misc corresp, papers rel to enclosure, rectories and tithes 16th-20th cent, and papers rel to sales 16th-17th cent, 20th cent; Dorset, Hants and Herts (Standon) estate papers 14th-16th cent, incl leases 16th cent, plan of Knowlton water mills c1600, surveys 15th-16th cent, rentals and accounts; Kent estate papers 15th-17th cent, incl leases and accounts 16th-17th cent, surveys and rentals 15th-16th cent and papers rel to sales early 17th cent; Yorks E and NR estate papers 15th-20th cent, incl surveys 18th cent, rentals 17th-18th cent, accounts (Helmsley and Ravensworth) 15th cent, and papers rel to Wharram-le-Street enclosure 1756-1812; Herefs rental and accounts 14th cent; Middlesex (Holborn) estate papers 17th cent; survey of Smallwood (Cheshire) 1598; papers rel to Munster plantation 1590-1611; Gloucs, Somerset and Wilts estate papers 18th-19th cent (Colston family), with papers rel to Edward Colston's charitable settlement; extensive papers rel to collieries in Notts and other counties 14th-20th cent; papers rel to woad late 16th cent and to iron works late 16th-early 17th cent.

Wollaton Hall building accounts 16th-17th cent and plans 19th cent; accounts for rebuilding Stapleford Hall 18th cent; household accounts 1304-5 (Grey of Codnor), 16th-18th cent (mainly Wollaton and Middleton); inventories, incl Wollaton Hall 16th-19th cent, Middleton Hall (Warwicks) and Penshurst (Kent) 16th cent, and Bore Place (Kent) 1596-1610.

Shrievalty papers for Notts, etc 14th-17th cent, incl Notts and Derbys sheriff's accounts 1390-

1, 1400-1, for Dorset 15th-16th cent and for Kent and Warwicks 16th-17th cent; tax assessments for Dorset 1437-8, Warwicks 16th cent, Notts 1598, 1729 and Yorks ER 1642; Kent, Notts and Warwicks militia corresp and papers late 16th-early 17th cent; quarter sessions papers, Kent and Warwicks 16th cent and Notts 17th cent; commissions of sewers, Notts 1394-5 and Lincs 1629-32; other papers rel to Notts affairs 15th-20th cent, incl Sherwood Forest papers 15th-17th cent, survey of chantries 16th cent, election accounts and Shire Hall subscription 18th cent, and papers rel to Willoughby Hospital, Cossall 20th cent; papers rel to oyer and terminer sessions at Derby and Nottingham 1332 and to pleas before the justices itinerant at Uppingham (Rutland) 1266; inquests rel to Surrey liberties 1279 and to lands of the Bishop of Lincoln at Thame (Oxon), etc early 14th cent; Northumberland escheator's account 1426-7.

Patents, appointments and commissions from 15th cent; family corresp and papers 14th-20th cent, incl personal accounts 16th cent, MS family history by Cassandra Willoughby, later Duchess of Chandos (incorporating much family corresp, since lost) *c*1702, naval and personal papers of Admiral Sir Nesbit Willoughby (1777-1849), papers rel to Captain Francis Willoughby of the 9th Lancers (1819-46), and personal (largely family) corresp of the 9th, 10th and 11th Barons Middleton 1883-1951; minutes and papers of the Archbishop of Canterbury's Consultative Committee on Migration (11th Baron chairman) 1933-6; natural history collections of Francis Willoughby (d1672) and his collaborator John Ray (1627-1705); literary and misc papers from 12th cent, incl French romances 13th cent, legal MSS 14th-18th cent, letters patent of Queen Philippa acknowledging receipt of jewels (listed) 1332, and Wardrobe accounts 1579; accounts of the Countess of Oxford's Market Overton (Rutland) property 1410-11; foundation deeds, Ewelme (Oxon) almshouses 15th cent; rentals, Burnham Abbey (Bucks) 1450-1 and Newark Priory (Surrey) 15th cent; register of Burton-upon-Trent Abbey (Staffs) 15th cent.

Nottingham University Library, Department of Manuscripts and Special Collections (Mi). Deposited by the 11th and 12th Barons Middleton 1947-73. HMC *Eighteenth Report*, 1917, pp14-21; *Middleton*, 1911. NRA 7428.

[b] Wills, settlements and legal papers 17th-20th cent, with related corresp; Yorks, Notts, etc maps and plans 19th-20th cent; Yorks, Notts, Warwicks, Lincs, etc estate papers 18th-20th cent, incl rental and accounts for whole estate 1873-80; papers rel to the purchase of Wharram Percy 1832-6 and land belonging to the prebend of South Muskham (Notts) 1858-61; extensive papers rel to sales 1858 (Gloucs), 1867 (Notts), 1920s (Notts, Warwicks, Lincs) and 1950s (Wellingore, Lincs); papers rel to the

Applecross estate 1862-1929, with inventory of furniture in Applecross House 1928, and to London properties 19th-20th cent; papers rel to minerals and collieries 18th-20th cent and to the Birdsall Estates Company Ltd 20th cent; papers rel to canals, railways, etc 18th-20th cent and the Willoughby Hospital, Cossall (Notts) 19th-20th cent.

Nottingham University Library, Department of Manuscripts and Special Collections (Mi 3, Mi 4 (part)). Deposited by Messrs Purchase, Pollock & Treadwell, solicitors, London 1963, 1974. NRA 7428.

[c] MS history of the Willoughby family by Cassandra Willoughby, Duchess of Chandos early 18th cent (second vol).

Nottingham University Library, Department of Manuscripts and Special Collections (Mi/LM 27). Given by Mrs Willoughby Gardner 1956. AC Wood (ed), *The Continuation of the history of the Willoughby family by Cassandra Duchess of Chandos*, Eton, 1958. NRA 7428.

[d] The 'Wollaton Antiphonal' 15th cent, containing calendar of obits, incl Willoughby family.

Nottingham University Library, Department of Manuscripts and Special Collections (MS 250). Given by the 11th Baron Middleton to Wollaton parish church 1924 and deposited by the parochial church council 1974. *Eleventh Report of the Keeper of MSS*, pp10-11; HMC *Middleton*, pp236-7.

[e] Copies of deeds, rentals, surveys and papers for Notts, Warwicks, Derbys, etc *c*1568-1610 (1 vol).

Nottinghamshire Archives (M 475). Purchased 1923.

[f] Notts lease 1460; Willoughby letters *c*1521-48 and militia papers (mainly Notts) *c*1542-1628.

Nottinghamshire Archives (M 1205-1229). Given by Dr G Ward 1937, through the British Records Association.

[g] Letter book of JN Martin, Lord Middleton's agent at Wollaton 1808-23.

Nottinghamshire Archives (M 11,530). Given by Mr Harkin 1960. *Annual Report 1959-60*, p5.

[h] Notts manorial records (Wollaton, Willoughby-on-the-Wolds, etc) 1568-90, incl honour of Peverel.

Public Record Office (SC 2/196/76-91).

[i] Kent (Chiddingstone, Penshurst, Sundridge, etc) deeds 1441-1647; misc family settlements, probate papers and legal papers 16th cent; Chiddingstone, etc manorial records 1440-1586;

Sundridge custumals ?1258, 1262 and estreat roll 1505; Kent estate records 13th cent-*c*1600, incl surveyor's drawings of Willoughby estates *c*1590, surveys and valuations *c*1500-*c*1600, rentals ?1258-*c*1575, accounts 15th-16th cent, and inventory of cattle and grain at Bore Place 1518; particulars of Bore Place *c*1600 and part of an inventory of the house at Penshurst *c*1550; assessments of fifteenth collected at Sundridge 1417, *c*1420; quietus rolls for Thomas Willoughby as sheriff of Kent 1573-4, 1590-1; substantial Kent milita corresp and papers 1571-96, with a few items rel to Notts.

Centre for Kentish Studies U 1000/3. Given by the 11th Baron Middleton, through Dr G Ward, to Sevenoaks Public Library 1930 and transferred 1963. HMC *Middleton*, 1911. NRA 18189.

[j] The 'Ceolfrid Bible' 8th cent, formerly used as covers of 16th cent Willoughby cartularies; the 'Oswald cartulary' 11th cent.

British Library, Manuscript Collections (Add MSS 45025, 46204). Purchased 1937, 1946. HMC *Middleton*, pp196-212, 611-2.

[k] MS of Bartholomew Anglicanus (Glanville), *De Proprietabus Rerum* 15th cent.

Columbia University Libraries, Rare Book and Manuscript Library, New York (Plimpton MS 263). Sold at Christie's 15 June 1925 (lot 371), with three other manuscripts, two of which, the Juvenal *Satyrs* 1673 (lot 398) and the *Missale Romanum* 15th cent (lot 567), are untraced. HMC *Middleton*, p240. A 15th cent MS of Lydgate's translation of Boccaccio's 'Fall of Princes' (lot 169, HMC *Middleton*, p622) was acquired by Princeton University Library (Robert H Taylor collection).

Related collections: Genealogical and other papers of Cassandra, Duchess of Chandos (British Library Stowe MS 656; Huntington Library, San Marino, California; Shakespeare Birthplace Trust Records Office DR 18).

[117] WYNDHAM, Barons Leconfield and Egremont

By the early eighteenth century the Wyndham family of Orchard Wyndham (Somerset) had extensive estates in Somerset and Devon (see Wyndham of Orchard Wyndham, no 118). Sir William Wyndham, third Bt (d1740), married in 1708 Katherine, a daughter of the sixth Duke of Somerset. In 1750 their elder son Sir Charles Wyndham, fourth Bt (1710-63), succeeded his uncle, the seventh Duke, as second Earl of Egremont, inheriting the former Percy estates in Sussex, Yorkshire and Cumberland (see Percy, Dukes of Northumberland, no 82), and making Petworth (Sussex) his principal seat. He was succeeded as third Earl in 1763 by his son George O'Brien Wyndham (1751-1837).

In 1774 the third Earl inherited the estates of his uncle Percy Wyndham, Earl of Thomond, including the ancestral Irish estates of the earls of Thomond principally in Counties Clare and Limerick, together with property in Essex (Shortgrove), Cambridgeshire (Ickleton), Somerset and elsewhere. These estates had descended to Percy Wyndham (for whom the earldom of Thomond was revived in 1756) through his aunt Elizabeth, another daughter of the sixth Duke of Somerset, who had in 1707 married Henry O'Brien, seventh Earl of Thomond (d1741).

The third Earl of Egremont also enlarged the Sussex estates by purchase, and acquired land in Surrey and Hampshire (sold by the late nineteenth century) and Middlesex (Hurlingham, acquired for his wife in 1807 but sold after her death in 1822). He died without legitimate issue in 1837, when the Wyndham estates descended to his nephew George O'Brien Wyndham, fourth Earl of Egremont (see Wyndham of Orchard Wyndham, no 118). The Sussex, Yorkshire and Irish estates, however, passed to his eldest natural son George Wyndham, created Baron Leconfield in 1859, and the Cumberland estates to his second son Henry. On Henry's death in 1860 the Cumberland estates were inherited by Lord Leconfield. John Wyndham (1920-72), created Baron Egremont in 1963, succeeded his father as sixth Baron Leconfield in 1967.

Estates in 1883: Sussex 30,221 acres, Yorks ER 13,247 acres, Cumberland 11,147 acres, Yorks NR 7,643 acres, Yorks WR 3,843 acres, Co Clare 37,292 acres, Co Limerick 6,269 acres, Co Tipperary 273 acres, total 109,935 acres worth £88,112 a year.

[a] Deeds for English estates 13th-20th cent, mainly Sussex and Yorks but incl some for Hants and Middlesex (Egremont purchases) 16th-19th cent, Essex and Northants (Thomond), Cumberland, London houses, and various Percy, Seymour and Wadham properties; Irish deeds (Cos Clare, Limerick and Tipperary) 16th-19th cent; wills, settlements, trust papers and executorship papers 17th-20th cent; legal and case papers 16th-20th cent, English and Irish estates; manorial records, mainly Sussex (honour of Petworth, etc) 14th-20th cent and Yorks (Catton, Leconfield, Topcliffe, etc) 14th-19th cent but incl misc rolls, accounts or papers for Isleworth Syon (Middlesex) 17th-18th cent, Burton Latimer (Northants) 16th cent, Haselbury Bryan (Dorset) late 16th-early 17th cent, Ickleton (Cambs) 17th-18th cent, Duke of Somerset's courts in Wilts and Somerset 1730-42, and Ireland *c*1670-90.

Sussex (Petworth) estate records 16th-20th cent, incl surveys from *c*1500, maps from early 17th cent, rentals and accounts from 16th cent, farm accounts from 1772, labour accounts 19th-20th cent, timber accounts and papers

17th-20th cent, Petworth granary accounts 1699-1707, corresp 18th-20th cent, and papers rel to buildings, tithes, roads, railways, rivers, etc; Yorks ER, NR and WR estate records 16th-20th cent, incl surveys from early 16th cent, maps and plans from early 17th cent, rentals from 17th cent, accounts from 16th cent, mining leases 20th cent, and papers from 17th cent rel to leases and agreements, tithes and advowsons, enclosure, etc; misc Surrey estate papers 17th-19th cent; misc Cumberland estate records 16th-20th cent, incl surveys, accounts, papers rel to minerals 19th-20th cent and herd book 1928-32.

Misc accounts, etc rel to Percy estates in Northumberland 1562-1749, Middlesex 17th-mid-18th cent, Somerset and Dorset 15th-17th cent and Wales 16th-17th cent; accounts, etc rel to Seymour estates in Somerset and Wilts 17th-18th cent (mainly 1710-45), and to Wyndham estates in Somerset, Devon, Dorset and Wilts 17th cent-*c*1847; accounts for Poynings estates 1472-1528, Kent and Suffolk (Percy estates) 1523-4, Ickleton (Cambs) 1545 and Marston Bigott (Somerset: Countess of Orrery) 1682-4; estate papers for Shortgrove (Essex) 1749-53, Winchelsea (Sussex) 1761-71, Hurlingham 1807-20 and Much Cowarne (Herefs: Hon Percy Wyndham) 1857-75; Irish (Thomond) estate records 17th-20th cent, incl surveys, valuations, maps, rentals, accounts, and corresp and papers rel to sales 19th-20th cent; accounts for Orrery estates in Cos Cork, Clare and Limerick *c*1668-85.

Accounts and papers rel to Petworth House 16th-19th cent (incl building accounts 1688-96), Petworth Park (incl landscaping by Capability Brown 1753-64), Syon House 17th cent, Northumberland House 1650-85, Egremont House (London) 1770s and Marlborough (Wilts) late 17th-early 18th cent, with inventories and catalogues for Petworth and Egremont House 1606-1903 and for Orchard Wyndham 1773; Petworth guest lists and visitors' books 1839-1944; garden and stable accounts 17th-20th cent, mainly Seymour and Egremont but incl Syon gardens 1709; papers rel to Sussex affairs 18th-20th cent, incl yeomanry and militia, elections 18th-19th cent, Rother navigation 1792-1869, Five Oaks turnpike trust 1811-36, Sutton poor law union 1790-1841 and West Sussex War Agricultural Committee 1939-45; papers rel to Petworth 18th-20th cent, incl Somerset Hospital 1746-1886, emigration committee and savings bank 19th cent and friendly society 19th-20th cent; papers rel to Somerset militia and politics mid-18th cent (Earl of Thomond as lord lieutenant) and to misc Yorks affairs 19th cent; papers rel to Irish elections, emigration, etc 19th cent.

Patents and commissions 17th-19th cent; personal and family papers 16th-19th cent, Wyndham and related families, incl personal, household and estate accounts of the 9th and 10th Earls of Northumberland 1582-1667, Admiralty papers of the 10th Earl, corresp of the 1st Earl of Orrery (brother-in-law of the 10th Earl of Northumberland) *c*1661-77, and personal and political papers of the 6th Duke of Somerset 1682-1733, Sir William Wyndham, 3rd Bt early 18th cent and the 2nd and 3rd Earls of Egremont; corresp, diaries and papers of later members of the Wyndham family, Barons Leconfield 19th-20th cent; papers of Thomas Harriott, astronomer and mathematician early 17th cent; accounts of the Duke of York 1647-8; private and business corresp of George Thornton (Duke of Somerset's agent) 1686-1706; diplomatic papers of the 2nd Earl of Bristol 1756-61; misc and printed papers.

In private possession. Enquiries to West Sussex Record Office. Uncatalogued papers and those less than one hundred years old are not available for consultation. HMC *Sixth Report, App*, 1877, pp287-319; *Papers of British Politicians 1782-1900*, 1989, p114. Francis W Steer and others, *The Petworth House Archives*, 2 vols, 1968, 1979. NRA 15719. For papers (mostly described in the *Sixth Report*) sold in 1928 see HMC *Guide to the Location of Collections*, 1982, p36, and [h], [i] and [j] below.

[b] Records of Coates school 1875-1907 and Up Waltham school 1886-1904.

West Sussex Record Office. Deposited from Petworth House (see *The Petworth House archives*, ii, pp53-5).

[c] Misc deeds for Wyndham estates in Somerset, Devon, etc 1325, 16th-18th cent; legal papers mainly 18th-19th cent; manorial accounts, Somerset, Devon, Dorset, etc 1593-1636; misc Wyndham estate papers late 16th-early 19th cent, mainly Somerset, incl leases, rentals, accounts, vouchers 1758-1835 and Watchet harbour papers 1614-1812; surveys of Wadham property in Salisbury (Wilts) 1590, 1606; account book of John Wyndham of Williton 1571-89.

Somerset Archive and Record Service (DD/WYp). Deposited from Petworth House by the 1st and 2nd Barons Egremont 1958, 1982. NRA 1199.

[d] Cumberland deeds 13th-20th cent, mainly post-medieval; Lucy cartulary *c*1400; legal papers mainly 16th-20th cent, incl draft deeds, schedules, feodaries, evidence rolls, precedent books and case papers, with solicitors' papers (Saul & Lightfoot, Carlisle) 19th-20th cent; Cumberland manorial records 15th-20th cent (extensive), incl court rolls, etc for the honour of Cockermouth, the barony of Egremont, Bolton (a Latimer manor) and Caldbeck, etc (manors sold to the Wharton family 1530 but repurchased 1741), with court papers, accounts of fines and papers rel to enfranchisement 18th-20th cent; court rolls for Latimer manors in

Westmorland and Yorks NR 1439-1596; Wressell (Yorks ER) court book 19th cent.

Cumberland estate records 15th-mid-20th cent (extensive), incl leases from 1576, lease books 1606-1856, surveys and valuations 1578, 1758, etc, maps and plans 17th-20th cent, rentals and accounts from mid-15th cent, Latimer (Bolton) estate accounts 1440-1591, cornage rentals from 1437 (Latimer, later Percy), Wharton estate accounts 1721-41, petitions 16th-19th cent, appointments of agents, etc from 1533, agents' corresp from 1578, letter books from 1778, agents' diaries 20th cent, and papers rel to enclosure 18th-19th cent, grazing rights, timber, buildings, quarries, wrecks and foreshore, fisheries and game, Derwentwater and Bassenthwaite Lake, railways, sales, etc; papers rel to Cumberland mines and mineral rights 17th-20th cent, incl leases, plans, reports, royalty returns, agents' notebooks and records 19th-20th cent rel to mines worked by the estate; Cumberland estate farm records mainly 19th cent; estate records for Latimer properties in Westmorland and Yorks NR and for Percy (formerly Poynings and Bryan) properties in Dorset, Somerset, Bucks, etc 1440-17th cent; Northumberland (Percy) receivers' accounts 1634-1721 and rentals 17th cent; Yorks (Percy, later Wyndham) receivers' accounts 1634-1721 and rentals, accounts, etc 19th-mid-20th cent.

Inventories, Cockermouth Castle 1676-early 20th cent and Fellside (Cumberland) early 20 cent; ? household account roll 15th cent; Cumberland and Cockermouth election papers 1641-1880; papers rel to Cockermouth burgage properties, market tolls, etc 17th-19th cent; misc family papers 18th-19th cent, incl personal and political corresp and papers of Gen Sir Henry Wyndham *c*1831-60; 'Description of Cumberland' early 18th cent; papers of Richard Atkinson, surveyor, of Bassenthwaite 1808-59, John Alexander Dixon, consultant mining engineer, of Whitehaven (Cumberland) 1853-90 and Thomas Foster Brown, consultant mining engineer, of Cardiff (Glamorganshire) 1881-96, all rel principally to the Wyndham estates in Cumberland.

In private possession. Enquiries to Cumbria Record Office, Carlisle. NRA 12202.

[e] Cockermouth and Egremont coroners' records 1693-1875.

Cumbria Record Office, Carlisle (D/LEC/CRI). Deposited from Cockermouth Castle. NRA 12202.

[f] Deeds and papers 15th-20th cent, incl legal, manorial and other papers rel to the Wyndham estates in Cumberland.

Cumbria Record Office, Carlisle (D/BEN). Formerly with Bensons, solicitors, of Whitehaven. Purchased by the Leconfield estate

1928 and deposited from Cockermouth Castle 1993.

[g] Irish rentals and rent accounts 1872-1917; Ennis (Co Clare) account book 1846-73; turbary book 1910-13.

National Archives of Ireland (Acc 1074/1). Deposited by the Leconfield Estate Office, Ennis 1976. NRA 29976.

[h] Papers of the 10th Earl of Northumberland as Lord High Admiral (9 vols), incl instructions and journals of voyages 1636-7.

National Maritime Museum (LEC). Sold at Sotheby's 23-4 Apr 1928 and acquired by the Museum 1931-9. HMC *Sixth Report, App,* 1877, pp287 ff, nos 13-48 *passim. Guide to the manuscripts in the National Maritime Museum,* vol 2, 1980, pp94-5.

[i] Boyle family papers 1620-99, rel mainly to the 1st Earl of Orrery.

National Library of Ireland (MSS 32-36A). Acquired 1928 (Sotheby's, 23-4 Apr, lot 20). Edward McLysaght, *Calendar of the Orrery papers,* 1941; *Manuscript sources for the history of Irish civilisation,* ed RJ Hayes, 1965, iii, 821. The Library also has microfilms of the Orrery papers remaining at Petworth (see *Analecta Hibernica,* 23, 1966, pp303-5).

[j] Register of Ely Priory 13th-15th cent; tracts and other papers 16th-17th cent; map of and report on Dover harbour 1552.

British Library, Manuscript Collections (Add MSS 41612-17, 41667G, 69824A, B). Purchased 1928 (Sotheby's, 23-4 Apr), 1989. HMC *Sixth Report, App,* pp287 ff, nos 9-135 *passim.*

[k] Papers of the 2nd Earl of Egremont as Secretary of State mainly 1761-3.

Public Record Office (PRO 30/47). Deposited by the 4th Baron Leconfield 1947. HMC *Sixth Report, App,* p316. NRA 8663.

Related collections; Percy, Dukes of Northumberland, no 82; Wyndham of Orchard Wyndham, no 118; Manners, Dukes of Rutland, no 68.

[118] WYNDHAM of Orchard Wyndham

Sir John Wyndham (knighted 1547), second son of Sir Thomas Wyndham of Felbrigg (Norfolk), married Elizabeth, daughter and co-heir of John Sydenham, through whom he acquired property in north Somerset (Orchard, Williton, Watchet, etc) and Devon (Bondleigh). Their son John (d1572) married Florence, sister and co-heir of Nicholas Wadham, through whom he acquired properties including Ilton (Somerset) and Silverton (Devon). (For another co-heir of the Wadham estates see Fox-Strangways, Earls of

Ilchester, no 40.) In the seventeenth century the Somerset and Devon estates were extended by purchase, and the family also had properties in Dorset (Mappowder), Wiltshire (Mere) and Hampshire (Southampton). John Wyndham (d1649) married Catharine, daughter and co-heir of Robert Hopton of Witham (Somerset), a property sold in 1762. Their son William Wyndham was created a baronet in 1661, and Sir Charles Wyndham, fourth Bt, succeeded as second Earl of Egremont in 1750, on inheriting part of the Percy estates (see Wyndham, Barons Leconfield and Egremont, no 117).

The third Earl of Egremont died in 1837, being succeeded in the Wyndham estates by a nephew, George O'Brien Wyndham, who became fourth Earl of Egremont. Some property in Devon and Somerset held at one time by the Earl of Thomond (d1774) and later by the Hon Percy Wyndham (d1833), second son of the second Earl of Egremont, appears to have passed to the third and then to the fourth Earl. Another son of the second Earl, the Hon Charles William Wyndham (1760-1828), was a co-heir of the Seymour estates of the seventh Duke of Somerset, inheriting the manors of Allington and Slaughterford (Wiltshire). These properties also passed to the fourth Earl, but were sold in 1840. (For another co-heir of the Seymour estates in Somerset and Wiltshire see Manners, Dukes of Rutland, no 68).

The fourth Earl of Egremont died without issue in 1845, and on the death of his widow in 1876 his estates passed to a kinsman, William Wyndham (1834-1914) of Dinton (Wiltshire). The Wyndhams of Dinton were descended from William Wyndham, who purchased Dinton in 1689-90 and married Henrietta Stratford of Hawling (Gloucestershire: sold in 1808). He was the third son of Sir Wadham Wyndham (d1688), of St Edmund's College, Salisbury, who was a younger brother of John Wyndham of Orchard Wyndham and the purchaser, in or before 1659, of Norrington (Wiltshire). Following the death of John Wyndham of Norrington in 1750 some property of the Norrington branch descended to John's daughter Anne, wife of James Everard Arundell (see Arundell, Barons Arundell of Wardour, no 2), but some former Wadham property and eventually (on Anne's death in 1796) Norrington itself passed to the Dinton line. William Wyndham of Dinton (1769-1814) married in 1794 Laetitia, daughter of Alexander Popham, a Master in Chancery. In the early nineteenth century the Dinton estate was enlarged by the purchase of Arundell lands in Wiltshire and Somerset, and in the late nineteenth century property in Hampshire (Hinton Admiral, Ripley), Shropshire (Beckbury) and Somerset was inherited from another branch of the Wyndham family.

Estates in 1883: Wyndham of Orchard Wyndham and Dinton: Somerset 11,231 acres, Devon 6,740 acres, Wilts 5,734 acres, Surrey 3 acres, total 23,708 acres worth £37,420 a year; Wyndham of Hinton Admiral (in 1873): c926 acres in Hants, Salop and Somerset. (Of the total of 23,708 acres held by the Wyndhams of Orchard Wyndham and Dinton in 1883, 5,734 acres in Wiltshire and 2,866 acres in Somerset represented the estates of the Dinton branch.)

[a] Deeds 12th-19th cent (c650 medieval), mainly Somerset and Devon but incl Dorset, Wilts, Hants and a few for Kent (Knatchbull family 17th-18th cent); wills and settlements 15th-18th cent, Wyndham, Sydenham, Wadham, etc, incl Norfolk property early 17th cent; trust and legal papers 15th-19th cent, incl Wadham family 16th-early 17th cent, exchanges, etc with the Fox-Strangways family 17th-19th cent, Penruddocke family 17th-19th cent, Sanford of Nynehead (Somerset) 1767-85 (Alexander Popham a trustee) and Alexander Popham decd 1815-31; manorial court records, mainly Somerset 14th-19th cent and Devon 15th-17th cent but incl other Wadham properties 16th-17th cent, Wilts and Somerset (Duke of Somerset's courts) 17th-18th cent and Hants 17th-18th cent.

Wyndham estate records (Orchard Wyndham, Ilton, Silverton, etc) 15th-early 20th cent, mainly Somerset and Devon but some for properties in Dorset, Wilts and Hants, incl leases and agreements (numerous), surveys and valuations, maps and plans, rentals and accounts, agents' and solicitors' corresp mainly 19th cent, farm accounts 19th cent, and papers (particularly full for 19th cent) rel to tithes, enclosure (Neroche Forest, etc), drainage, roads, canals, railways, game, taxation, fairs, schools and sales; papers rel to Williton chapel and St Decuman's parish late 16th-19th cent, Watchet harbour 17th-19th cent, and Watchet lime kilns, paper mills and iron foundry 19th-early 20th cent; surveys, rentals, accounts and other papers rel to estates of the Wyndhams of Dinton 15th-early 20th cent, mainly Wilts, Dorset and Somerset from 17th cent but incl former Wadham properties in Somerset and Devon 15th-19th cent, and Gloucs (Hawling) mainly 18th cent; papers rel to Hants (Hinton Admiral, etc) and Salop estates 16th-19th cent; papers rel to the Wadham estates generally in Devon, Cornwall, Somerset, Dorset, Wilts and Hants late 16th-early 17th cent; rental of Fox-Strangways property in South Bradon and Buckland St Mary (Somerset) 1817; fee roll for Devon hundreds 1458-9; shrievalty papers from 18th cent, Somerset and Wilts; Somerset and Minehead election papers 18th-19th cent; papers rel to Wadham's and Whetstone's almshouses, Ilton 17th-early 20th cent.

Inventories, Orchard Wyndham from late 17th cent and Silverton Park 19th cent, with drawings rel to alterations to Silverton Park c1837-40 and papers rel to its sale 1892; household accounts, Norrington 18th cent, Silverton 19th cent and Orchard Wyndham 19th-early 20th cent; misc Wyndham personal corresp and papers 17th-20th cent, incl Wyndhams of Orchard Wyndham from early 17th cent, Wyndhams of Dinton 17th-19th cent, Wyndham of Yateley (Hants) early 18th cent (accounts for Hawkchurch (Dorset), etc), Wyndhams of Hinton Admiral 19th cent, and the 3rd Earl of Egremont (letters from his brother the Hon WF Wyndham 1794-1822); Popham family papers 18th cent, incl legal notebooks of Alexander Popham; papers of Benjamin Love of Hinton St George (Somerset), agent and surveyor, incl accounts and plans rel to the Penruddocke estates early 19th cent; maps (incl non-Wyndham estates) by Thomas Hawkes of Williton, surveyor.

Somerset Archive and Record Service (DD/WY, DD/DEL). Deposited by G Wyndham 1951, 1953 and by the De Lancy and De La Hanty Foundation 1984. NRA 1199. (For further papers of Thomas Hawkes of Williton see Somerset Archive and Record Service DD/SAS.)

[b] Trowbridge (Wilts) manorial records 1583-1747.

Wiltshire and Swindon Record Office. Transferred on temporary loan from Somerset Record Office (DD/WY/C/306) 1985. (Although Trowbridge was never a Wyndham property these records, with records of other Seymour manors in Wiltshire and Somerset, had been transferred with the Wyndham of Orchard Wyndham deeds from Petworth to Orchard Wyndham in 1838.)

[c] Wilts estate farm accounts 1821-1910.

Wiltshire and Swindon Record Office (WRO 939). Deposited by the National Trust from Phillips House, Dinton. NRA 81.

[d] Somerset, Dorset and Hants (Hawkchurch, etc) account book 1619-1791; game book 1806-17; hound book 1827-48; diaries of William Wyndham 1820-48 (6 vols).

The National Trust, Phillips House, Dinton. NRA 81.

[e] Corresp of Henry Wyndham of the Close, Salisbury (1709-88) with his son Henry Penruddocke Wyndham on the grand tour 1765-7, with a letter of 1783 rel to Bubb Dodington's diary.

Wiltshire and Swindon Record Office (WRO 96). NRA 1335. Given by the Hon HA Wyndham 1949, who had been given these letters by Dr T Borenius, who had acquired them from Bernard Halliday 1930.

[f] Inventories, Orchard Wyndham and Silverton Park 1845.

Public Record Office (C 107/153, Egremont *v* Thompson).

Related collections: Arundell, Barons Arundell of Wardour, no 2; Fox-Strangways, Earls of Ilchester, no 40; Manners, Dukes of Rutland, no 68; Wyndham, Barons Leconfield and Egremont, no 117; Wyndham of Bathealston (Wiltshire and Swindon Record Office DD/FC, NRA 1199); Wyndham of the College, Salisbury (Wiltshire and Swindon Record Office 727/2/6-19, NRA 3523).

Addenda
(Family names A–K)

Part I of this guide, Families A–K, represented the Commission's state of knowledge on 31 December 1994. This appendix contains material that came to the Commission's notice or was acquired by record offices and libraries between 1 January 1995 and 31 December 1997.

[1] ANDERSON-PELHAM, Earls of Yarborough

[i] The Conisborough (Yorks) manorial records, with related papers, are at Doncaster Archives Department (Accs 753, 765-6; DD YAR).

[2] ARUNDELL, Barons Arundell of Wardour

Related collection (Barons Clifford of Chudleigh): the papers are in private possession, enquiries to Devon Record Office, NRA 20060.

Addendum: Misc executorship and legal papers 17th-18th cent, incl wills of Sir John Arundell of Lanherne 1686 and Richard Bellings Arundell 1724-5 (Cornwall Record Office DD CF, nos 4057-68, NRA 21923, deposited by Coodes, Hubbard, French & Follet, solicitors, St Austell 1956).

[4] ASHLEY-COOPER, Earls of Shaftesbury

[j] Strictly speaking these are Templemore papers and should be noted as a related collection. (The first Marquess of Donegall's second son, created Baron Templemore 1831, inherited unsettled property in County Donegal, County Londonderry and County Down, and at Fisherwick, Staffordshire.)

Addendum: Fisherwick survey 1760 (William Salt Library, Stafford 114/31, NRA 3516).

[7] BERKELEY, Earls of Berkeley

[g] These papers were mostly withdrawn and returned to Berkeley Castle 1996-7.

[8] BOWES-LYON, Earls of Strathmore and Kinghorne

Addendum: Yorks and Co Durham estate plans 19th-20th cent (Durham County Record Office D/XP 136, deposited by Frere, Cholmeley, Bischoff, solicitors, London, through the British Records Association 1996, BRA 2585).

[10] BRIDGEMAN, Earls of Bradford

[a] (additional) Plans of Weston Park alterations 19th cent, Weston Park landscaping plan 1760s and family corresp and papers 19th-20th cent (Staffordshire Record Office D1287, deposited 1995 and 1996).

[17] CAVENDISH, Dukes of Devonshire

The Holker (Lancashire) estate came to Lord George Augustus Henry Cavendish from the Lowther baronets of Marske, not the Lowther Earls of Lonsdale (see introduction, p24, col 2).

Addenda:

Derbys mineral accounts 1651, with misc related papers 17th-19th cent, incl Baslow court roll 1867 (Derbyshire Record Office D 1289 B/ L 183, 245, etc, deposited 1973-95, NRA 19306).

High Peak (Derbys) rental 1765-8 (Derbyshire Record Office D 4458/4, presented 1996).

Sussex (Eastbourne, Wilmington, etc) manorial records 16th-20th cent, incl rentals and stewards' papers 19th-20th cent (East Sussex Record Office Acc 2327/2, NRA 37772, deposited by Blaker, Son & Young, solicitors, Lewes 1978).

[18] CAVENDISH-BENTINCK, Dukes of Portland

Addendum (Harley of Brampton Bryan, related collection, p29, col 2): in 1991 the British

Library acquired a volume of Harley papers c1622-1713 (Add MS 61989) and was presented with further Harley papers 1605-1887 (Add MS 61899).

[20] CHETWYND-TALBOT, Earls of Shrewsbury

In 1856 all the entailed estates passed to a distant cousin the third Earl Talbot of Hensol, who succeeded as eighteenth Earl of Shrewsbury, while the unentailed property (and some of the records) went to Lord Edmund Howard (see introduction, p31, col 1).

[a] (additional) Deeds and family settlements 18th-19th cent (Staffordshire Record Office D 5457, NRA 8481, purchased from the 22nd Earl of Shrewsbury 1995). D 240 has now also been purchased from Lord Shrewsbury.

[n] The covering dates are 16th-20th cent (Cheshire Record Office DSH, NRA 41663).

[q] The covering dates are 1626-1796 (Oxfordshire Archives SL/30, NRA 21610).

Addenda:

Misc Berks deeds and papers 17th-18th cent (Berkshire Record Office D/EX 1471, 1528, deposited by Withers & Co, solicitors, London, through the British Records Association 1996, 1998, BRA 2630).

Little Neston (Cheshire) deeds and legal papers 1765-1861 (Cheshire Record Office Acc 5363, deposited by Withers & Co, solicitors, London through the British Records Association 1997, BRA 2630).

North Chester estate papers 1917 (Cheshire Record Office DBC, Acc 5434/3, deposited by Birch, Cullimore & Co, solicitors, Chester 1997).

Legal corresp and papers of the 18th Earl of Shrewsbury (d1868) (Georgetown University, Special Collections, Washington DC, presented by FB Scheetz and NB Scheetz, *Descriptive Catalogue*, 1996, p57).

Family papers of Colonel Sir Patrick Chetwynd-Talbot (1817-98) and Lady Emma Chetwynd-Talbot (1835-1928), incl some rel to the foundation of Wellington College (in private possession, enquiries to the Historical Manuscripts Commission).

[21] CHICHESTER-CONSTABLE of Burton Constable

Addendum: Tixall (Staffs) valuation 1766 and maps 1833 (William Salt Library, Stafford unnumbered collections nos 522, 655-6, NRA 7279).

[23] COKE, Earls of Leicester

Addendum: Trust deeds and mortgages 1671-1786 (National Library of Wales Peniston Lamb Lincoln's Inn Deeds, NRA 40533, presented by Mrs Checkland Williams 1994-5).

[24] COMPTON, Marquesses of Northampton

[f] Personal and family correspondence and papers of the 1st and 2nd Barons Ashburton, including correspondence of Thomas Carlyle, were sold by the Marquess of Northampton to the National Library of Scotland 1996-7 (Accs 11388 and 11489).

[25] COWPER, Earls Cowper

The 696 acres in Yorkshire ascribed to Earl Cowper in 1883 included 496 acres (the Clifton estate) left jointly to Lady Cowper and the Vyner family (see introduction, p40, col 1, and VYNER of Gautby and Newby, no 112).

[d] Lamb family papers, including papers of the 2nd Viscount Melbourne, were sold from Melbourne Hall to the British Library 1996.

Related collection (Grenfell of Taplow Court): for NRA 2317 read NRA 23171.

Addendum: Papers rel to the Fordwich, Ratling and Swalecliffe (Kent) manors of the 7th Earl Cowper 1701-1931 (Canterbury Cathedral Archives U 62/14, NRA 36317, deposited by Kingsford & Wightwick, solicitors, Canterbury 1996).

[27] CUST, Earls Brownlow

Related collection (additional) Cust (of Arthingworth, Northants) deeds and estate papers 18th-20th cent (Lincolnshire Archives Acc 96/83).

[28] DE GREY, Barons Lucas

For the division of the Robinson and Weddell estates in 1859 (introduction, p46, col 1, 2nd para) see now ROBINSON, Marquesses of Ripon (no 89) and VYNER of Gautby and Newby (no 112). Studley Royal was not among these properties, having been inherited by the first Earl of Ripon in 1845.

[j] (additional) Corresp and papers of the 1st Baron Grantham (British Library, Manuscript Collections, Add MSS 23780-23877, presented by Anne, Countess Cowper 1860).

Addendum: Crudwell (Wilts) maps early 19th cent and nd (Wiltshire Record Office WRO 374/309-10, NRA 1556).

[30] DOUGLAS-HAMILTON, Dukes of Hamilton and Brandon

Addendum: Letter books rel to the Duke of Hamilton's affairs 1811-46 (National Library of Scotland Dep 301/91-100, NRA 29083, deposited by Tods, Murray & Jamieson, WS, Edinburgh 1979).

[31] DOUGLAS-HOME, Earls of Home

For 'Tantallon (Lanarkshire)' (introduction, p52, col 1) read 'Tantallon (East Lothian).'

[33] EGERTON, Earls of Ellesmere

The Brackley estate (introduction, p54, col 1, 2nd para) had been Lovel, not Strange, property.

[34] FANE, Earls of Westmorland

Addendum: Stringer family account book and commonplace book 16th-17th cent (West Yorkshire Archives Service, Leeds MS 311).

[36] FINCH-HATTON, Earls of Winchilsea and Nottingham

[h] Now Add MS 71474.

Addendum: Lincs deeds (Haverholme, etc) 17th-19th cent (Lincolnshire Archives Acc 95/36, BRA 2609, deposited by Lawrence, Graham, solicitors, London, through the British Records Association 1995).

[37] FITZALAN-HOWARD, Dukes of Norfolk

The Holme Lacy estate (introduction, p60, col 1, 4th para) did not remain in the Howard family after the death of Frances, Duchess of Norfolk in 1820.

Addenda:

Sheffield and Ecclesfield manorial court records 1680-1926 (Sheffield Archives MD 585-601, NRA 23246, deposited by Wake & Sons, solicitors, Sheffield 1926).

Inventories and misc papers of Elizabeth, Countess of Shrewsbury (d1608) (Sheffield Archives MD 6277-9, 6311, NRA 23246, purchased at Sotheby's sale of Phillipps MSS 26 June 1974, lots 3038-9).

Horsham (Sussex) borough papers 1736-1819 and estate agency papers of Thomas Medwin 1786-1811 (Horsham Museum, NRA 38877, acquired from Medwin & Co, solicitors, Horsham c1900).

Agency accounts of Thomas Medwin (West Sussex Record Office Add MSS 572-717).

[38] FOLJAMBE of Osberton

Addendum: Estate accounts and papers of the Barnsley family as Foljambe agents 17th-18th cent (Sheffield Archives MD 2693, NRA 23246, collected by TW Hall and presented by his executors 1954).

[39] FORTESCUE, Barons Fortescue

[a] (additional) Family and estate papers 18th-20th cent (Devon Record Office D1262 add 8, deposited by the 8th Earl Fortescue 1995).

[40] FOX-STRANGWAYS, Earls of Ilchester

[a] (additional) Estate papers 19th-20th cent (Dorset Record Office D/FSI, deposited by the Hon Mrs Charlotte Townsend through the Ilchester Estates 1997).

Related collection (Bunbury of Barton): for NRA 2582 read NRA 41001.

[44] GRENVILLE, Dukes of Buckingham and Chandos

Addenda:

Misc papers rel to the Nugent family and estates mainly 18th cent (Royal Institution of Cornwall BRA^A/328/1-24, deposited by Farrer & Co, solicitors, London through the British Records Association 1941).

Leases and papers rel to the Nugent (later Buckingham) estates in Cornwall (St Mawes, Mevagissey, etc) 18th-19th cent (Royal Institution of Cornwall BRA^A/328/25-81 and JAGO/1-87, received from the collections of the Reverend William Jago, d1918).

[45] GREVILLE, Earls Brooke and Earls of Warwick

GEC (*sub* Willoughby de Broke) gives the date of the Willoughby marriage as 1526. For the Beauchamp estates see also above, LYGON, Earls Beauchamp, no 67.

[46] GROSVENOR, Dukes of Westminster

Wymondley (Hertfordshire) was acquired through the marriage of Sir Richard Grosvenor, fourth Bt, to Diana Warburton in 1724 but sold in 1767.

Addendum: Dorset manorial and estate papers 1781-1929 (Dorset Record Office D 484, NRA 20486, deposited by Burridge, Kent & Arkell, solicitors 1975).

[47] HAY, Marquesses of Tweeddale

[h] Correspondence of the 1st Marquess 1672-92 was purchased by Cambridge University Library in 1996 (Add 9362).

[48] HEATHCOTE-DRUMMOND-WILLOUGHBY, Earls of Ancaster

On the death of the fourth Duke of Ancaster in 1779 (see introduction, p78, col 1, 3rd para) the dukedom and the Grimsthorpe estate passed to his uncle, who died without male issue in 1809. At that point the dukedom became extinct and the Grimsthorpe estate passed to his niece Priscilla, Baroness Willoughby de Eresby, who had succeeded to the other Willoughby estates in 1779.

Addendum: Kent (Burrell) deeds and papers 13th-19th cent (Centre for Kentish Studies U 36, NRA 3509, deposited by Warrens, solicitors, London, through the British Records Association 1940, BRA 301).

[51] HERBERT, Earls of Powis

The Clive family papers in [a] and [n] were purchased respectively by the National Library of Wales and the British Library, Oriental and India Office Collections, from the Earl of Powis in 1996, when also certain of the Clive papers in [d] were presented by Lord Powis to Shropshire Record Office (see HMC *Annual Review 1995-1996*, pp 33-5).

Addendum: Corresp of the 3rd Earl of Powis rel to the North Wales College movement (University College of North Wales, Bangor, Bangor MSS 4248-4545, deposited 1942-3).

[52] HILL, Marquesses of Downshire

Addendum: Papers (6 vols) of Sir William Trumbull (d1716) (British Library, Manuscript Collections, Deposit 9145, received 1992).

[53] HOPE, Earls of Hopetoun, later Marquesses of Linlithgow

Addendum: Scottish state papers 15th-16th cent (British Library, Manuscript Collections, Add MS 33531, acquired 1888, formerly in the library of the 7th Earl of Hopetoun).

[55] HOWARD, Earls of Carlisle

[g] (additional) The Lanercost priory cartulary *c*1252-1370, annotated by Lord William Howard when in his possession but later presumed destroyed, was acquired by Cumbria Record Office, Carlisle, in 1983 (MS D2/1).

[56] INGILBY of Ripley

[a] (additional) Ripley rentals, accounts and estate papers 18th-20th cent, with a Lincs rental 1887-1913, were deposited by Sir Thomas Ingilby 1995-6 (Acc 3978, 4080, NRA 11614).

[58] KERR, Marquesses of Lothian

Emily, Marchioness of Londonderry (introduction, p95, col 1, 2nd para), is thought to have had a life interest only in the Bellaghy estate (*ex inf* Dr APW Malcomson).

[l] Some of the HMC-reported papers described are now Norfolk Record Office NRS 17434 (Sco 1-6, 16-25), NRA 5403, deposited through the Norfolk Record Society 1954.

Addenda:

Blickling estate papers 18th-19th cent, incl manorial minute book 1789-1861 (Norfolk Record Office MS 688, deposited by the National Trust 1997).

Estate and personal papers of the Marchioness of Lothian 1862-1906 (Norfolk Record Office MC 689, purchased at Phillips's, 13 Mar 1997, lot 331).

Select index
(Family names L–W)

The primary purpose of this index is to act as a means of reference to families mentioned in the text and to their principal estates and seats. Individuals are included only in a landowning context, and place-names are indexed only when significant records for those places are described in the text. Institutions and corporations are also indexed where the text notes significant surviving records.

A reference to an entry number followed by a letter (eg 60a, 70k) indicates the specific group of papers in which the reference occurs. Where a number only is cited (eg 60, 70), there is a reference in the introductory or closing paragraph or paragraphs and generally also in one or more of the groups of papers described in the entry.

LIVERPOOL
UNIVERSITY
LIBRARY

Printed in the United Kingdom for The Stationery Office
J74411 C5 5/99 10170